D1083118

MODERN DESCRIPTIVE ENGLISH GRAMMAR

MODERN

DESCRIPTIVE

ENGLISH GRAMMAR

HULON WILLIS
BAKERSFIELD COLLEGE

CHANDLER PUBLISHING COMPANY
An Intext Publisher
SAN FRANCISCO • SCRANTON • LONDON • TORONTO

Library of Congress Cataloging in Publication Data

Willis, Hulon.
   Modern descriptive English grammar.

   1. English language—Grammar—1950–   I. Title.
PE1106.W5   428′.2   77-165178
ISBN 0-8102-0442-8

for **PROFESSOR TOM SWEDENBERG**

CONTENTS

PREFACE

The study of grammar at all levels in our colleges and universities has increased significantly during the last two decades. New discoveries in grammar have been made and new types of grammatical analysis have been introduced. Transformational grammar has been the most popular new grammar, but its successes have not lessened the need for continued study of scholarly-traditional grammar. Even though the tradition requires examination and revision, it "provides the most widespread, influential, and best understood method of discussing Indo-European languages in the Western world." I concur with this opinion of Professor Francis P. Dinneen (from his *An Introduction to General Linguistics*—1967), and have prepared this book because I believe that students and prospective teachers of English need a solid background in scholarly-traditional grammar for use in their classrooms, whether or not they will also dip into some of the highly theoretical, and somewhat fragmented, grammars.

My book retains the aspects and terminology of traditional grammar which have proved themselves tenable over the centuries, but it also adopts widely accepted new terminology, such as *form classes*. It introduces some analyses which, so far as I know, have not until now been given attention in textbooks, and it organizes grammatical analysis along lines which have not heretofore been used in texts but which I hope will make the surface structure of our language clearer to students than it has before been made in traditional grammars. I hope the book will be fresh enough to be meaningful alike to those students who will pursue advanced linguistic study and those who will be charged with teaching the language to school children and college freshmen.

The utility of traditional grammar in teaching our literary heritage—especially our traditional poetry—is considerable. The highly theoretical and fragmented grammars cannot compete here. Let me give some examples. Here is a part of a stanza from Frost's "Two Tramps in Mud Time":

> The blows that a life of self-control
> Spares to strike for the common good,
> That day, giving a loose to my soul,
> I spent on the unimportant wood.

This passage is not as clear as it might at first seem, and bright students often puzzle over its meaning. An ability to handle syntax in a traditional way best lets the teacher clarify the passage for the student. Since *spares* can mean either "refuses to act" or "gives from a store," the prepositional phrase *for the common good* can logically modify either the verb *spares* or the verb *to strike* (which most students at first assume it modifies). Through traditional syntactical analysis the teacher can show that the prepositional phrase modifies *spares* and can thus elucidate the passage for students. Other grammars would call for considerably more complex analysis.

Or consider this passage from Shelley's "Ozymandias":

> Near them, on the sand,
> Half sunk, a shattered vizage lies, whose frown,
> And wrinkled lip, and sneer of cold command,
> Tell that its sculptor well those passions read
> Which yet survive, stamped on these lifeless things,
> The hand that mocked them, and the heart that fed:

I know a brilliant and skillful teacher who taught this poem for years without understanding the intricate syntax of this passage. He was surprised when he learned it and began making the poem much more meaningful to his students. To explain the passage one must understand the concepts of complementation, adverbial modification by a passive past participle, and coordination with ellipsis, concepts that can be handled most simply with modern scholarly-traditional analysis.

One more example, from Emily Dickinson:

> The Soul selects her own Society—
> Then—shuts the Door—
> To her divine Majority—
> Present no more—

The bright student who wants to understand is sometimes puzzled by this opening stanza. The syntactical puzzle centers on the word *present*: Is it an adjective or a verb? There seems to be no structural reason for the poet to bring in an imperative sentence at this point, and it is a fact that my students in reading the poem aloud always pronounce the word PREsent. To consider the alternatives, the teacher must bring traditional grammatical analysis into play, and he finds his job much easier if his students can understand syntactic structures without elaborate branching-tree diagrams. Incidentally, comparison of this stanza with a variant reading shows that the imperative sentence is indeed the intended structure.

Ambiguities, too, are often more easily cleared up with traditional analysis than with transformational analysis. Newspaper headlines frequently call for an application of simple syntactical understanding. For example, here are two real headlines:

Inmate Demands Stir Rally

Negotiations Continue to Bring
Solution of Year-long Dispute

Who would not pause over these (or is the slang term *to be in stir* now vanished)? It took me probably five seconds to understand the second of these headlines, and then only a knowledge of the difference between infinitives as nominals and adverbials let me solve the problem at all.

Or consider these sentences:

How would you like to see a model home?
You can buy that dirt cheap

To unravel the syntax of these sentences, transformational grammar would take pages of branching-tree diagrams. One soundly grounded in scholarly-traditional grammar can explain the syntactical possibilities easily. And a point not to be dismissed too lightly is that people interested in language (and on a certain level that probably includes most of us) get fun out of playing with such sentences.

Finally, let me say a word about the over-all organization of this book. Since grammar cannot be presented in a linear fashion, as, say, some phases of mathematics can be, it is necessary to bring in some concepts—such as that of complements, for example—before it is really time to present a thorough discussion of such concepts. Thus there is apparent repetition in the book. For example, in the first four chapters on the parts of speech many concepts are presented briefly, or alluded to, which are given more detailed discussion in later chapters, usually from different points of view as well as with more thoroughness and more plentiful illustrations. Such repetition is purposeful and intended to aid the student in his mastery of complex subject matter. A glance through the table of contents will show the degree, nature, and planned design of this repetition.

I can't resist a postscript. Here is an answer from a test given to a college freshman in a course in basic grammar and usage. "A phrase modifier differs from a clause modifier in the fact the phrase modifier modifies in the sence of first person the action of the subject. While the clause modifier acts as passive voice to modify the action of the subject." I'll leave you to ponder that thought.

H. W.

January, 1972

MODERN DESCRIPTIVE ENGLISH GRAMMAR

1 THE PARTS OF SPEECH BY FORM

The Four Great Form Classes

Until about 1940 it was an article of faith with most grammarians that the English language is composed of eight parts of speech. Indeed, even today some school grammars still take this approach. Like Ptolemaic astronomy, which, after all, lasted over 1000 years, the system can be made to work, and, unlike Ptolemaic astronomy, it has the virtue of simplicity. But it masks much of the truth about the structure of English. An example will illustrate one aspect of its many weaknesses. Under the system both

> many girls *and* pretty girls

are analyzed as equivalent structures: a noun modified by an adjective. But they are not equivalent. The word *pretty* may be compared: *prettier, prettiest.* It may be made into an adverb by the addition of the inflectional suffix *ly: prettily.* And it may be made into a noun by the addition of the derivational suffix *ness: prettiness.* All of these permutations are characteristics of most adjectives. But the word *many* cannot undergo any of these permutations. Indeed, there are so many differences between the two constructions that it is incredible that in the eighteenth and nineteenth centuries they should have been analyzed as similar. As you will learn in Chapter 4, *many* is a **structure word**, a determiner or noun marker.

So, as a starter, it is necessary to see that parts of speech in English

1

divide into **lexical words** and **structure words**. Lexical words are those with full dictionary definitions; they are **content words**. Structure words have some lexical meaning but are also, and sometimes mainly, used to establish the grammatical structure of a sentence.

Another distinction that we must make is that between the **form** of lexical words and their **function** in a sentence. As we will see in Chapter 2, certain names are used for elements of the language with reference to form and other names for these elements with reference to function. *The reason such a distinction must be made is that the lexical words cross freely over into each other's territory when actually used in sentences: nouns may function as adjectives; verbs may function as nouns; nouns may function as adverbs; adverbs may function as adjectives; and still other function changes occur.* This important fact of English structure makes the old system of analysis untenable. An example will illustrate. Under the old system in

an iron fence   *and*   a pretty fence

both *iron* and *pretty* were called adjectives, even though it was recognized that by itself *iron* is a noun. But notice again that *pretty* will go through all the permutations listed above, whereas *iron* won't. And also you can say *a fence of iron* but not *a fence of pretty*. The simple truth is that a noun (and other parts of speech besides adjectives) can modify a noun. So we need to identify parts of speech by **form** and by **function**. As you will learn in Chapter 2, *iron* in the above construction is called an **adjectival** by function because it functions in a position normally occupied by an adjective. It is called a noun by form, as you will learn in the next section.

This chapter, then, will continue with analysis of the **four great form classes**: **nouns**, **verbs**, **adjectives**, and **adverbs**. When these classes were first established, some grammarians wanted to call them Forms I, II, III, and IV to get away from traditional terminology. But the traditional terms are satisfactory, for there was, indeed, much truth in the old traditional system.

The four great form classes are **open classes:** new vocabulary items are added to these classes almost daily. *Webster's New International Dictionary* of 1961 contains thousands of vocabulary items not listed in its predecessor of 1934. Most new items are nouns, but from them are often coined verbs, adjectives, and adverbs. The structure words, we will learn in Chapter 4, are a **closed class**, for new ones seldom enter the language.

With the concept of the form classes, the chief aim of grammarians has been to determine ways to identify a vocabulary item in each of the four classes *by form alone*. The **citation form** of a word comes into play here: the word by itself or completely isolated in a sentence. If we are to have success in all attempts to identify words by form class, then examination of the citation form of a word will always tells us what form class the word fits into.[1] Unfortunately, such complete success is not attainable, at least at the present moment. But success in identifying parts of speech by form is almost 100 percent, sufficient to warrant the establishment of the four great form classes.

Nouns

Notional Definition of the Noun

Early traditional grammar tried to identify a noun not by its form but by its meaning, by the kind of notion it conveys. Even today almost every school child knows that a noun is the name of a person, place, or thing. Indeed, the word *noun* comes from the Latin word *nomen*, meaning "a name." The word **substantive** was used by some uneasy grammarians to mean *noun*: a noun has "substance." Other uneasy grammarians tried to supplement the insufficiency of the original definition by adding to it such concepts as "quality," "action," and "abstract concept." Other said that a noun is the name "of anything that exists or can be conceived." Actually, there is much truth in these definitions, and most of us even today do recognize a noun by knowing that it is the name of something. But there is enough vagueness in the definition to worry grammarians. For example, *time* is undoubtedly a noun, but what is it really the name of? Is *concentration* a quality or an abstract concept? Certainly it is not a place or thing. And consider *dancing*. It looks like a verb (and is), but does it not seem to be the name of something? So grammarians sought formal clues that would identify nouns.

The Noun Paradigm

There are two major methods of identifying nouns by form. The first of these, and perhaps the most important, is the fitting of a word into the **noun paradigm**. A paradigm is a set of related forms. The noun paradigm consists of the four possible forms that a noun may take (not all nouns have the four forms):

SINGULAR	POSSESSIVE	PLURAL	PLURAL + POSSESSIVE
man	man's	men	men's
dog	dog's	dogs	dogs'
table	table's	tables	tables'
action	—	actions	—
—	—	measles	measles'

[1] Of course, English words often fit into more than one form class, as for instance *love* and *to love*, which fit into the noun and verb classes.

If a word will fit into *any two* of these four slots, it is a noun by form. For example, *action* and *measles* qualify as nouns, as illustrated.

However, many words that certainly seem to be nouns do not readily fit into the paradigm. A word like *derision*, for example, doesn't seem to have a plural form. And though you can say "derision's capacity for deflating egos," some might look askance at the word's being used in the possessive. (Actually, such a use of the possessive is fully grammatical, and *derision* certainly fits into the paradigm.) Or consider *advice*. Can it be made plural or possessive? Apparently some means other than fitting into the paradigm is needed to identify nouns by form.

But before we go on to a second means, this is the proper place to introduce the concept of **inflectional suffixes**. The plural and possessive endings in the noun paradigm above are inflectional suffixes. **Inflection** is a pattern of change in form (usually but not always word endings) undergone by words to express grammatical relations, most commonly those of case, number, gender, person, or tense. Besides the plural and possessive endings[2] of nouns, the inflectional suffixes are the various endings of verbs, the comparative forms (*er*, *est* or *more*, *most*) of adjectives and adverbs, and the *ly* suffix which makes an adverb out of an adjective. Pronouns also have inflection.

English is not a highly inflected language, though it once was. Some languages have large numbers of word endings. Estonian, for example, has twelve cases for its nouns—twelve different endings or internal form changes for a noun according to its use in a sentence. But even though English is not highly inflected, it does have inflectional suffixes that help grammarians identify parts of speech by form. The plural and possessive endings of nouns give one means of identifying nouns by form, and we will also see that inflection helps identify verbs, adjectives, and adverbs by form. Now to the second means of identifying nouns by form.

Noun-Forming Derivational Suffixes

A derivational suffix is usually one that is used to derive one part of speech from another, such as *act-actor* and *courage-courageous*, or to

---

[2]Some plural forms are not made by endings, for example *men*, *geese*, and *mice*. These modes of making plurals are called **replacive allomorphs**. **Morphology** is the study of words and their meaningful parts. In that study, a **morpheme** is the smallest unit of meaning in any language. For example, *boy* is a single morpheme, for it has meaning but is not divisible into smaller meaningful parts. *Boys*, however, is two morphemes: *boy* and the *z* sound, which means the plural. An allomorph is a variant form of a morpheme: it has the same meaning but a different form. For example, the *ren* of *children* and the *z* sound of *boys* are both allomorphs of the plural morpheme. Morphology is an interesting study, but this text is restricted to the study of **syntax**, or word arrangement in sentences.

derive another kind of meaning from the same part of speech, such as *book-booklet*, *pamphlet-pamphleteer*, and *slave-slavery*. Several derivational suffixes form nouns of these sorts. The noun-forming derivational suffix is the second main way of identifying nouns by form. If a word ends in a noun-forming suffix, it is a noun by form. This test takes care of some nouns that do not seem readily to fit into the noun paradigm, such as *mileage*.

Following is a list of some of the more common noun-forming derivational suffixes:

```
compose + ure = composure
advise + er = adviser
beg + ar = beggar
deposit + or = depositor
lovely + ness = loveliness
tense + ion = tension
introduce + tion = introduction
achieve + ment = achievement
receive + tacle = receptacle
deny + al = denial
contrive + ance = contrivance
superintend + ent = superintendent
assist + ant = assistant
mile + age = mileage
active + ity = activity
lemon + ade = lemonade
deform + ation = deformation
deliver + y = delivery
refer + ee = referee
purify + cation = purification
slave + ery = slavery
commune + ist = communist
social + ism = socialism
just + ice = justice
redundant + cy = redundancy
true + th = truth
king + dom = kingdom
America + n = American (an, ian)
China + ese = Chinese
kin + ship = kinship
laundry + ess = laundress
boy + hood = boyhood
labor + ite = laborite
dull + ard = dullard
meet + ing = meeting
```

Note the last example. In the vast majority of cases, *ing* is an inflectional suffix of a verb, but sometimes it is a noun-forming derivational suffix. If the word ending in *ing* can be made plural, it is a noun by form as well as a verb. Examples:

> meetings
> gatherings
> hearings
> beckonings
> cravings

On the other hand such words as these are verbs only:

> swimming
> possessing
> considering
> rebelling
> contributing

They cannot be made plural.

(Actually, this initial analysis of the *ing* verb is far too simple. This kind of word is very complex in its syntactic behavior, and on pages 17–18 we will show that it has several nounlike characteristics. Essentially, however, we will consider it a verb unless it can be made plural, and so we will delay discussion of its complexity until we get to the section on verbs by form.)

Some derivational changes are not additions at the ends of words but are changes of sound within the word, for example the change from the *z* sound in *advise* to the *s* sound in *advice*, or the change from the *ate* sound in the verb *associate* to the *it* sound in the noun *associate*. Although these changes are not suffixes, strictly speaking, grammarians' statements about derivational suffixes often apply also to them. Other such purely phonological derivational suffixes exist in our language.

Most nouns formed by derivational suffixes will also fit into the paradigm, but the suffixes have their use in noun identification. An instance is seen in *mileage*, which does not readily fit into the paradigm.

Some difficulty in identifying nouns by suffix exists. *Assist + ant* certainly makes the noun *assistant*; but *resist + ant* makes the adjective *resistant*. Also *cup + ful* makes the noun *cupful*; but *sin + ful* makes the adjective *sinful*. But in these very few cases the paradigm identifies the nouns.

A few words that seem to be nouns neither fit into the paradigm nor have derivational suffixes. Some that have been so listed are *hose* (stockings), *tennis*, *golf*, *chaos*, *means*, and *remains*. A few grammarians have, therefore, established a category of **uninflected words** to take care of these, refusing to call them nouns since their form is not identifiable. However, many such words, if not most, will fit the paradigm, though some grammarians have not recognized this fact. You can say *golf's fascination for executives* or *chaos's effect on political stability*. That permutation puts the nouns in the paradigm. But a few anomalies do exist, and most grammarians do at times rely on the old notional definition, which has much truth to it and is useful. Noun identification by form, however, is over 99 percent successful.

Proper, Count, and Mass Nouns

One method of categorizing nouns is to divide them into count, mass, and proper nouns. **Proper** nouns are names of people, of geographical locations, and of particular or unique things. They are capitalized and will usually fit into the paradigm since they can be made possessive. They are such nouns as *John Doe*, *Princess Margaret*, the *Queen Mary* (ship), *Deer Mountain*, the *Cascades*, the *Mona Lisa*, the *Netherlands*, and *Lake Huron*.

Count nouns are those that name objects which can be counted or numbered: *girls*, *books*, *locks*, *conceptions*, *referrals* are examples. They almost always occur in both the singular and the plural, and in the singular they always occur with a determiner or noun marker: *one toy*, *the toy*, *a boat*, *some boat*, or the like. The count noun in the singular is never used without a determiner, as

> *Boy hit the ball.[3]

In the plural, a count noun may or may not take a determiner:

> These books are interesting.
> Books can be stimulating.

The determiner *many* may almost always be used with a plural count noun, but the determiner *much* almost never is:

> many songs
> *much balls

Mass nouns include those that name things which are not countable: *sugar*, *steam*, *dirt*, *whisky*. They never have a plural form. Thus they fit into the noun paradigm only by having a possessive form: *sugar's nutritional value*. They may or may not take a determiner:

> Whisky is intoxicating.
> The whisky is spoiled.

[3]An asterisk (*) is used by grammarians to denote that a construction is ungrammatical.

They never take the indefinite article:

> *a dirt
> *an envy

But when these words have the sense of "type of ———" or "kind of ———," they are count nouns:

> a Scotch whisky; the whiskies of Scotland
> a refined sugar; the simple sugars

Abstract nouns, which really have no mass, are nevertheless categorized as mass nouns. *Love*, *justice*, *music*, *courage*, *tolerance*, *pity*, *compassion*, *sympathy*, and the like may fit into the paradigm by taking the possessive or they may have derivational suffixes, as do *information* and *drainage*.

The determiner *much* may almost always be used with a mass noun, but the determiner *many* almost never is:

> much love   *many sympathy

Some nouns that are normally thought of as mass may in certain contexts become count nouns:

> his many **loves**
> two **beers**
> several **creeds**
> He took the **waters**.
> the **joys** of living
> the **truths** of the Bible

When made plural in this way, a noun is no longer a member of the mass group.

A few nouns seem to be neither count nor mass:

> *much mumps
> *many mumps
>
> *much hose
> many hose (?)
>
> much manhood (?)
> *many manhood

Abstract and Concrete Nouns

Nouns may also be usefully categorized as abstract and concrete. A **concrete** noun is one that names a tangible object or substance: *soil*, *toy*, *pliers*, *tree*, *molecule*, *star*. Concrete nouns can be either count or mass, and there is seldom any difficulty fitting them into the paradigm.

The word *abstract* comes from the Latin *abstrahere*, which means "to draw out of or away from." An abstraction, then, is the name of an intangible, a quality which has been drawn out of the concrete substance which might contain it. *Beauty* is a typical **abstract** noun. It means an intangible quality that may reside in an object, but it is often used without reference to any object. Our language is full of abstract nouns: *courage*, *love*, *devotion*, *sympathy*, *virtue*, *justice*, *socialism*, *foolishness*, *duty*, *liberty*, *cowardice*, *influence*, *danger*, *enlightenment*, *bravery*, *comfort*. Most abstract nouns are mass. There is often difficulty fitting them into the paradigm, but many have derivational suffixes that identify them as nouns.

Compound Nouns

Many **compound** nouns exist in English, but they are not always easy to identify. In German, a compound is always written as one word, but in English it may be written as one word, as two words, or as hyphenated words: *drugstore*, *shoe store*, *father-in-law*. Compound nouns pattern as do ordinary nouns. They make take inflectional suffixes, may be modified, and may function in a sentence in the same way an ordinary noun does:

drugstore—drugstores
shoe store—a pretty shoe store
the shoe store's manager

Compound nouns are to be differentiated from **grammatical structures**. In this case a grammatical structure is a noun with a modifier. In a compound noun the first part does not modify the second part but is simply one half of the compound. For example, the term *high chair* is a compound when it means the chair built for a baby. But a *high chair* may also mean any chair which is high. In the latter case, *high* is an adjective modifying the noun *chair* and the two words form a grammatical structure, whereas in the former *high* is not a modifier but part of a compound.

In a compound noun *neither part may be modified by itself*; a modifier, if there is one, must modify the whole compound. For example, the structure *very high chair* cannot refer to the baby's chair. Neither can a *high*, *comfortable chair*. But *an expensive high chair* can refer to the baby's chair, for *expensive* is modifying the whole compound, not just a part of it.

The best way to differentiate a compound noun from a grammatical structure, however, is by **stress pattern**. There are four degrees of stress in English utterances:

´	primary stress	`	tertiary stress
^	secondary stress	˘	weak stress

The usual stress pattern for a compound noun (inevitably, there are some exceptions) is primary-tertiary (´ `)

bláckbìrd	hóthòuse
hígh schòol	bláckboàrd
róckĭng chàir	pápĕrbàck
sídewàlk	spínnĭng whèel
dínĭng ròom	fúnnў bòne
Whíte Hòuse	hándўmàn

The usual stress pattern for a grammatical structure is secondary-primary (^ ´):

blâck bírd	blâck bóard
hîgh róllĕr	pâpĕr báck
rôckĭng cháir	spínnĭng wheél
whîte hóuse	fûnnў bóne
hôt hóuse	hândў mán

Usually a grammatical structure will undergo this transformation:

A rôckĭng cháir is a chair which is rocking.

The compound noun will not undergo this transformation. It does, however, suggest a grammatical structure:

A róckĭng chàir is one that can rock (though it need not be rocking at any given time).

A spínnĭng whèel is one used for spinning (not necessarily one that is spinning).

The tendency in English spelling is more and more for compound nouns to be spelled as one word. For example, there was a progression from *week end* to *week-end* to *weekend*.

Collective Nouns

In English a **collective** noun is one which is singular in form but which in meaning suggests a number of individuals: *family, crowd, team, crew, group, number, faculty, staff, pride* (of lions), *gaggle* (of geese), *swarm, audience, committee, bunch, jury,* and numerous others. Such English words have been called **nouns of multitude** and some grammarians have maintained that they represent a third **number** in English grammar (besides singular and plural). They do show that number in nouns is not always a simple matter, but they take only a singular or plural verb or pronoun (there are no others) and thus should be considered singular or plural according to what verb form or pronoun form is used with them.

The grammatical term **concord** is often used to mean **agreement**. Among other things, concord involves the fitting of a verb to its subject and a pronoun to its antecedent. The concord of collective nouns is variable. Some handbooks maintain that a singular verb should normally be used with a collective noun, and we often find professional writers very carefully writing such sentences as

> A number of books **was** lost.
> A crowd of spectators **was** injured.
> A gaggle of geese **was** honking.

But there is no real problem in usage with these nouns. A writer need only be consistent within a whole composition. In the above example sentences, the plural verb *were* would be equally correct.

Sometimes in using a collective noun, a writer or speaker may wish his audience to think of the individual members of the noun and sometimes of the group as a whole. Verbs and pronouns should be used accordingly:

> My family **are** taking separate vacations.
> My family **is** now at home.
>
> The team took **their** lumps in stride.
> The team improved **its** record.

Collective nouns are of interest grammatically, but, contrary to the strictures of many textbooks, they present no problem in usage.

Nouns in the Plural Only

As is apparent by now, the noun system in English is very complex. One oddity in the system is the existence of nouns that occur only in the plural form, even sometimes when a single item is meant: *scissors, pliers, pants, shears, vespers, tidings, means, remains, hose, dregs, oats, annals, trousers, athletics, clothes, culottes, environs, thanks.* These nouns usually take plural verbs and pronouns, though occasionally a singular verb is used:

> Any **means** of achieving our end **is** satisfactory.
> **Vespers is** at 9:00.

But note that we would probably say, when referring to someone's wealth,

> His means **are** considerable.

Some anomalies exist in this group of nouns. For example, most grains are referred to with singular mass nouns: *corn, wheat, rice,* and

the like. But *oats* is generally considered plural, even though in meaning it is thought of as a mass noun. Some uncertainty perhaps exists
as to whether one should say *oats is* or *oats are*, though the latter
probably has preference. The word can exist in the singular, as in

> The wild oat is nourishing food.

But more likely the term *wild oats are* would be used (not referring of
course to the young man sowing his wild oats). We never speak of *an
oat*, meaning one grain.

The word *pants* is also interesting. It is a shortened form of *panta-
loons*, which originally was a singular word. We undoubtedly think of
pants as plural because there are two legs to a pair. But nowadays
many clothing salesmen are introducing the singular *pant*. You will
often hear a salesman say something like

> Now this pant is made of our finest material.

The word *panties* is also now frequently used in the singular *panty*. It
remains to be seen if *trousers* will become *trouser*.

The word *goods* is also of interest. In many senses, the singular
noun *good* has long been used; but in the sense of *goods* = *wares, a
good* was long unused until relatively recently when economists needed
the singular *a good* to be comparable to *a service*.

Nouns Plural in Form but Singular in Meaning

There is also a small group of nouns in English that are plural in
form but usually singular in meaning: *measles, mumps, molasses, news,
summons, civics, mathematics, physics, gymnastics, tactics, acoustics,
politics, economics, linguistics, ethics*, and some others. Many of these
words have frequently caused concern as to whether they should be
used with a singular or plural verb. Of course, if one of them is used
with a plural verb, it should be called a plural rather than a singular
noun. For a long time the handbook strictures were to use these words
only with singular verbs, but in informal usage now some of the *ics*
words are used with plural verbs. Actually, no real problem in usage
exists, though in formal writing it is still customary to use a singular
verb. In an essay one would write

> Politics **is** one of the most stimulating areas of endeavor a young
> college man can go into.

But in speaking, most people would say

> My politics **are** my own affair.

The concord of some of these words is peculiar indeed. For example, one could say without expecting criticism

> Measles **is** a childhood disease, but I haven't had **them**

—a singular verb but a plural pronoun. Would you say

> I looked for the molasses but couldn't find **it** (or **them**?).

Or would you way

> Acoustics **is** an interesting field, but I haven't had a course in **it** (or **them**?).

These instances of pronoun concord are certainly awkward, and probably most speakers and writers would just avoid the issue. But eighteenth-century prescriptive grammar is dead so far as concord for these and other peculiar English nouns is concerned.

Case in Nouns

Case is the aspect of inflection that has to do with the form of nouns or pronouns (and in some languages adjectives) according to their use in a sentence. Languages vary in the number of cases they have. Latin has six cases: (1) the nominative (the noun used as a subject); (2) the accusative (the noun used as a direct object); (3) the genitive (the noun used to show possession); (4) the dative (the noun used as an indirect object, after *to* or *for*); (5) the ablative (a case expressing separation, position, motion from, instrumentality, and some other relations, usually translated by the prepositions *from*, *with*, *in*, and *by*); and (6) the vocative (the noun in direct address).   Eighteenth-century grammarians, thinking Latin represented perfect, universal grammar, tried to fit these cases into English, but they were misguided. The only case remaining in English nouns is the **possessive** (called the genitive in Latin). For nouns in the singular and for plural nouns not ending is *s*, we have the following forms:

> James's car
> the boy's book
> the rat's tail
> the men's stag
> the mice's nests

Three different pronunciations occur in these forms of the possessive: *s*, *z*, *iz*. The pronunciation used is dictated by the phonology (that is, the sound system) of the noun being made possessive. For nouns in the plural ending in *s*, no additional sounded ending is added for the possessive, though in writing an apostrophe is added:

the Joneses' house
the teachers' roll books

Note that the pronunciation of the plural plus possessive is the same as that for the *s-z-iz* plural alone.

Though in pronunciation and spelling the possessive case is simple, in meaning it is quite complex. The case is used for several meanings other than the simple possession conveyed in *Bill's car*. It can designate characterization or description, as in *the policeman's swagger* or *Mary's deportment*. It can denote the origin of an activity or object, such as *Western Civilization's beginning* or *Shakespeare's plays*. It can denote that the noun in the possessive case performed an action, as in *Mary's swimming* or *Mantle's home run*. It can denote that the noun in the possessive case received an action, as in *Perry's reprimand* or *his son's talking to*. And it can be used to express a measure of time or money or space, as in *a month's salary*, *one nickel's worth*, and *an acre's production*. In spite of this complexity, we still use the term possessive case.

For all other uses, the form of the English noun does not vary; the noun's form for a subject, a direct object, an indirect object, an object of a preposition, and a name in direct address is the same. This form may be given the label **common case**. It is pointless to talk about the subjective and objective cases of English nouns (for case in pronouns, see page 70).

Gender in Nouns

In highly inflected languages, nouns have **gender**. Some languages, such as French, for example, classify all nouns as either masculine or feminine. In French we have

le main (the hand)—masculine
la tête (the head)—feminine

Other languages, such as German, for example, have three genders: masculine, feminine, and neuter. In German we have

das Fraülein (the young girl)—neuter
die Tür (the door)—feminine
der Stuhl (the stool)—masculine

As you can see, the gender of a noun in these languages does not necessarily refer to the sex of the object at all, but is wholly an inflectional function. In German the form of the definite article changes according to the case of the noun, and adjectival modifiers also change form according to both case and gender.

English nouns have no inflectional gender. However, there is real gender by reason of sex reference in some of our nouns (all nouns, if neuter is included), and pronoun choice for reference depends on the gender of the noun. **Masculine gender** includes such nouns as *man*, *boy*, *father*, *gander*, *comedian*, *fiancé*, *patron*, *masseur*, *hero*, *host*, and *landlord*. The singular pronouns used to refer to these are *he*, *him*, and *his*. **Feminine gender** includes such nouns as *woman*, *girl*, *mother*, *goose*, *comedienne*, *fiancée*, *patroness*, *masseuse*, *heroine*, *hostess*, and *landlady*. The singular pronouns used to refer to these are *she*, *her*, and *hers*. **Neuter** nouns are those without any sex. The singular pronouns used to refer to them are *it* and *its*. The plural pronouns *they*, *them*, *their*, and *theirs* refer to all genders. Also we have a group of nouns that may be said to have **common gender**: *child*, *parent*, *person*, *relative*, *mouse*, *American*, *baby* are examples. Pronoun usage with these nouns varies. In general, noun gender is of small interest in English grammar.

Verbs

Notional Definition of the Verb

In earlier days traditional grammar gave a notional definition of the verb, just as it did of the noun. The simplest such definition was that "a verb is a word that expresses action or being," such as *he* **talks** and *he* **is** *intelligent*. Later grammarians added "state of being" to the definition to take care of verbs like *he* **appears** *intelligent*, which do more than state flat existence. Realizing the shakiness of these definitions, other grammarians added that a verb also may express "condition, state, or process" to take care of such slightly different meanings as *he* **stinks**, *he* **resides** *here*, and *it* **comes out** *green*.

Though there is some truth to this notional definition of the verb, it nevertheless is somewhat unsatisfactory, being more philosophical than grammatical and also not fully making a distinction between parts of speech. For example, does not the word *growth* express a state or condition or process? And does not *a fight* express an action? There is some obscure process in our minds that lets us recognize verbs according to the notional definition, but modern grammarians are dissatisfied with the definition and want a basis for identifying verbs by form. And the verb is the only one of the four great form classes for which we can have 100 percent success in identifying by form alone. All verbs will fit into the verb paradigm.

The Verb Paradigm

The verb paradigm consists of five slots:

STEM	PRESENT THIRD PERSON SINGULAR	PRESENT PARTICIPLE	PAST TENSE	PAST PARTICIPLE
walk	walks	walking	walked	walked
run	runs	running	ran	run
break	breaks	breaking	broke	broken
set	sets	setting	set	set

Any word which will fit into *any three* of these slots is a verb by form, and all verbs will fit into at least three of the slots. In fact, all verbs will fit into all five slots, though in some cases the forms of a verb for two or even three of the slots is the same. Slots two and three are completely regular for all verbs, but there are irregularities in slots four and five. Note that words such as *could*, *might*, and *can* are not verbs, for they do not fit into the paradigm. They are modal auxiliaries and will be covered in Chapter 4 as structure words. There is one apparent exception, however. A common construction in English is

> I would rather (that) you take the job.

The verb of the main clause seems to be *would*, which will of course not fit into the paradigm. The apparent explanation for its use in this construction is that *would rather* is the equivalent of *prefer* and is just an odd English idiom. It is correct to say that the modal auxiliaries are not verbs.

English frequently converts a noun into a verb, and when the conversion is made, the word will fit into the verb paradigm. For example, the word *author* was for a long time only a noun, but then it was converted into a verb: *He recently authored a book.* When so converted, the new verb immediately took its place in all five slots of the verb paradigm:

> He will **author** a book.
> He **authors** a book every year.
> He is currently **authoring** a book.
> He **authored** a book last year.
> He has **authored** many books.

Some verbs do have verb-forming derivational suffixes. Examples:

> person + **ify** = personify
> atom + **ize** = atomize
> length + **en** = lengthen

But these suffixes are not needed for identification by form. The paradigm alone suffices, since all verbs will fit it.

Now, as we promised in the section on nouns, we must give attention to the *ing* (present participle) verb form, for it has peculiarities. Unless such a form can be made plural (such as *meetings*), it seems to be a verb, and yet it often can be made possessive. Examples:

> **drinking's** effect on the liver
> **swimming's** value as exercise
> **kissing's** contribution to courtship

This permutation means that many *ing* forms will fit into the noun paradigm as well as into their slot in the verb paradigm. Yet many grammarians are reluctant to call the words nouns by form. But we have not reached the end of the problem, for in other syntactical uses other peculiarities appear. Consider the sentence

> **Studying** can be fun.

Studying certainly appears to be a verb (present participle) functioning in a normal noun position. Furthermore the sentence

> **Studying** psychology can be fun

reinforces this analysis, for *studying* is taking the direct object *psychology*, and only a verb can take a direct object. And further, the sentence

> **Studying** effectively brings good grades

shows *studying* to be a verb, for it is modified by the *ly* adverb *effectively*. But consider this sentence:

> Effective **studying** brings good grades.

Now *studying* is modified by the adjective *effective*, and adjectives do not normally precede and modify verbs. So *studying* seems to be a noun. And aside from fitting into the noun paradigm, many *ing* forms can be modified by determiners, or noun markers, as in

> **My** studying was not effective

and

> **Some** swimming is beneficial.

So a real problem exists in identifying the present participle as a part of speech by form. Our position, however, will be that *ing* forms are verbs (unless they can be made plural or unless they are adjectives that can be modified by *very*), for normally they function as verbs in several sentence positions. We will simply have to allow for the fact that present participles can often be made possessive, can often take determiners or noun markers, and can sometimes be modified by adjectives. English grammar is so complex that such apparent anomalies are not unusual. We are on safe enough ground in calling most *ing* words verbs by form.

Nonfinite Verb Forms

A **finite** verb form is one that can serve as a sentence verb. Examples:

> He **went** to the game.
> He **has been gone** several days.
> He **could have gone** early.

A **nonfinite** verb form is one that cannot serve as a sentence verb. There are twelve such forms that you will meet in Chapter 2 and later chapters:

1. **The infinitive**: *to eat, to see, to refer*
2. **The present progressive infinitive**: *to be eating, to be seeing, to be referring*
3. **Present perfect infinitive**: *to have eaten, to have seen, to have referred*
4. **Present perfect progressive infinitive**: *to have been going, to have been seeing, to have been referring*
5. **Present infinitive, passive voice**: *to be eaten, to be seen, to be referred*
6. **Present perfect infinitive, passive voice**: *to have been eaten, to have been seen, to have been referred*
7. **The present participle**: *eating, seeing, referring*
8. **The present perfect progressive participle**: *having been eating, having been seeing*
9. **The past participle**: *eaten, seen, referred*
10. **The past participle, passive voice**: *being eaten, being seen, being referred*
11. **The past perfect participle**: *having eaten, having seen, having referred*
12. **The past perfect participle, passive voice**: *having been eaten, having been seen, having been referred*

Other verb forms are finite.

If certain auxiliaries are used with the participial nonfinite forms, the combinations become finite verb forms. For example, if the present perfect participle (*been seeing*) is used with a proper auxiliary, it will make a finite verb form (*has been seeing, had been seeing*). Numbers 10, 11, and 12 are sometimes called present participles because of the *ing* auxiliaries, but since the main verb form in them is a past participle, it seems best to call them past-participial forms. Numbers 2, 3, 4, 5, and 6 may for convenience just be called infinitive phrases. Numbers 8, 10, 11, and 12 may for convenience be called participial phrases. The technical names are unimportant. Numbers 4, 6, 8, and 12 are not much used in our language. The others, especially numbers 1, 7, and 9 (the infinitive, the present participle, and the past participle) are very frequently used as nonfinite verb forms.

As you will learn in Chapter 2, these nonfinite forms variously take subjects, complements, and modifiers.

Regular and Irregular Verbs

On the basis of the paradigm, English verbs may be classified as **regular** and **irregular**, or **weak** and **strong**. The regular or weak verbs have the same form for both the past tense and the past participle. Though the ending of these forms is usually spelled *ed*, three different pronunciations are used: *t*, *d*, and *id*. The pronunciation used is dictated by the phonology of the verb being made into the past tense or past participle. Here are some examples:

> walk—walked—walked (*t*)
> drag—dragged—dragged (*d*)
> hunt—hunted—hunted (*id*)

There is some tendency for irregular verbs to become regular, as, for example, the gradual change from *dove* to *dived*.

Irregular or strong verbs occur in various forms. Some have non-regular suffixes added, as the *en* in *spoken*, but some have replacive allomorphs (see footnote on page 4). The fairly large number of English irregular verbs can be grouped into classes, as in the following examples:

> sting—stung—stung
> cling—clung—clung
>
> spin—spun—spun
> win—won—won
>
> creep—crept—crept
> keep—kept—kept
> deal—dealt—dealt
>
> drive—drove—driven
> ride—rode—ridden
> write—wrote—written
>
> sing—sang—sung
> ring—rang—rung
> swim—swam—swum
> spring—sprang—sprung

But no names have ever been given to such categories and they are of only minor interest.

Intransitive Verbs

Verbs may also be classified into these three categories: **intransitive, transitive,** and **linking.** Some subclassifications are possible, as will be mentioned, but are not necessary for a general understanding of the English verb system.[4]

An intransitive verb is one that does not take a direct object. It expresses an action, at least of sorts, but the action is not directed at any person or object that appears in the sentence structure. Here are some examples:

> The boy **laughed.**
> The girl **sat** still.
> The boat **moved** rapidly.
> The sun **rose.**
> We **were singing** merrily.

Modifiers may or may not appear with intransitive verbs.

Some verbs may function either as intransitive or transitive (see the next section for transitive verbs). Note the different uses of the following verbs:

> He **fought** long and hard.
> He **fought** a tiger.
>
> He **ate** early.
> He **ate** his dinner.
>
> He **smoked** furiously.
> He **smoked** his pipe.

Each second sentence in these examples is a transitive verb because it takes a direct object. The intransitive verbs in the first sentences have modifiers but no objects.

Transitive Verbs

A transitive verb takes a direct object and may also take an indirect object or an object complement.[5] The transitive verb is generally

---

[4] For **tense, mood,** and **aspect** of verbs see Chapter 7. Chapters 6, 7, and 8 deal with the three basic components of sentences: **subjects, verbs** (or **predicators**), and **complements.** English grammar cannot be presented in a linear fashion. You can't just proceed from point A to point B to point C and so forth and develop a clear understanding of the syntactic structure of English. Hence some repetition is apparent in this text when grammatical topics are being presented from different points of view.

[5] These types of **complements** will be treated in Chapters 8 and 9. A complement is a completer of a verb.

thought of as an action verb, though simple action is not always expressed. For example,

> I **possess** a car

has a transitive verb, for the verb has a direct object, but no real action is expressed. Here are some typical transitive verbs:

> I **repaired** the tire.
> She **bought** the perfume.
> He **played** a sonata.
> We **jumped** the creek.

Note that the direct object in these sentences has a different referent from that of the subject. Transitive verbs can take objects that have the same referent as the subject, but such an object is always a reflexive or a reciprocal pronoun. Examples:

> He cut **himself**.
> She controlled **herself**.
> They aided **each other**.

Transitive verbs also sometimes take **cognate objects**. These are objects that are noun forms of the verb. Examples:

> He **lived** a long **life**.
> She **dreamed** a **dream**.
> We **fought** a good **fight**.

Transitive verbs also appear with indirect objects and object complements (see Chapter 8). Examples:

> Harry gave **me** a ride.
> We elected John **president**.
> He considered her **beautiful**.

The indirect object in sentence one has a different referent from the direct object (*ride*). The noun object complement in sentence two has the same referent as the direct object (*John*). The adjective object complement in sentence three completes the direct object (*her*).

Some grammarians think that transitive verbs that can take an indirect object (*give, buy, find, purchase, lend, sell, make, tell, write, send, ask, build, teach, offer, pay*, and a few others) and transitive verbs that can take an object complement (*choose, elect, name, appoint, designate, select, vote, make, consider, find, prove*, and a few others) should be given subclassifications under transitive verbs, but no name has ever become accepted for these small groups of verbs. The grammar of the English verb can be well understood without labels for these verbs.

Linking Verbs

The third broad classification of verbs is the **linking** or **copulative verb**. It is not an action verb but is a "being" or "state of being" verb. It links the subject of a sentence with a complement that renames the subject (a **predicate noun**) or that modifies the subject (a **predicate adjective**). The linking verb can be subclassified, for some will take only predicate adjectives:

> He **grew** tall

but not

> ·*He grew a beard (transitive).

> That **tastes** good

but not

> *That tastes a steak.

And some linking verbs will take either predicate adjectives or predicate nouns:

> He remained sick.
> He remained president.

> He seemed intelligent.
> He seemed a giant.

The whole group of linking verbs is quite small, the main ones being *to be*,[6] *to remain, to become, to appear, to seem, to continue, to stay, to stand, to grow, to turn, to taste, to look, to smell, to sound,* and *to get.* Some of these verbs may also function as intransitive or transitive verbs:

> He grew a tree. (transitive)
> He remained there. (intransitive)

In a few instances a verb not normally thought of as linking may take a predicate adjective and thus function as a linking verb. Examples:

> The well went **dry**.
> Gaylen proved **capable**.

---

[6]*To be* is a special case as an English verb. In fact, some grammarians even refuse to call it a verb at all. It has special characteristics that no other verb has. It is the only verb left in English which has the grammatical function of person: *I am, you are, he is.* It is also the only one that has number in the past tense: *I was, you were, he was, they were.* And it has special meanings (see Chapter 8). It may, however, be satisfactorily classified as a linking verb, for it can take a predicate noun or a predicate adjective.

Both *dry* and *capable* are predicate adjectives modifying *well* and *Gaylen*, and thus *went* and *proved* are functioning as linking verbs, though usually they do not.

Sometimes a sentence will be ambiguous because the reader or hearer cannot tell whether a verb is intransitive or linking. Example:

> The child looks backward.

If *looks* is an intransitive verb, then *backward* is an adverbial modifier telling the direction in which the child is looking. But if *looks* is a linking verb, then *backward* is functioning as a predicate adjective modifying *child*, and the sentence means that the child looks retarded. As was mentioned above, a verb may fall into more than one of the three classifications.

Adjectives

Functional and Notional Definitions of the Adjective

One of the great weaknesses of early traditional grammar was that it used notional definitions of nouns and verbs but functional definitions of adjectives and adverbs. Such a dual system of classification led to many flaws in grammatical analysis. But classification by form and function establishes a unified method of classifying all four of the lexical parts of speech and provides for much sounder analysis.

The functional definition of the adjective was that it modifies a noun or pronoun. Now it is true that many if not most modifiers of nouns and pronouns are adjectives, but many such modifiers are not (see pp. 44–47 and 261–274 for illustrations). So the system was allowed to call nouns and verbs and even adverbs adjectives at certain times, but to call them nouns, verbs, and adverbs at other times. Also it was allowed to call many structure words adjectives when they manifestly had no characteristics of adjectives proper. The whole system was, indeed, very shaky, for it did not allow for classification according to both **form** and **function**. Remember, the parts of speech by form cross freely into each other's territory when used in sentences.

Realizing that their dual system of classification of nouns, verbs, adjectives, and adverbs was hardly tenable, some grammarians tried to give a notional definition of the adjective, to complement the notional definitions of nouns and verbs. But the best they could do was to say that an adjective expresses "a quality or description." These words are far too abstract to denote a satisfactory notional definition, even though we do recognize an adjective as a describing word. Certainly a quality is expressed in *devotion*, but the word is surely not an adjective. And the word *stumbles* has an element of description in it, but is assuredly a verb. So modern grammarians sought to establish a definition of the adjective by form so that it could be fitted into the great form classes with nouns, verbs, and adverbs. As with nouns, the two main means of identifying an adjective by form are to fit it into the adjective paradigm or to identify it by adjective-forming derivational suffixes.

The Adjective Paradigm

The basic part of the adjective paradigm is the so-called **comparable paradigm**, which expresses the comparative and superlative forms of adjectives with the addition of *er* and *est* or *more* and *most*:

> sweet—sweeter—sweetest
> beautiful—more beautiful—most beautiful

But this part of the paradigm alone is not enough to identify the adjective by form, for adverbs compare in the same way:

> soon—sooner—soonest
> rapidly—more rapidly—most rapidly

So the adjective paradigm must be extended:

STEM	ER/MORE	EST/MOST	LY	NESS
pretty	prettier	prettiest	prettily	prettiness
gentle	gentler	gentlest	gently	gentleness
icy	icier	iciest	icily	iciness
small	smaller	smallest	—	smallness
convenient	more convenient	most convenient	conveniently	—
good	better	best	—	goodness
ill	worse	worst	—	illness
little	less	least	—	littleness

If a word will compare and will also *either* make an adverb by the addition of *ly or* make a noun by the addition of *ness*, then it is an adjective by form, for it fits into the adjective paradigm.

Adjective-Forming Derivational Suffixes

The adjective can also be identified by derivational suffix alone. Here are some of the most common adjective-forming suffixes:

> athlete + **ic** = athletic
> boy + **ish** = boyish
> snow + **y** = snowy
> person + **al** = personal
> resist + **ant** = resistant
> exist + **ent** = existent
> fortune + **ate** = fortunate

mercy + **less** = merciless
assert + **ive** = assertive
quarrel + **some** = quarrelsome
moment + **ary** = momentary
courage + **ous** = courageous
sin + **ful** = sinful
prohibit + **ory** = prohibitory
eat + **able** = eatable
preserve + **ative** = preservative
rich + **ly** = richly

Note in the last example that the *ly* does not make an adverb; it is a different *ly* from the inflectional suffix. Other examples are *kindly, lovely, deadly, comely, newly, lively, queenly, manly, portly.* Also note that many, if not most, of the adjectives formed by suffixes will also fit into the paradigm.

Some adjective-forming suffixes occur in words with **bound roots**, that is, roots which by themselves cannot stand as words. Examples:

contr- + **ary** = contrary
sul- + **en** = sullen
du- + **al** = dual
ter- + **ific** = terrific
pens- + **ive** = pensive
fal- + **ible** = fallible
frag- + **ile** = fragile
cert- + **ain** = certain
ranc- + **id** = rancid

Two other adjective-forming derivational suffixes require special attention: *ing* and *ed*. These as we know are also (and usually) inflectional endings of verbs, making the present and past participles. These two verb forms frequently function as adjectivals, though they are still verbs by form. Examples:

a **swimming** boy
a **created** disturbance
a **bound** book

These examples are verbs by form but are functioning as adjectivals because they are modifying nouns. But some *ing* and *ed* forms are true adjectives by form. Examples:

an **interesting** book
a **charming** girl
an **excited** dog
a **devoted** mother

The test used to differentiate between these words with identical forms is to see whether the qualifier *very* will modify them. If *very* will modify one of these words, it is an adjective by form and the *ing* or *ed* is a derivational suffix; if *very* will not modify it, it is a verb by form. *Very* can never modify a verb, only adjectives and adverbs. Examples:

> a very charming girl

but not

> *a very swimming boy;
>
> a very excited dog

but not

> *a very created disturbance.

An adjective ending in *ing* or *ed* also usually can be compared: *more excited, most excited*. Verbs cannot be compared. As we also know, these adjective forms are also frequently verb forms. Examples:

> He is **charming** the snake.
> He **excited** the dog.

Note that the qualifier *very* cannot modify these verbs. The grammatical fact here is that many words in English fit into more than one form class.

Almost all adjectives, then, can be identified by the paradigm or by adjective-forming derivational suffixes. There are a few exceptions, chiefly those in the next section, but they are so few that identification of adjectives by form is virtually 100 percent successful.

Adjectives Used Only in the Predicate

There are a few adjectives which cannot be used as modifiers preceding the noun but only as predicate adjectives. Here are the common ones:

> The boy is **afraid**.
> The teacher is **aghast**.
> I am **aweary**.
> I was **agape** at his cheekiness.
> Sanskrit is **akin** to Latin.
> I was **awake** early.
> That snake is **alive**.

As was mentioned, few of these adjectives will fit into the paradigm, though they will compare.

Absolute Superlatives

Three adjectives that since the eighteenth century have provoked arguments about comparison (degree) are *unique, correct*, and *perfect*. Prescriptive grammarians argued that those adjectives cannot be compared, for something is either correct, perfect, or unique or it isn't. Thus such expressions as *I have a very unique book* or *my paper is more perfect than yours* were considered by some early authorities to be grammatical errors. But of course these three words have for a long time been used in a relative sense. *Unique* now can mean "quite unusual" as well as "being the only one of its kind," its original meaning. And certainly excellent writers and speakers use such phrases as *more perfect* and *less correct*.

There are, however, a few **absolute superlatives** in English—words which cannot logically admit of comparison. Some of them are *everlasting, vertical, endless, dead, eternal, perpetual, mortal, universal, matchless, infinite, single*, and *empty*. Words like *honest, round, square, right, erect, holy, divine*, and *sincere* are really in the same category as *unique, perfect*, and *correct*.

Adverbs

Functional and Notional Definitions of the Adverb

The early traditional grammarians gave a functional definition of the adverb as well as of the adjective, in contrast to the notional definitions of the noun and verb. The functional definition is that "an adverb is a word that modifies a verb, adjective, or other adverb." The weakness here is obvious inasmuch as many words that modify verbs, adjectives, and adverbs are not adverbs by form. For example, in

Hemingway wrote **standing,**

standing modifies the verb *wrote* but is unmistakably a verb by form. The flaw in the old system disappears, however, when we classify by form and function. In the above sentence, *standing* is a verb by form but an adverbial by function, since it modifies a verb. Also in the old system a number of **qualifiers**, which are structure words and will be discussed in Chapter 4, were called adverbs because they modify adjectives and adverbs. The chief of these are *very, rather, quite*, and *somewhat*. Note that these words, except for *somewhat*, cannot modify verbs and thus are considerably different from pure adverbs. For example:

He ran rapidly.
*He ran very.

As with the adjective, the old functional definition of the adverb is not tenable.

Grammarians also tried to give a notional definition of the adverb, and here they had some success. An adverb, they said, "expresses time, place, or manner." Most adverbs, but not all, are covered by this notional definition. The words *then*, *there*, and *thus* will replace most adverbs:

> He is leaving **soon**. (*then*)
> He is **outside**. (*there*)
> He plays **beautifully**. (*thus*)

It might seem that *thus* is not an accurate substitute for *beautifully*, but when thought of in the meaning *in this manner*, it is. The test is very useful, but unfortunately it cannot be applied with 100 percent success. For example, in

> **Perhaps** he will leave,

perhaps cannot be so replaced, though it seems to be an adverb.

Also most adverbials (which may be other parts of speech by form or may be word groups) can be replaced by *then*, *there*, or *thus*. Examples:

> He walked **home**. (*there*)
> He left last **year**. (*then*)
> He stood **talking**. (*thus*)

Home is a noun; *year* is a noun; and *talking* is a verb. Thus the notional definition of the adverb really breaks down, useful as it is. Again, we must classify by form and function. Notional definitions have limited use.

Since not all adverbs express time, place, and manner, later grammarians expanded the time-place-manner notional definition to include "degree, amount, purpose, result, attendant circumstances, means," and other concepts. So the definition became too unwieldy and further revealed the weakness of notional definitions.

Modern grammarians want a formal definition of the adverb so it can take its place in the great form classes. But success in classifying adverbs by form is less than 100 percent. The adverb is the most refractory of the form classes.

The Adverb Paradigm

The pure adverb is formed by adding the inflectional suffix *ly* to an adjective stem. This is the basis of the adverb paradigm; most adverbs will fit the paradigm and are thus easily identifiable by form. Here is the paradigm:

ADJECTIVE STEM	LY	MORE	MOST
pretty	prettily	more prettily	most prettily
careful	carefully	more carefully	most carefully
quick	quickly	more quickly	most quickly
sad	sadly	more sadly	most sadly

Thousands and thousands of adverbs of this form exist in the language, and they are all regular. But that is not the end of the adverb story. The language has many words which appear to be adverbs but which are not formed from an adjective stem. A few, but not many, may be identified by derivational suffixes:

> up + **ward** = upward
> fore + **ward** = forward
> money + **wise** = moneywise
> clock + **wise** = clockwise
> cross + **ways** = crossways
> side + **ways** = sideways

Ward, *wise*, and *ways*, however, do little to help us identify adverbs by form, since only a few words have these suffixes.

Other Adverbs of Time, Place, and Manner

Some words that do not end in *ly* are nevertheless classified as adverbs because they express time, place, and manner and function more often as adverbials than as any of the other function classes. Some of them (*soon, fast, well* and a few others) will also compare. Here are the most common ones: *soon, fast, well, often, inside, outside, there, here, now, ahead, back, seldom, always, hereafter, thereafter, somewhere, anywhere, meantime, sometime, before, then, still, after, yet, never, already, thus, forth, overhead, headlong, behind, henceforth,* and *unaware*s. Also such words as *below, up, out, within, down, in, above,* and *across* are adverbs (a form class) as well as prepositions (a structure class). Some of them are particles as well. A **particle** is a short, uninflected structure-class word that joins with a verb to make a semantic unit (see Chapter 3). The word *not* is often called an adverb, but it is best considered a **structural negative**, for it functions with all the form-class words and some of the structure-class words. Some grammarians want to call most of these adverbs uninflected words, since they cannot be identified by form. But most grammarians, including those who work for dictionary makers, admit that they rely on the old functional and notional definitions of the adverb.

Other words have been called adverbs but are really structure words and will be discussed in Chapter 4. Some of the more common ones are *however, nevertheless, consequently, therefore, moreover, thus* (as a connective), *hence, because, when, since, though, if, as, in that, so, so that,* and *while*. These words are connectives and do not belong to the form classes.

Miscellaneous Adverbs

Besides the refractory groups mentioned above, there are still a few words in English which do not denote time, place, or manner and do not fit the paradigm, but which nevertheless seem to be adverbs. A few are *perhaps, indeed, also, too, maybe, instead, offhand,* and *besides*. Never forget, however, that many English words fall into more than one classification. For example, in

> He came, too

too is an adverb; but in

> I am too tired to go

too is a qualifier, a structure word. Or in

> He is rich besides

besides is an adverb; but in

> No one besides me came

besides is a preposition, a structure word. Many, many such over-lappings exist in English.

– – – – – – – – – – – – –

Most of the words in the four great form classes, then, are identifiable by form, enough of them so that this system eliminates many of the grave flaws and weaknesses of the old dual classification system. Anomalies do exist in the language, but they do not cause much trouble in grammatical analysis. Chapter 2 on the parts of speech by function, Chapter 3 on verb-particle composites, and Chapter 4 on structure words will complete this system of analysis of parts of speech and will make the system more comprehensible.

EXERCISES

1. The form classes are open classes, new words being added to them almost daily. Find five nouns that have been added to our language

since 1934 (the use of Webster's Second and Third *New International Dictionary* is advised here). Find out what the process of *back formation* is and determine whether it has been used on your five nouns. As a humorous exercise, create two new nouns of your own which could be used in the language. See if back formation can be applied to them.

2. Consult two modern unabridged dictionaries to see how they define *noun*.

3. Into how many slots of the noun paradigm will each of the following words fit:

rabbit	consternation
cellar	mathematics
degree	achievement
moon	marijuana
goose	Gillis
approach	jar
quality	love

4. List as many nouns as you can that have the derivational suffixes *ure*, *age*, and *dom*.

5. Find three nouns whose derivational suffixes are simply a change in sound, as *advise* to *advice*.

6. Try to find two nouns not listed in the text which will not fit into the paradigm and which do not have derivational suffixes. How do you identify them as nouns? Or can you?

7. List five nouns (not from the text) which may be used as either count or mass nouns.

8. Explain the following as both compound nouns and grammatical structures (as grammatical structures all the items will have to be spelled as two words). What are the different stress patterns?

bluebird	tenderfoot
sweetheart	hardtop
sweet potatoes	hot dog
softball	stronghold
sparkling water	black market
old-timer	sharpshooter
hard ball	bulls-eye

9. List two verbs (not in the text) that have five forms for the paradigm, two that have four, and two that have only three.

10. Find two verbs (besides *to author*) that have recently been converted from nouns.

11. List a half-dozen verbs (not from the text) which can function as both intransitive and transitive verbs.

12. Identify the verbs in the following sentences as either intransitive, transitive, or linking:

    a. Mary suffers agonizing pain.
    b. Perry suffers occasionally.
    c. Napoleon has been dead a long time.
    d. Nixon laughed uncontrollably.
    e. We chose Susan captain.
    f. He considered her a pig.
    g. He found her a pig.
    h. He spoke in the most insinuating way.
    i. He felt bad.
    j. He felt badly.
    k. He felt Clay's muscles.
    l. We walked into the theater.
    m. The pitcher walked the batter.
    n. The clerk sold the girl a dress.
    o. Mamie sold out to the club owners.
    p. Linda remained sweet-tempered all day.
    q. Horace remained outside.
    r. The music sounds loud.
    s. He sounds like an expert.
    t. The butler sounded the gong.
    u. Mother appeared tired.
    v. Her date appeared quickly.
    w. Watson appeared a fool.
    x. The student argued vehemently.
    y. The lawyer argued the case forcefully.

13. Which of the following words are by form verbs only, which adjectives only, and which both verbs and adjectives? Remember that *ing* and *ed* can be adjective-forming derivational suffixes as well as inflectional verb suffixes.

chattering	devoting
convincing	located
dedicated	skilled
referred	cunning
denied	consecrated
received	debating
retiring	entranced
denying	rugged
demanding	printed
condescending	detached
motivated	coveting
stunning	embarrassed

14. Explain how these words will or will not fit into the adjective paradigm:

<table>
<tr><td>mighty</td><td>black</td></tr>
<tr><td>cold</td><td>bald</td></tr>
<tr><td>little</td><td>holy</td></tr>
<tr><td>big</td><td>desperate</td></tr>
<tr><td>anxious</td><td>lucky</td></tr>
<tr><td>common</td><td>old</td></tr>
<tr><td>bare</td><td>foreign</td></tr>
<tr><td>clear</td><td>mere</td></tr>
<tr><td>aghast</td><td>terrible</td></tr>
<tr><td>above</td><td>upstairs</td></tr>
</table>

15. Which words in the following sentences can be replaced by *then*, *there*, or *thus*? Are they adverbs by form or are they in one of the other three form classes?

a. He danced gracefully.
b. He will arrive Sunday.
c. He can run fast.
d. I will love you always.
e. He sat thinking.
f. He looked curiously.
g. He works days.
h. He went inside.
i. He will arrive early.
j. She behaved divinely.

16. Place each of the following words into the form classes and explain the basis of your classification.

<table>
<tr><td>jumpy</td><td>dive</td></tr>
<tr><td>cursory</td><td>morbid</td></tr>
<tr><td>mainly</td><td>seizure</td></tr>
<tr><td>scratch</td><td>meddlesome</td></tr>
<tr><td>syrup</td><td>canine</td></tr>
<tr><td>friendly</td><td>congenially</td></tr>
<tr><td>marvelous</td><td>marvel</td></tr>
<tr><td>edgy</td><td>edge</td></tr>
<tr><td>fluent</td><td>effluent</td></tr>
<tr><td>rank</td><td>dank</td></tr>
<tr><td>depth</td><td>associate</td></tr>
<tr><td>newly</td><td>compelling</td></tr>
<tr><td>devotee</td><td>printed</td></tr>
<tr><td>consecrated</td><td>device</td></tr>
<tr><td>broad</td><td>heretofore</td></tr>
<tr><td>never</td><td>conductivity</td></tr>
<tr><td>mileage</td><td>heartily</td></tr>
<tr><td>nonsense</td><td>nonsensical</td></tr>
<tr><td>fit</td><td>lay</td></tr>
<tr><td>break</td><td>being</td></tr>
</table>

2 THE PARTS OF SPEECH BY FUNCTION

The Four Great Function Classes

As has already been emphasized, grammatical analysis calls for classification of parts of speech by **form** and by **function**. The reason for this need is that functions normally performed by, say, nouns are also often performed by words of the other three form classes and by certain structure-class words too. And also in actual sentences these functions are frequently performed by word groups—prepositional phrases, verbal phrases, and dependent clauses. For example, the subject of a verb is most often a noun, but a verb can also function in that position. Example:

> **Skating** is good exercise.

Though functioning as a subject here, **skating** fits into the verb form class, not the noun form class. Or consider this perfectly grammatical English sentence:

> **Under the tree** is better than in the sun.

Under the tree is a prepositional phrase by form, but here it is functioning as a subject. So in addition to form, we need to classify by function and we need terminology to distinguish form from function. We have such terminology: In the sentences above both *skating* (a verb by form) and *under the tree* (a prepositional phrase by form) are **nominals** by function, for they operate in a function usually performed by nouns.

34

Words in all the form classes (and word groups too) cross freely into each other's territory. So never forget: **form** and **function**.

Words and word groups operating in normal noun functions are called **nominals**; those in verb functions, **verbals**; those in adjective functions, **adjectivals**; and those in adverb functions, **adverbials**. Remember these terms well, for throughout this book we will distinguish between form and function.

An operational knowledge of the parts of speech by function is absolutely necessary for understanding. Consider, for example, this short sentence:

> They are fighting roosters.

It is ambiguous because we do not know how *fighting* is functioning as a part of speech. If it is functioning as the **sentence verb** (**predicator**), the sentence means that a group of people or animals is engaged in a fight with some roosters, and the *they* refers to the group of people or animals. But if *fighting* is functioning as an adjectival, the sentence means that some roosters are fighting, and the *they* refers to the roosters. Finally, if *fighting* is a part of a compound noun, just a type of rooster is being identified and a fight may not be going on at all. Though an analytical knowledge of parts of speech is not necessary for the ordinary reader or listener, an operational understanding is.

Now we will examine the four great function classes in detail.

Nominals

The Common Functions of the Noun in Sentences

Nouns have numerous functions in sentences. Here we will discuss the eight most common functions (omitting **direct address**, which is not of interest grammatically, and leaving to Chapter 8 the function of the noun as **complement of the adjective**). Any word or word group that performs one of these noun functions is a nominal. It may be a word in any one of the four form classes, a word in one of the structure classes, or a word group of some kind. Before we discuss the nominals, we will examine the noun performing each of the eight functions.

1. *The subject of a verb or a verbal.* Normally, the word that acts as a subject is of the noun form class.

> The **student** entered his class late.
> The **sun** having set, we left the park.
> Mary wanted **John** to drive the car.

The first example illustrates a simple sentence subject; *student* is a noun by form and a nominal by function. In the second sentence, *sun* is the subject of the nonfinite verb *having set*; *sun* is a noun by form and a nominal by function. In the third sentence, *John* is the subject of the infinitive *to drive* (the infinitive with a subject is discussed in Chapter 6); *John* is a noun and functions as a nominal.

2. *The direct object of a verb.* The second most common function of the noun is as the direct object of a verb. (See Chapter 8 for discussion of direct objects, indirect objects, object complements, and predicate nouns.) Here are three examples:

> The ranger killed the **snake**.
> The ranger having killed the **snake**, we sighed with relief.
> Mary wanted John to drive the **car**.

In sentence one, *snake* is the direct object of a simple sentence verb. In sentence two, *snake* is the direct object of the nonfinite verb *having killed*. And in sentence three, *car* is the direct object of the infinitive *to drive*. All three of these words are nouns by form and nominals by function.

3. *The indirect object of a verb.*

> Father gave **Edward** a dollar.
> Father having given **Edward** a dollar, we went to the Slurp Shop.
> Father wants you to give **Edward** another dollar.

In the first sentence, *Edward* is the indirect object of the finite verb *gave*; in the second, of the nonfinite verb *having given*; and in the third, of the infinitive *to give*. All three *Edward*s are nominals.

Observe that these indirect objects (*Edward*) come *before* the direct objects (*dollar*). We do not say or write **Father gave a dollar Edward.*

4. *The object complement of a direct object.* When a noun comes after the direct object of a transitive verb, the position signifies that it is the object complement of this direct object.

> The Dean appointed Professor Gordon **chairman**.

Chairman is a noun by form and a nominal by function.

Observe that *chairman* and *Professor Gordon* refer to the same person; or that, in the technical language of grammar, this object and its object complement have the same **referent**. In contrast, the two successive nouns *Edward* and *dollar*—indirect and direct objects—in the preceding example have different referents.

5. *The predicate noun.* A predicate noun comes after a linking verb and has the same referent as the subject.

> Professor Gordon remained **chairman** for ten years.

Again, *chairman* is a noun by form and a nominal by function.

6. *The object of a preposition.* One of the commonest functions of a noun is as the object of a preposition.

> The cop punched me in the **stomach**.
> From the **sky** came eerie noises.

Stomach and *sky*, objects of *in* and *from*, are nouns by form and nominals by function.

7. *The retained object in a passive-voice sentence* (see Chapter 9). When an active-voice sentence which has both a direct object and an indirect object, such as

> I bought **Steve** a **car**,

is converted into a passive-voice sentence, either the direct object or the indirect object becomes the subject and the other remains as a **retained object**.

> Steve was bought a **car** (by me).
> A car was bought **Steve** (by me).

Both *car* and *Steve* are retained objects. They are nouns by form and nominals by function.

8. *The headword in an appositive phrase.* The appositive phrase (which will be discussed more fully in Chapter 10) is a repeater; it renames a noun and is said to be **in apposition to** that noun. Here are some examples:

> William Faulkner, **a writer from Mississippi**, died in 1962.
> Anticholinergics, **drugs which reduce muscle spasm**, were used in ancient times.
> That is what I want, **a date with Goldie Hawn**.

Each of the boldface constructions is an appositive. The first is in apposition to *William Faulkner*, for it renames him in different terms. In the third sentence, the appositive is in apposition to *that*. These appositives are nominals, as also are the nouns that they rename.

Sometimes titles are appositives:

> The movie **Gunga Din** was filmed in 1932.
> Faulkner's first novel, **Soldier's Pay**, did not sell well.

These appositive titles are nominals.

Nominals that Are Not Nouns

Now we will see words from the other three form classes and various kinds of word groups function as nominals.

1. *The subject of a sentence.*

>The **young** in spirit are my friends.
>**Eating** is his favorite pastime.
>**Soon** is not soon enough.
>**To sleep late** is my desire.
>**Sleeping late** is a pleasure.
>**What you do** is of no concern to me.
>**By the fence** is a good place.
>**They** came to the game.

In sentence one, the adjective *young* is functioning as a nominal; in sentence two, the present participle *eating*; in sentence three, the adverb *soon*; in sentence four, the infinitive phrase *to sleep late*; in sentence five, the present-participial phrase[1] *sleeping late*; in sentence six, the dependent clause *what you do*; in sentence seven, the prepositional phrase *by the fence*; and in sentence eight, the pronoun *they*. These simple, common sentences illustrate how freely the form classes cross over into each other's territory.

2. *The direct object of a verb.*

>The priest blessed **them.**
>The priest blessed the **poor.**
>The priest condemned **drinking.**
>I hated **doing my calisthenics.**
>We wanted **to sleep late.**
>We did **what we pleased.**
>I caught **him cheating.**
>Multiply the **above** by ten to get your answer.

In sentence one, a pronoun is functioning as a nominal; in sentence two, an adjective; in sentence three, a present participle; in sentence four, a present-participial phrase; in sentence five, an infinitive phrase; and in sentence six, a dependent clause. Sentence seven is somewhat more complicated. *Him cheating* (a present-participial phrase) is a nominal, the direct object of *caught*. *Him* is the subject of the present participle *cheating*. In sentence eight the adverb *above* is functioning as a nominal.

3. *The indirect object of a verb.*

>The governor gave the **rich** a hard time.
>The priest gave **drinking** a hard time.

---

[1]Older traditional grammar called this form a **gerund phrase**. Any *ing* verb acting as a noun was called a **gerund**. The terms are no longer useful. *Sleeping late* is indubitably a present-participial phrase by form and is a nominal by function.

In sentence one, an adjective, and in sentence two, a present participle are functioning as nominals.

4. *Object complement of a direct object.*

> I considered Sadie the **best**.
> We elected Jean **what she wanted to be**.

Here an adjective and a dependent clause are functioning as nominals.

5. *A predicate noun.*

> John is the **bravest**.
> Susie is **what every man admires**.

Also here an adjective and a dependent clause are functioning as nominals.

6. *Object of a preposition.*

> That's a good figure for this **soon**.
> Beautiful girls belong to the **amorous**.
> He is devoted to **eating**.
> Give the package to **whoever comes first**.

Here, in order, we have an adverb, an adjective, a present participle, and a dependent clause functioning as nominals.

7. *Retained direct and indirect objects.*

> I was given the **largest** (by John).
> The book was given **whoever called first** (by John).

Here an adjective is a retained direct object and a dependent clause a retained indirect object, both being nominals.

8. *The appositive.* Both present-participial phrases and dependent clauses can function as appositives. Examples:

> His mistake—**flunking French**—caused him to drop out of college.
> The belief **that like produces like** is an old superstition.
> Our first assumption—**that the rebellion would die down**—proved wrong.

In sentence one the boldface participial phrase is in apposition to *mistake* and is a nominal. In sentences two and three the boldface dependent clauses are in apposition to the nouns *belief* and *assumption* and are nominals.

Structure words used as nominals will be given further treatment under *noun substitutes* in Chapter 4.

Verbals

Verbs may function in all four function classes—that is, a verb by form may be a nominal, a verbal, an adjectival, or an adverbial. But an adjective, adverb, or noun cannot be a verbal; a verbal is always a verb by form. In a sentence like

> His letters **picture** the scene to me clearly.

picture is not a noun but a verb by form (it will fit the verb paradigm). Auxiliaries, which are not verbs by form, may be called verbals, but they are really structure words as is explained in Chapter 4.

Sentence Verbs

Sentence verbs (also called **finite verbs** and **predicators**) are verbals by function and verbs by form. Examples:

> She **drank** the gin.
> She **did drink** the gin.
> She **is drinking** the gin.
> She **will be drinking** the gin.
> She **had drunk** the gin.
> She **could drink** the gin.

Each part of the finite verb of a sentence may be called a verbal, but it is not wrong to call the whole phrase a verbal. That is, in sentence six both *could* and *drink* may each be called a verbal, or the phrase *could drink* may be called a single verbal. The latter practice is simpler and more sensible.

Nonfinite Verb Forms as Verbals

Certain forms of a verb—the infinitive and various infinitive phrases, the present participle and various participial phrases, and the past participle—cannot be used as finite verbs but may be verbals in other sentence positions. *If a verb form takes a subject or a complement or a modifier, it is a verbal by function.* Grammatical analysis becomes rather complex here. Elementary explanations will be given here, and more detailed discussion of these grammatical functions will be given in later chapters.

1. *Verbals with subjects.* Not only the finite verb of a sentence but also nonfinite forms can take subjects. Examples:

> The bell **having rung**, we left the classroom.
> Nancy caught Vince **kissing** Joan.
> We asked Mary **to sing**.

Each of the boldface verb forms is a verbal by function, for each has a subject. Real complexity enters the second and third sentences, however. The whole phrase *Vince kissing Joan* is the direct object of *caught* and is therefore a nominal. But *Vince* is the subject of *kissing* (*Joan* is its object), making *kissing* a verbal. In sentence three the whole phrase *Mary to sing* is the direct object of the verb *asked* and is therefore a nominal. But within that nominal, *to sing* is a verbal because it has a subject, *Mary*. Note that an infinitive or present participle used by itself as a direct object (or subject) is not a verbal. Examples:

> We wanted **to sing**.
> The Arabs prohibit **drinking**.

To sing and *drinking* here are nominals because they are the direct objects of the verbs *wanted* and *prohibit*, but they are not verbals because they do not have subjects, complements, or modifiers, even though they are verbs by form.

2. *Verbals with complements.* The most common complements are the **direct object, the indirect object**, the **predicate noun**, the **predicate adjective**, and the **object complement**. If a nonfinite verb form takes one of these, it is a verbal by function.

2a. *The verbal with a direct object.*

> **Having shut** the door, I sank to sleep.
> **To shoot** buzzards is illegal.
> **Hitting** small children is despicable.

Each of the boldface verbals has a direct object. In sentence one, *having shut the door* as a whole is an adjectival because it modifies the pronoun *I*. Within that adjectival is the verbal *having shut*, which has the direct object *door*. In sentence two, *to shoot buzzards* is a subject and therefore a nominal. But within that nominal, *to shoot* is a verbal because it has the direct object *buzzards*. In sentence three, *hitting small children* is a subject and therefore a nominal, but within that nominal *hitting* is a verbal because it has the direct object *children*.

2b. *The verbal with a direct object and an indirect object.*

> **Giving** me a book, he said, "Read it."
> She wanted **to give** me a date.

In sentence one, *giving me a book* is an adjectival modifying *he*, but within that adjectival *giving* is a verbal because it has the indirect object *me* and the direct object *book*. In sentence two, *to give me a date* is a nominal as the direct object of *wanted*. But within that nominal *to give* is a verbal because it has the indirect object *me* and the direct object *date.* In that sentence there is, in effect, a direct object within a direct object.

2c. *The verbal with a predicate noun.*

> **Being** a liberal, he voted Democratic.
> She wanted **to be** a queen.

The grammar of these simple sentences is complex. *Being* is a verbal because it has the predicate noun *liberal.* The *he* of the sentence is also the displaced subject of *being a liberal.* The two sentences implied are *he was a liberal* and *he voted Democratic.* The whole present-participial phrase *being a liberal* is, however, an adjectival by function because it modifies the pronoun *he.* In sentence two, *to be* is a verbal because it has the predicate noun *queen*, and the whole infinitive phrase *to be a queen* is a nominal as the direct object of *wanted.* Note that in

> She wanted **to eat**

to eat is not a verbal, for it has no subject, complement, or modifier. As a direct object, it is a nominal only (a verb by form).

2d. *The verbal with a predicate adjective.*

> **Being** sweet-tempered, she kissed him.
> She wants **to be** successful.

In sentence one, *being sweet-tempered* is a present-participial phrase by form and an adjectival by function, since it modifies the pronoun *she.* Within that adjectival, *being* is a verbal because it has the predicate adjective *sweet-tempered.* In sentence two, *to be successful* is an infinitive phrase by form and a nominal by function, since it is the direct object of *wants.* Within that nominal, *to be* is a verbal because it has the predicate adjective *successful.*

2e. *The verbal with a direct object and an object complement.*

> **Having chosen** Dick captain, we started the game.
> We wanted **to choose** Fred captain.

In sentence one, *having chosen Dick captain* is an adjectival as a modifier of *we.* Within that adjectival, *having chosen* is a verbal because it has the direct object *Dick* and the object complement *captain.* In sentence two, *to choose Fred captain* is a nominal as the direct object of *wanted.* In that nominal *to choose* is a verbal because it has the direct object *Fred* and the object complement *captain.*

3. *Verbals with modifiers.* If a nonfinite verb form has an adverbial modifier, it is a verbal by function.

3a. *Single-word modifiers with verbals.*

> **Sleeping** late is pleasurable.

To drink rapidly is gauche.
To eat standing is juvenile.

In sentence one, *sleeping*, a present participle by form, is a verbal because it is modified by *late*. The whole participial phrase *sleeping late* is a nominal because it is a subject. In sentence two, *to drink* is a verbal because it is modified by *rapidly*; with no modifier, it would be a nominal. The whole infinitive phrase *to drink rapidly* is a nominal because it is a subject. In sentence three, *to eat* is a verbal because it is modified by *standing*. *Standing* is a verb (present participle) by form but an adverbial by function because it is modifying a verb. The whole construction *to eat standing* is a subject and therefore a nominal.

3b. *Prepositional-phrase modifiers with verbals.*

Getting into the car, I sprained my ankle.
I want **to eat** in the cafeteria.

Both *getting* and *to eat* are verbals because they are modified by the adverbial prepositional phrases *into the car* and *in the cafeteria*. The entire present-participial phrase *getting into the car* is an adjectival modifying the pronoun *I*, and the entire infinitive phrase *to eat in the cafeteria* is the direct object of *want* and therefore a nominal.

3c. *Dependent-clause modifiers with verbals.*

Eating when you feel like it is normal.
Blushing while he told the story, I covered my face.

Both *eating* and *blushing* are verbals because each is modified by a dependent clause; without modifiers they would be a nominal and an adjectival, respectively. The entire construction *eating when you feel like it* is a subject and therefore a nominal. The entire construction *blushing while he told the story* is an adjectival because it modifies the pronoun *I*.

Adjectivals

The Normal Function of the Adjective

The normal function of an adjective is to modify a noun or pronoun. This is the original functional definition of the adjective given by early traditional grammar. But words other than adjectives by form can modify nouns, and thus we must distinguish between form and function.

Here are some typical examples of adjectives by form functioning as adjectivals:

The **funny** clown delighted the **excited** children.

Marriage to Charlotte will make a **happier** me.
The **most beautiful** girl did not win the crown.

The adjectives in boldface will all compare and will all make adverbs with the addition of *ly*. Usually, a word modifying a noun or pronoun is an adjective by form. For that reason we apply the term **adjectival** to any word or word group modifying a noun or pronoun.

Adjectivals that Are Not Adjectives

Words in the noun, verb, and adverb form classes and also various kinds of word groups and structure words can function as adjectivals.

1. *Nouns as adjectivals.* Millions of school children have been baffled and frustrated by grammar because they have been taught to call, say, *cat* a noun in *the cat in the box* but to call it an adjective in *cat food.* The simple remedy for this confusion is to identify parts of speech by form and by function and to recognize that a noun can modify a noun. Here are a few example*s*:

the **steel** rails	the **plastic** telephone
the **rubber** tires	the **owl** feathers

All the nouns in boldface are adjectivals because they modify nouns. Sometimes a two-part construction is a compound noun rather than a noun modifying a noun, as for example, *car hop, tree house,* and *motor court.* But it is a very minor mistake in grammatical analysis to say that *car* is modifying *hop* or that *tree* is modifying *house.*

The modification of nouns by nouns is really a very complex aspect of grammar. Note the various transformations of the following constructions. A **transformation** is the change of a construction from its surface structure in the language to its so-called deep structure, that structure which is implied beneath the surface, or a change from its deep structure to its surface structure.

an August sale = a sale during August
a shirt sale = a sale of shirts
a June-bride sale = a sale for June brides
a warehouse sale = a sale at a warehouse
a moonlight sale = a sale in the moonlight
an anniversary sale = a sale honoring an anniversary
a celebration sale = a sale intended to celebrate
a discount sale = a sale giving discounts
a clearance sale = a sale for the purpose of clearance
an inventory sale = a sale to reduce inventory
a big sale = a sale which is big (*adjective*)
that sale (*no transformation possible*)

On the surface each of these constructions except the last two seems to be just a noun modifying a noun. But as the transformation demonstrates, some complex process is going on beneath the surface.

2. *Verbs as adjectivals.*

> The boy **swimming** is my nephew.
> That **laughing** clown is really sad.
> The **recommended** procedure is to apply in triplicate.
> These **stolen** shells are valuable.
> The girl **to date** is Susie.

The first two boldface adjectivals are present-participle verb forms, the next two past-participle forms, and the last one an infinitive. Note that they are really verbs by form and not adjectives. Adjectives by form can end in *ing* or *ed* (see page 25), but when they do they can usually be compared, can be modified by *very*, and (usually) can take *ly* to form an adverb. The boldface verbs above can do none of these. They are all adjectivals because they are modifying nouns.

3. *Adverbs as adjectivals.*

> The racketeers pulled an **inside** job.
> The car **ahead** is speeding.
> The **above** directions must be followed faithfully.
> The apartment **below** is vacant.

The *ly* adverb is never used as an adjectival; for example, you would never say *a happily man*. The words in boldface above have been called uninflected words by some grammarians on the grounds that they cannot be identified by form. But most grammarians recognize them as adverbs, as was explained in Chapter 1. They are adjectivals here because they are modifying the nouns *job*, *car*, *directions*, and *apartment*.

4. *Prepositional phrases as adjectivals.*

> the girl **in the next apartment**
> the man **from Mars**
> the man **of the hour**
> the boy **for her**

These prepositional phrases, since they modify nouns, are adjectivals by function.

5. *Verbal phrases as adjectivals.*

> The girl **wearing the sweater** is Trudy Bess.
> The man **to see about tickets** is Jerry Collis.

In sentence one, the present-participial phrase *wearing the sweater* is an adjectival modifying *girl*. Within that adjectival, *wearing* is a verbal

with the direct object *sweater*. In sentence two, the infinitive phrase *to see about tickets* is an adjectival modifying *man*. In that adjectival, *to see* is a verbal because it is modified by *about tickets*; with no modifier, it would be the adjectival.

    6. *Dependent clauses as adjectivals.*

> The student **who finishes first** will receive the highest grade.
> The reason **why I lied** was that I was afraid.
> The day **when you graduate** should be declared a holiday.

In sentence one the adjective clause *who finishes first* is an adjectival modifying *student*. In sentence two the noun clause *why I lied* is an adjectival modifying *reason*. And in sentence three the adverb clause *when you graduate* is an adjectival modifying *day*. Noun, adjective, and adverb dependent clauses can cross over into territory of others, just as form-class words can.

    7. *Structure words as adjectivals.* Various structure words modify nouns and therefore may be called adjectivals. Usually, however, they are just referred to by their class name. Examples:

> **That** cat is mine.
> **One** dog is enough.
> **John's** girl is intelligent.
> **All** Gurkhas are brave.
> **Which** book did you lose?

The boldface words are adjectivals because they modify nouns, but it is not necessary to apply that term to them. All are functioning as **determiners** here, but have other classifications as well.

Adverbials

The Normal Function of the Adverb

    The normal function of the adverb is to modify a verb or, less frequently, an adjective or other adverb, but words other than adverbs by form can modify verbs, adjectives, and adverbs and thus function as adverbials.

    Here are some typical examples of adverbs by form functioning as adverbials:

> The players ate **rapidly**.
> It will rain **soon**.
> The children are playing **outside**.
> Henry is **completely** capable.
> Jerry fought **extremely** courageously.

In the first three sentences the adverbs are modifying the verbs *ate*, *will rain*, and *are playing* and are thus adverbials. *Rapidly* is the "pure" adverb, made by adding *ly* to an adjective. *Soon* and *outside* are recognized as adverbs by most grammarians and lexicographers. *Completely* and *extremely* are pure *ly* adverbs modifying the adjective *capable* and the adverb *courageously*.

Adverbials that Are Not Adverbs

Nouns, verbs, adjectives, qualifiers, and various word groups can also function as adverbials.

1. *The noun as adverbial.*

> Patty will arrive **Saturday.**
> The mail did not come **today.**
> I walked Susie **home.**
> He sleeps **days.**

Note that the four words in boldface are nouns by form, for they will fit into the noun paradigm. But here they are adverbials because they are modifying the verbs *will arrive*, *did not come*, *walked*, and *sleeps*. Note that *then* or *there* can be substituted for these adverbials, usually evidence that a word or phrase is an adverbial.

2. *The verb as adverbial.*

> Hemingway wrote **standing.**
> We think better **sitting.**

Standing and *sitting* are of course verbs by form, but here they are modifying verbs (*wrote* and *think*) and thus are adverbials. Verbs, however, do not often function as adverbials.

3. *The adjective as adverbial.*

> Tim plays **dirty.**
> We arrived **late.**

Both *dirty* and *late* are adjectives by form; they can be compared and can take the suffix *ly* to make adverbs. But since they are here modifying verbs they are adverbials. But adjectives seldom function as adverbials.

4. *The prepositional phrase as adverbial.*

> We walked **into the store.**
> Jane came **by my house.**
> An attendant looked **over the cabana door.**

Prepositional phrases modify verbs very frequently and, doing so, are adverbials.

5. *Verb phrases as adverbials.*

> Ray came **running like a rabbit**.
> Tom arrived **driving a jeep**.
> We waited **to see the last show**.
> We worked hard **to win the election**.

The boldface constructions in the first two sentences are present-participial phrases, but since they are modifying *came* and *arrived*, they are adverbials. Note that *running* is a verbal (not an adverbial) since it has a modifier and that *driving* is a verbal since it has a direct object. The infinitive phrases in the last two sentences are adverbials modifying *waited* and *worked*. One way to test to see if an infinitive is an adverbial is to see if *in order to* will go with it. If so, as in the above two cases, the infinitive is an adverbial. Note that in

> He's the man **to see**

and in

> I want **to go**

in order to cannot be used. *To see* is an adjectival modifying *man*, and *to go* is the direct object of *want* and is therefore a nominal. On rare occasions, however, as will be shown in Chapter 10, an infinitive can modify a verb and still not be able to take *in order to*.

6. *Dependent clauses as adverbials.* Only the adverb dependent clause can function as an adverbial, and it does not do so very often. Noun and adjective clauses do not function as adverbials. As will be demonstrated in Chapter 11, adverb clauses usually function as sentence modifiers. But when one modifies a verb only, it is functioning as an adverbial. Examples:

> Talking **while you chew** is impolite.
> Blushing **as he listened**, John grew embarrassed.

In sentence one the adverb clause *while you chew* is modifying the present participle *talking* and is therefore an adverbial. The entire present-participial phrase *talking while you chew* is a subject and therefore a nominal; *talking* is a verbal (not a nominal) because it has an adverbial modifier. In sentence two *as he listened* is an adverbial modifying the present participle *blushing*. The whole participial phrase *blushing as he listened* is an adjectival modifying *John*, and *blushing* is a verbal since it has a modifier.

7. *Qualifiers as adverbials.*

> Your car runs **very** smoothly.
> Susan is **rather** pretty.

The weather is **somewhat** cold.
She will arrive **quite** soon.

The boldface words are **qualifiers**, which, as you will learn in Chapter 4, are a rather extensive group of structure words that modify adjectives and adverbs (but seldom verbs). They may be called adverbials, but usually are just referred to as qualifiers. If an *ly* adverb (made from an adjective)—such as *extremely* and *completely*—modifies an adjective or adverb, it is an adverb by form and an adverbial by function. Most other words that modify adjectives or adverbs are qualifiers.

EXERCISES

1. The following sentences illustrate how an operational knowledge of parts of speech by function is necessary for understanding the meaning of a sentence. Figure out the possible meanings (in some cases three) in these sentences and see if you can give analytical explanations.

 a. Bathing beauties can be fun.
 b. Susan's spending money was a source of discussion.
 c. Smoking turkeys can give a good income.
 d. The moving van belongs to John.
 e. These game fish belong in the black market.
 f. They are cooking apples.

2. Identify eight common functions of nouns in these sentences, which have the nouns under examination italicized.

 a. He found *ants* in his pants.
 b. *Gary* gave his *wife* a hardtop.
 c. She wanted a husband with *money*.
 d. Ernest Hemingway, *a famous writer of the '20s, '30s, and '40s*, committed suicide.
 e. The faculty elected Marvin *president*.
 f. Dennis remained the best *player* in town.
 g. Susie was given a *kiss* by her father.
 h. Steve asked *Dave* to pay the bill.
 i. The *bars* being closed, we went home for a nightcap.

3. In the following sentences identify nominals that are not nouns. Identify the forms if you can.

 a. Only the brave deserve the fair.
 b. Europeans think consuming is America's favorite pastime.
 c. To practice tolerance is beyond the communists.

d. Where the book is located is not now known.

e. Over the fence is out.

f. I dislike studying.

g. Some people don't consider Clay the greatest.

h. John is not what you would call brilliant.

i. Perry has a good sales record for this soon.

j. Bishop Clark introduced me to praying.

4. In the following sentences identify verbals other than sentence (finite) verbs. Explain why each is a verbal.

a. The concert having ended, we dropped by Leone's for supper.

b. The coach asked John to substitute for Bill.

c. Mr. Hunter was fined for catching a catfish.

d. To hunt alligators is now illegal.

e. I thanked my father for buying me a car.

f. Remaining the department chairman, Professor Colfax tightened regulations.

g. I wanted to be the first to arrive in Uganda.

h. Being lovely, Sue enjoyed popularity.

i. Tom seems to want to be guilty.

j. Driving on the shoulder is dangerous.

k. To study after midnight is inefficient.

l. To talk rapidly is not recommended for teachers.

m. Swimming just after you have eaten can be dangerous.

n. Getting married only because you are in love is not acceptable in some societies.

5. In the following sentences identify adjectivals that are not adjectives by form. Identify the forms if you can.

a. The ostrich attitude of some politicians is deplorable.

b. Brock's held a suit sale.

c. The student talking is the dullest in the class.

d. He broke his spoken promise.

e. The dictated letter was badly punctuated.

f. The movie to see is *Lincoln*.

g. The clowning professor amused the students.

h. The footnote below is in error.

i. The inside story was leaked by Jack Anderson.

j. The talk of the town is Cheri.

k. We walked to the end of the racetrack.

l. The only student listening to the teacher is Etaoin Shrdlu.

  m. The horse to bet on in the fifth race is Gadfly.
  n. The statesman whom I admired most was Churchill.
  o. The axiom which we challenged was number 10.

6. In the following sentences identify adverbials that are not adverbs by form. Identify the forms if you can.

  a. We will shoot the rapids Tuesday.
  b. John called yesterday to say he couldn't come.
  c. Some people work nights.
  d. By which route will you walk home?
  e. He was caught lying.
  f. The cheetah ran into the nylon net.
  g. He entered the room talking rapidly.
  h. The missile was fired over the Atlantic Ocean.
  i. We studied to make an A on the exam.
  j. I haven't been happy since you went away.

7. Identify the function class of each of the italicized words or constructions in the following sentences. Identify them by form, too, if you can.

  a. We communicated *by satellite*.
  b. I think *dating* is a good American custom.
  c. The *iron* gates of life are closing *for me*.
  d. I begged Susan *to give* me another chance.
  e. The time *having come*, I went to my *prison* cell.
  f. The boys *wrestling* are twins.
  g. I don't know *what do do with you*.
  h. He contributed *because he favored the strike*.
  i. I decided *to enroll in the Foreign Legion*.
  j. *Waiting* for an hour, I finally gave up.
  k. *Waiting for an hour*, I finally gave up.
  l. It is warm for *this late in the year*.
  m. He was seen *cheating*.
  n. I lied *to go to the game*.
  o. The stop sign *ahead* was only recently embedded *in the ground*.
  p. The only player *trying* was Manski.
  q. I will call you *tomorrow*.
  r. The course *that I like best* is anthropology.
  s. The *enclosed* money came *from your mother*.
  t. The *metal* box contained flowers.
  u. *Sitting* quietly, he looked *asleep*.

v.   *Sitting quietly*, he looked *a corpse*.
w.   *Being* intelligent, he advanced rapidly.
x.   Williams badly wanted *to be* president.
y.   Williams badly wanted *to be president*.
z.   *Peeking* is forbidden.
aa. Tom was made sick by *eating spoiled fruit*.
bb. Tom was made sick by *eating* spoiled fruit.
cc. *Under the house* is safer than in the attic.
dd. The *curious* may die *peeking*.

3 VERB-PARTICLE COMPOSITES AND SIMILAR STRUCTURES

The Complexity of Verbs with Prepositions, Adverbs, and Particles

This short chapter could have been included in Chapter 1, for it treats of verbs by form. But the verb-particle composite involves such complex and interesting syntax that it deserves a chapter by itself. The term **particle** may be defined as a word that joins with a verb to make a semantic unit. The identically spelled adverb or preposition is not a particle.

The constructions we are about to see are often called **idioms**— structures "peculiar" to English and not literally translatable into another language. Six different types of constructions are involved, and it is sometimes difficult to distinguish among them. Two of them have a similar appearance and will fit into one group; the other four also have a similar appearance and will fit into another group. The constructions have regular verb forms plus either a preposition or an adverb or a particle. All of these three classifications may variously include such words as *out*, *in*, *down*, *up*, *over*, *across*, *off*, and *on*. Thus such words may fall into any one of three classifications—one (the adverb) being a form-class word and two (the preposition and the particle) being structure-class words. When the verb is accompanied by a particle, the combination is called a **verb-particle composite** or a **merged verb**.

First let's see these six different kinds of constructions illustrated—

two of each—and ponder their syntax before we separate them by analysis.

> The question was **taken up**.
> The tame deer was **shot at**.
> The lost dog **turned up**.
> The car **turned down** the alley.
> The publisher **turned down** my proposal.
> As the car slowed, I **jumped out**.
> The squirrel **ran up** the tree.
> Susan **looked up**.
> I decided **to carry on**.
> I **ran across** an old friend.
> This bed has never been **slept in**.
> The book was **turned in**.

Puzzle over these constructions for a while before you go to the next sections. Can you pair off those that are alike? Can you inductively explain the different grammatical structures?

Similar Elements within the Sentence

Verbs with Prepositional-Phrase Modifiers

One of the most common constructions in English is a verb modified by a prepositional phrase. Here are examples:

> John looked **at the coed**.   We ran **into the classroom**.
> We walked **over the bridge**.

The boldface prepositional phrases modify the verbs *looked*, *walked*, and *ran*. Two characteristics of this kind of construction are to be noted. First, the prepositional phrase *sounds* like a unit; the listener or reader just feels that the words go together. Ask such a question as "Where did John look?" and the answer *at the coed* shows itself to be a prepositional phrase modifying *looked*. Second, both the verb and the preposition in this kind of construction have their regular meanings. For example, *looked* simply means what it says, and *at* has the prepositional meaning of direction. In the type of construction discussed in the next section these two characteristics will not be evident.

Active-Voice Transitive Verb-Particle Composites

English has idioms that look quite similar to the verb plus preposi-tional phrase illustrated above but that are entirely different syntactical constructions. Compare these two sentences:

> The tractor ran across a furrow.
> I ran across a rare book.

They have a superficial similarity but in actuality are different. Note that in the first sentence *across a furrow* sounds like a prepositional phrase. Where did the tractor run? Across a furrow. Also *ran* and *across* have their regular meanings. But note that these two characteristics are not present in the second sentence. *Across a rare book*, though in some contexts it could be a prepositional phrase, does not sound like a unit here and does not modify the verb *ran*. Ask "Where did you run?" and *across a rare book* doesn't sound like an answer. Instead, you would ask "What did you run across?", a question which shows *ran across* to be the unit. So *ran across* is a **transitive verb-particle composite** with the direct object *a rare book*. The total meaning of the composite is not the sum of the meaning of the two parts. In the composite, there is really no *running* and *across* does not have its usual meaning of place or direction. In the first sentence, however, the totality of the meaning of *ran across* is the sum of the meanings of the two words; there is *running* and there is the direction of *across*. Thus there is a great difference between a verb with a modifying prepositional phrase and a verb-particle composite with a direct object. (The example sentence of the transitive verb-particle composite is in the active voice, since the subject of the sentence performs the action. This construction in the passive voice, with the subject receiving the action, will be discussed later in this chapter.)

Sometimes in a transitive verb-particle composite the verb will have its definite meaning but the particle will not have the meaning of a preposition. Examples:

> She **cooked up** a stew.
> He **bought out** the store.

Up a stew is definitely not a prepositional phrase; instead *stew* is the direct object of the composite *cooked up*. *Cooked* has its regular meaning, but there is no directional meaning in *up*. Also *out the store* is definitely not a prepositional phrase; *store* is instead the direct object of *bought out*. *Bought* has its regular meaning but *out* has no prepositional meaning. So *cooked up* and *bought out* are transitive verb-particle composites.

Here are some more examples of transitive verb-particle composites, all in the active voice:

> The Assembly **passed on** the amendment.

Mary couldn't **make up** her mind.
She could only **stir up** trouble.
Can you **look over** my proposal?
That **wrapped up** the deal.

Notice that the total meaning of each composite is not the sum of the two parts and also notice that *on the amendment* and the likes are not prepositional phrases.

There is, however, another way to distinguish transitive composites from verbs with prepositional phrases. With a verb and a modifying prepositional phrase there is no possibility of rearrangement of the words. For example:

I walked through the gate

but not

*I walked the gate through.

With a transitive composite, however, the direct object usually can be placed between the verb and the particle. Examples:

Mary couldn't make up her mind.
Mary couldn't make her mind up.

Can you look over my proposal?
Can you look my proposal over?

A few transitive composites cannot undergo this transformation. Example:

I ran across an old friend

but not

*I ran an old friend across.

When a pronoun rather than a noun is the direct object of a composite, the particle usually follows the object pronoun. Examples:

I called him up

but not

*I called up him.

I wore them out

but not

*I wore out them.

What seems to be a particle followed by a pronoun may in reality be a prepositional phrase, however. For example,

> I turned **up it**

could mean that the speaker turned *up a driveway*.

Similar Elements at the End of the Sentence

Verbs with Prepositions Having Displaced Objects

Now we will see four different types of constructions in which a verb is followed by a preposition, an adverb, or a particle, but without a noun object following. The first of these is the verb with a preposition having a displaced object.

A preposition normally has an object. The syntactic function of a preposition is to serve as a connective between its object and the word it modifies. Examples:

> John **walked into** the **room**.
> We **looked at** the **painting**.

In sentence one the preposition *into* serves as a connective and expresses a relationship between *walked* and *room*. In sentence two *at* connects and expresses a relationship between *looked* and *painting*.

Sometimes, however, a preposition stands alone and has a **displaced object**. Observe these two sentences:

> Someone wrote **in this book**.
> This book has been written **in**.

In sentence one there is a typical prepositional phrase with the preposition *in* and the object *book*, the whole phrase modifying *wrote*. This sentence is in the active voice. The second sentence is the first transformed into the passive voice (with the phrase *by someone* suppressed). *In* is still a preposition, however. Its real object is still *book*, which has been made the subject of the passive-voice sentence. So *book* is the displaced object of *in*.

Here are some other examples of this English idiom, with a regular prepositional phrase in the active voice in the first sentence and a preposition with a displaced object in the passive voice in the second sentence.

> Someone shot **at my dog**.
> My dog was shot **at**.

> Someone wrote **on the walls**.
> The walls have been written **on**.

> Someone flew **over my house**.
> My house was flown **over**.

When a word that looks like a preposition appears at the end of a sentence (or construction), as in each second sentence above, a test can be applied to see whether it really is a preposition with a displaced object—just see whether the sentence can be transformed into the active voice. For example:

> This bed has never been slept in

will transform into

> No one has ever slept **in this bed**.

This transformation is conclusive proof that in the original sentence the *in* is a true preposition with a displaced object, *bed*.

Many active-voice sentences will not transform this way into passive-voice sentences with prepositions at the end. For example:

> John went to the dance

but not

> *The dance was gone to (by John).

> John walked with a limp

but not

> *A limp was walked with (by John).

Some such sentences might be accepted as grammatical by some native speakers but not by others. Examples:

> Someone peered through the door.
> The door was peered through. (?)

> John walked behind his girl.
> His girl was walked behind (by John). (?)

But even when there is doubtful grammaticality, the identification of the preposition is certain.

Prepositions with displaced objects also appear in sentences with adjective clauses (see Chapter 11). Examples:

> There's the girl whom I wanted to talk **to**.
> That's the river which I swam **in**.

In sentence one *whom* is the displaced object of *to*, and in sentence two *which* is the displaced object of *in*. Both *to* and *in* are unmistakably prepositions here, for the sentences can be written in this pattern:

> There's the girl **to whom** I wanted to talk.
> That's the river **in which** I swam.

Early prescriptive grammarians maintained that this second pattern is the only correct one, since a sentence must not end in a preposition. And even today some students report that they have been taught not to end a sentence with a preposition. The prescriptive grammarians and their followers were obviously misguided, for the sentences with the prepositions at the end are natural and thus grammatical. The stricture that a sentence must not end with a preposition is entirely illogical.

Two kinds of infinitive phrases may also take prepositions that seem to have no objects. Here is the first kind:

> I have no one to talk **to.**

To is a preposition with an understood object, for the construction may be written as

> I have no one **to whom** to talk.

So *whom* is the understood object of *to* in the first sentence. Here is the second kind:

> She wanted to be danced **with.**

Such an infinitive phrase (*to be danced with*) is a passive-voice construction which can be transformed into an active-voice construction:

> She wanted someone to dance **with her.**

So in the original sentence *with* is a preposition that has no stated object. The object is the *her* of the understood active-voice construction. Here are other examples of these two kinds of infinitive constructions with prepositions having no stated objects. A transformation of each is given in parentheses.

> He saw a hippie to relate **to.**
> (He saw a hippie **to whom** to relate.)
> I had to be reasoned **with.**
> (Someone had to reason **with me.**)
> I saw no place to begin **at.**
> (I saw no place **at which** to begin.)
> Joan wanted to be talked **to.**
> (Joan wanted someone to talk **to her.**)

The transformations show that in the original sentences the boldface words are prepositions.

Verbs with Modifying Adverbs

Often at the end of a sentence a word looks like a preposition but is really an adverb functioning as an adverbial and not a preposition at all. In such a construction the word in question does not have a displaced object but in reality modifies the verb. The sentence is always in the active voice. Here are some examples:

The teacher looked **up**.
The actor stomped **out**.
My neighbor came **over**.
We all went **in**.
My pastor came **by**.
At the gateway I stepped **down**.

All of these boldface words look like prepositions, but note that they do not have objects in either regular or displaced position. Thus they cannot be prepositions. They are adverbs functioning as adverbials. They are modifying the verb, not serving as a connective between it and an object. In sentence one, *up* tells the direction in which the teacher looked. In sentence two, *out* tells where the actor stomped. And so with the other four. Note that the substitute *there* can replace each of these adverbs, showing that they are adverbials. (Of course, the modification of the verb also shows that they are adverbials.)

The verb with a modifying adverb is to be distinguished from a verb with a preposition that has a displaced object. They are two different kinds of idioms. For example, in the passive-voice sentence

This kitten has never been talked **to**,

to is not an adverb modifying *talked* but is a preposition with *kitten* as its displaced object. The active-voice sentence is

No one has ever talked **to this kitten**.

The verb with a modifying adverb is quite a different construction.

Intransitive Verb-Particle Composites

In English there are also idioms that look very much like the verb with a modifying adverb or the verb and preposition with a displaced object, but that are in reality verb-particle composites or merged verbs. They are in effect compound words. The particle is not modifying the verb but is a part of it. Here are some examples:

The rugs were **passed off** as genuine Persians.
The drunk **passed out**.
I don't know how you can **carry on** so.

> With a dozen eggs I can **make out.**
> After an hour the prizefighter **came to.**

First note that the words *off*, *out*, *on*, *to* are not modifying the verbs
and do not have displaced objects. If modification were taking place,
these words would be adverbials and would undoubtedly express time,
place, or manner. But the words *then*, *there*, and *thus* cannot be substituted for these words. The words are particles and the boldface constructions are true composites, or word compounds. Note that the
composites in these examples do not have direct objects; they are intransitive.

Differentiating between verbs with modifying adverbs and those that
are composites is not always easy. The best way to differentiate is to
perceive that in the verb with a modifying adverb the total meaning of
the construction is the sum of the meanings of the two parts. Example:

> The flotsam **drifted by.**

The total meaning is that of the verb *drifted* and the directional meaning of *by*. In the verb-particle composite the total meaning of the construction is not the sum of the meanings of the two parts. Example:

> Since I'm sleepy, I think I'll **turn in.**

There is no real *turning* involved and there is no directional meaning
for *in*. Such is also the case in the examples above. In sentence one,
for example, there is really no *passing* of the rugs and no directional
meaning for *off*. Or in sentence four there is no *making* and no directional meaning for *out*.

Passive-Voice Transitive Verb-Particle Composites

For our fourth kind of construction with a verb followed by a word
that looks like a preposition we go back to the transitive verb-particle
composite discussed earlier. The transitive composite can be transformed into the passive voice (subject receiving the action), and then
the particle comes at the end of the construction if the *by* phrase is
suppressed. Here are some examples:

> *Active voice*:
> John **gave up** the idea.
> *Passive voice*:
> The idea was **given up.**

> *Active voice*:
> The teacher **looked over** the proposal.
> *Passive voice*:
> The proposal was **looked over.**

Active voice:
  The gossips **passed on** the rumor.
Passive voice:
  The rumor was **passed on**.

In the passive-voice sentences the boldface composites are transitive as in the active-voice sentences, and the subjects of the sentences are the composites' displaced direct objects. Note that the total meaning of these composites is not the sum of the meanings of the two parts. For example, in the first pair of sentences there is no real *giving* and no directional meaning for *up*. *Gave up* is a verb-particle composite. Also note that in the three examples given the particle could follow the direct object. Examples:

  John **gave** the idea **up**.
  The teacher **looked** the proposal **over**.
  The gossips **passed** the rumor **on**.

If the constructions were prepositional phrases, this rearrangement of word order would be impossible.

A Summary of the Four Sentence-End Situations

Thus four seemingly similar but actually different constructions must be distinguished. Examples:

Preposition with displaced object:
  The children were screamed **at**.
Modifying adverb:
  The teacher looked **up**.
Intransitive composite:
  Joan's father **gave in**.
Passive transitive composite:
  More evidence was **turned up**.

In the first example the preposition *at* forms a regular phrase when the sentence is transformed into the active voice:

  The mother screamed **at the children**.

In the second example the total meaning of *looked up* is the sum of the meanings of the two parts; there is *looking* and the direction is *up*. *Up* is an adverb modifying *looked*. In the third example the total meaning of *gave in* is not the sum of the meanings of the two parts; the meaning is something like *acquiesced*. *In* does not modify *gave* but is a part of the composite. In the fourth example the composite is shown to be transitive when the sentence is transformed into the active voice:

  Someone **turned up** more evidence.

The total meaning of *turned up* is not the sum of the meanings of the two parts, and thus the whole is a composite. The four sentences, though superficially similar in construction, represent four entirely different constructions.

Identifying Two or More Elements Associated with Verbs

Sometimes two particles (or a particle plus a preposition) rather than one function with a verb. Examples:

> I can't **put up with** that.
> He **came up with** an idea.
> He **ran off with** his secretary.
> **Look out for** the streetcar.
> **Get in beside** me.
> My girl friend **stood up for** me.

Such sentences are often hard to analyze. The best approach is this: If the second particle-like word and the object sound like a prepositional phrase, as *with his secretary* in

> He ran off with his secretary,

then the verb and the first particle-like word may be an intransitive composite or a verb plus a modifying adverb, and the second particlelike word a preposition with a regular object. But if the second particle-like word and the object do not sound like a prepositional phrase, as *with an idea* in

> He came up with an idea,

then the construction should be considered a three-part transitive composite. Also when all three parts of the construction can be readily replaced with a single verb with the same meaning, such as

> I can't **tolerate** that

instead of

> I can't **put up with** that,

then the whole construction should be considered a transitive composite. Occasionally there are even three particle-like words with a verb, such as

> He got **up out of** the chair.

Usually in these idioms the last two words, such as *out of* above, are really a compound preposition and the verb and the first word are a verb plus its adverb modifier and not a composite. In other words, *he got up* has a verb with a modifying adverb, and *out of the chair* is a prepositional phrase.

Verb-Particle Composites as Verbals

Just as do ordinary single verbs, composites can occur in nonfinite forms and can function as verbals. To do so they must have either a subject or a complement or a modifier. Examples:

> **Calling** him **up** on the phone, I made my proposal.
> **Making up** her mind quickly, she gave the correct response.
> **To make up** your mind quickly is not always advisable.
> Our grandfather **having passed on**, we devoted more attention to Grandmother.
> **Passing out** more quickly than we expected, the alcoholic caused a disturbance.
> We wanted to kiss and **make up** at once.

In sentence one, *calling up* is a verbal because it has the direct object *him* and the modifier *on the phone*. The entire construction *calling him up on the phone* is an adjectival because it modifies the pronoun *I*. The same analysis applies to sentence two. In sentence three, *to make up* is a verbal because it has a direct object and a modifier. The entire construction *to make up your mind quickly* is a subject and therefore a nominal. In sentence four, *having passed on* is a verbal because it has a subject. In sentence six, *make up* (*to* is understood) is a verbal because it has the modifier *at once*. The entire construction [*to*] *make up at once* is one part of a compound direct object and is therefore a nominal. Note that in such constructions as these the particle is a part of the verbal because it is a part of a word compound.

EXERCISES

1. In the following sentences, distinguish between verbs with prepositions having displaced or understood objects and verbs with modifying adverbials.

    a. I was jeered at.
    b. The grass was walked on.
    c. The clouds floated by.
    d. I wanted to be spoken to.
    e. The teacher walked out.
    f. I found a character to identify with.
    g. The cement slab sank down.
    h. The snake was stepped on.
    i. The last member walked in.
    j. The blind man asked to be guided in.

2. In the following sentences distinguish between verbs with prepositions and intransitive verb-particle composites. (None of the sentences have adverbials.)

    a. The sick boy spit up.
    b. Her parents split up.
    c. Sally was laughed at.
    d. Black Bart was hung up.
    e. That's the boy I want to be introduced to.
    f. The key broke off.
    g. That's a good hideout to flee to.
    h. Suddenly his wife turned up.
    i. That's the way it came out.
    j. The little boy was barked at.

3. In the following sentences distinguish between verbs modified by prepositional phrases and active-voice transitive verb-particle composites. (None of the sentences have adverbials.)

    a. I turned off the water.
    b. I turned off the driveway.
    c. He threw up the coin.
    d. He rowed up the river.
    e. She turned in her library books.
    f. We gave up the chase.
    g. She turned in the street.
    h. We went up the stairs.
    i. The author left off the ending.
    j. The farmer burned off the grass.

4. In the following sentences distinguish between passive-voice transitive verb-particle composites and sentences ending with prepositions or with modifying adverbials.

    a. The snow was brushed off.

b. The little boys ran by.
c. There's the girl I spoke to.
d. A fuss was kicked up.
e. A watch was made off with.
f. The stenographer looked out.
g. The bridge was crossed over.
h. Our objectives were lost sight of.
i. The babies were jerked up.
j. Her clothes were torn off.

5. In the following sentences distinguish among (1) verbs with prepositional-phrase modifiers, (2) active-voice transitive verb-particle composites, (3) verbs with prepositions having displaced objects, (4) verbs with modifying adverbs, (5) intransitive verb-particle composites, and (6) passive-voice transitive verb-particle composites. Some three- or four-part constructions are included.

a. The hours flew by.
b. He came across with a good proposal.
c. That plant was cared for.
d. My maiden aunt passed on.
e. She eagerly passed on the rumor.
f. The college passed over me for promotion.
g. She turned into a witch.
h. The storekeeper looked out.
i. The pupil looked out the window.
j. That officer has been shot at seven times.
k. Look over the plans carefully.
l. Look over the transom at that cutie.
m. Come over when you can.
n. The sale was rung up.
o. We talked over the proposal.
p. The gossips talked over the fence.
q. We must do away with that eyesore.
r. The partners fell out.
s. The ball fell out.
t. The child fell out the window.
u. You must cut down on smoking.
v. She is someone you can depend on.
w. I don't care about her.
x. Please look out for my little brother.
y. At seven o'clock wake me up.
z. I joined up Friday.

aa. When we came to the washout, we turned back.

bb. Get down off of that table.

cc. Yesterday she was fought over for the third time.

dd. I went to the library to turn in a book.

ee. She turned down my proposal.

ff. She turned down the inside lane.

gg. You can't catch up with me.

hh. Put in a good word for me with Sally.

ii. It's hard to break in new shoes.

jj. Will the windows break in your new den?

kk. Don't you know that antique chair shouldn't be sat in?

ll. His wife ran up an enormous debt.

mm. The squirrel ran up the tree.

nn. Call up my friend for me.

oo. He called up.

pp. She called up the dumb waiter.

qq. The patrol car ran down the fleeing suspect.

rr. She's always running down her friends.

ss. Who's running down the street?

tt. We hoped the new President would bring about a change.

uu. The painting was bid for.

vv. We wore out the tape recorder.

ww. We made up a good imitation.

xx. The soldiers' ammunition gave out.

yy. If my dead uncle knew of my apostasy, he would turn in his grave.

zz. I think I will turn in my old car on a new one.

aaa. The bolt was taken off.

bbb. The plumber was laid off.

ccc. The rocks were painted on.

ddd. The buzzards were shot at.

eee. The injured were cared for.

fff. The bottle cap was screwed off.

ggg. The pool was swum in.

STRUCTURE WORDS

Lexical Words and Structure Words

Except for the particles and prepositions discussed in Chapter 3, you have in three preceding chapters been studying **lexical words**—content words that have full dictionary definitions. These lexical words belong to the four great form classes and in various ways perform in the four great function classes. The inflectional endings (and also the replacive allomorphs) of these words are **structural morphemes** in that they help determine the grammatical structure of a sentence, but the words themselves deliver the principal meanings in our communication with one another.

A substantial number and variety of other words in our language are **structure words** in that, though they do carry some lexical meaning, they form the syntactical framework for English sentences. Some grammarians have called them **function words**, but since the form-class words also function in sentences it seems more meaningful to call the non-lexical words structure words. The structure classes are **closed classes**. Rarely does a new structure word enter the language. Most of the structure classes are small in the number of words they comprise, especially when compared with the form classes.

In the analysis to follow it will be seen that many of these words fall into more than one classification. In fact, probably no language other than English has so many words that have so many different meanings and functions. For example, the *Oxford English Dictionary* lists eighteen long columns of definitions for the word *by*. You have already seen how *by* can be a preposition, an adverb modifying a verb, and a particle forming a part of a verb composite. Other such multiple meanings and functions will be seen in other structure words.

Pronouns

The various types of **pronouns** form one of the sizable general classifications of structure words, with several subclassifications. The personal pronouns could be given subclassification under nouns in the form classes, but since they have various structural characteristics and since other kinds of pronouns are clearly structure words, it seems best to include all kinds of pronouns in the structural classification. The chief structural characteristic of pronouns is that they have **reference** and thus help establish syntactic structure in sentences. Also they sometimes serve as determiners and connectives, words more structural than lexical. The pronoun classes are all closed.

The word *pronoun* comes from the Latin *pro* and *nomen*, meaning "for a name." The pronoun is supposed to stand for a noun. In some cases it does specifically; for instance, in

> As Mary and John strolled along, **he** told **her he** loved **her,**

the pronouns are directly standing for the nouns *Mary* and *John*. In other cases pronouns merely have reference without standing so directly for specific nouns. Examples:

> **They** say it always rains directly after an earthquake.
> I made an A in physics, **which** is hard to do.
> **Everyone** should help **each other.**

The boldface pronouns in these sentences do not stand for specific nouns. So actually the term *pronoun* has meaning more than "for a noun" and applies to various syntactical functions.

We will discuss and illustrate five classes of pronouns: personal, reflexive, relative, demonstrative, and indefinite. The possessive pronouns (other than those used as noun substitutes) are classed as determiners and are discussed under that heading later in this chapter. The interrogative pronouns are QW words and are discussed under that heading.

Personal Pronouns

The **personal pronoun** is one used by a speaker or writer to refer to himself, to refer to persons he directly addresses, and to refer to other persons, animals, and things, present or not present. The other kinds of pronouns (discussed below) also refer to persons or things, and also ideas, but they have different characteristics and thus different classifications.

The personal pronouns, being rather highly inflected, show **person**, **case**, **number**, and **gender**. The three persons are **first** (the person speaking), **second** (the person spoken to), and **third** (the person or thing spoken about). The three cases are the **subjective** (the function of being a subject or predicate nominal[1]), the **objective** (the function of being a direct or indirect object or object complement of a finite or nonfinite verb form and the object of a preposition), and the **possessive** (the function of showing possession). The two numbers are **singular** and **plural**. The three genders are **masculine**, **feminine**, and **neuter**. The **declension** of the personal pronouns can be shown by paradigm.

FIRST PERSON

	Singular	*Plural*
Subjective	I	we
Objective	me	us
Possessive	my, mine	our, ours

SECOND PERSON

	Singular	*Plural*
Subjective	you	you
Objective	you	you
Possessive	your, yours	your, yours

THIRD PERSON

	Singular	*Plural*
Subjective	he, she, it	they
Objective	him, her, it	them
Possessive	his, her, hers, its	their, theirs

Note that only the third person singular has inflection for gender. The forms *mine*, *ours*, *yours*, and the like are used only as noun substitutes and will be mentioned again below. Nowadays the archaic forms *thou*, *thee*, *ye*, *thy*, and *thine* play little part in English grammar.

The personal pronouns *we*, *you*, *it*, and *they* may be used as **indefinite pronouns**. Examples:

> **We** never know when disaster will strike.
> **You** should never shirk your duties.
> I'll never make **it** alone.
> **They** say "like father, like son."

---

[1]The objective form of the pronoun serves as the subject of an infinitive. Example: *He asked* **me** *to lend him some money.* The *me* is the subject of *to lend*; it is in the objective case because it follows a verb and is part of a direct object. The objective form of the pronoun can also serve as the subject of a present participle and a past participle.

In the first two sentences the *we* and the *you* refer to people in general; either of them could be used in either of these two sentences. The *it* in the third sentence has no specific reference, but it is not an expletive *it* (see page 107). This *it* makes general reference to something like "my course through life" or "my attempt at a college education." The *they* in the fourth sentence also refers indefinitely to people in general.

It may also be a subject referring to a predicate noun that follows a form of *to be*. Examples:

> It is the scholar who must lead society.
> It is such cases as that which make us despair of eliminating poverty.

In sentence one the *it* refers to *scholar* and in sentence two to *cases*. This construction is a wordy English idiom designed to effect a kind of emphasis. Note that one could say

> The scholar must lead society,

but that such a construction does not have the same emphatic effect. Also note that in this construction a singular form of *to be* is used regardless of the number of the predicate noun.

It may also be used to refer broadly to a general idea, as can the demonstrative pronouns *this* and *that* and the relative pronoun *which*. Example:

> We worked very hard, but it made no difference in the results.

The *it* refers to the general idea of our having worked hard. This *it*, too, is different from the expletive discussed later in this chapter.

Reflexive Pronouns

The **reflexive pronouns** are the compound forms *myself, yourself, himself, herself, itself* and their plural forms (*selves*). These forms are sometimes used as reflexive direct objects. Examples:

> Mary cut **herself**.
> The Cubs boxed **themselves** in.

The *herself* is the direct object of *cut* and the *themselves* is the object of the verb-particle composite *boxed in*. They are reflexive because they reflect back to the subjects of the sentences.

These forms are also sometimes used for emphasis. Examples:

> The President **himself** was unable to persuade Mr. Wherry to run.
> The students **themselves** supported the new regulation.
> I went to the play **myself**.

In the first sentence *himself* implies that others had tried to persuade

Mr. Wherry and that even the President failed. In the second sentence *themselves* emphasizes the implication that there was something unusual about the students' supporting the regulation. Note that the third sentence shows that the intensive reflexive can be separated from its antecedent.

In colloquial usage the reflexive form *myself* is sometimes used to replace either *I* or *me*. Also *yourself* on rare occasions replaces *you*. Examples:

> Mary and **myself** will both attend.
> The letter was addressed to my father and **myself**.
> May I go with John and **yourself** to the movie?

Such usage, though acceptable colloquially, does not appear in expository writing.

Relative Pronouns

The **relative pronouns** are *who*, *whom*, *whose*, *which*, *that*, and (rarely) *who(m)ever* and *whichever*. They are connectives that introduce adjective clauses, which will be discussed in Chapter 11. These forms have specific antecedents (though *which* can refer broadly to a whole idea). The *who* forms refer to persons, *that* refers to both persons and things, and *which* refers to things and concepts. Reference to animals varies with the speaker. The possessive form *whose* can refer to inanimate objects as well as to persons. Examples:

> I have a **brother who** is an airline pilot.
> He's a **man whom** all can trust.
> He's a **diplomat whose** tact never leaves him.
> Those are **hinges whose** screws must be specifically ordered.
> That's a **superstition which** I've never heard of before.
> He's a **man that** everyone loves.
> Here is a **book that** you will like.
> He gambled away his wealth, **which** caused his wife to divorce him.

Both the relative pronouns and their antecedents are in boldface in these sentences. Though sentence four illustrates acceptable usage, many writers would use *for which* rather than *whose*. In sentence eight the *which* refers to the whole idea of his gambling his wealth away, but it is still considered a relative pronoun.

The relative pronouns have a grammatical function in their own clauses. In sentences one and eight, *who* and *which* are subjects. In sentences two, six, and seven, *whom*, *that*, and *that* are direct objects of verbs. In sentence five, *which* is the object of the preposition *of*. And in sentences three and four, *whose* is modifying (as a determiner) the subjects *tact* and *screws*.

Colloquially, the distinction between *who* (subject) and *whom* (object) is fast disappearing. Most speakers use *who* in all positions except those directly after a preposition. When speakers or writers wish to be precise and formal, they attempt to observe the distinction; otherwise, most people use *who* in all constructions, or else use no pronoun. Nearly everyone understands, if he reads or hears them, such sentences as these:

> He's the man **whom** I mentioned to you.
> She is the woman **whom** I love.

But such sentences are rarely encountered. People who are indifferent to the distinction, or antagonistic about it, may say *who* rather than *whom*; more likely, they omit saying either. But the following kind of sentence is a little more often used:

> He is the man **to whom** I referred.
> Smith is the professor **with whom** I studied physics.

Few people would say *who* instead of *whom* immediately after a preposition like *to* or *with*. If they feel uncomfortable about *whom*, they order their sentences in this way:

> He is the man I referred to.
> Smith is the professor I studied physics with.

This merging of *who-whom* forms is also occurring in questions that call for *who* or *whom* (see the discussion of QW words later in this chapter).

The relative pronouns (except *whose*) are often omitted from sentences, as has been intimated above. This usage is considered good speech and writing. Examples:

> He's the man I talked to you about.
> That's the watch I lost.

In the first sentence *whom* (or *who*) and in the second *which* or *that* are understood. This omission can occur only when the relative pronoun is an object, never when it is a subject.

Some authorities have maintained that a preposition must come before the relative pronoun, as in

> Here's the girl **to** whom I was talking.

But certainly it is natural usage to put the preposition at the end of the construction, as in

> Here's the girl (who) I was talking **to.**

Such usage is entirely correct.

Relative pronouns are also used with infinitive phrases, though usually they are omitted and simply understood. Examples:

> I have no one with **whom** to talk.
> I have no paper on **which** to write.
> He's the man to **whom** to address your request.

In actual usage we almost always omit the relative pronoun and shift the preposition to the end of the sentence, as in

> I have no one to talk with.

In this construction the relative pronoun is always the object of a preposition, and the prepositional phrase modifies the infinitive.

Demonstrative Pronouns

The pronouns *this*, *that*, *these*, and *those* "point" to their referents— *this* suggests nearness, *that* suggests remoteness—and are therefore called the **demonstrative pronouns** because the Latin word *demonstrare* means "to point." They may be used as noun substitutes.

> **That** is yours.
> **These** are mine.

As noun substitutes, *this* and *that* also frequently refer to a general idea in a preceding clause or sentence. Examples:

> I always agree with my political opponents. I've found **this** is the best way to get along in the world.
> The Administration expelled some students for demonstrating. **That's** a despicable action for college officials to take.

The *this* and *that* are referring broadly to the whole idea in each preceding sentence.

Demonstrative pronouns may also be used as determiners:

> **This** book is valuable.
> **Those** dogs are rabid.

Such determiners will be mentioned again in the proper sections later in the chapter. They are given a brief separate section here because the term *demonstrative pronouns* is quite useful.

Be sure to note that *that* as a demonstrative is an entirely different word from *that* as a relative pronoun (and also from *that* as a connective introducing a noun clause). Homographs are common among the structure words.

Indefinite Pronouns

A fairly numerous group of structure words in English are commonly called **indefinite pronouns** because they do not refer to definite or specific persons or things. These words do have reference, at least of a sort, and thus may reasonably be called pronouns. Like many other English structure words, some of these indefinite pronouns also fit into other classifications. Some function at times as determiners and almost all of them may also be noun substitutes. The most common ones are the following:

one	everything	less
anyone	other	much
everyone	another	either
someone	any other	neither
no one	no other	several
anybody	some	all
everybody	none	both
somebody	more	each one
nobody	most	one another
anything	many	each other
nothing	enough	each
something	few	

One another and *each other* are also called **reciprocal pronouns** since they denote reciprocal action between people. Examples:

We should all be eager to help **one another.**
The twins were devoted to **each other.**

Note that these are noun substitutes, one being the direct object of the infinitive *to help* and the other being the object of the preposition *to.*

The indefinite pronoun *one* also occurs in the reflexive. Example:

If one thinks only of **oneself,** one will not lay up treasures in heaven.

The other indefinite pronouns do not undergo this permutation.

Other and *one* are the only indefinite pronouns commonly used in the plural form. Examples:

No **others** will be accepted.
These are the **ones** I want.

The *body* words can be made plural, but the construction rarely occurs.

A number of the indefinite pronouns take the possessive. All the *one* and *body* words can, plus *other*, *another*, *one another*, and *each other*. Examples:

> **anyone's** girlfriend
> **nobody's** business
> **another's** mistake
> **each other's** homework

Each, *either*, *neither*, *other*, and *others* are usually awkward in the possessive.

The form *else* frequently goes with the *one*, *body*, and *thing* words to form a compound indefinite pronoun. *Else* is not an adjective but a part of the pronoun construction. Examples of its use:

> Don't speak to **anybody else**.
> **Everyone else** stayed home.
> I don't want **anything else**.

When this compound construction is used in the possessive, the *'s* always goes with *else*. Examples:

> **nobody else's** business
> **someone else's** fault

Some authorities have approved or demanded the construction *nobody's else business*, but no native speaker of English has ever used such a construction naturally. It originated with eighteenth-century prescriptive grammarians, who fallaciously reasoned that since *else* itself is not a noun or pronoun, it shouldn't take an *'s*. English grammar is not so rigorously logical as the prescriptive grammarians thought.

Few, *less*, and *many* as indefinite pronouns (and also as determiners) may be compared:

few	fewer	fewest
less	lesser	least
many	more	most

Others of the group will not compare.

QW Words

These question formers—called **QW words** because most of them begin with a W—are *who*, *whom*, *whose*, *which*, *what*, *where*, *why*, *when*, and *how*. Those which imply antecedents—*who*, *whom*, *whose*, *which*, and *what*—are often called **interrogative pronouns**. *Where*, *why*, *when*, and *how* may be called **adverbial interrogatives**. All of the group may

just be referred to as QW words. All are used in direct questions.
Examples:

> **Who** did you invite?
> **Whose** book is that?
> **Which** is mine?
> **Where** did he go?
> **How** does he look?

In colloquial usage, *whom* has almost disappeared as an interrogative
pronoun, as in sentence one above, where *who* is an object but *whom*
could be used. Syntactically, the QWs may function as subjects, objects, or adverbial modifiers. In sentences four and five above, *where*
and *how* may be analyzed as adverbial modifiers of *go* and *look*, but it
is not necessary to analyze them so. They may just be called question-
formers or QW words.

These QW words may also be used in indirect questions. Examples:

> I wonder **when** he is coming.
> I want to know **who(m)** you have invited.

When so used, these QW words are actually connectives introducing
noun clauses, though they do imply questions. In sentence one, *when
he is coming* is a noun-clause object of *wonder* and in sentence two *who
you have invited* is a noun-clause object of *to know*. Thus these words
will also be classified as subordinating conjunctions introducing noun
clauses (which are discussed later in this chapter).

All of the QW words except *why* may also function as the subject or
object or adverbial modifier of an infinitive. Examples:

> I don't know **who(m)** to call.
> I don't know **whose** to borrow.
> He wondered **which** to take.
> We don't know **what** to do about him.
> I wondered **where** to go.
> He didn't tell me **when** to leave.
> He doesn't know **how** to write effectively.

This usage often involves a negative statement or a *wonder* statement
and also implies a question or decision. The QW words here function
in the same ways they do in QW questions.

Quantifiers

A number of the indefinite pronouns, plus a few other structure
words, frequently function as **quantifiers** or **quantity indicators**. A

quantifier is a noun substitute which is modified by an *of* prepositional phrase and which indicates the quantity of the object of the preposition. Examples:

> **much** of the sugar
> **many** of the students
> **none** of the books

The indefinite pronouns which will so function, besides the illustrated three, are *few, less, all, one, some, more, most, each, either,* and *neither.*

Also functioning as quantifiers are *a lot* and *lots* (sometimes also qualifiers), *one* and other cardinal numbers (sometimes also determiners and sometimes noun substitutes), *plenty* (also a noun substitute and occasionally a colloquial qualifier), and occasionally *enough* (sometimes also a qualifier and sometimes a noun substitute).

Often three other structure words quantify by modifying the indefinite pronouns *all* and *none.* Examples:

> **About** all that I had went up in smoke.
> **Nearly** all of us passed.
> **Almost** all of the books were lost.
> **Almost** none of the books were lost.

In this function these boldface words can be called **secondary quantifiers**. As has already been stressed, many of the structure words fall into more than one classification.

Prepositions

A **preposition** is a kind of noncoordinate connective that, usually, forms a phrase with its object and modifiers of its object. The preposition shows a relationship between its object and the noun, pronoun, verb, or adjective that the prepositional phrase modifies. The phrase itself is either an adjectival or adverbial or sentence modifier (see Chapter 10).

There are both simple and compound prepositions in English. Here is a list of the most common simple prepositions:

after	off	up	beside
at	on	upon	besides
but	like	within	near
except	as	until	around
by	beneath	toward(s)	across
down	since	before	amid
over	through	beyond	outside

to	till	above	inside
from	under	against	without
of	below	along	behind
for	with	among	aboard
in	into	between	during
past	save		

Quite a number of present participial forms are also now considered prepositions, since they are used in set phrases that act as sentence modifiers. Examples:

Considering the cost of living, all workers need raises.
We should protect all the big cats, **including** the lion.

Some others of this sort are these:

barring	pending	excepting
concerning	regarding	assuming
saving	respecting	following

The most common compound prepositions are these:

out of	inside of	in comparison with
together with	aside from	in front of
as for	because of	on behalf of
away from	owing to	in place of
up at	on account of	in lieu of
up to	by way of	belonging to
up on	by means of	in addition to
contrary to	in case of	for the sake of
ahead of	in spite of	in the event of
due to	in consideration of	with respect to
apart from	with regard to	in reference to
away from	in advance of	in back of

The three-part compound prepositions may be analyzed as a prepositional phrase followed by another preposition, but they are such set phrases that it is best just to call them compound prepositions.

Two compound prepositions—*instead of* and *rather than*—may be called **coordinating prepositions** since they connect two grammatically equal constructions. Examples:

He spoke rapidly **instead of** thoughtfully.
He spoke rapidly **rather than** thoughtfully.
I want red **instead of** black.
I want red **rather than** black.
I want books **instead of** sermons.
I want to eat **rather than** play.

As illustrated, words of all four form classes may be connected by these prepositions. Note that *rather than* in this usage is not a subordinating conjunction, as are *more than*, *less than*, and *better than*. In

> I like blondes **better than** brunettes,

than I like brunettes is implied and *better than* is therefore a subordinating conjunction (see the treatment later in this chapter).

Objects of Prepositions

Usually the object of a preposition is a noun by form, and hence all objects of prepositions are nominals by function. But words from all four of the form classes and also various kinds of structure words and word groups can function as the objects of prepositions.

1. *Nouns as objects of prepositions.*

> We drove **into** the **parking lot**.
> No one **but** the **constable** was awake.
> We bought soft drinks **in addition to** some **beer**.

2. *Pronouns as objects of prepositions.*

> Give the package **to her**.
> Don't shoot **at them**.
> These guns **of his** must be destroyed.
> The movie **to which** I referred is no longer showing.
> I object **to that**.
> **To whom** did you speak?
> This game is not **for everyone**.

In sentences three, four, five, six, and seven respectively, a possessive personal pronoun, a relative pronoun, a demonstrative pronoun, an interrogative pronoun, and an indefinite pronoun are functioning as objects of prepositions.

3. *Adjectives as objects of prepositions.*

> We gave food **to** the **poor**.
> No one can afford mink **except** the **rich**.
> This store sells suits **for** the **tall**.

4. *Adverbs as objects of prepositions.*

> The weather is cold **for** this **soon**.
> I never liked poetry **until lately**.
> I haven't been home **since then**.

5. *Present participles and participial phrases as objects of preposi-tions.*

> The rector preached a sermon **on drinking.**
> John insisted **on phoning the manager.**
> We saw the whole game **in spite of arriving late.**

6. *The prepositional phrase as the object of a preposition.*

> I won't come **until after Easter.**
> Don't call **except** just **before prayer meeting.**

This is not a common usage in English.

7. *Noun clauses as objects of prepositions.*

> The question **of who is guilty** is important.
> Our chances of survival will depend **upon whether it rains.**
> Give the money **to whoever calls first.**

8. *Adverb clauses as objects of prepositions.*

> We can't come **until after the game is over.**
> Don't talk **till** just **before class is over.**
> Take it **to where the inspectors are.**

Only a limited number of prepositions will take adverb clauses as ob-jects, and those clauses must denote time or place.

With *adjective clauses* only the relative pronoun, not the whole clause, can be the object of a preposition.

Modifiers of Prepositional Phrases

Occasionally a prepositional phrase itself is modified. Examples:

> I left school **just** before being expelled.
> Break the glass **only** in case of fire.
> I am **wholly** in the wrong.
> The professor was **completely** in error.

These modifiers are adverbials.

Prepositional Phrases as Modifiers

Prepositional phrases can modify nouns, pronouns, verbs, adjectives, and sentences.

1. *Modification of nouns.*

> The **tear in the tent** was caused by high winds.

> The **tree by the parsonage** is two hundred years old.
> I wanted to talk to the **girl ahead of me**.

These prepositional phrases are adjectivals since they modify nouns.

2. *Modification of pronouns.*

> **Somebody in the balcony** is smoking.
> **Each of these books** is excellent.
> **Who in the choir** will volunteer?

Indefinite pronouns are frequently modified by prepositional phrases, but other kinds of pronouns are not often so modified.

3. *Modification of verbs.*

> **Bring** your alms to them **in the early morning**.
> **Impress** your date **by bringing her an orchid**.
> Our minister was **talking about original sin** yesterday.

Note in the first two sentences that the prepositional phrases are modifying the verbs and not the pronoun and noun they are next to. The way to check on such modification is to ask what the phrase *goes with*. Testing shows that the word relationship is *bring in the early morning*, not *them in the early morning*. Phrases modifying verbs are adverbials.

Ambiguity is possible when a reader has no way to distinguish between a preposition and an adverb. Example:

> The mailman will come **by** early tomorrow.

The *by* can be a preposition or an adverb. The sentence can mean that early tomorrow the mailman will come by (adverb). Or it can mean that the mailman will come no later than early tomorrow (preposition).

4. *Modification of adjectives.*

> The **young in spirit** are my friends.
> The **wealthy in their mansions** forget the poor.
> I am **sick at my stomach**.

The prepositional phrases here are adverbials because they are modifying adjectives.

5. *Modification of sentences.*

> **In spite of the weather**, we went to the game.
> **Instead of a trophy** I decided to take cash.
> **Considering the circumstances**, our earnings were good.

Though these prepositional phrases have some adverbial characteristics, they are really sentence modifiers (see Chapter 10).

Prepositional Phrases with Displaced Objects

There are four kinds of idioms in English in which a preposition ends a sentence or construction and has a displaced object.

1. *The passive-voice construction.* When a sentence in the active voice is transformed into the passive voice so that an object of a preposition in the active-voice sentence becomes the subject of the passive-voice sentence, the preposition is left at the end of the passive-voice sentence and has a displaced object. Examples:

> *Active Voice:* Someone stared at Jane.
> *Passive Voice:* Jane was stared **at**.
>
> *Active Voice:* Someone lives in this house.
> *Passive Voice:* This house is lived **in**.

In each of the passive-voice sentences the displaced object of the bold-face preposition is the noun subject of the sentence.

2. *The adjective clause.*

> This is the bank I work **in**.
> There's the girl I waved **to**.

In the first sentence the displaced object of *in* is the understood relative pronoun *which* (*which* I work *in*). In the second sentence the displaced object of *to* is the understood relative pronoun *whom* (*whom* I waved *to*).

3. *The infinitive with an understood relative pronoun.*

> I have no tools to work **with**.
> Jerry has a girl to write **to**.

In the first sentence the construction *with which to work* is implied. The understood *which* is the displaced object of *with*. In the second sentence an understood *whom* is the displaced object of *to* (a girl *to whom* to write).

4. *Questions ending in prepositions.*

> What are you doing that **for**?
> Where did she come **from**?
> Who is he speaking **to**?

In this very common construction, the introductory QW word is the displaced object of the ending preposition. Note the awkwardness of putting the preposition before the QW word:

> For what are you doing that?

In the third sentence, *who* is clearly an object of *to* but is as acceptable as *whom*.

Meaning in Prepositions

Prepositions are structure words and often have little lexical meaning; when they have any, that meaning is often hard to pin down. For example, consider this preposition:

Your book is different **from** mine.

What is the meaning of *from*? It has little; it shows a relationship between *different* and *mine* but not in such a way that you can express its meaning clearly. In fact, its lexical meaning is so obscure that many people say instead

Your book is different **than** mine.

Than is usually a conjunction, not a preposition. At one time authorities thought such an idiom incorrect because the sentence really says

Your book is different than my book is different,

which is meaningless. But the idiom is now acceptable and shows that neither *from* nor *than* in these sentences has much meaning. In this one use, *than* has to be considered a preposition.

At times, though, prepositions do have some lexical meaning. Here are a few of the many meanings of *by*:

at the edge of	in the course of
in the vicinity of	not later than
near	according to
close to	in conformity with
beside	with respect to
by the side of	originating with
in the region of	in consequence of
in the general direction of	

By has many other idiomatic meanings that are hard to express. In our communication we simply understand without analyzing.

Some of the common meanings of prepositions are position or place (*at, above, in, on, behind, over, near, against*), direction (*to, toward, into*), time (*at, during, until, after, before*), source (*from, of, by*), possession (*of, belonging to*), cause (*because of*), description (*with, of, like, as*), exclusion (*except, but*), manner (*with, like, as*), measure (*by, of, within*), purpose (*for, through*), and probably others. Native speak-

ers of English are lucky they already know how to use their
prepositions.

Coordinating Conjunctions

Simple Coordinating Conjunctions

The **simple coordinating conjunctions** are a small but important group
of connectives. They are among the most used words in the language.
They are *and*, *but*, *or*, *nor*, *yet*, and *for*. *For* is the maverick of the
group, for, unlike the others, it can connect independent clauses only
and not other kinds of grammatical constructions. It is kept in the
group because no grammarian knows where else to classify it. *So*,
which is listed by some authorities as a coordinating conjunction, fits
easily into the group called conjunctive adverbs, but *for* doesn't. *And*,
but (often with *not*), *or*, and *yet* (often with *not*) can connect nearly
all kinds of constructions. *Nor* as a correlative (see the discussion later
in this chapter) can connect all kinds of constructions, but is limited
when used by itself.

1. *Connection of single words.*

boys **and** girls	carelessly **or** carefully
boys **but not** girls	calm **yet** tense
boys **or** girls	calm **or** tense
pretty **and** sweet	devotedly **yet** objectively
pretty **yet not** sweet	to eat **and** to digest
rapidly **and** eagerly	to eat **yet not** to digest
sitting **and** thinking	him **and** her
	if **and** when

As you can see, nouns, verbs, adjectives, adverbs, and structure words
can be joined by the coordinating conjunctions, except *nor*, which
usually requires *neither* in such constructions as *boys nor girls* and
pretty nor sweet. The conjunction *for* connects only independent
clauses.

2. *Connection of prepositional phrases.*

in the house **and** in the yard
in the house **but** not in the yard
at the theater **or** at home
in good humor **yet** on the wagon

Sometimes a regular adjective or adverb is connected to a prepositional
phrase which functions as an adjectival or adverbial:

in good humor **but** not happy   slowly **but** in good time

3. *Connection of verb phrases.*

> sitting quietly at home **and** thinking of a past girl friend
> to read books **or** to watch television
> drinking the cola **but** not enjoying it
> listening carefully **yet** missing the import

4. *Connection of dependent clauses.*

> while the sun was still shining **but** before the guests had left
> which I had seen before **and** which I wanted to see again
> while you are here **or** after you return home

5. *Connection of independent clauses.*

> The rains came **and** the rivers rose.
> I proposed **but** she didn't accept.
> He studied hard, **yet** he failed the test.
> The bill must be paid **or** your wages will be garnisheed.
> He did not pay, **nor** were his wages garnisheed.
> I was in love, **for** it was spring.

Note that *for* can function only in this kind of construction, and, for the most part, *nor* too. Note that with *nor* the subject and verb are reversed in the second independent clause. The coordinating conjunctions express various logical relationships as they connect. *And* expresses **addition** or **accumulation** and sometimes expresses **cause-and-result** in addition. Examples:

> I went to school **and** my wife went to work.
> The thunder crashed **and** the dogs were frightened.

In the second sentence, as in the first, two statements are added together, but also a **causal** relationship between them is expressed. *But* and *yet* express the general relationship of **contrast**, which includes contradiction, opposition, paradox, qualification, and concession. *Or* and *nor* express the relationship of **alternatives** and in addition *or* sometimes expresses the relationship of **condition**. Example:

> I must work harder **or** you will fire me.

A condition as well as an alternative is expressed here. Frequently this relationship is expressed by *or else*. *For* expresses the relationship of **cause-and-result**. Example:

> I want a good education, **for** I know its economic and social value.

The second clause (the *knowing*) is the cause of the first clause (the *wanting*).

Correlatives

The **correlatives** are the two-part connectives *either...or, neither... nor, not only...but also,* and *both...and.* They may connect independent clauses or lesser constructions, though *both...and* normally connects only words or phrases. Usually when two clauses are joined by *neither...nor* or *not only...but also,* the verb-subject word order is used in the first clause. The two-part connectives emphasize the relationship between the two constructions that are being joined. Examples:

> **Either** you go **or** I go.
> **Neither** rain **nor** sleet **nor** hail shall stop me.
> **Not only** did I join the army **but** I **also** sold all my property.
> **Not only** cash **but also** goods are acceptable.
> **Both** men **and** women are eligible for the grants.

Note that in the last three sentences the simple conjunction *and* could be used; but the correlatives are more emphatic.

Other less frequently used correlatives are these:

> You must go **whether** you want to **or** not.
> Shakespeare was **not** of an age **but** for all time.
> We must **not** lose faith **nor** must we shirk our duties.
> He **never** complains **nor** expects favors.

In most such constructions a word of negation is used as a part of the correlative.

Conjunctive Adverbs

Conjunctive adverbs is the traditional name given to a sizable group of connectives that join independent clauses and express a logical relationship between the ideas of the clauses. They are not true adverbs but structure words. They may be grouped according to the relationship they express. All of the conjunctive adverbs except *so* require a semicolon (or period) between the independent clauses they join, and many of them can be shifted to the interior of the second clause, as will be shown in the example sentences below. Conjunctive adverbs are the only connectives than can be so shifted.

The relationship of **addition** or **accumulation** is expressed by the conjunctive adverbs *moreover, furthermore, besides,* and *also.* Examples:

> The union struck; **moreover** it picketed the factories of allied industries.

John didn't phone last night; **besides,** he asked Ellen to get his letters back for him.

Peter won the singles; **also** he was second in the doubles.

Note that in logic any of the four connectives listed will present the relationships in all these sentences, though in style there are preferences. *Besides* is used only colloquially in this function. *Furthermore* and *moreover* could be shifted to the interior of each second clause.

The relationship of **cause-and-result** is expressed by the conjunctive adverbs *accordingly*, *consequently*, *therefore*, *hence*, *so*, and *thus*. Examples:

Round-the-clock negotiations were scheduled; **thus** the chances of an early settlement increased.

Betty didn't call, **so** I went to bed.

The nurse failed to administer the prescribed medicine; the patient was, **therefore**, left in critical condition.

Note that any of the six connectives will function to present the relationships in these sentences, though stylistic preferences exist. *So* is chiefly colloquial and is the only conjunctive adverb used with just a comma between the clauses it connects.

The relationship of **contrast** (which includes such concepts as contradiction, opposition, paradox, qualification, and concession) is expressed by the conjunctive adverbs *however*, *nevertheless*, *still*, and sometimes *otherwise*. Examples:

In June the negotiators appeared on the verge of a settlement; the strike, **however**, continued through July.

I wanted to believe Tom; **still**, I was not sure he was dependable.

Light rains still fell along the coast; **otherwise** the hurricane seemed to have run its course.

Otherwise is not often used for this relationship.

The relationship of **condition** is expressed by *otherwise*. Example:

We must resist Russian aggression; **otherwise** we may lose our position of world leadership.

An *or else* or *unless* condition is expressed here.

A **time** relationship is expressed by the conjunctive adverbs *afterward(s)*, *earlier*, *later*, and *then*. Examples:

At first Edward was truculent; **afterwards** he apologized.

The mob destroyed the ROTC Building; **then** they marched toward the Administration Building.

All of the logical relationships (except addition) that the conjunctive adverbs express are also expressed by subordinating conjunctions, as will be demonstrated below.

For reference here is a list of the conjunctive adverbs:

moreover	therefore	still
furthermore	hence	otherwise
besides	so	afterward(s)
also	thus	earlier
accordingly	however	later
consequently	nevertheless	then

Appositive Conjunctions

A number of structure words are used to introduce appositive constructions. Since appositives are repeaters and are grammatically equivalent to the nominals they are in apposition to, these connectives are coordinating. Here are examples of the chief ones:

> We brought various supplies, **such as** blankets, cots, canned food, and water.
>
> The Great White Father, **as** the President is known, has forgotten the Indians.
>
> **As** a teacher, Professor Gordon is great.
>
> Primitive peoples, **for example** the Hottentots, are usually shrewd.
>
> The senior professors, **especially** Professor Longueil, have widespread reputations.
>
> Liquor, **that is**, all alcoholic beverages, is not sold in Iraq.
>
> The top members of the class, **namely** John Ray, Mary French, and Marty Buckley, were given scholarships.
>
> The cat's vibrissae, **or** whiskers, are sensors.

The boldface connectives introduce appositive constructions and so are serving as coordinating connectives. In sentence two the clause introduced by *as* is really in apposition to *Great White Father*; it is not the same as an adverbial clause introduced by *as*. In sentence three *teacher* is in apposition to *Professor Gordon*. In the other sentences the apposition should be clear. These connectives could be called expletives (see pages 107–110), but since they do seem to have some meaning they are best called appositive conjunctions.

Subordinating Conjunctions

Subordinating conjunctions are connectives that join unequal constructions, usually a dependent clause to an independent clause. The relative pronouns discussed above are similar connectives but were included in the general section on pronouns because they have characteristics different from those of true subordinating conjunctions.

Subordinating Conjunctions that Introduce Adverb Clauses.

The subordinating conjunctions that introduce adverb clauses (see Chapter 11) may be grouped according to the relationships they express. Note that in all the following examples the subordinating conjunctions, unlike the relative pronouns, do not perform a grammatical function within their own clauses but only connect with an expression of relationship.

The relationship of **cause-and-result** is expressed by the subordinating conjunctions *because, inasmuch as, in that, now that, since,* and *so that* (often *so ... that*). Examples:

> We can now forget our differences for another four years, **because** the election is over.
>
> **Inasmuch as** the election is over, we can now forget our differences for another four years.
>
> The election is **so** far in the past now **that** we can forget our differences for another four years.

Note that the other connectives listed will function to present the same relationship in this kind of sentence. The forgetting is the result; the election's being over is the cause. Stylistic preferences nevertheless exist in the choice of connectives.

The relationship of **contrast** is expressed by *although, though, whereas, while, however,* and *no matter how.* Examples:

> **Although** he expected to lose the election, Casey won by a margin of one percent.
>
> Casey won the election by a margin of one percent, **whereas** he had expected to lose.

Note that *while* could be substituted in these sentences, but is used only colloquially. *However* and *no matter how* also are used as subordinating conjunctions to present the relationship of contrast, though they differ from *though, whereas,* and *while.* They may be used with or without reversed sentence order in their dependent clauses. Examples:

> **However** tired I am, I will come.
>
> **However** you vote, you will vote wrong.
>
> **No matter how** hungry you are, we will drive on.
>
> **No matter how** you rave on, I will not give in.

Note that there is a contrast between the two clauses in each of these sentences. One way to distinguish *however* as a subordinating conjunction from *however* as a (coordinating) conjunctive adverb is to see that as a subordinating conjunction *however* cannot be separated from its clause by a comma, whereas it can always be separated by a comma when it is used as a coordinating connective. *No matter how* is never used as a coordinating connective.

The relationship of **condition** is expressed by *if*, *in case*, *unless*, and *provided* (*that*). Examples:

If we get a ninety-percent voter turnout, we can win the election.
In case we get a ninety-percent voter turnout, we can win the election.
We can't win the election **unless** we get a ninety-percent voter turnout.
We can win the election **provided** we get a ninety-percent voter turnout.

The relationship of **manner** or **method** is expressed by *as*, *as if*, *as though*, and *like*. Examples:

Casey conducted his campaign **as** a gentleman should.
Casey conducted his campaign **like** a gentleman should.
He worked **as though** he were a demon.

Like, as in sentence two, is considered by some to be colloquial and by some purists to be unacceptable as a conjunction. But *like* has been so used by the best English writers for hundreds of years.

The relationship of **purpose** is expressed by *so that* and *in order that*. The use of *so* for *so that* is colloquial. Examples:

Casey refused to indulge in mud-slinging **so that** he would not repulse intelligent voters.
In order that he might not repulse intelligent voters, Casey refused to indulge in mud-slinging.

In colloquial usage, *so* can replace *so that* in sentence one. *In case* also can be said to present the relationship of purpose:

Casey refused to indulge in mud slinging **in case** it might repulse intelligent voters.

A **time** relationship is expressed by *after*, *as*, *as soon as*, *before*, *since*, *once*, *until*, *when*, and *while*. In addition, a relationship of **cause-and-result** often accompanies some of these connectives of time. Examples:

Once he starts talking, he won't shut up.
When he was confronted with the evidence, Marty confessed his part in the crime.
After the attorney for the defense completed his summation, the jury members were in tears.

Both *when* and *after* express time here, but also there is a cause-and-result relationship between the two clauses in each sentence.

A **place** relationship is expressed by *where* and *wherever*. Examples:

> I'll go **where you want me to go.**
> He plays **wherever there is sand**.

A relationship of **comparison** is expressed by *as . . . as*, *more . . than* and *more than*, *less . . . than* and *less than*, and by *than* after the comparative form of an adjective or adverb. Examples:

> I work **as** hard **as** you do.
> Paul donated **more** money **than** I (donated).
> Paul awakens **more** cheerfully **than** I (awaken).
> Paul sleeps **more than** I (sleep).
> Americans sing **less than** Italians (sing).
> Americans eat **less** garlic **than** Italians (eat).
> Dick is **less** (**more**) interested **than** I (am interested).
> The Joneses arrived earli**er than** we (arrived).

A nominal between the two parts of any of these conjunctions may be understood from context but omitted from the sentence:

> Paul donated **more than** I (donated).

The context will let the reader or hearer infer that *money* or *blood* or the like was donated. But an adverbial or adjectival cannot be left to be similarly understood—the sentence must say *more cheerfully than* or *less interested than*.

The adverb clauses introduced by these subordinating conjunctions mostly function as sentence modifiers.

For reference, here is a list of the subordinating conjunctions that introduce adverb clauses:

because	unless	until
inasmuch as	provided (that)	when
in that	as	where
so . . . that	as if	as . . . as
now that	no matter how	more than
in case	as though	more . . . than
since	like	less than
although	so (that)	less . . . than
though	in order that	fewer than
whereas	once	fewer . . . than
while	as soon as	than
however	before	
if	after	

Some of these subordinating conjunctions are used in elliptical constructions. Examples:

> **When** possible, pay off your debts.
> **Though** tough, John is gentle.
> **While** studying, keep the TV off.
> **If** pursued, try to walk in water.
> **Unless** proved wrong, we will continue to support the strike.

A full dependent clause is understood in each of these elliptical constructions: *when it is possible*, *though he is tough*, and so on.

Subordinating Conjunctions that Introduce Noun Clauses

Some of the structure words classified above as relative and interrogative pronouns and subordinating conjunctions that introduce adverb clauses also introduce noun clauses. They form a separate classification. For example, when *who* introduces a noun clause it is not a member of the relative- or interrogative-pronoun class but is a member of the class of subordinating conjunctions that introduce noun clauses. As a relative pronoun in an adjective clause, *who* has definite reference to a noun in the sentence; in a noun clause it has reference only outside the sentence. Here are a number of sentences with noun clauses:

> **Who** arrives first is of little importance.
> **Whoever** follows my creed will be saved.
> **Whomsoever** the proctor reports will be expelled.
> I didn't hear **what** you said.
> He knew **where** I had gone.
> Perry doesn't know **when** it's time to shut up.
> I don't know **whether** I should go.
> I understand **that** you are a Buddhist.

Sometimes the subordinating conjunction plays a grammatical role in its noun clause and sometimes it doesn't. In sentences one and two, *who* and *whoever* are subjects; in sentences three and four, *whomsoever* and *what* are direct objects; in sentences five and six, *where* and *when* are adverbial modifiers (equivalent to *I had gone there* and to *to shut up then*); *whether* and *that* are connectives that do not play a grammatical role within their own clauses.

Note that in the last sentence the *that* is an entirely different word from other *that*s classified earlier in this chapter. It is an **empty morpheme** because it has no meaning whatsoever. It is the connective most often used to introduce noun clauses and is very frequently omitted, as it can be in the example sentence. In such a sentence as

> I know this is the wrong thing to do,

the demonstrative pronoun *this* is not introducing the noun clause; an understood *that* is the true subordinating conjunction.

Note that the *where* in sentence five is functioning differently from the *where* that introduces an adverb clause. In

> I'll go **where** you want me to go,

the entire dependent clause can have *there* substituted for it, showing that the clause is an adverbial. In sentence five above *where I had gone* can have *something* substituted for it, showing that the clause is a nominal. The same analysis applies to the connective *when*, which introduces both adverb and noun clauses. Examples:

> I will come **when** I can.
> I don't know **when** he will come.

In the first sentence, the clause introduced by *when* can have *then* substituted for it, showing that the clause is an adverbial. In the second sentence, the clause introduced by *when* can have *something* substituted for it, showing that the clause is a nominal.

For reference, here is a list of the subordinating conjunctions that introduce noun clauses:

who	whatever	whensoever
whom	whatsoever	which
whosoever	where	whichever
whoever	wherever	why
whomsoever	wheresoever	that
whose	when	whether
what	whenever	how .

Determiners

Determiners, often called **noun markers**, are a sizable group of structure words with complex syntactic behavior. Though they most usually pattern with nouns, most of them also pattern with adjectives, adverbs, and verbs, which they thus mark as nominals. There are subclasses of determiners, but for the sake of convenience and simplicity all may just be called determiners. Since they modify nouns, they may be called adjectivals by function.

The most frequently used group of determiners form a subclass that can be preceded by a few so-called **predeterminers**. This group includes the articles, *a*, *an*, and *the*; the possessive pronouns *my*, *your*, *our*, *her*, *his*, *its*, and *their*; the possessive of any name or common noun, such as *Bill*'s and *the dog*'s; the possessive of an indefinite pronoun, such as *somebody's*; and the demonstrative pronouns *this*, *that*, *these*, and *those*. As simple determiners they pattern in this way:

a book	**Sally's** poodle
the creek	**this** house
my mother	**those** berries

They announce that a noun is coming. Note, however, that with common nouns in the possessive an article determiner can precede the possessive determiner. Examples:

a dog's life   **the** book's cover

In a sense, then, in these constructions *a* and *the* are predeterminers; but we do not really need that name for them. The simple syntactic fact is that two or more determiners can pile up in front of a noun.

All, *both*, *half*, and *double* have been classed as predeterminers since they can precede a regular determiner. Examples:

all his debtors   **half** the liquor
both your aunts   **double** this contribution

In actual usage, however, *all*, *both*, and *half* are almost always used with an *of* phrase, which makes them quantifiers and not determiners at all. Examples:

all of his debtors   **both** of your aunts

Double does not pattern with *of*, but it may just be called a determiner like *the* in *the book's cover*. The classification of predeterminers is thus doubtful.

Another group of determiners may be given a subclassification on the grounds that they are not preceded by predeterminers. They are *either*, *neither*, *no*, *some*, *much*, *enough*, *another*, *any*, *each*, *what* (*a*), *whose*, and *which*. Examples:

either book	**what a** character
no money	I don't know **whose** book to take.
some cash	I wonder **which** sandwich is best.

No other determiner can precede these. In the last two examples, *whose* and *which* are connectives introducing noun clauses, but they are also functioning as determiners.

Some anomalies exist in the group. Example:

I have **this** much money.

The *this* seems to be pointing and thus may be a demonstrative, but it is modifying *much* rather than *money*. It may be a qualifier (see pages

98–100) or it may be a determiner. The fact is that the determiners have such complex syntactic behavior that it is almost impossible to sort out all the functions they can and cannot have.

The following group have been called **postdeterminers** on the grounds that they are sometimes preceded by a regular determiner: *first* and *last* (and all ordinal numbers), *one* (and all cardinal numbers), *more, most, many* (*a*), *every, few, less, single, other, same, several, little* (quantity), and *such* (*a*). These may come after a determiner in the modification of a noun or noun substitute. Examples:

a **single** one   his **every** wish
the **first** teacher   those **same** villains
any **two** books   their **little** sugar
some **more** towels

But only a few determiners will pattern with any one word of this group; the limitation makes any attempt to map them out completely extraordinarily complex. Furthermore, most of these so-called post-determiners will pattern singly with nouns. Examples:

one cat   **every** book
more wine   **few** men
many a girl   **less** sugar

In view of this kind of function and of the complexity of determiners in general, it seems best to just call all the noun markers determiners and to understand that two or three of them can precede a noun.

In word order, all determiners precede any adjective or noun that is modifying a noun. Examples:

the last blue passenger car
Elizabeth's porcelain dishes
any such erratic behavior
those same dirty hoodlums
double his many large church donations

Note that the word order in these phrases cannot possibly be rearranged. This shows not only that determiners precede adjectives but that there is also a strict order when more than one determiner modifies a noun.

For reference, here is a list of determiners:

one (*and all cardinal numbers*)
first *and* last (*and all ordinal numbers*)
John's (*and the possessive of all proper nouns*)
dog's (*and the possessive of all common nouns*)
another's (*and the possessive of all indefinite pronouns*)

a	this	no	many (a)
an	that	some	every
the	these	much	few
my	those	enough	less
your	all	another	little
our	both	any	single
her	half	each	other
his	double	what (a)	same
its	either	whose	several
their	neither	which	such (a)

Many of these determiners have other classifications in structure words too.

Most of the determiners pattern with verbs, adjectives, and adverbs and thus mark these as nominals. The definite article *the* and possessive forms will pattern with some adjectives. Examples:

> **the** young
> **the** amorous
> **America's** poor

The definite article *the*, possessives, demonstratives, and *such, enough, all, no, some, much, any, whose, more, most, less,* and *little* will pattern with the present-participle form of verbs. Examples:

> **his** studying
> **The** swimming is good.
> **this** coming and going
> **Such** eating is dangerous.
> **Enough** eating is enough.
> **All** talking is forbidden.

The singular demonstratives pattern with some adverbs. Examples:

> **this** soon
> **that** soon
> **this** fast

Some grammarians argue that in this last usage *this* and *that* are qualifiers, like *very*, but they seem to behave like demonstratives.

Restrictors

A few words that may precede determiners in a noun phrase are *even, just, only, especially, particularly, merely,* and possibly a few others.

These words may modify a noun alone, as in

> **even** snakes
> **just** pepper
> **merely** anthologies

But they seem different from determiners in that they restrict, and thus a good name for them is **restrictors.** When a noun has other modifiers, including determiners, the restrictors always come first. Examples:

> **even** all the many beautiful college coeds
> **particularly** all the football players
> **only** both the sophomores
> **just** the few straight-A students

These words may also modify prepositional phrases, as in

> He came **just** in time.

In that function they may be called either restrictors or adverbials.

Qualifiers

Qualifiers, which may be called **adjective** and **adverb markers**, are structure words that modify adjectives and adverbs but usually not verbs; thus they do not fit into the form class of adverbs. Some words that modify adjectives and adverbs are true adverbs by form. Examples:

> **completely** comfortable   **extremely** courageously
> **excessively** stingy   **probably** soon

When an *ly* word formed from an adjective modifies an adjective or adverb, it is an adverb by form and an adverbial by function. Most other modifiers of adjectives and adverbs are qualifiers. They may be called adverbials by function since they modify adjectives and adverbs. Four of the most common are these:

> **very** tired   **rather** courageously
> **quite** courageous   **somewhat** embittered

Somewhat can modify a verb, as in *it glows somewhat*, but it is primarily a qualifier. *Quite* and *rather* can also function as secondary quantifiers, as in *quite a lot of money*, but they too are chiefly qualifiers.

There are many other qualifiers, almost all of which have other classifications, either in the form classes or the structure classes. Some of these are used only in set phrases, such as

> **stark** naked   **fresh** out
> **dirt** cheap   **clean** out

dead right   **boiling** hot
fighting mad   **just** right

Modifiers of this sort are functioning as qualifiers though they are more commonly used otherwise. For example, *dirt* is usually a noun and *fighting* is usually a verb.

Some qualifiers are compounds. These are the common ones:

a little tired   **a good deal** younger
less than candid   **kind of** bored
more than generously   **sort of** hungry
a lot better   **a bit** looney
a whole lot worse   **a good bit** smarter

Some of these are used only colloquially. Note that these compounds are qualifiers only when they modify adjectives and adverbs. In such a phrase as *a lot of corn*, *a lot* is a quantifier. And so with some of the others.

Not all of the qualifiers will modify the comparative-degree adjectives and adverbs. Here are a few that will:

much greater   **a lot** worse
a little longer   **somewhat** stronger
a whole lot better   **no** earlier

Most of the others will not modify the comparative degree.

Four of the qualifiers will modify superlative-degree adjectives but only under special conditions. Examples:

the **very** strongest
my **dead level** best
much the greatest
quite the best

In the first two examples, a determiner must precede the qualifier, and in the last the determiner *the* must follow the qualifier. These are special idioms in English and illustrate further the complex functioning of determiners and qualifiers.

Enough is the only qualifier that follows the adjective or adverb it modifies. Example:

Man will not learn enough quickly **enough**.

The boldface *enough* is a qualifier modifying *quickly*. The other *enough* is a noun substitute. When *enough* modifies the comparative degree, it precedes the word it modifies. Example:

He is **enough** better to walk around.

This usage is rare.

For reference, here is a list of the most common qualifiers:

very	least	real
quite	less	right
rather	lots	so
somewhat	mighty	kind of
too	plenty	sort of
still	pretty	a bit
some	awful	a little
just	awfully	a great deal
enough	more	a lot
almost	most	a whole lot
even	no	a good deal

Many of these are colloquial, and most of them also have other classifications.

Auxiliaries

To be, *to have*, and *to do* serve not only as regular verbs in English but also as **auxiliaries**, or, as the school grammars say, "verb helpers." As auxiliaries they are structure words and have meanings (usually very little lexical meaning) different from their verb meanings. They may be called **verb markers**, just as determiners are called noun markers.

Be as an Auxiliary

The various forms of *to be* serve as auxiliaries in various ways. The so-called progressive tenses (*ing* form of the main verb) are formed with *be* as an auxiliary. The names for the various tenses will not be given here but in Chapter 7. Examples:

> He **is** going.
> He **was** going.
> He has **been** going.
> He had **been** going.
> He will **be** going.

Be is also used as an auxiliary in passive-voice sentences. Again, the names for the tenses will not be given here. Examples:

> This boat **was** built (by someone).
> This boat **is being** built (by someone).
> Two boats **were being** built (by someone).
> This boat has **been** built (by someone).
> A boat will **be** built (by someone).
> I **am** forced to study (by someone).

If these sentences are transformed into the active voice, the *be* auxiliaries disappear, as in *someone built this boat*.

Be as an auxiliary combines with the *to* of an infinitive to build a verb form that denotes an impending action or an action that was impending. Examples:

> He **is to** leave tomorrow.
> We **were to** arrive yesterday.
> I **am to** go with Pauline.

The two-part boldface forms here are together the auxiliary and the verb following *to* is the main verb of the sentence, not really an infinitive.

Be as an auxiliary also combines with *going to* to denote future action or action that was to have been in the future. Examples:

> I **am going to** study tonight.
> He **was going to** leave yesterday.

In such sentences *going* is not the main verb of the sentence with an infinitive modifying it. Instead, *be going to* as a whole is an auxiliary, and the main verb of the sentence is *study*, *leave*, and the like. This compound auxiliary can be grouped with the modal auxiliaries (see below).

Be also combines with *about to* to form a compound auxiliary denoting impending action. Examples:

> He **is about to** leave.
> She **was about to** kiss him.

In these sentences *leave* and *kiss* are the main verbs of the sentences, not infinitives. *Be about to* may also be classified with the modal auxiliaries.

Finally, in a very few cases *be* is used instead of *have* to make a perfect tense form. Examples:

> My dog **is** gone.
> The minister **is** come.
> The sun **was** risen before we got up.

In the last two examples *have* could replace *be* as the auxiliary.

Have as an Auxiliary

Forms of *have* are used as auxiliaries to form the so-called perfect tenses (see Chapter 7), both in active- and passive-voice sentences. Examples:

> I **have** gone.

He **has** been going.
I **had** gone.
I shall **have** gone.
The boat **has** been built (by someone).
The boat **had** been built (by someone).

These auxiliary forms of *have* do not have the same meaning as *have* as a verb, as in *I have four dollars.* The auxiliary is a structure word only, with little if any lexical meaning.

Have also combines with *to* to form an auxiliary which denotes compulsory action. Examples:

I **have to** leave now.
He **had to** pay a fine.

The two-part boldface forms are auxiliaries. *Leave* and *pay* are the main verbs of the sentences, not really infinitives. *Have to* as an auxiliary may also be classed with the modal auxiliaries.

Do as an Auxiliary

The forms *do*, *does*, and *did* function as auxiliaries to denote emphasis and the unexpected and to form questions and negative sentences. Examples of emphatic use of *do*:

I **do** attend class regularly.
He **did** invite me to the party.

These emphatic auxiliaries imply a contradiction of the immediately preceding utterance. The verb form used with them is the infinitive form of the verb without the *to* (that is, the stem). Past tense is expressed in the auxiliary, not in the main verb.

Example of *did* denoting the unexpected:

Shirley **did** qualify after all.

The *did* denotes that Shirley was not expected to qualify.

Examples of *do* as an auxiliary in questions:

Do you go to college?
Did he read the book?

The auxiliaries here are completely empty morphemes lexically, used only as question-formers (and to show tense). English could have evolved so that we would normally say

Go you to college?
Read he the book?

But it didn't. The stem form of the main verb is also used with these auxiliaries, and tense is expressed in the auxiliary.

The same kind of empty morpheme is used in negative sentences. Examples:

> He **doesn**'t belong to Phi Beta Kappa.
> We **did**n't see you pass.

In English we just don't say

> He belongs not to Phi Beta Kappa.
> We saw not you pass.

In the regular negative sentences the main verb is always the verb stem, and tense is expressed in the auxiliary.

Not all questions and negative statements require *do* as an auxiliary. If another auxiliary is to be used because of tense form, then it rather than *do* will serve to make a question or to express a negation. Examples:

> I **have** not been to class.
> I **will** not attend the funeral.
> **Have** you found the money?
> **Can** he solve the equation?

If there is more than one auxiliary in a negative sentence, the *not* goes after the first one. Example:

> I **have** not **been** teasing Linda,

but not

> *I have been not teasing Linda.

This word-order convention sometimes collides with the needs of logicians and philosophers, who perceive a difference between "I have not been teasing" and "I have been not teasing." In a question the subject and the first auxiliary are reversed. Example:

> **Can** he **have been** looking in the window?

No other word order is grammatical.

Modal Auxiliaries

Another group of verb markers—called **modal auxiliaries**—are extraordinarily subtle in their meanings and complex in their functions.

Those commonly listed are

can	could
may	might
shall	should
will	would
must	ought to

Shall and *will* denote futurity; *must* and *ought to* denote obligation or necessity and *must* can have other meanings as well; the others variously denote volition, possibility, permission, probability, potentiality, ability, and perhaps other subtly shaded meanings.

The modals are sometimes said to have tense. The first four in column one above are in the present tense and the first four in column two supposedly represent the past tense of these forms. *Must* and *ought to* do not have such parallel forms. Tense, however, is not necessarily expressed in these words. For example,

> **Can** I help you?

and

> **Could** I help you?

have about the same meaning with no tense implied. Or consider the sentence

> He **should** get a wife.

Certainly the *should* does not denote past tense. In fact, futurity seems to be the time element most commonly expressed in all these modals. The meanings of these verb markers are so elusive that native speakers should be thankful that they already have a command of the forms.

The main-verb form used when a modal is the only auxiliary is the stem. Examples:

> He **will** go.
> You **should** go.
> They **ought to** go.

Tense, if there is any, is expressed in the modal rather than in the sentence verb.

When one or more other auxiliaries are used with a modal, the modal always comes first and the main sentence verb may be the present- or past-participle form. Examples:

> I **could** have gone.
> She **could** have been gone.
> He **should** be going.
> They **must** have been leaving.

Note that the *must* in the last sentence denotes strong probability rather than necessity, as in *I must go*.

Two pairs of the modals—*shall* and *will, can* and *may*—used to be the subject of debates about usage. As late as 1940, or even later, school children were taught "rules" about the use of *shall* and *will*. One rule, for instance, said that to express simple futurity, *shall* should be used with the first person and *will* with the second and third, as in

> I **shall** go.
> You **will** go.
> He **will** go.

But probably no native speaker of English ever naturally and unconsciously adhered to such a rule. It and other such rules were the products of the imaginations of eighteenth-century prescriptive grammarians. *Shall* and *will* are increasingly used interchangeably.

For a long time it was also taught that *can* should be used only to denote ability to perform an action and *may* to ask or grant permission. But *can* also is used by all native speakers to ask permission, as in

> **Can** I go to the movies tonight?

Can and *may* are thus used interchangeably in the meaning of asking or granting permission, and nobody makes errors in their use.

There are auxiliaries other than the ten listed above that can be classed as modals. *Have to* was mentioned above as denoting obligation. In

> I **have to** (must) go,

it seems to be a modal. Also *be going to* and *be about to*, expressing futurity and pending action, are really modals. And there are other modal auxiliaries. *Dare* and *need* are still in somewhat common use as modals, as in

> **Dare** I go?   **Need** you eat that?
> I would not **dare** leave. He **need** not listen to you.

Go, leave, eat, and *listen* are the main verbs in these sentences, and *dare* and *need* are auxiliaries denoting uncertainty or risk and obligation. *To dare* and *to need* also function as regular verbs, just as *to do, to have*, and *to be* do.

Other auxiliaries that may be called modals have been little recognized. *Used to, be supposed to*, and *be able to* are auxiliaries when followed by a verb stem. Examples:

> He **used to** preach hell-fire sermons.
> I **am supposed to** take three of these pills a day.
> He **is able to** pay his own way.

In sentence one, *preach* is the main verb, a relationship being shown between it and the subject *he*. *Used to* is an auxiliary denoting continuing action in the past, like *kept preaching* (see the next paragraph). Similarly, in sentence two, a subject-verb relationship is shown between *I* and *take*, making *am supposed to* an auxiliary denoting obligation (like *should*). And in sentence three, *is able to* is identical in meaning to the modal *can* and is itself a modal. *He* and *pay* are the subject and the main verb. It should be noted that *used to* is not always an auxiliary. When it is followed by a noun, as in *I am used to pain*, *used* is a predicate adjective modified by a prepositional phrase.

Also *keep* and *get* (sometimes with a previous auxiliary and *to*) are often used as auxiliaries. Examples:

> He **keeps** talking when he should shut up.
> He **got** killed.
> I **have got to** study.

Note that the relationship (subject-verb) is between *he* and *talking*, *he* and *killed*, and *I* and *study*. The boldface words are auxiliaries, with *keeps* denoting continuing action, *got* denoting the same meaning as the auxiliary *to be*, and *have got to* denoting obligation (like *must*). Sentence two is especially interesting grammatically. It is really a passive-voice sentence, the active voice being

> Someone killed him.

Got is functioning as an auxiliary just as *was* would. Also modals, as well as *have*, will function with *get to* as an auxiliary. Example:

> I **will get to** go.

Will get to must be considered an auxiliary, since the subject-verb relationship is between *I* and *go*. The whole phrase denotes futurity and permission. Of course *to get* and *to keep* also function as regular verbs, as in *I will get an A in the course* and *he keeps a menagerie*.

To show how extensive auxiliaries may be in a single English sentence, here is a real sentence taken from a newspaper:

> You **are going to have to** get used to jets flying overhead.

Though dictionaries list *used* in this meaning as a verb, it is really a predicate adjective with approximately the meaning of *accustomed*. *You-get-used* is the combination of subject plus verb plus predicate adjective; *get* is functioning as a linking verb like *become*. *Are going to have to* is two auxiliaries, and even these auxiliaries could be grammatically expanded to *are going to have to keep (getting)*, in which case the three auxiliaries would denote futurity, necessity, and continuing action. Note that all the auxiliaries discussed in the last three paragraphs have about the same denotations specified for the "pure" modals listed on page 104.

Expletives

Several structure words serve as expletives, or "fillers." They are empty morphemes in that they have no meaning. The most common two are *it* and *there*.

It frequently fills out as a subject when the true subject follows its verb. Sometimes noun clauses are the true subjects. Examples:

> It is true that we are in a recession.
> It was clear that John was cheating.
> It is a fact that women live longer than men.

The transformed structures are

> That we are in a recession is true.
> That John was cheating was clear.
> That women live longer than men is a fact.

The expletive *it* is a rhetorical device in these sentences, allowing the speaker or writer to delay his main idea for emphasis.

Sometimes infinitive phrases are the true subjects that the expletive *it* fills in for. Examples:

> It is necessary to suspend George.
> It is all right to use my credit card.

The transformed structures are

> To suspend George is necessary.
> To use my credit card is all right.

We are so used to the expletives that the transformed structures seem awkward. Both the noun clauses and infinitive phrases above are nominals because they are subjects.

Sometimes a *for* phrase functioning as a nominal is the true subject that the expletive *it* fills in for. Examples:

> It is difficult for me to go now.
> It is early for him to be working.

The transformed structures are

> For me to go now is difficult.
> For him to be working is early.

The second transformed structure sounds especially awkward; the use of the expletive makes a comfortable sentence. This structure will be mentioned again below.

Sometimes the expletive *it* is in an object position rather than a subject position. Examples:

> He thinks **it** unlikely that you are insane.
> I have **it** in mind to go to Ensenada.

In the first sentence, *it* is filling in for a noun clause, and the transformed structure is

> He thinks that you are insane is unlikely.

In the second sentence *it* fills in for an infinitive phrase, and the transformed structure is

> I have to go to Ensenada in mind.

Both the noun clause and the infinitive phrase are of course nominals because they are direct objects. The transformed structures sound ungrammatical because we are so used to the expletive *it*. Indeed, the expletive structure is much clearer in both these sentences. To achieve clarity without the expletive, one might use participial phrases:

> He thinks your being insane is unlikely.
> I have going to Ensenada in mind.

The *it* used in speaking of the weather may be called an expletive. Example:

> **It** is raining.

In a sense the *it* here is referring to the weather and might be called a pronoun, but also in a sense it seems to be a filler.

Do not confuse the expletive *it* with pronouns that have reference. In

> **It** is war that we must avoid,

the *it* is a pronoun referring to *war*. In such a sentence as

> I can't make **it** without you,

the *it* refers to some activity the speaker has in mind.

There also frequently functions as an expletive filler when the true subject of a linking verb follows the verb. Examples:

> **There** are two cannons in the orchard.
> **There** is no way to solve the problem.
> **There** seem to be too many of us.

The transformed structure of the first sentence is

> Two cannons are in the orchard.

The transformed structure of the second sentence is

> No way to solve the problem is (exists),

which sounds incomplete to our ears. The transformed structure of the third sentence is

> Too many of us seem to be,

which also sounds ungrammatical. The expletive *there* supplies a comfortable structure for us.

The expletive *there* is also used to introduce participial phrases made with linking verbs. Examples:

> **There** being no electricity, we went to bed.
> He raced his car without **there** being any reason for it.
> **There** seeming to be no way out, we resigned ourselves to death.

Though the *there* in these sentences has no meaning, we demand it as a filler for such structures. Note that the *it* in sentence two is not an expletive since it has reference to his racing his car.

There as an expletive should not be confused with *there* as an adverb of place. Consider:

> **There** we were.
> **There** in the orchard stood two cannons.

In these sentences the *there* is not a filler but a word of lexical meaning.

When *for* introduces a phrase that serves as a nominal (a subject), the *for* may be considered an expletive. Examples:

> It's difficult **for** me to study.
> **For** me to be catty seems natural.

The *for* seems to be a filler to introduce an infinitive phrase with a subject. It would not be wrong, however, to consider *for* a preposition and the prepositional phrase a subject (nominal).

Another expletive is *as* when it stands between a direct object and its object complement. Example:

> We chose Ray **as** captain.

Note that the *as* can be omitted, though that test alone is not proof that *as* is an expletive. But *as* seems to be just a filler. When the object complement occurs in reversed sentence order, the expletive *as* is mandatory. Example:

> **As** Homecoming Queen, we elected Charlotte.

The *as* can be dispensed with if *Homecoming Queen* is placed after *Charlotte*.

The infinitive *to be* is often used as an expletive in conjunction with a linking verb. Examples:

> She seems **to be** happy.
> He appeared **to be** a giant.

The meaning of *to be* is already contained in the linking verbs *seems* and *appeared*, and so *to be* is redundant and an expletive. But our ears are so accustomed to it that we often demand it in such constructions. (See page 199 for a possible alternate analysis of this construction.) With a nonlinking verb, *to be* is never an expletive. For example, in

> He wants to be a doctor

to be a doctor is an infinitive phrase functioning as the direct object of *wants*. Note that the meaning of *to be* is not contained in *wants*.

Other structure words mentioned as appositive conjunctions on page 89 are sometimes called expletives, but they seem to have somewhat more meaning than the empty morphemes discussed here.

Noun Substitutes

Many of the structure words discussed above (and a few form-class words) sometimes function as **noun substitutes**. Or perhaps **nominal substitutes** would be a better term, since sometimes the substitute refers to a word group rather than a single noun. Consider this ambiguous sentence from an advertisement:

> People who drink Old Fitzgerald don't know any **better**.

The common idiomatic meaning of *any better* is adverbial in connection with the understood clause *than to drink Old Fitzgerald*. *Better than* is a subordinating conjunction introducing an adverb clause. But the ad writer wants to stir your interest by having you understand *better* also as a noun substitute, meaning *better whiskey*. *Any* is then a determiner. Such noun substitutes are common in our language. Sometimes a whole sentence may be little more than noun substitutes. Consider this question about the high earnings of some entertainers:

> Who's worth what where?

Who, *what*, and *where* are all functioning as noun substitutes, though they belong to various structure classes. In fact the question is composed almost wholly of structure words; some grammarians consider even *is* a structure word.

Any word or short phrase, then, that stands for a noun or nominal construction may be called a noun substitute. The personal, relative, and interrogative pronouns, though not normally given that name, do function as noun substitutes. The whole purpose of the possessive pronoun forms *ours*, *yours*, *hers*, *theirs*, *mine*, and (in certain usages) *his* and *its* is to function as noun substitutes. Examples:

> That one is **mine.**
> Sally is **yours.**

Mine substitutes for whatever object is under discussion; *yours* substitutes for *your girl* or some such phrase.

The possessive of a proper or common noun also may function as a noun substitute. Examples:

> I tried to borrow **John's.**
> That's my **dog's.**

Both *John's* and *dog's* are noun substitutes standing for whatever objects are under discussion.

The demonstrative pronouns are frequently noun substitutes. Examples:

> **That** is yours.
> We decided to leave early, and **this** was a wise decision.

That substitutes for whatever object is under discussion. *This* substitutes for *our decision to leave early*, a nominal. The indefinite pronouns (see page 75 for a full list) usually function as noun substitutes. Examples:

> I want **both.**
> Give me **another.**
> How **many** do you have?

These are structure words substituting for nouns.

The cardinal numbers and fractions frequently function as noun substitutes. Examples:

> Give me those **two.**
> **Half** is all I want.

These structure words may also function as determiners. *Any more* (negative) and *some more* (positive) very frequently function as noun substitutes. Examples:

> I don't have **any more**.
> Do you want **some more?**

Much more, many more, and *no more* also function as substitutes, as does *a lot*. Both *plenty* and *enough*, both of which may function as qualifiers, are frequently used as noun substitutes. Examples:

> Do you have **enough?**
> I have **plenty**.

Though these are listed in dictionaries as nouns, they are really structure words. They do not fit into the noun paradigm, do not have derivational suffixes, and are not the name of anything. The old system was in error in calling these structure words nouns.

The word *so*, variously used as a colloquial qualifier, a connective, a substitute for *true*, and a part of a verb substitute (see below), also frequently serves as a noun substitute. Example:

> "Do you think Casey will be elected?" "Yes, I think **so**."

So is substituting for the noun clause (*that*) *Casey will be elected*. This usage is very common.

Verb Substitutes

Many of the auxiliaries and modal auxiliaries serve as verb substitutes. For example, a conversation cannot begin with such an utterance as

> I think I **can**.

Can is a verb substitute, standing for a verb in the preceding utterance, which might be

> Can you go with me to the movies?

Can in the first sentence substitutes for *can go*. All of the modals can function in this way. Examples:

> Yes, I **might**.
> I **may**.
> I **ought to**.
> I **had to**.
> I'm **going to**.

These are very common usages in our daily talk.

Forms of *be*, *have*, and *do* also function as verb substitutes. Examples:

> He **is** (invited to my party).
> They **have been** (married).
> Yes, I **have** (voted).
> He **does** (work at night).
> I hope I can **do so** (attend your meeting).

So is quite frequently used with *do* to form a verb substitute. These usages are very common.

Particles

The particles discussed in Chapter 3 on verb-particle composites may be classified as structure words. The prepositions are of course prepositions. The particle-like words that function as modifiers of verbs are perhaps best called adverbs since they function in that capacity. Examples are

> Don't look **up**.
> He walked **out**.
> The canoe floated **by**.

These words modify the verbs and have lexical, adverbial meanings of place or direction and so can be classed as adverbs. But the particles in composites have mostly structural function. Examples:

> The little boy turned **up**.
> That's hard to come **by**.
> I ran **across** a rarity.
> He barked **out** the orders.

These words seem to have little lexical meaning and are really structure words. Some of the words that look like prepositions fit into this class. You can pick them out from the list on pages 78–79.

– – – – – – – – – – – – –

Our inventory of structure words is now completed. The classifications given here are intended to clarify the extraordinary complexity and the multiple functions of English words that do not fit into the four great form classes. Early traditional grammar tried to label each of these words as belonging to one of the eight parts of speech (only seven if interjections are omitted), but that labeling obscures the wide variety of functions that our structure words have. When given in citation form, many of these words must be listed in more than one structure class, but when they are functioning in sentences they mostly can be satisfactorily labeled.

The coming chapters will in various ways analyze the four great grammatical functions: **predication**, **complementation**, **modification**, and **coordination**. It might seem that subordination has been left out of this group, but modification is subordination and all subordination is modification. Chapter 5 discusses predication as a function, and then Chapters 6, 7, and 8 analyze it further with discussions of the three major parts of sentences, **subjects**, **finite verbs**, and **complements.**

EXERCISES

1. How many structure classes can you fit each of these words into? Do any fit into the form classes as well?

by	out	one another
who	many	instead of
several	which	but
over	provided	still
about	merely	whose
this	to	a lot
nobody	enough	so
that	even	since
plenty	it	near
his	could	there

2. How many definitions can you compile for the following words? Try the *Oxford English Dictionary*.

to	over
that	but

3. Use four completely empty morphemes in sentences.

4. As a creative exercise see if you can invent a structure word and show how it could function in a sentence.

5. Use in sentences five pronouns, none of which are indefinite pronouns by class, which have indefinite reference or which refer to a whole idea rather than a specific noun.

6. Which pronouns besides the personal pronouns have any inflection (person, case, number, and gender)?

7. Use a personal pronoun in the objective case as a subject.

8. Use one personal pronoun in the objective case in four different functions.

9. Use the five relative pronouns in a sentence each, and explain the grammatical function of each relative in its own clause.

10. Use five indefinite pronouns (besides the *body*, *one*, and *thing* words) in sentences and comment on the number of the verb used.

11. Use five QW words in questions and explain the grammatical function of each QW word in its own question.

12. Explain which words the prepositional phrases in the following sentences modify. Are any of them sentence modifiers? Indicate which phrases are adjectivals and which adverbials. Do not confuse infinitives and verb-particle composites with prepositional phrases.

    a. After turning on the lights in the back of the house, I settled down to studying.

    b. When he knocked me down by throwing a brick at me, I spread blood on the brick to keep as evidence.

    c. Save the children by donating to UNESCO.

    d. In spite of my caution, I received a considerable loss at the hands of my broker.

    e. The old in their hermitages carry on correspondence with friends in other countries.

13. What is the displaced object of the preposition at the end of each of these sentences?

    a. The policeman was shot at.

    b. Piedmont's the college I went to.

    c. Jerry has no one to play with.

    d. Who are you listening to?

    e. She's the girl everybody flirts with.

14. Write two sentences in which one of the coordinating conjunctions and one of the subordinating conjunctions each expresses two different kinds of relation at the same time.

15. Write two compound sentences using *otherwise* as a connective and tell what relationship *otherwise* expresses.

16. Which conjunctive adverbs cannot be shifted to the interior of the second clause?

17. Create three noun phrases that have a restrictor, at least two determiners, an adjective, and a noun in front of the noun headword of the phrase.

18. Choose two of the modal auxiliaries and list all the meanings given for them in the *Oxford English Dictionary*.

19. Following are two paragraphs selected at random. Identify and classify the structure words in them.

    Almost every "Communism" course repeats an account of Marxism. When it centers on doctrines like "dialectical materialsm," which even Communists have trouble understanding, the course usually turns into a farce.   Afterward we often get the accompanying horror images.   One widely used film states that the only three non-Communist countries in the West are Spain, Switzerland and America!   In an attempt to get down to what is presumed to be our level, one text shows a cartoon of an Oriental-looking Lenin, left hand on a cannon, leading regimented lines of darkly colored robot people against others who, huddled in small groups around the base of the Statue of Liberty, are riding in a car, watching TV, debating, and mowing a lawn.   Most of us think that such things insult our intelligence.   [Steven Kelman, "You Force Kids to Rebel"]

At the same time, my generation was discovering that reforming the world is a little like fighting a military campaign in the Appenines: as soon as you capture one mountain range, another one looms just ahead.   As the big problems of the 'thirties were brought under some kind of rough control, new problems took their place—the unprecedented problems of an affluent society, of racial justice, of keeping our cities from becoming uninhabitable, of coping with war in unfamiliar guises.   Most disturbing of all was our discovery of the population explosion.   It dawned on us rather suddenly that the number of passengers on the small spaceship we inhabit is doubling about every forty years—and that already there aren't enough seats to go around. So long as the earth's population keeps growing at this cancerous rate, all of the other problems appear virtually insoluble.   Our cities will continue to become more crowded and noisome.   The landscape will get more cluttered, the air and water even dirtier.   The quality of life is likely to become steadily worse for everybody.   And warfare on a rising scale seems inevitable, if too many bodies have to struggle for ever-dwindling shares of food and living space.   [John Fischer, "Four Choices for Young People"]

5 PREDICATION

This chapter is a prelude to the following three chapters, which examine in detail the three (sometimes only two) component parts of a predication. First we need an overview.

The First Great Grammatical Function

The term **predication** has been strangely neglected in grammatical studies. It is the first great grammatical function that should be discovered if one totally unfamiliar with language study were to undertake to analyze inductively what goes on in English sentences. Yet few grammar texts even use the word, and those that use it dismiss it in a sentence or two without considering it as a grammatical function.

This neglect of our primary grammatical function is manifested in dictionaries. If you look in the best collegiate dictionaries, you will find *predication* defined only as "the act of predicating," a most frustrating type of definition. Then, going to the verb *predicate*, you will find that it means "to declare, affirm, or proclaim." From these definitions you would deduce that a predication is a statement, something declared or affirmed. That is certainly one common meaning of *predication,* but the word also applies as a technical term to the grammatical function which results in a statement. Such dual meanings in our vocabulary (lexical) terms is common, and we have syntactic ways of indicating which sense of the word we mean. For example, when we use *predication* in the sense of a declaration or affirmation, we are likely to say *a predication* or *this predication*, but when we mean the word in its sense of a grammatical function we would not normally use a determiner with it (though it is possible to do so). Also we would think of the word in the first sense as a count noun, capable of being made plural, whereas in the second sense we would think of it only as a mass noun, not capable of being made plural. The first meaning denotes a thing, the second a function.

The grammatical term *predicate* has perhaps interfered with a proper use of *predication* to mean a grammatical function. The predicate of a sentence is the finite verb of the sentence with all its modifiers and complements. The term has traditionally been used because the verb of a sentence, often called the **predicator**, seems to be most central to the total statement that can be called a predication. But in predication as a grammatical function the subject is equally important. And also a predication need not include a finite verb, a grammatical fact which many grammarians seem not to have recognized. *Predication as a grammatical function is simply the fitting of a subject to a predicate.*

Many of our utterances are not predications and do not employ the grammatical function of predication. Such utterances as *oh yeah*, *hardly*, *yes indeed*, and *absolutely not* are not predications. An utterance like *in a minute* does imply such a predication as *I will come in a minute*, but as an utterance it is not a predication. The request sentence —such as *hurry up*, *close the door*, or *don't rush me*—is not really a predication either, for it has no subject (see page 177). Also, in a sense, a question is not a predication even though it grammatically has a subject and predicate. From one point of view the grammatical function of predication (mass noun) results in a predication (count noun) and in this sense questions do not represent predications. But in a technical sense predication (grammatical function) can be said to be in operation in a question, since a subject is fitted to a verb.

Predication occurs in six kinds of constructions in English (aside from questions and elliptical constructions, which will be discussed a few pages further on). Two of these—simple declarative sentences and dependent clauses—may be called **finite predications** because the predicate to which a subject is fitted contains a finite verb. The other four— (1) the absolute phrase, (2) the infinitive with a subject, (3) the present participle with a subject, and (4) the past participle with a subject— may be called **nonfinite predications** because the predicate to which a subject is fitted contains a nonfinite verb.

Finite Predications

The Simple Declarative Sentence

The first kind of finite predication is the **simple declarative sentence**, which makes a statement. For example, in

> Life is short

a subject, *life*, is fitted to a predicate, *is short*, and this grammatical function results in a statement, that is, a predication. Such a simple declarative sentence may be embedded in a longer sentence, or may stand alone.

Most sentences in writing, however, and many in speaking, contain **sentence expansions** in the form of modifiers and appositives which flesh out the sentence. Within the long sentence is a **central predication** or **sentence nucleus** which exhibits the grammatical function of predication. Consider this example:

> After the votes were counted, the Democratic candidate, who had run on a clean-government issue, graciously conceded the election, a gesture that not many of his backers approved of.

The central predication of this long sentence is

> The Democratic candidate / graciously conceded the election.

The other three large constituents are sentence expansions (modifiers and an appositive), and each of them has a predication of its own:

> the votes / were counted
> who / had run on a clean-government issue
> not many of his backers / approved of (that)

Since each of these constituents has a subject fitted to a predicate, each is a predication, as will be explained in the next section on dependent clauses.

A useful way to think of predication is to see that each predication is composed of **topic** and **comment**. In most sentences the subject is the topic (that is the meaning of the word *subject*) and the predicate is the comment. Example:

> The right of Americans to travel where they please / is being undermined by bureaucrats in the State Department.

The topic under discussion is *the right of Americans to travel where they please*, and the comment on that topic is the predicate of the sentence. Here is another example:

> The nationalistic movement in Mexican music / has lost both its vitality and its sureness.

Again, topic (the subject) and comment (the predicate) are evident in the sentence.

In the grammatical function of predication, however, the subject of a sentence is not necessarily the topic of the statement. Rhetorically, we have ways of using grammatical subjects so as to leave the true topic in a different but equally emphatic position. Example:

I / was aghast that he should deny his parentage.

Grammatically, the predication is the subject *I* fitted to the long predicate. But rhetorically the topic of the sentence is *that he should deny his parentage* and the comment is that this fact made me aghast. In fact, the sentence could be written as

That he should deny his parentage / made me aghast,

but that structure doesn't sound comfortable to our ears, especially in conversation. Here is another example:

Much / has been written about the social and economic aspects of Harlem.

Not the grammatical subject *much*, but rather *the social and economic aspects of Harlem*, is the topic, and the comment is that much has been written about that topic. The grammatical function of predication, however, is the fitting of the subject *much* to a long predicate.

Dependent Clauses

All kinds of dependent clauses also employ the grammatical function of predication, since in each a subject is fitted to a predicate. The fact that the clause is not grammatically independent has no bearing on its employing the function of predication. Here are three sentences with noun clauses:

That I could fail never entered my mind.
I understand **that you are going abroad**.
My suggestion, **that we buy common stock**, was rejected.

In the first sentence the noun clause participates as a subject in the predication of the whole sentence. But within the noun clause is a subject and predicate:

I / could fail.

That construction also exhibits the grammatical function of predication because a subject is fitted to a predicate. In the second sentence the noun clause *that you are going abroad* participates as the direct object in the predication of the whole sentence. But it too has a subject-predicate combination:

You / are going abroad.

Therefore it exhibits predication. In the third sentence the noun clause is an appositive and not a part of the central predication of the sentence, but it has its own function of predication:

> We / buy common stock.

If the modal *should* is understood (*should buy*) the predicative statement is clear.

Adjective clauses also exhibit predication. Here are three examples:

> The student **who scores highest** will receive an award.
> The Sterile Cuckoos, **who are my favorite combo**, are trained musicians.
> Billy reads two thousand words a minute, **which is a record in our school.**

In the first sentence the adjective clause is a part of the predication of the whole sentence since it is restrictive; it is an indispensable part of the subject. But it also exhibits predication:

> Who / scores highest.

In the second sentence the adjective clause is not a part of the central predication, since it is nonrestrictive; it is not a part of the subject. It does, however, have the predication

> Who / are my favorite combo.

In sentence three also, the adjective clause is not a part of the central predication. Its predication is

> Which / is a record in our school.

Similarly, adverb clauses contain predication. Examples:

> **After the dance was over**, we went to Shakey's.
> **Since the stock market fell**, I became wary of investing in it.
> Sam hesitated **because he did not see the signal.**

In the first sentence the adverb clause contains the predication

> The dance / was over.

In sentence two it is

> The stock market / fell.

And in sentence three,

> He / did not see the signal.

After, *since*, and *because* are merely connectives used to relate the two predications in each sentence. On page 126 elliptical adverb clauses will be discussed.

Nonfinite Predications

The Absolute Phrase

A rather rare construction in English, especially in conversation, is the absolute phrase, which has a subject fitted to a predicate containing a nonfinite verb form. Here are three examples:

> **The ducks having already flown north**, the hunters had to search for other game.
> **The election being over**, we returned to our peaceful ways.
> She wouldn't talk about her coming wedding, **the date not having been set**.

Absolute phrases such as these exhibit the grammatical function of predication since a subject is fitted to a predicate. True predications occur in these constructions since, even though the verb form is nonfinite, a statement is made. In the above sentences the predications are

> the ducks / having already flown north
> the election / being over
> the date / not having been set

Changing the verbs to finite forms would create independent clauses, which would contain finite predications. As they stand, the absolute phrases contain nonfinite predications.

The Present-Participial Phrase with a Subject

A present-participial phrase which is not a part of an absolute phrase may also take a subject. Such a phrase is usually a direct object. Examples:

> John saw **me flirting with Jane**.
> We caught **our cat eating a mouse**.
> We found **Henry standing on his head**.

Each of these boldface constructions is a participial phrase with a subject. The three nonfinite predications are

> me / flirting with Jane
> our cat / eating a mouse
> Henry / standing on his head

All three of these boldface constructions are functioning as direct objects of *saw*, *caught*, and *found*.

Such a phrase can also be the object of a nonfinite verb form. Example:

> Having **the big boys hanging around** bothers me.

The entire construction *having the big boys hanging around* is the subject of *bothers me* (note that the verb must be singular). But within that subject is the nonfinite predication

> the big boys / hanging around,

which is the direct object of *having*. This kind of nonfinite predication is not unusual in English,

The Infinitive Phrase with a Subject

A common nonfinite predicative construction in English is the infinitive phrase with a subject. Examples:

> The host asked **me to leave**.
> I wanted **John to drive the car carefully**.
> **For Alec to attend graduate school** is unthinkable.

Each of these sentences as a whole is a single predication. In the first two the infinitive phrase is a direct object and in the third it is a subject, all parts of central predications. But the infinitive phrases themselves exhibit predication because in each a subject is fitted to a verb (or predicate). In the first,

> me / to leave

is a subject-verb combination. True, a statement is not made in the conventional sense, but the grammatical function of predication does occur. In the second sentence, the infinitive *to drive* not only has a subject (*John*) but also a direct object (*car*) and an adverbial modifier (*carefully*), all components of a predication.

> John / to drive the car carefully

is just as surely a subject-predicate combination as is any declarative statement. The same analysis applies to the infinitive phrase in sentence three. *For* can be considered either a preposition or an expletive, but it does not affect the fact that

> Alec / to attend graduate school

exhibits nonfinite predication.

Quite similar to the nonfinite predication in which an infinitive has a subject is the construction in which a verb stem (the infinitive without the *to*) has a subject. Examples:

> Making **Steve wash the car** was unkind.
> Letting **Jenny stay out after midnight** was unwise.

> Carol let **us cook our dinner.**

Each of the boldface constructions is a direct object (of *making*, *letting*, and *let*) and therefore a nominal. Each is also a nonfinite predication, for the verb stem in each is not a finite verb agreeing in number with the singular subject. The nonfinite predications are these:

> Steve / wash the car
> Jenny / stay out after midnight
> us / cook our dinner

Probably the accurate analysis of these predications is that the verb stems (*wash*, *stay*, and *cook*) are infinitives with the *to* elided.

The Past Participle with a Subject

Just like the infinitive and present participle, a past participle (which is a nonfinite verb form) can take a subject and thus participate in the grammatical function of predication. Examples:

> She got **coffee spilled on her.**
> He had **his letters filed away secretly.**
> He found **his textbook printed backwards.**
> He had **his bicycle run over.**

Several grammatical matters are to be noted here. First, the entire boldface phrases are direct objects (of *got*, *had*, and *found*) and thus are nominals. In the first example *coffee* alone is not the direct object of *got*, for *she got coffee* would have an entirely different meaning—that she obtained or was given coffee as her drink. The whole phrase is the direct object of *got*. Second, the boldface phrases must not be confused with noun clauses. For example,

> He thought **his son broke the window**

might superficially seem to be a similar construction, but is not. An understood conjunction *that* comes between *thought* and *his* in this sentence, but such an understood *that* is not possible in the four example sentences. Third, the verb form *broke* is past tense, whereas *spilled*, *filed*, *printed* and *run* are past participles and not past-tense forms, though three of these forms are identical with past-tense forms. Finally, *spilled on her* is not modifying *coffee* but is taking *coffee* as its subject (and such is the case in the other three sentences). Therefore these constructions are exhibiting predication, since a subject is fitted to a predicate. The predications are

    coffee / spilled on her
    his letters / filed away secretly
    his textbook / printed backwards
    his bicycle / run over

Note that if *was* or *were* were included, a full sentence would result; this possibility shows that *coffee* and the like are subjects.

Interestingly, all of these constructions are in the passive voice, the active transformation being

    Someone / spilled coffee on her.

The subject in each of the above constructions (*coffee* and the like) is really the displaced direct object of the past participle (*spilled* and the like), just as the subject in a passive-voice sentence is the displaced object of a transitive verb (see page 181).

Similar constructions in the subject position are grammatically different. Example:

    The coffee **spilled on her** was hot.

Here, *spilled on her* is an adjectival modifying *coffee*, for the whole adjective clause *which was spilled on her* is implied, and *coffee* is the subject of *was*. Such is not the case in the direct objects above. This is the same grammatical situation as in

    The girl **wearing the sweater** is Joan

and

    We saw **her wearing a sweater**.

In the first sentence, *wearing the sweater* is an adjectival modifying *girl*, for the understood construction is *who is wearing the sweater*. But in the second sentence *her wearing a sweater* is the direct object of *saw*, and *her* is the subject of the present-participial phrase *wearing a sweater*. *She was wearing a sweater* is the construction implied, showing that *her* is a subject.

In the sections on infinitives, verb stems, and past participles with subjects we have illustrated with simple infinitives and past participles only. But there are other nonfinite verb forms (see page 18 for a list; memorizing the various names is not necessary), and they can take subjects and form nonfinite predications. Examples:

    For Hobart **to have been arrested** seems funny.
    We found Nancy **being consumed** with anger.
    I didn't like Henry **having been chosen** captain.

These complex nonfinite verb forms—(1) present perfect infinitive, passive voice; (2) past participle, passive voice; and (3) past perfect participle, passive voice—are functioning in the nonfinite predications

> Hobart / to have been arrested (subject of *seems*)
> Nancy / being consumed with anger (direct object of *found*)
> Henry / having been chosen captain (direct object of *didn't like*)

But such constructions are not as common as are nonfinite predications with simple infinitives, present participles, and past participles.

Predication in Ellipsis

As was mentioned on page 93 in Chapter 4, many adverb clauses are elliptical in that a part of them is simply understood and not stated. These elliptical constructions imply predication. One such kind of adverb clause is the comparative construction in which a predicate or a subject and verb are not repeated but understood. Examples:

> I am **as** capable **as you**.
> Jerry donated **more than I**.
> Father pays **more** attention to Jane **than to me**.

In sentence one the predicate *are capable* is understood. The central predication is

> I / am capable.

The understood adverb clause is

> as you / are capable,

which, with its fitting of a subject to a predicate, exhibits predication. The subordinating conjunction *as ... as* makes a comparison which calls for two predications, one independent and one dependent. In sentence two *donated* is understood so that we have predication in

> more than I / donated.

In sentence three the subject-verb *he pays* is understood so that predication is evident both in

> Father / pays attention to Jane

and

> more than he / pays to me.

Again, the comparison calls for two predications.

Noncomparative adverb clauses are also sometimes elided (that is, show ellipsis). Examples:

> **Though angry**, I held my tongue.
> **When downcast**, try meditation.
> **Once installed**, he refused to relinquish his chairmanship.

The predications that are understood are

> though I / was angry
> when you / are downcast
> once he / was installed

Though in the normal sentences it is not seen on the surface, predication is at work beneath the surface.

Sometimes in a parallel construction a verb is elided. Examples:

> Some of them are slow, **some just stupid**.
> In the first hour we will have a lecture; **in the second, an exam**.
> I'll take my chances; **you, yours**.

Sometimes a comma replaces the elided verb, as in sentence three, and sometimes not, as in sentence one. The predications that are understood are

> Some / are just stupid.
> In the second (hour) we / will have an exam.
> You / will take your chances.

The elliptical constructions are true predications.

Faulty Predication

Of some grammatical interest but of more psychological interest is a linguistic phenomenon known as faulty predication, a kind of error that is frequently seen in amateur writing. The error occurs when the subject of a sentence does not fit its predicate. Here is a live example from a student paper:

> The casting of a ballot for a candidate / sometimes tends to be a popularity contest.

A computer analysis would perhaps not turn up the faulty predication, since grammatically the sentence says a nominal tends to be another nominal, a very common syntactic structure. But the casting of a ballot cannot be a popularity contest (the election may be), and so semantically the predication is faulty.

Here are some more of these peculiar sentences. They make interesting topics for a discussion of the relationships between grammar and semantics.

> An excellent way to enrich the soil / would be man himself.
> My first impression of my physics teacher / was overbearing and conceited.
> The next type of advertising / is the radio.
> The hair oil that states "try the sixty-second workout" / is a misleading advertisement.

Psychologically, it would be interesting to follow the thought processes of one who writes such sentences.

Syntactic Devices in Sentences

Now it is time to bring together some concepts discussed in Chapters 1 and 4 and to introduce another. By what devices do English sentences deliver meaning? What are the signals that register instantaneously in the mind of a listener? Why does a beginning student of a foreign language often have considerable difficulty following a conversation even when he knows all the words individually? The answer is that all languages have syntactic devices that act as signals and control the delivery of meaning. The beginning student of a foreign language may have difficulty because he is not used to the signals even though he knows the words, for the signals in the new language may be quite different from those in his native language.

In English there are four syntactic devices[1] that serve as signals to let the listener or reader follow discourse and even to anticipate structures that are coming. These four are **word order**, **structure words**, **inflection**, and **derivational suffixes**, the last three of which have already been discussed in detail. Languages not only differ in the syntactic devices they have but also vary in the degree of importance of a particular device. Chinese, for example, depends on word order and does not have inflection or derivational suffixes. Latin depends mainly on inflection, word order not being very important. All four devices are important in English, with word order and structure words probably being more important than inflection and derivational suffixes.

Word Order

Word order in English is rather rigid (though it was not in the Old English period). Occasionally we see the normal subject-verb-comple-

---

[1]Besides the phonological devices of juncture (voice pause), stress, and pitch, which belong to another study.

ment order reversed for rhetorical purposes, but for the most part we expect a noun or pronoun at the beginning of an independent clause to be a subject. For example, if someone starts off an utterance with *the cat* our minds immediately receive the signal that *cat* will function as a subject and will do something, be something, or have something done to it, as for instance

> The cat ate the bird.

Word order is all important. The order

> The bird ate the cat

would deliver an entirely different meaning. And

> Ate the cat the bird

would not be meaningful in English. Our normal word order is subject-verb-complement, and it is word order more than anything else that determines which is which.

Such is not true in all languages. For example, in German

> Der Kater fraß den Vogel   (The cat ate the bird.)

and

> Den Vogel fraß der Kater

mean exactly the same thing (though a stylistic preference for a certain order exists in German). Also

> Fraß der Kater den Vogel

would be interpretable word order in German, though not common. The difference is that inflection in German will distinguish a subject from an object, whereas in English it is mainly word order that does.

Except for some adverbials, modifiers in English also must hold rather rigidly to a certain word order. We can have some variations, such as

> the boy swimming

and

> the swimming boy,

which may mean about the same thing. But normally adjectivals and most adverbials are placed close to the word they modify and in a rather strict order. Our minds interpret this order with lightning speed, and thus the word order serves as a syntactic signal. The order of prenominal modifiers and of auxiliaries best illustrates the rigidity of word order in English. Here is a noun phrase:

only the many articulate school teachers

A restrictor, two determiners, an adjective, and a noun modify the
headword *teachers*, and they must adhere strictly to the word order
shown. Our minds are used to interpreting this word order as a series
of syntactic signals and would reject any other order. And here is a
verb phrase:

could not have been spilling beans.

The three auxiliaries, the modifier *not*, and the object *beans* must adhere
to this strict word order, which serves as a syntactic device.

Structure Words

The many structure words classified and discussed in Chapter 4 are
syntactic signals, even when they denote some lexical meaning. The
determiners usually signal that a noun is coming. A listener's mind
is conditioned to hear such words as *a, the, this*, and *many*, accept
them as signals, and anticipate the structure to follow. Typographical
errors in newspapers frequently demonstrate the importance of determiners as syntactic signals. For example, a newspaper article once
started a sentence in this way:

The President selected Cabinet without . . .

The omission of the determiner *his* or *the* tripped the reader, for the
proper signal was not present. Similarly, if a sentence were to start with
such a typographical error as

A swarms of ants . . . ,

the faulty signal would confuse the reader. True, sometimes *this, many*,
and similar words serve as noun substitutes rather than determiners,
but that use is also a syntactic device that our minds accept.

The auxiliaries or verb markers also operate as signals. Such modals
as *could, may*, and *should* work intricately to signal certain expectations
to the mind—expectations which, when fulfilled, help the mind to absorb meaning instantaneously. *Have, be*, and *do* operate not only as
auxiliaries but also as main verbs, but in some way our minds handle
such dual functions and interpret the signals properly.

The prepositions, conjunctions, and other structure words also function as syntactic devices. A preposition normally signals that a noun
object is coming, and our minds respond. When a preposition has a
displaced object, other not-well-understood signals operate to keep
meaning clear. The coordinating conjunctions signal the approach of a

structure equivalent to the immediately preceding one. A subordinating conjunction signals subordination and modification and also the logical relationship to be expressed between two clauses. The purely lexical morphemes of our language are encompassed by syntactic signals.

Inflection

Though English is not highly inflected, it does have inflectional morphemes that serve as syntactic devices. You will remember from Chapter 1 that inflection is the change in the form of a word to produce such grammatical distinctions as tense, mood, comparison, plurality, possession, and case. The inflectional suffixes comprise all the verb endings, the plural and possessive endings of nouns, the *ly* ending of adverbs, and the comparative and superlative endings of adjectives and adverbs. The various pronoun forms are inflections. Verbs and nouns often have inflectional replacive allomorphs instead of endings. All of these inflectional morphemes are syntactic signals.

When we hear such forms as *talked*, *sang*, and *threw*, the past tense is signaled to us because our minds are thus conditioned, and we interpret the meaning of the whole sentence accordingly. The final *t* sound in *talked*, the change from *sing* to *sang* (replacive allomorph), and the change from *throw* to *threw* do not constitute differences in lexical meanings but only in syntactic meaning. Our minds respond to the signals. Or consider the difference between

> **was being robbed**

and

> ***was been robbed**

There is no lexical—only an inflectional—difference between *being* and *been*, and yet our minds immediately reject the second verb phrase because its signal is not right.

The *ly* suffix of the pure adverb is also such a signal; it does not contain any lexical meaning. For example,

> **he fought courageous**

has all the necessary lexical morphemes for meaning, but our minds reject the pattern, for the syntactic signal is not there. But we can discriminate about expecting this kind of signal. We understand the highway warning

> **Drive slow**

as readily as we would understand the very rare warning

> Drive **slowly**.

And we don't expect *ly* when we interpret

> John has done **well**.

and

> John has been **well**

—adverb and adjective identically spelled and pronounced. Nevertheless we usually expect and usually are given the *ly* signal and we use this signal to help interpret sentences.

Also consider the various pronouns. We accept the pronoun *you* as both singular and plural, as both a subject and an object, and as both masculine and feminine. But in the third person we have *he*, *him*, *she*, *her*, *it*, *they*, and *them*, distinguishing between masculine, feminine and neuter, between subjects and objects, and between singular and plural. Why the difference? The only answer is that English happens to have evolved thus. We respond to the structure signals of the various third-person pronouns but somehow manage to do without signals for pronouns in the second person. Other pronouns—such as *which*, *that*, *this*, and even to a degree *who*—do not have all the inflectional signals, but we make do without the signals, or rather substitute other signals for them.

Curiously, an inflectional signal and a word-order signal can be identical and still be differentiated in our minds. For example,

> John's

and

> John's

are identical, but one of these can mean *John is* and the other *belonging to John*. Presumably our minds are quite aware of the duplication and, to make a differentiation, call on some other signal which follows immediately.

All in all, inflection is a rather important syntactic device in our language, though it is possible for a language to evolve to a point of having no inflection at all.

Derivational Suffixes

A minor syntactic device in our language is the derivational suffix, which you studied in Chapter 1. Many of the noun-forming and adjective-forming suffixes have no lexical meaning at all but serve only to signal a part of speech so that we will understand immediately the syntactic structure of a sentence. For example, the *ous* of *courageous* has no lexical meaning but a syntactic function only. When we hear the base word with the *ous* added, as in

Courageous beyond the call of duty, he saved his whole platoon,

our minds immediately receive the signal that an adjectival—not a nominal or adverbial—must be placed in its syntactic structure, and this signal helps our minds interpret the meaning properly. So it is with many of the other derivational suffixes. For example, the *ion*, *tion*, *ation*, and *sion* of nouns have no lexical meaning at all, but they help us interpret syntax instantaneously. *Confuse* and *confusion* have the same lexical morphemes, but the derivational suffix *ion* helps us to differentiate between the functions of the words in a sentence.

Ambiguity in Syntactic Devices

Ambiguity arising from not knowing how a form-class word is functioning has been illustrated earlier. Here are a couple of further examples:

I will remember tonight.
Canning peaches can be therapeutic.

The ambiguity in sentence one occurs because we don't know whether *tonight* is functioning as an adverbial or nominal. In sentence two *canning* can be a verbal with *peaches* its direct object, or just a variety of peaches (compound noun) may be under discussion. To understand, we must know how the form-class words are functioning.

Ambiguity can also occur when there is a breakdown in syntactic devices. Such a breakdown illustrates well how important the signals are in delivering meaning. For example, consider these structures:

cook chops carefully
guide canoes with care

Think of them as headlines and puzzle over them a minute. How does our system of syntactic devices break down? A pecularity of English structure is involved. In English many singular nouns and verb stems have the same form, as *cook* (verb) and *cook* (noun). Also we use an *s* (*s*, *z*, or *iz* sound) to make both the plural of a noun and the third-person singular present tense of a verb. Thus in the above examples we can't tell which words are nouns and which verbs, because the signals are not clear. Other signals must be added. We could have

This cook chops carefully

or

Cook these chops carefully.

And we could have

Guide these canoes with care

or

This guide canoes with care.

The signals are all-important. Our system requires that we often have more than one signal.

The multiplicity of meanings in our structure words also can cause signals to break down. Examples:

John doesn't understand juncture or voice pause.
Watch her eye provocatively.
You left her cookies.

From the structure of the first sentence a reader might not know whether John doesn't understand either juncture or voice pause, which are different; or whether he doesn't understand juncture, which is voice pause. *Or* can mean alternatives and it can also mean something like "that is." In the second sentence *her* can be the subject of the infinitive (*to*) *eye*, with the whole phrase *her* (*to*) *eye provocatively* being the direct object of *watch*; or *her* can be a determiner (possessive pronoun) modifying *eye* as a noun (direct object of *watch*). In the first case, *provocatively* would be modifying the verb *eye*, and in the second case it would be modifying the verb *watch*. So in the first case she is eyeing provocatively, and in the second case you are watching provocatively. In the third sentence *her* can be the indirect object (a nominal), in which case the sentence means

You left cookies for her,

cookies being the direct object. Or *her* can be a determiner (possessive pronoun), in which case the sentence means

You left cookies belonging to her.

Thus structure words must function clearly as syntactic devices or the reader will not understand. The multiplicity of meanings in our structure words can produce such ambiguities.

Though real ambiguities are rare in writing and even rarer in speech (because of juncture, stress, and pitch), occasionally a reader needs a pause to think out the word relationships and syntactic signals in headlines and even in the text of an article. Some writers are careless about their signals. For example, in such a sentence as

> Above the buzzards were circling,

a reader will at first assume that *above* is a preposition, but then he will have to pause to see that it is really an adverbial. A careful writer would put a comma after *above*, representing juncture, or voice pause. Paradoxically, it is the intelligent and skilled reader who pauses most often to ponder word relationships and syntactic signals; because his mind is more keenly attuned to signals than is the mind of an inefficient reader, he is more likely to see ambiguities. He is like the very bright student taking a multiple-choice test, who often sees possibilities that the writer of the test did not see.

– – – – – – – – – – – –

In conclusion, we may agree that apparently no language has to have any one particular syntactic device, but it must have at least one of some sort, and most languages have more than one. Our language seems nicely balanced with its four. To illustrate fully each of the syntactic devices that exist in English would take many volumes, a testimony to the intricacy—and the miracle—of language.

– – – – – – – – – – – –

The next three chapters concern the component parts of a predication. You have seen how most English sentences break into subjects and predicates. The predicate may also break into the verb and its complement(s). Subjects, verbs, and complements will now be discussed in detail.

EXERCISES

1. Here are two paragraphs chosen at random. List the predications in each, with a slash (/) between each subject and predicate. In dependent clauses, the connective words need to be included only if they are subjects or objects and thus part of the predication.

> What happens to the crapshooters, Henslin theorizes, is similar to what happens to the pigeons. A crapshooter who had a winning streak while he was wearing certain clothes, or scratching his head, or talking to the dice is likely to continue to do those things in the expectation that his reward will be repeated. It would take only very occasional reinforcement to establish such practices very firmly. And because crapshooters are people and not pigeons, their magical beliefs

tend to become part of a craps-playing culture. Novices at the game, like Henslin, are taught the appropriate rituals—so this culture of magic is passed on to new generations of crapshooters. ["The Crapshooter as Magician," from *Trans-action* magazine]

When we moved to the Casa Grande I was still quite small. Our first room there was very tiny and in terrible condition. The floor was full of holes, out of which came large rats. We would lose lots of things down those holes, money, marbles, combs. There was no electricity there then, until my father paid to have them connect it up. I liked being in the dark, or having only candlelight, but my father has always insisted on modern comforts. He liked a place to be roomy and very clean, and that is why we moved into a larger room. [From *The Children of Sanchez* by Oscar Lewis]

2. Identify all the predications in the following sentences.

    a. He found out who the culprit was.
    b. John saw Paul picking a lock.
    c. Jerry found his bicycle broken.
    d. Jerry thought John broke his bicycle.
    e. We made Joan leave the dance.
    f. The student sporting a beard is on the football team.
    g. We saw the student sporting a beard.
    h. The school year being over, we caught John burning all his books.
    i. We wanted Chandler to publish our book.
    j. He had mud spread on his face.
    k. Since August is hot, we decided to go to Alaska then.
    l. No one who is sane can oppose equal justice before the law.
    m. My father not caring, I decided to skip a year of school.
    n. He discovered marijuana planted in his garden.
    o. It's easy for you to make an A.
    p. We caught the professor skirting the issue.
    q. For John to vote against me seemed incredible.
    r. The movie being over, we returned to our books.
    s. Sam got hot tar spattered on him.
    t. Whoever wins Fran will have an excellent wife.

3. Compose five sentences using absolute phrases as predications, five using infinitive phrases with subjects, five using present-participial phrases with subjects, five using past participles with subjects, and five with elliptical constructions that imply predications.

4. Discuss the following sentences as examples of faulty predication.

  a. Too many people working on a good thing may prove faulty.
  b. The white lie is not living up to what one believes.
  c. Twenty-five years ago was quite different from what it is now.
  d. An understanding of our country's standing in the world is one of leadership.
  e. Another way to help preserve wildlife is during the winter months.
  f. Another example of how people are dishonest is in the schools.
  g. One of the reasons restricting the fulfillment of goals is conformity.
  h. Another argument that one may use is the Bill of Rights.
  i. Another well-known advertisement is hair oil.
  j. My opinion about the age of drafting young men into the service should stay as it is today.

5. To illustrate the relative rigidity of word order in English, arrange the following words so that syntactically they function clearly in a sentence beginning with *I borrowed* ... and ending in ... *poles*.

bamboo	of my friend's	brand new
red	long	father's
two	beautiful	imitation
thin	four	Japanese
fishing		

6. Supply structure words to these constructions to show two different meanings for each:

ship sails today
log comments now
jail orders quickly
union demands increase
fill shows early

7. Following are two paragraphs chosen at random. Show how the structure words, inflectional endings (or replacive allomorphs), and derivational suffixes act as syntactic signals in the sentences.

Many records, in fact, had been broken in the game. The final score of 169–147 set a new total-points record of 316 points. Wilt's 36 field goals and 28 foul goals were records. His 59 points in the second half and 31 points in the fourth quarter were also records. And his 100 points for the game pushed his scoring average to 50 points for the season.

Bill Russell had been right. Wilt Chamberlain had what it takes to score 100 points.   This made him the greatest basketball player in history. And fans began going to games in large numbers—to watch Wilt play. Just as Babe Ruth's homeruns brought success to baseball, Wilt Chamberlain's dunk shots turned basketball into the major sport it is today. [Martin Walsh, "Give the Ball to Wilt!"]

⑥ SUBJECTS

Definition of *Subject*

The grammatical term *subject* is hard to define. The word is employed for its meaning as *topic*, but we have already seen on page 120 that the true topic of a sentence may not be the grammatical subject. Still, many school grammars today say that the subject is what the sentence is talking about and the predicate is what is said about the subject. In many cases this statement is true, but in such a sentence as

> The cake was eaten by Harry

the sentence is just as surely talking about Harry as it is the cake. For example,

> Harry ate the cake

says the same thing. And in such a sentence as

> The sermon said much about the evils of drink,

the evils of drink is perhaps more the subject of discussion than the sermon. Also in

> Much of the sand is coarse,

the sentence is certainly not talking about *much*, though *much* is the grammatical simple subject.

Another definition of the term is that a subject is (1) what performs the action in an active-voice sentence or (2) what receives the action in a passive-voice sentence or (3) what exists in a state of being when the verb is a linking verb. For example, in

> The man-eating tiger stalked the deer for miles,

tiger is performing the action and is the subject. In

> The deer was stalked by the tiger,

deer is receiving the action in the passive-voice sentence and is the subject. And in

> The fish remained deep in the pond,

fish is in a state of being with a linking verb and is the subject. There are flaws in this definition, however. For example in

> Many of the students demonstrated vociferously,

the students are performing the action, but *many* is the grammatical subject. And aside from any flaw, by the time a student has learned to handle all the grammar of active, passive, and linking verbs, he can recognize a subject without referring to a definition.

The great Danish grammarian Otto Jespersen maintained that in doubtful situations the subject is the most specific word or phrase. For example, in

> A denizen of Hollywood is Sola Manhoff

and

> A very good teacher is Professor Gordon,

Jespersen would say that *Sola Manhoff* and *Professor Gordon*, being the more specific, are the subjects. However, the subject of such sentences depends on the writer's intent. For example, if the writer is just identifying a denizen of Hollywood at random, then *a denizen of Hollywood* is the subject, but if he is intending to make a statement about Sola Manhoff, then that proper noun is the subject. Furthermore, in such a sentence as

> Much of the underbrush was burned,

certainly *underbrush* is the most specific word in the sentence, but just as certainly *much* is the grammatical subject.

Perhaps the best approach to a definition is to say that *the subject is the word or word group that* **controls** *the verb*. For example, in

> **One** of the students **is** a Ghanaian

and

> **Two** in my class **are** Ghanaians,

the verb control is clear and so are the grammatical subjects. However, a difficulty with the idea of verb control is that past-tense verbs and modal auxiliaries do not vary at all with different subjects, and thus it might sometimes be difficult to tell what word controls the verb. For example, in

> The chief of engineers **talked** the longest

and

> The last of the Mohicans **could** not be found,

it might not be clear to a beginner which word controls each verb. But there are useful ways of approaching this problem, as will be illustrated below. Also, once a student learns to identify prepositional phrases and other modifiers, he will usually be able to identify subjects accurately.

Simple Subjects

The normal word order in English sentences is subject-verb or subject-verb-complement. When a sentence maintains this order and when the subject is a noun with no or few modifiers, identification of the subject is easy. In such a sentence as

> Boys are greedy,

the very beginner in language study (say in the third or fourth grade) can identify the subject without fail. Even in the face of a little complexity, such as in

> Greedy boys deserve whipping

or

> The prettiest girls are modest,

the beginner will not be baffled. A little more complexity, though, calls for more sophisticated analysis.

It is with such simple sentences, however, that the relationship between subject and verb is best illustrated. The subject is the noun (or nominal) that is tied to the verb, or controls it. In certain cases the verb form changes according to the form of the subject. In

> This bird flies north,

the verb ends in *s* because the noun subject, *bird*, is singular. Make the noun plural and the sentence changes to

These birds fly north.

Now the verb is plural because *birds* is plural. This verb control identifies *bird* or *birds* as the subject.

Not all verb forms, however, occur in both the singular and the plural. All verbs have both forms in the present tense and *be* has number in some other tenses. When used as auxiliaries in their present tenses, *have* and *do* have number. But all past-tense forms and all modal auxiliaries are identical for both singular and plural subjects. Here are illustrations of the relationships between simple subjects and the verb forms mentioned:

> *Present singular*:
>   A cow moos.
> *Present plural*:
>   Cows moo.

> *Present singular*:
>   This man is a chief.
> *Present plural*:
>   These men are chiefs.

> *Past singular*:
>   This girl was queen.
> *Past plural*:
>   These girls were queens.

> *Past singular*:
>   This man had been sleeping.
> *Past plural*:
>   These men had been sleeping.

> *Singular with modal*:
>   This boy can swim.
> *Plural with modal*:
>   These boys can swim.

As you can see, the past-tense forms, except for *to be*, and modal auxiliaries do not have number.

When there is more than one auxiliary in a verb form, only the first auxiliary changes form under control of the subject, and sometimes it does not change. Examples:

> *Present singular*:
>   This girl **has** been eating.
> *Present plural*:
>   These girls **have** been eating.

Past singular:
  This boy **was** being scolded.
Past plural:
  These boys **were** being scolded.

Future singular:
  The cloud **will** have blown over.
Future plural:
  The clouds **will** have blown over.

This relationship between subject and verb sometimes serves to identify subjects when the full subject is a noun with many modifiers. There is a way to test for modals and past-tense forms, as is illustrated on pages 146–147.

The infinitive and present-participle verb forms can serve as simple subjects (nominals). Examples:

  To cheat is immoral.
  To love is Christian.
  Jogging is good exercise.
  Studying can be enjoyable.

Such subjects always take singular verbs (if the verb has number). These verb forms with complements and modifiers can also function as subjects, as will be explained below in the section on word-group subjects.

On occasion, an adjective by form can function as a subject. Examples:

  The **poor** are often neglected.
  The most **sinful** reach the lower depths of hell.
  The **simple** is often not so simple as it seems.
  The **smaller** was the brighter of the pair.
  The **most courageous** is he who feels fear but masters it.

Adverbs rarely function as subjects. Here are some possibilities:

  Forward remained the only way to go.
  Outside is good enough for me.
  Backward seems a poor way for a crab to travel.

In the last example, *backward* seems clearly to be the subject, since

  *A poor way for a crab to travel seems backward

is not grammatical. The same analysis applies to the first sentence. In sentence two there is no other nominal to be the subject.

Usually when an adverb comes directly before a verb there is reversed sentence order. For example, in

> Headlong went the frogman into the bay

frogman, not *headlong*, is the subject.

Note that only linking verbs are used with the adverbs as subjects.

The Noun Phrase as Subject

A noun phrase (sometimes called a noun cluster because the modifiers cluster around the noun) is an **endocentric structure**, that is, a structure with a **headword** which can function grammatically in the same way that the whole phrase does. Here are examples of endocentric noun phrases, with *men* as the headword:

the greedy	men	who sold spoiled beef
all	men	in the third row
no	men	in college who have not taken the Graduate Record Exam
even all the many	men	who have bought bootleg liquor
	men	in general
the intelligent	men	

And here are examples of how a headword will function grammatically as the whole endocentric structure does:

> **All the many men in grey overcoats** were inspectors. (*endocentric structure*)
> **The men** were inspectors. (*headword replacement*)
> I talked to **both the girls who were driving racing cars.** (*endocentric structure*)
> I talked to **the girls.** (*headword replacement*)

The headwords function just as the entire noun phrases do.

Sometimes the headword of an endocentric noun phrase is not such a noun as *men* or *girls* but is a noun substitute. Examples:

> **Very many of the cats which were prowling the alleys** were poisoned by spoiled fish. (*endocentric structure*)
> **Many** were poisoned by spoiled fish. (*headword replacement*)
> **Half of the students at the game** were on probation. (*endocentric structure*)
> **Half** were on probation. (*headword replacement*)

Even though they do not have nouns by form as headwords, these last examples are nevertheless nominal phrases and endocentric structures.

Sometimes an adjective by form can function as the headword in a nominal endocentric structure. Examples:

> In war **the brave that we depend on** are poorly paid. (endocentric structure)
> (In war) the **brave** are poorly paid. (headword replacement)
> **Even the most courageous of the contestants** were afraid. (*endocentric structure*)
> The **courageous** were afraid. (*headword replacement*)

These adjectives are simple subjects and nominals.

An endocentric noun phrase frequently functions as the **full subject** of a sentence (it can also function as a complement), and its headword controls the verb of the sentence. The headword is the **simple subject**, just as are the single nouns in the example sentences in the section above.

First let's see noun phrases that consist just of a noun or noun substitute and a prepositional phrase. Examples:

> The **students** in the back **were** noisy.
> The **student** in the dark sweater **was** silent.
> **Neither** of the girls **is** a cheerleader.
> **Both** of the boys **are** football players.

The prepositional-phrase part of each endocentric structure can be omitted and the nouns and noun substitutes still function as the entire structure does. Even beginners in language study can quickly learn not to take the prepositional phrase into account in analyzing for verb control.

Sometimes, however, the noun phrase can be very long. Examples:

> **Even all the patient, devoted college professors who were denied a salary increase by the Board of Regents** were at the rally.
> **Not even the glamorous and intelligent television star on the Friday night show "Our Better Selves"** was willing to face the investigating committee.

In the first example, the headword is *professors*, which controls the verb: plural, *were*. In the second, the headword is the singular noun *star*, which controls the verb: singular, *was*. Both headwords can function just as the entire phrases do.

With such a long noun-phrase full subject, a beginner in language study might have trouble identifying the simple subject (the headword). Example:

> In spring **the most beautiful native flower to bloom in our section of the United States** is gathered by the hundreds by tourists.

A tenth- or eleventh-grader might become confused if asked to pick out the simple subject. But he can test in various ways to see which word controls the verb. He can ask *what is gathered* and inspect the sentence for an answer. Once he lights on *flower*, he can test further by changing that noun to plural to see if the verb is affected:

> ... flower ... is gathered ... ?
> ... flowers ... are gathered ... ?

With such testing he can analyze the subject-verb combination correctly.

Here are some other examples of finding the simple-subject head-word in a long noun phrase:

> **The imported California frog with the gold ring fastened to its nose** jumps always on order.

What jumps?

> ... frog ... jumps ...

Change the verb to plural:

> ... frogs ... jump ...

The simple subject is identified. Sometimes, however, the process is harder:

> **At lunch perhaps the most eager boy in the whole group working on the project** was the one who had eaten the biggest breakfast.

Analysis is more difficult here because there is no action verb to test with, only a form of *to be*. Ask *what was*, and students might variously answer *lunch was*, *boy was*, *group was*, or *project was*, since they might not be aware of the complement. But with a little training most students will see that the verb *was* is controlled by *boy* and can see that changing *boy* to *boys* will change the verb to *were*.

When an action verb is in the past tense, or when a modal auxiliary is used, somewhat more complicated testing is needed. Example:

> At first the **cross-country runner from Idaho wearing the purple and green harrier's outfit and carrying two rods** started to take the lead.

The past-tense verb *started* will fit both a singular and plural subject, and the inexperienced student might say *rods started*. But for testing, *started* can be changed to the present tense. So the student will ask *who starts* and should get the answer

> ... runner ... starts ... ,

which would become

> ...runners...start...

Thus he could be fairly certain that he had isolated the simple subject, which controls the verb. Here is an example with a modal:

> **Even all the beautiful college coeds wearing the school colors of garnet and orange** could see that the game was lost.

Since *could* can take either a singular or a plural subject, for testing purposes the student can leave off the modal and use only the verb *see*. *Who see*?

> ...coeds...see...

but

> ...coed...sees...

Thus the verb control is established and the simple subject is isolated.

Compound Subjects and Subjects with Correlatives

Subjects are often compounded with the use of the coordinating conjunction *and*, and then a plural verb is normally called for. Examples:

> The Secretary of State and the chief White House advisor on foreign affairs attended the conference in Belfast.
>
> The first local bank president who attends Rotary twenty consecutive times and the local CPA who devotes the most logged time to Kiwanis will share a five-thousand-dollar prize.

To test for the simple subject in sentence one, the student asks *who attended*, and examination shows that

> The Secretary of State and the chief White House advisor... attended....

If the verb is changed to the present, it becomes *attend* or *are attending*, showing that a compound subject controls it.

One other point to notice here is that prepositional phrases such as *together with*... and *as well as*..., even though they may add additional persons to the full subject, are not to be counted in the verb control. For example, the sentence

> My **father** as well as my mother **belongs** to the PTA

requires a singular verb, for only *father* is controlling the verb. And if we slightly revise the first sentence above, to read

> **The Secretary of State** together with the chief White House advisor on foreign affairs **attended** the conference in Belfast,

then *Secretary of State* alone controls the verb, for *the chief White House advisor* is the object of the preposition *together with* and does not compound the subject.

In the second sentence above, the student tries to find out what word or words control the verb *will share*. By dropping the modal *will* so that *share* can have number, he finds that *president* and *CPA* control the verb *share* and thus are the simple compound subject. If one of the two is omitted, the verb becomes the singular *shares*.

Occasionally a compound subject has meaning which may be considered singular in its totality, and then a singular verb may be used. Examples:

> Some **gas** and **dust** actually **shows** up in photographs.—*Scientific American*
> Disparate **clatter** and **chatter has** fascinated linguists.—*Time*
> Your **rattling** and **banging is** giving me a headache.

Sometimes, as in the third example, a plural verb would actually sound awkward.

The correlative conjunctions are *(n)either...(n)or, not only...but also*, and such constructions as *not...but* and *whether...or*. Though when these connectives are used in full subjects there are two parts to the subject, the verb is controlled by the second part only. Examples:

> Neither **plagues** nor **war is** to be feared by Christians.
> Neither **war** nor **plagues are** to be feared by Christians.
> Not only these **rocks** but also this **sand is** of ancient origin.
> Not **tactics** but **strategy is** important.

In the last two examples, interchange the parts of the subject and the verb will become *are*, since the plural part of the subject will then be controlling the verb. The correlative *both...and* makes a true compound subject which takes a plural verb. Example:

> Both **tactics** and **strategy are** important.

Sometimes triple or even quadruple subjects occur in a sentence.

Subjects in Reversed Sentence Order

Though normal word order in English is subject-verb-complement, sometimes this order is reversed in some way for rhetorical effect, and especially in traditional poetry is word order often reversed. As an example from poetry here is a famous stanza from Gray's "Elegy":

> The boast of heraldry, the pomp of pow'r,
>   And all that beauty, all that wealth e'er gave,
> **Awaits** alike th' inevitable **hour**.
> The paths of glory lead but to the grave.

Some editors have actually used the plural verb *await* in this stanza, mistakenly thinking that the verb is controlled by *boast*, *pomp*, and *all*. But is is really controlled by the reversed subject *hour*, which takes the singular verb *awaits*.

When a complement of the predicate-adjective variety comes first, the subject of a sentence is easy to identify. Examples:

> Greedy is the **man** who will cheat the blind.
> Cold and dreary is the **world** I live in.

Since the sentences begin with adjectives, students with a little experience in language study will immediately spot the subject following the verb. Also when an adverbial complement or modifier comes directly before the verb, the subject is easy to spot. Examples:

> First came the fifth-grade **band**.
> And away ran the little **children**.
> Softly blew the **wind**.
> Offside were **Blotnik, Olson**, and **Dubbin**.

Mostly, such reversed order occurs in relatively short sentences so that the simple subject is easily detected. The two kinds of reversed order illustrated in this paragraph are by far the most common, except for those sentences that use the expletives *it* and *there*.

When a complement of the predicate-noun variety comes first in a sentence, the sentence verb is almost always a form of *to be*, and thus the predicate noun may not be distinguishable from the subject. For example, in

> A great pitcher was Walter Johnson,

Walter Johnson may be called the subject and *pitcher* the predicate noun, but no demonstrable proof can be given for this analysis, since the writer may either be trying to identify one of many great pitchers or may be saying something about Walter Johnson. Change the *a* to *one* and *pitcher* is demonstrably the subject. Context will usually help identify the subject in such sentences.

Almost never does a sentence, with or without a direct object, begin with a verb (except questions and request sentences). For example, such constructions as

> *Ran away the boys
> *Crowded the children the theater

and

> *Crowed the rooster

would be considered so unnatural as to be ungrammatical in English.

Seldom is the structure direct object-verb-subject used in English, for instead a passive-voice sentence will normally be used, such as

> The cake was eaten by Jane

instead of

> *The cake ate Jane,

which would not be considered grammatical. A rare example of direct-object-verb-subject order occurs in the stanza of poetry quoted on page 149.

Sometimes a sentence with an object complement may have the object complement come first if it is used with the expletive *as*. Examples:

> As captain, **we** chose Harry.
> As President, this small African **republic** elected a respected legislator.

In such sentences the subject really occupies the normal position and is easily identifiable.

Sentences with the expletives *it* and *there* have a kind of reversed order, since the true subject follows the verb. When *it* is used as an expletive, the sentence verb is usually a form of *to be* and the subject is either a noun clause, an infinitive phrase, or else a prepositional phrase beginning with *for* and having an infinitive phrase with a subject as its object (see page 107). Also when the expletive *it* is used, the true subject follows an adjective (usually) or a noun (rarely), both of which are subjective complements. Examples:

> It is a fact **that Hemingway committed suicide.**
> It is easy **to see that you're prejudiced.**
> It is hard **for me to learn genetics.**

The boldface subjects can replace *it* and still produce grammatical sentences.

When *there* is used as an expletive, the sentence verb is usually a form of *to be* and the true subject is usually a noun. Examples:

> There are three **reasons** why we should seek a detente with Russia.
> There is a **flaw** in your logic.

In rare instances a verb other than *to be* can follow the expletive *there*. Example:

> There came three **strangers** to my door.

Subjects in Questions

In yes-no questions, which begin with a verb or auxiliary, the subject always follows the verb or auxiliary immediately. Examples:

> Are **you** sure of your facts?
> Did **John** apply to Yale?
> Have the **Renegades** won a game?

No complexity exists here.

More complexity exists in QW questions. Sometimes the QW word in a question modifies a noun which is rather clearly the subject. Examples:

> What **student** wrote this paper?
> Which **bird** escaped?

The subjects are clear here; no uncertainty exists. But in such questions as

> Which student did the Dean discipline?

and

> What book have you read?

uncertainty exists. Such cases can be tested by transforming the question into a pseudo statement. Here are the transformations:

> The **Dean** did discipline which student.
> **You** have read what book.

This transformation shows that in the questions the noun modified by the QW word is a direct object, not a subject, and it also identifies the subject clearly.

In some QW questions the QW word does not modify a noun. Examples:

> Who is the best student?
> What were the directions?

It might be argued that *who* and *what* are the subjects, but a transformation shows that they are not. The transformation converts the question into a dependent clause, and in dependent clauses the subject almost always precedes the verb. Examples of the transformation:

> We wonder who the best **student** is.
> We did not know what the **directions** were.

This transformation shows what the true subject is in such QW questions. Yet in other QW questions, the QW word itself is the subject. Examples:

> **Who** killed Cock Robin?
> **What** causes a bird to sing?

The transformation into dependent clauses is

> We know **who** killed Cock Robin

and

> We know **what** causes a bird to sing.

Thus the QW words are demonstrated to be the subjects of the questions.

Subjects of Nonfinite Verbs

Infinitives and present and past participles (or phrases made with these forms) can, as nonfinite verb forms, take subjects. When an infinitive has a subject, it is always a noun, noun phrase (endocentric structure), or pronoun. Examples:

> We wanted the **bear** to beg for food.
> He asked the **student whom you mentioned** to investigate the charge.
> Do you want **me** to answer first?

Bear is the subject of the infinitive *to beg*; *student whom you mentioned*, of *to investigate*; and *me*, of *answer*.

When a present participle has a subject, it is usually a noun, noun phrase, or pronoun. Examples:

> The **debate** being over, we relaxed in the student lounge.
> John found **me** sitting at my desk.

Debate is the subject of the present participle *being*, and *me* is the subject of *sitting*. Past participles can take subjects in the same way. Examples:

> The **game** finished, we prepared to leave for the airport.
> We found our **work** completed.

Game is the subject of the past participle *finished*, and *work* is the subject of *completed*. Nonfinite verb forms do on occasion take word-group subjects, as will be shown in the next section.

Word-Group Subjects

So far we have been discussing nouns, noun phrases, pronouns, infinitives, present participles, adjectives, and adverbs as subjects. Word groups also can function as subjects. The term **word group** is usually applied to structures such as prepositional phrases, dependent clauses, infinitive phrases, and participial phrases, the latter two often being endocentric structures. When such a word group is a subject, the verb is always singular (if it has number). Examples of noun clauses as subjects:

> **That Peter failed astronomy** was no surprise to me.
> **Whether he is insane** is not the question we are debating.
> **What we intended to do** not having been decided, we reopened the discussion.

The noun clause in the last sentence is the subject of a nonfinite verb.

Examples of infinitive phrases as subjects:

> **To be great in his own field** is all a man can ask.
> **To complete the course with a C** was my only desire.
> **To be great** having been his desire, he was a disappointed man.

In the last example an infinitive phrase is the subject of a nonfinite verb.

Examples of present-participial phrases as subjects:

> **Behaving in a conventional manner** is still required in some cultures.
> **Driving faster than the set speed limit** can lead to an accident.
> **Joining the choir** not being required, I refused to sign up.

In the last example a participial phrase is the subject of a participial phrase.

On rare occasions even a prepositional phrase can function as a subject. Examples:

> **In the house** is better than in the yard.
> **Around the park once** is good enough for me.

In these sentences there is no other nominal that can be considered the subject. Sometimes, however, the true subject in such a construction may not be clear. Consider such a sentence as

> Down the street live the **Joneses.**

Rather clearly it has reversed sentence order, so that *Joneses* is the subject.

In one common colloquial construction in English an adverb clause serves as a subject. Example:

> Just **because you're highly intelligent** is no reason for you to be conceited.

In this case we have an adverb clause by form functioning as a nominal.

Subjects in Dependent Clauses; Elided Subjects

In dependent clauses subjects can behave just as they do in independent clauses, though usually they come before the verb. Some examples:

> When **participating in out-of-school activities** is onerous . . . .
> Since **what we should do** is not clear . . . .
> Because in such a situation **what to say** is hard to know . . . .

In order, a participial phrase, a noun clause, and an infinitive phrase with a subject are functioning as subjects in dependent clauses. And all other forms that can function as subjects in independent clauses can function as subjects in dependent clauses.

In some constructions, subjects can be omitted. In conversation we often hear such utterances as

> Seems a real shame, doesn't it?
> Had to leave the game early last night.

The subjects of such elliptical utterances are clear.

In one kind of adverb clause the subject is absent. Example:

> He is richer than is thought.

The predicate *is thought* has no subject. What has happened structurally is that a passive-voice verb (active voice would be *than someone thinks*) has its *by* phrase (*by someone*) suppressed, and no subject is needed, since the original active-voice clause had no direct object to become the subject of the passive-voice predicate.

On page 93 we have shown how both the subject and verb can be omitted in an elliptical adverb clause.

Contrary to popular opinion, the request or imperative sentence—such as *come over here* and *give me a break*—does not have an understood subject, as will be explained in Chapter 7.

EXERCISES

1. Identify the simple subjects in the following sentences, which have noun phrases as full subjects.

    a. Even all the extra hands hired for the farm work donated a part of their wages to charity.

    b. In autumn the most colorful of all the leaves are those of the sweetgum tree.

    c. The strongly built, heavy iron cage used to keep the lions in is over one hundred years old.

    d. The most expensive of all the rings shown at the trade fair were made in Sweden.

    e. The cute little California chipmunks at Lake Tahoe belong to a rare species.

    f. Merely the most beautiful college coed in the nation is to be a guest on Hamilton Fish's talk show.

    g. In the evening much of the chemical pollution in the air drops to the earth.

    h. The extraordinarily ambidextrous abilities of some of the Chicago Cubs show clearly in the club's record.

    i. Not very many of the soldiers who received R & R leaves to Hawaii were greeted by native girls.

    j. Not even one of the very many prisoners who were judged dangerous caused any disturbance.

2. Complete the following sentences with a predicate containing a form of *to be*, either as the verb or as an auxiliary. What does the completion of the sentences tell you about the subjects?

    a. Neither rain nor sleet nor little frogs . . .

    b. Neither little frogs nor rain nor sleet . . .

    c. Not only the comptroller but also the Regents . . .

    d. Not only the Regents but also the comptroller . . .

    e. Not only the comptroller but also the Board of Regents . . .

    f. Not friends in high places but skill . . .

    g. Not skill but friends in high places . . .

    h. Both the cop and the suspect . . .

    i. The student-body president as well as the members of the student court . . .

    j. A woman's sweetness and gentleness . . .

    k. Either a bus or three cars . . .

    l. The Chairman of the Chemistry Department together with six of his staff . . .

    m. Cussing and growling . . .

n. Whether grain or potatoes ...
o. Not only beards but also long hair ...

3. Identify the full subjects in the following sentences or questions.

a. What program did you say we will watch?
b. What is the cost of that car?
c. Happy is the man who can repair his own car.
d. Controlling insects with insecticides that will not decompose is dangerous to all life.
e. It is the truth that some millionaires are Democrats.
f. Where will the money for our project come from?
g. There is a power that guides us through life.
h. Far in the back of the corridor of the third floor lay a booby trap placed by radicals.
i. To lose your head over a new fad or fleeting custom is a sign of low intelligence.
j. What directions did the judge give to the jury?
k. Courageously is the way to behave in battle.
l. At dawn is the time for executions.
m. There wandered into the kitchen three blind mice.
n. Whatever is thought to be the best for the future of the club is all right with me.
o. It is difficult for ministers to make a living.
p. It was a wild and windy night.
q. Which is the tastier?
r. There was talking late into the night.
s. To sandbag is a cardinal sin in poker.
t. Because we're young is no reason for us to break the law.
u. On the town is in the gravy.
v. Condemning Parker's record seemed the best way to defeat him.
w. Happy to be of service are all the professors.
x. In the vanguard of the troops came General Patton.
y. Whatever made you give up your apartment?

7   FINITE VERBS

This chapter treats of the second part of a sentence predication: the **finite verb**. A finite verb is defined as any verb form that can serve as the sentence verb in an independent or dependent clause. It may or may not have modifiers and complements.

The Verb Phrase

Just as a noun can take modifiers to form a noun phrase that is an endocentric structure, so the finite verb can take modifiers and complements to form a verb phrase, or verb cluster, that is an endocentric structure. The verb form is the headword (or head-phrase, if auxiliaries are used) of the phrase. Sometimes the headword can function grammatically as the whole phrase functions, though sometimes it has a mandatory complement and cannot function meaningfully by itself. But the chief characteristic of an endocentric structure is that it has a headword, and in that sense verb phrases are endocentric. The verb phrase (unless the verb form is nonfinite) is the second half of a predication, that is, it is the predicate of a sentence.

In Chapter 1 we saw that verbs may be classified as intransitive, transitive, and linking. A linking verb always takes a subjective complement (predicate adjective or predicate noun) as a part of its verb phrase. Occasionally *to be*, the most common linking verb, does not have a complement. For example, the sentence

There is no way to solve the problem

transforms into

No way to solve the problem is (exists).

Is is the complete verb phrase of the sentence, without modifiers or a complement. In such a case *to be* must just be considered in a class by itself, not transitive, intransitive, or linking. Other linking verbs and usually *to be* have complements and often modifiers. Here are examples of verb phrases made with linking verbs:

He **remained cool under the threat of prosecution**.
The question of capital punishment **became the chief issue in the campaign for Attorney General.**
The most convincing evidence **is the fact that the suspect had kept a diary recording his intention to murder his boss.**

The headwords in these verb phrases are *remained*, *became*, and *is*. There is hardly any limit to the length of such verb phrases, since one can be composed of complements, modifiers of the verb, modifiers of the modifiers, complements of the verbal modifiers, and so on without limit.

Here are examples of verb phrases with intransitive verbs as headwords:

The candidate **talked with increasing force about the issue of pollution and the need for federal money to assist industry in reducing pollutants.**
The culprit **begged for clemency on the grounds that he did not at the time of his crime have control of the inhibitory functions of his mind.**

Here the verbs *talked* and *begged* are the headwords of very long, but quite reasonable, verb phrases. Modifiers of modifiers of modifiers pile up. Note that *talked* will function grammatically as its whole verb phrase does. So will *begged*, though its meaning might be less adequate.

And here are instances of verb phrases with transitive verbs as the headwords:

The old gentleman **had been telling stories about his early life in India as an army officer for the British detachment responsible for controlling the state of Bengal.**
In college the young lawyer **had given lessons to draft-eligible students who wanted to learn ways of avoiding the draft which would leave them free to remain in their own city without harassment from draft officials.**

Actually the direct objects in these sentences—*stories* and *lessons*—contribute little to the length of the verb phrases, which are composed mostly of modifiers piled upon modifiers. In the last example note that the prepositional phrase *in college* is a part of the whole verb phrase since it modifies *had given*. The phrase could be placed after *had given* or after *lessons*. Quite frequently an opening modifier of that sort is a sentence modifier rather than a verb modifier, but in many cases it is a part of the verb phrase. In these two sentences the verbs *had been telling* and *had given* will not really function grammatically as the whole phrase does, since the direct objects are mandatory. The verbs are still the headwords of the phrases.

Just as nouns or noun phrases can be compounded in the subject part of a predication (and in other positions too), so compound verbs or verb phrases may appear in sentences. Examples:

> We **will pay** any price, **bear** any burden, **support** any friend, **oppose** any foe, to assure the survival and success of liberty.
>
> Professor Wattron **has been gathering** data on the production of plays in fifteenth-century Italy and **will be publishing** his findings within a few months.

The famous first example shows how one modal, *will*, can be applied to several stems. The second example shows two entirely different verb forms compounded. In such a compound structure each verb form controls a whole verb phrase, usually with a complement and modifiers. For example, the two verb phrases in the second sentence are

> has been gathering data on the production of plays in fifteenth-century Italy

and

> will be publishing his findings within a few months.

The Wide Variety of Finite Verb Forms

Though some languages, such as Navajo and Eskimo, have verb systems incredibly more complex than ours,[1] ours is rather complex. The complexity arises from our broad system of auxiliaries and modal auxiliaries. These are subject to almost endless combinations and permutations—they run into the hundreds. Oddly, the intricacy is manifested

---

[1] For example, a Navajo verb equivalent in meaning to our *to throw* may have in it morphemes which tell the shape of the object thrown, the size of the object thrown, the distance it is thrown, the sex of the thrower, and other facts, and simultaneously comport with such concepts as tense, aspect, mood, and voice, which our verbs show.

more in our speech than our writing. For example, such forms as

I knew I was going to be kept jailed

and

He was about to have been consulted

are not uncommon in our conversation, but do not appear often in writing, except in reported dialogue. In the first sentence, the two words between which a subject-verb relationship is being shown are *I* and *jailed*. All the words in between are auxiliaries which denote exactly what the relationship is—tense, aspect, mood, and voice. In sentence two, five words are denoting the subject-verb relationship between *he* and *consulted*.

Before we go into the concepts of tense, aspect, mood, and voice, it will be impressive to see a partial list of the multitudinous verb forms in English. Of the five forms in the verb paradigm, two will not take auxiliaries: the third person singular of the present tense, and the simple past tense. For example, combinations such as these are ungrammatical:

> *did freezes
> *could freezes
> *has froze
> *have been froze

The last two examples show that in such constructions as *had talked* and *had been thought* the main verb forms are past participles and not past-tense forms. The stem of a verb (first form in the paradigm) is limited in the auxiliaries it can take. Such a form as *go* or *see* can take only the modals and *do* as auxiliaries, not *have* or *be*. Here is just a small sample of the permutations of English verbs:

break	was breaking
breaks	was being broken
does break	were about to be broken
did break	were going to be broken
do break	kept breaking
has broken	kept getting broken
had broken	getting broken
be broken	had to be broken
was broken	was about to have been broken
were broken	was supposed to have been broken
has been broken	was used to breaking
has been breaking	was used to being broken
have been broken	was used to getting broken

could break
could be breaking
could have been broken
could have been being broken
could have kept being broken
will break
will be broken

will be breaking
will have been breaking
will have been being broken
will be about to be broken
will be going to get broken
does keep getting broken

All of these forms, and almost countless other combinations, are used to show a relationship between a subject, such as *I* or *John*, and the main verb form, such as *break* or *breaking* or *broken*. Some of the aspects of such a relationship will be explained in the following sections on tense, aspect, mood, and voice, though it is virtually impossible to catalogue all the meanings that are so subtly implied in these manifold verb forms. Also, you will be glad to know, it is not at all necessary to learn a name for each of these forms. In fact, specific names for some of them do not exist. Also it is not necessary to keep sets of forms categorized in your mind, except for the six "regular" tenses listed on page 163.

Tense

Tense is the denotation in a verb form of time of occurrence; and since, simply put, time seems to divide naturally into past, present, and future, three simple tenses might seem sufficient for a language. But the expression of time of occurrence in our verb system is far more complicated than this simple analysis would suggest. Tense is complex because time itself is complex. Both past and future are huge blocks of time admitting to various divisions and subtle organizations, and present time itself is a baffling peculiarity since logically it may not exist and can be only the scantest interval between past and future. But regardless of the philosophical implications of time, we do live in the present and we do think about various aspects of the past and future. And our tense system allows us to relate time to our daily lives.

Some of the complexities of tense can be illustrated in common verb forms. For example, it is difficult to say what time the verb specifies in such a sentence as

I **go** by Brock's on my way to work.

In the common conjugation *go* is called present tense, but obviously here the time is not the present. The verb certainly indicates both past and future times of occurrence, and probably at the time of utterance no present occurrence at all. Or consider this sentence:

> Jane **tells** me that you are coming to the party.

Tells is the same present-tense form (except for person) as *go* in the above sentence, but obviously it does not have the same time implications, since future occurrence is not denoted and since only one specific time of occurrence in the past is denoted. Present occurrence is not denoted at all. In fact, only occasionally is the so-called simple present tense used to specify an occurrence for the present time only. The so-called present progressive tense—*am going*—is the one normally used to specify occurrence at the present instant, and, as we will see in the next paragraph, it doesn't always do that.

For another example of the complexity of tense, consider the sentence

> I **am going** by Brock's on my way to work.

It might seem to represent actual present time, but it need not mean that at all. It is a common kind of statement that a man might make to his wife in his house before he has even dressed to go to work. So what is the time? It must be the future, even though the name of the tense is present progressive. Or consider this common finite verb:

> I **had been about to go** by Brock's on my way to work.

It indicates something about the past surely, but actually nothing has necessarily occurred in the past. Aside from the fact that aspect (see page 172) as well as tense complicates this verb form, it is hard to know what tense label to give it. And what are the subtle time differences between the preceding verb form and

> I **have** for a long time **been about to go** by Brock's on my way to work.

Had and *have* denote different time specifications in these two sentences —*had* a time before another specified time in the past and *have* past and present time. But what kind of labels should be given them? The term **perfect tenses** is used for such forms (and we will use it also for its simplicity), but the term *perfect* is defined as referring to an action completed in the past, and in the *have* sentence above the action has not even been completed at all, and may never be. In effect, it is very difficult to describe all the time denotations in finite verb forms. But for grammatical understanding there is really no need for many complex grammatical labels, and there is no need to conjugate elaborately all the possible tenses.

Six Simple and Perfect Tenses

The term **conjugation** is used to denote paradigms that classify the tenses. The basic conjugation of English verbs is made up of the six divisions of the indicative mood (see page 173 for indicative mood) listed in the table. These are sometimes called the "regular" tenses.

PRESENT TENSE

I hear	we hear
you hear	you hear
he hears	they hear

PAST TENSE

I heard	we heard
you heard	you heard
he heard	they heard

FUTURE TENSE

I will (shall) hear	we will hear
you will hear	you will hear
he will hear	they will hear

PRESENT PERFECT TENSE

I have heard	we have heard
you have heard	you have heard
he has heard	they have heard

PAST PERFECT TENSE

I had heard	we had heard
you had heard	you had heard
he had heard	they had heard

FUTURE PERFECT TENSE

I will have heard	we will have heard
you will have heard	you will have heard
he will have heard	they will have heard

Since our verb forms do not vary much with person and number, it might seem redundant to spell out all six forms of each tense. But it is done here once so that conjugation into paradigms can be illustrated. We will not go through whole conjugations in other discussions of tenses.

As has already been mentioned, the term **simple present tense** is something of a misnomer. It *can* be used to denote specifically present occurrence, as in

He **hears** the bell now.

But it is more often used to denote continuous or usual occurrence, as in

I **listen** to the Philharmonic on Tuesdays.

For denoting occurrence at this present instant, one is more likely to say

He **is hearing** the bell now

rather than to use the simple tense *hears*. The present tense can also denote future occurrence, as in

> I **go** to court next Monday.

This present is more common usage than

> I **will go** to court next Monday,

which could have various meanings (usually denoted by tone of voice and context). Also, as mentioned above, the present tense can denote a past occurrence, as in

> I **hear** you'll be the dean,

which usually means *I heard* (at some time or times in the past). The **historical present tense** is also frequently used, as in summaries, critical papers, and such. Example:

> In the first chapter Morgan **indicates** some displeasure with his daughters, but when faced with a decision he **works** for their welfare.

All in all, the so-called present tense is extremely variable, but not often used to denote occurrence at the present instant.

The **simple past tense** is the purest of all the tenses. It usually just means occurrence in the past, though the definite time of occurrence has to be expressed in other words. Examples:

> I **heard** the symphony last Tuesday.
> I **went** to the game Saturday night.

The simple past tense can also denote continued or repeated action in the past, as in

> He **listened** intently throughout the campaign.

The past forms of *to be* most often denote continuous occurrence or being, as in

> I **was** the top contender for valedictorian until the last test of the last year.

Other verbs in the past tense usually just denote an action that is over and done with. The simple past tense is the most uncomplicated of all the tenses.

The **simple future tense** denotes action or being that is to occur in the future, as in

> I **will turn on** the TV at 6:00 PM sharp.

and

I shall be at the game on Saturday.

The modals *will* and *shall*, however (which, thankfully, are no longer conjugated according to the old erroneous "rules"), complicate this tense. They may denote determination, passivity, resignation, alacrity, and other subtle meanings, as all the modals can. Future time of occurrence is also denoted in many of the other modal auxiliaries, as will be illustrated in the section below on the modal tenses. And, as mentioned above, the simple present tense can denote future occurrence.

The so-called **perfect tenses** use a form of *have* as an auxiliary,[2] and in the future perfect and various other complicated tenses such as the progressive perfect they use other auxiliaries as well. So perhaps here is the place to make the observation that when a verb form has an auxiliary the auxiliary for the most part denotes the tense. For example, in such sentences as these the auxiliary carries the tense:

> He **does** smoke.
> He **did** smoke
> He **has** been gone.
> He **had** been gone.

The main verb form in such cases does not really denote the tense. True, in such a form as the future-tense phrase *will be gone, gone* implies something about the past, but the real tense denotation is in the auxiliaries.

The **present perfect tense** conveys occurrence at any time in the past right up to the present moment. Examples:

> **I have gone** to Calabria many times.
> He **has seen** "Hello, Dolly!" before.

Usually a verb in this tense means that the occurrence may happen again or that its effects are still being felt. For example, in

> **I went** to Calabria many times,

the implication is that the action is over and done with, whereas in the first sentence above the implication is that it may happen again or that its effects are still evident. The *present* part of the name of the present perfect tense might seem to be a misnomer, since present time of occurrence is not usually denoted; it is used because of the so-called present tense of the auxiliary *have*.

The **past perfect tense** specifies that the occurrence took place at a

---

[2] With a very few verbs, a form of *to be* instead of *to have* may be used as an auxiliary in the present perfect tense: *is gone*, *is come*, *being risen* and perhaps a few others. *Have* is, however, replacing *be* in these few instances: *has gone*, and so on.

time before another past time. Examples:

> He **had heard** that joke before.
> They **had** already **left** when I arrived.

In sentence one, the *before* establishes one time in the past and *had heard* specifies an event at a time earlier than that. And the same analysis applies to sentence two. Sometimes the simple past tense is used instead of the past perfect. Example:

> After we **heard** the rumor, we **phoned** home.

The implication here is that the two occurrences were close together and that one was the result of the other. Actually, then, a meaning other than time is responsible for the difference between *had heard* and *heard* in the two sentences above. Another name for the past perfect is **pluperfect**, which means "more than perfect," *perfect* having to do with past occurrence.

The **future perfect tense** denotes that an occurrence will take place at any time before a specific time in the future. Examples:

> The store **will have closed** by the time we get there.
> By early autumn the birds **will have flown** south.

This tense is not often used in English. Note that when it is used, there must be another clause or phrase in the sentence specifying a time after the time denoted in the future perfect tense. Actually, the simple future tense can often be used instead of the future perfect. Example:

> The stores **will close** by the time we get there.

This option perhaps accounts for the rare use of the future perfect in English.

These six simple and perfect tenses can also be used in the passive voice. Examples:

> *Simple present*:
>   "Showboat" **is watched** by everyone.
> *Simple past*:
>   The game **was won** by us.
> *Simple future*:
>   This book **will be bought** by everyone.
> *Present perfect*:
>   This new car **has been driven** (by someone).
> *Past perfect*:
>   That rifle **had been cleaned** (by someone).
> *Future perfect*:
>   The steak **will have been eaten** (by someone) by the time we get
>   there.

More about the passive voice, including the passive-voice transformation, will be explained below.

The Progressive Tenses

The **progressive tenses** denote a continuing occurrence or continuing state of being. The forms always include a form of *to be* as an auxiliary and always take the present-participle—or *ing*—form of a verb. In the active voice the present participle is always the main verb form, as in *is hearing*. In the passive voice the present-participle form used is *being* with a past participle as the main verb form, as in *is being heard*. Always, however, an *ing* form is used, denoting continuing action.

All six of the basic tenses discussed in the section above have their progressive-tense counterparts, and in addition the progressive tense is used in conjunction with the modal auxiliaries, as will be explained below. The **present progressive tense** usually denotes continuing action at the present instant. Examples:

> I **am watching** a TV movie.
> He **is studying** for a test.

We seldom use the simple present tense, such as *watches*, to denote only present action, but instead use the progressive. In the case of some verbs, especially such as *go* and *arrive*, the present progressive form can denote future occurrence. Examples:

> **I'm playing** golf with Smith tomorrow morning.
> Mother **is arriving** next Sunday.
> I **am leaving** for Berlin tomorrow.

The present progressive can also denote action that continues but that is not continuous, as in

> I **am studying** for my CPA exams.

The speaker need not be actually studying when he utters such a sentence.

The **past progressive** denotes action that was continuing in the past but that is now ended. Examples:

> He **was studying** when the call came.
> They **were watching** TV at the time of the explosion.

Note that the simple past—*studied* and *watched*—will not function properly in sentences that convey continuing action.

The **future progressive** calls for the modal *will* or *shall*, the form *be*, and the present participle. Example:

> He **will be studying** by four o'clock.

The simple future—*will study*—will not give the same denotation of continuing action.

The present and past progressive tenses can be transformed into the passive voice. Examples:

> The alarm **is being heard** (by someone).
> That gun **was being cleaned** (by someone).

The future progressive is almost never used in the passive, for such a construction as *will be being heard* is too awkward, and the same denotation can be made in *will be heard*. The perfect progressive tenses are never used in the passive voice.

The **perfect progressive tenses** use as the first auxiliary a form of *have*, the form *been* as a second auxiliary, and the present participle as the main verb form. Examples:

> *Present perfect progressive*:
> He **has been listening** to the symphony.
> *Past perfect progressive*:
> He **had been telling** stories.
> *Future perfect progressive*:
> He **will have been studying** by the time you arrive.

The time denotations are the same here as for the simple perfect tenses discussed above, except that the action is expressed as a continuing one. Note that the passive-voice form of the verb in sentence two—*had been being told*—is hardly natural English.

The Modal Tenses

The modal auxiliaries may be used with the simple, present perfect, and progressive tenses. No additional tense names are used, however. All of the forms may just be called the modal tenses, or the **potential tenses**, since the modals generally denote potentiality, and the tense without the modal can be specified if one wishes. The future tenses, with *will* or *shall*, really belong to the modal tenses too. No full classification of these tenses will be given here, for the possibilities are almost endless.

Present time of occurrence can be denoted by the modals in conjunction with a verb stem or the present progressive form of a verb. Examples:

> He **must be** there at this very instant.
> I **can** now **hear** you quite well.
> He **might be leaving** now.
> He **could be talking** on the telephone.

Occurrence right now (chiefly) is denoted in these sentences, but note that other elements in the sentences really pinpoint the time. The conditions under which the modals can denote present occurrence are quite mixed. Note that in the last two sentences the present progressive is used with a modal, except that the form is *be leaving* instead of *is leaving*. Thus these are true modal tenses.

These same forms can also denote future occurrence. Examples:

> He **could donate** money if he wanted to.
> I **might decide** to join.
> You **should be leaving** soon.
> We **may be going** after all.

The modals as well as other elements in these sentences denote future time. Future occurrence is the most common tense denotation in the modals; even the so-called past tense of modals (*should* as opposed to *shall*, for instance) denotes future occurrence.

The modals can be used with the present perfect tense but not with the past perfect. For example, *could had been gone* is not grammatical. The future perfect tense is itself a modal tense. When a modal is used with the present perfect tense, past occurrence is denoted. Examples:

> The thief **could have stolen** my watch.
> You **should have gone** to the game.

The modals can also be used with the present perfect progressive tense. Examples:

> He **may have been leaving** at that moment.
> You **ought to have been studying**.

In such sentences it is really the auxiliary *have* that is denoting time, with the modals mostly denoting other meanings. The modals do have tense after a fashion—as do *will* and *would*—but it is not really their basic function to denote time in most uses.

The modals can also be used with some passive verb forms, just as can the simple, perfect, and progressive tenses. Examples:

> The speaker **could** not **be heard** (by anyone).
> These apples **should be peeled** fresh (by someone).
> Johnny **ought** not **to have been punished** (by anyone).

Note that such a passive form as *could be being heard* is not natural English. Progressive-tense passive-voice forms are not normally used with modals.

The highly idiomatic auxiliaries classed with the modals in Chapter 4 also denote time, at least to a degree. *Be to*, *be going to*, and *be about to* can denote future occurrence. Examples:

> He **is to run** for District Attorney.
> I **am going to leave** early.
> We **are about to rebel**.

These modals can also denote past occurrence. Examples:

> He **was to give** the main speech.
> I **was going to attend** the lecture.
> They **were about to call** it quits.

The perfect tenses can be used with *be going to* and *be about to*. Examples:

> He **had been going to leave**.
> They **have been about to rebel**.
> They **had been about to speak**.

The present perfect tense is not normally used with *be going to*. The future perfect can also be used with *be about to* (this tense is awkward with *be going to*). Example:

> He **will be about to leave** when you arrive.

As with all the modals, other meanings besides time are denoted in these auxiliaries.

Some of the other idiomatic auxiliaries mentioned in Chapter 4 also may denote various times of occurrence. Here are just a few possibilities; a full cataloguing of them would be far too extensive and not very rewarding.

> He **keeps swearing**.
> They **kept shouting** obscenities.
> You **will keep protesting**.
> He **gets drunk** frequently.
> She **got hanged**.
> You **have got to study**.
> He **used to cheat**.
> You **are supposed to come** early.

Various times of occurrence are denoted in such idiomatic auxiliaries.

Tense in the Auxiliary *Do*

The auxiliary *do* expresses tense in emphatic statements and in negations and questions. It denotes only simple present and simple past time, though it can imply continuing occurrence. Examples of emphatic tenses:

I **do hear** now.
I **do study** enough.
I **did attend** the lecture.
I once **did sing** well.

In sentences one and three, simple present and past occurrence are denoted. In sentences two and four, present and past times are denoted, but continuing action is also implied. The future and perfect tenses cannot be used with *do*.

Do expresses the same times of occurrence in negations and questions. Examples:

I **do** not **understand** that.
He **does** not **use** tobacco.
I **did** not **see** the flash.
He **did** not **follow** all the plays.
Do you **smoke?**
Did he **leave?**

Simple present and past time and also continuing occurrence can be expressed in such verb combinations.

Tense in Nonfinite Verb Forms

Nonfinite verb forms also denote time. **Present-participial forms**, whether they function as nominals, adjectivals, or verbs in nonfinite predications, may occur in present progressive and present perfect progressive tenses. Examples:

Present progressive tense:
Telling lies is a boy's secret sin.
My text **being** lost, I did not study.
He saw me **kissing** Joan.
Present perfect progressive tense:
Having been eating for an hour, I was no longer hungry.

This last usage is not common.

Past-participial forms, whether functioning as adjectivals or verbs in nonfinite predications, may express past tense in the passive voice and present perfect tense in the active and passive voice. Examples:

Past tense, passive voice:
The athlete, **tested** beyond endurance, collapsed.
His meal **finished**, he ordered a liqueur.
He found his meal **eaten**.
Present perfect tense, active voice:
Having told a lie, the boy was punished.
Present perfect tense, passive voice:
The apples **having been eaten**, we went hungry.

Those examples marked *passive voice* imply the passive forms *he was tested by something, his meal was finished by him*, and the like.

The **infinitive** can be formed into present and present perfect tenses and their progressive counterparts in the active and passive voices. Examples:

> *Present tense, active voice*:
>> **To see** Susan is to love her.
>
> *Present perfect tense, active voice*:
>> **To have seen** the play must have been rewarding.
>
> *Present progressive tense, active voice*:
>> **To be seeing** the landing on the moon seems a miracle.
>
> *Present tense, passive voice*:
>> **To be insulted** (by someone) is unpleasant.
>
> *Present perfect tense, passive voice*:
>> **To have been seen** (by someone) with Darcy would have embarrassed me.

It might seem as though the simple infinitive, as in the first example, denotes future time, but it is really the present-tense form.

Aspect

Aspect is a verb function not much discussed in grammatical study, for the good reason that it really is so closely connected with tense that the two may be considered together. In our discussion of tense above we have really considered aspect without using the term. For the record, aspect will be given a short separate section here. Aspect gives five kinds of information.

1. *Whether a process is beginning or is about to begin*:

> He **is about to speak**.
> We **are going to leave** now.

The Latin term for this is **inceptive aspect**.

2. *Whether the process is a continuous one*:

> He **has been talking** for an hour.
> She **will be gabbing** all night.

This is **durative aspect**.

3. *Whether the process is completed*:

> He **has given** that lecture before.
> The truth **will be known** in a minute.

This is **perfective aspect**. Though the tense in sentence two is future, the indication is that the process will be completed.

4. *Whether the process is considered as a whole without considering its beginning or end or how long it lasts*:

> She **talks** freely.
> He **will eat** heartily.

This is **terminative aspect**.

5. *Whether the process is a repeated one*:

> She **keeps talking**.
> He **kept interrupting**.

This is **iterative aspect**.

As you can see, this verb function is closely bound to tense.

Mood

Mood, sometimes spelled **mode**, is a grammatical term which refers to a set of verb forms used to indicate the speaker's attitude toward or understanding of the factuality or likelihood or desirability of the action or condition expressed. There are three standard moods in English: **indicative, subjunctive**, and **imperative**. Finite verbs in dependent clauses as well as those in independent clauses have mood. And some nonfinite forms are in the indicative mood.

The Indicative Mood

The **indicative** mood, though it has in recent decades taken over some of the subjunctive functions, is generally used to express a fact or what the speaker considers a fact (or falsehood) and to form a question concerning fact. The indicative-mood forms are considered the normal forms of the finite verb. The tense conjugations on page 163 are the indicative forms, and in addition almost all transitive and some intransitive verbs have passive-voice forms in the indicative.

Here are some normal indicative forms:

> Perry **owns** a GTO.
> The secretary **left** early.
> Jerry **has been loafing**.

The indicative mood may be expressed in the simple and perfect tenses and in their progressive counterparts.

Here are passive forms in the indicative mood:

> The electricity **was cut off** (by someone).
> The cake **has** already **been eaten** (by someone).

The other regular tenses also can express the indicative mood in the passive.

Here is a complex sentence:

> While the storm **was brewing,** we **were preparing** to evacuate
> our cabin.

In both the independent and dependent clauses, the verbs are in the
indicative mood.

Here is a sentence with a nonfinite verb form:

> Our guests **having arrived,** we **mixed** the cocktails.

The finite verb in this sentence is indicative and the nonfinite verb also
is, since it states a fact.

And here are a couple of questions:

> **Do** you **have** time to read this?
> **Hasn't** he **been punished** enough?

Since these questions are asking for factual replies, they are in the indicative mood.

The Subjunctive Mood

The **subjunctive** mood is the most complex of the three and the only
one that requires much explanation—and the only one of much grammatical interest, for that matter. The subjunctive verb forms express
doubt, unlikelihood, condition, wish, uncertainty, desirability, denial,
potentiality, and perhaps other such concepts (rather than facts or
falsehoods).

Many of the subjunctive verb forms are identical to those of the indicative mood. For example, in the sentence

> I suggested that they **buy** common stock

buy is in the subjunctive mood because it states desirability rather than
fact. Yet it is the same form as the indicative *they buy papers*. But
note this version:

> I suggested that he **buy** common stock.

The indicative form *he buys* will not function grammatically here.
The substitution shows that any verb in this construction is in the subjunctive mood, even though it may have the same form as in the indicative mood.

It is, then, only in singular verbs—the third person singular, present
tense of all verbs and the present and past of *to be*—that the subjunctive form changes from the indicative form. In the singular it takes
the plural verb forms, except for the present tense of *to be*, which in

the subjunctive mood is the form *be*. Here are some examples of subjunctive verbs:

> I desire that he **leave** at once.
> I urged that she **stay** with us.
> I begged that he **be** spared.
> I wish she **were** coming.
> If I **were** President, I would resign.
> He spoke as if he **were** inspired.

Note that in the first three sentences the indicative forms—*goes, stays, is*—will not function properly. When such verbs as *recommend, urge,* and *suggest* have a noun clause as a direct object, the verb in the noun clause is usually in the subjunctive mood (except that the indicative *was* can often be used instead of the subjunctive *were*). In the last three sentences the indicative form *was* can be used informally, for the use of the subjunctive is declining in our language.

In other noun clauses that state obligation, propriety, and other such concepts, the subjunctive is also commonly used. Examples:

> It is not proper that he **divorce** his wife.
> Is it necessary that I **be** punished?
> It is desirable that he **return** early.

The indicative forms—*divorces, am, returns*—would sound quite awkward in such constructions. But different idioms that avoid the subjunctive are more common in English today. We are far more likely to say

> It is not proper for him to divorce his wife

than to use the noun clause above with its subjunctive verb.

In earlier English, the subjunctive was more commonly used. Examples from past literature:

> If she **be** not so to me,
> What care I how fair she **be**?

> If it **were** done when 'tis done, then '**twere** well
> It **were** done quickly.

Also such subjunctive forms as these were common in the earlier days of English:

> Unless he **go** quickly, he will miss the opening.
> Whether it **be** fowl or fish, we will eat it.

Now the indicative is mostly used in such constructions. Also various traditional subjunctive forms still exist in our language. Examples:

> Long **live** the king.
> **Come** one, come all.
> **Be** he alive or **be** he dead.
> **Be** it ever so humble, there's no place like home.
> Judge not that you **be** not judged.

These are carry-overs from a time when the subjunctive was more prominent in English. Such set phrases are not likely to change.

As late as the 1950s, and even to a small extent today, the subjunctive forms were taught as a matter of usage in English, especially in *if* and *as if* (*as though*) clauses and in noun clauses following *wish*. For example, most authorities once demanded these forms:

> If he **were** sane, he would not deserve pity.
> He ate as though (as if) he **were** famished.
> I wish I **were** rich.

But so far as usage is concerned nowadays, any verb form that sounds natural is acceptable, at least in informal conversation. Such sentences as

> If I **was** principal, I would expel the Ancient Rubrics,
> He ran as if he **was** tired,

and

> I wish she **was** more courteous

are now acceptable, at least informally. True, not facts but conditions are expressed in these clauses, but nowadays the indicative mood is commonly used in such constructions. When an indicative form is awkward, as in

> I recommend that he **comes** with us,

no one actually uses it. The subjunctive mood really poses no problem in usage in English.

The modal auxiliaries also often express the subjunctive mood. In fact, the term *modal* refers to *mood*; both come from the Latin *modus*, meaning "manner." The subjunctive with the modals may be called the **modal subjunctive**. The verb forms in this mood, however, do not differ from those in the indicative mood, and thus the form generates little grammatical interest. Here are example sentences:

> He **could be** guilty.
> You **should go** to class.

May your life **be** long.
He **must register** to vote.
She **ought to return** to college.

Such constructions may be said to be in the subjunctive mood since they express potentiality, desirability, obligation, and other such concepts. However, if a modal auxiliary is used to express a fact, as in

I **can play** the piano by ear,
He **will arrive** on Wednesday,

and

We **shall be** happy to visit you,

the mood is indicative.

The Imperative Mood

The **imperative** mood is used only in request or command sentences. The verb form used is always the stem (first paradigm form); it does not have number. It may for simplicity be said to be in the present tense, but tense is really not a factor. Usually the request sentence is spoken to an audience of one or more. But it can appear in writing, and then the reader is being addressed as the audience. This fact of a required audience is germane to the question of whether the imperative verb has a subject, as will be explained below. Here are typical examples of the imperative mood:

Come as soon as you can.
Hand me that book.
Listen carefully.

The emphatic auxiliary *do* can be used in imperative sentences:

Do be quiet now.

It is normally used if the request is in the negative. Example:

Please **do** not **stop** writing to me.

The imperative verb may take the same complements and modifiers that indicative verbs can take. In the above sentence, *writing to me* is the direct object of *stop*.

Grammatically, the most interesting aspect of the imperative sentence is whether it has a subject. Hundreds of millions of school children have been taught that *you* is the understood subject of a request sentence. But the grammatical truth is that the request sentence does not have a subject. Early grammarians went on the assumption that every sentence must have a subject and, since a request sentence is addressed directly to someone who hears or reads it, they naturally chose the understood *you* as the subject of request sentences. But they were mistaken.

The request sentence doesn't have a subject because it can't take one. It is the one kind of standard, full sentence in English that doesn't have a subject. There is always an audience for a request sentence, and the audience is the one to whom the sentence is addressed, not the subject of the sentence. What is understood in the sentence is the audience. The understood *you* is the audience, and it is in **direct address** and not a subject.

Though it should be clear to a thoughtful student of language that the request sentence is not a kind that can have a subject, rational explanations can be given to substantiate this grammatical analysis. *You* is a pronoun, and anytime it is really the subject of a sentence its antecedent can replace it as the subject. Examples:

> **You** are the prettiest girl in the class.
> **Jane** is the prettiest girl in the class.

> **You** are all angels in disguise.
> **Jane and all her friends** are angels in disguise.

In the first example, do not let the change in verb number lead you astray. *You* is singular in the first sentence in spite of the plural verb *are*, and the antecedent must therefore take a singular verb. Now, contrary to the above sentences, the antecedent of *you* in a request sentence cannot be substituted as the subject. Example:

> You close the door.
> Jane closes the door.

The second sentence is obviously not the same as the first, for it states a fact (indicative mood), not a request. And if we leave the sentence as

> Jane close the door,

Jane is very clearly in direct address and a comma or pause would be placed after it. (A comma or pause belongs after *you* in the request sentence, too.) *Jane* cannot be the subject. Therefore *you* is not the subject, since *you* is standing for *Jane*.

Also *you* as the real subject of a verb-stem form functions quite differently from the understood *you* in a request sentence, which has the same verb-stem form. In

> You don't stare at the queen

as a request sentence, *you* is in direct address (and should have a comma after it). But in

> You don't stare at the queen, but Johnny does,

the *you* is a subject and the verb is in the indicative mood, stating a fact, not a request. These two uses of *you* would be ambiguous and cause trouble in understanding if the *you* in a request sentence were really a subject.

Some might agree that in

> You, close the door

the *you* is in direct address, but that in

> Jane, you close the door

Jane only is in direct address and *you* is the subject. But such is not so. The *you* is the same as in the sentence without *Jane*. Both *Jane* and *you* (which refer to the same person) are in direct address, the *you* being used as an intensive in direct address. True, there is not a comma after *you* in such a double direct address; the reason is that in this intensive structure there is no terminal juncture (voice pause) after *you*. Neither is there when *you* is used alone in an emphatic structure, such as

> You close the door (not me).

Still, *you* is the audience and is functioning in direct address, not as a subject.

It should also be observed that the understood *you* in a request sentence does not perform an action (the request may not be granted), nor receive an action, nor exist in a state of being, as subjects usually do, unless the verb is in the subjunctive mood. Also it should be observed that teaching that *you* is the understood subject in a request sentence does no real harm, for no point of usage is involved. The whole matter is of academic grammatical interest only.

Voice

The concept of **voice** in verb forms is simple, but it is difficult to know just where to discuss it in a grammar text, since not only verb forms but also subjects and complements are involved. We will place the discussion here in the chapter on finite verbs, knowing that some of the discussion of complements will be repeated in the next chapter.

The Concept of Voice and the Passive Transformation

Voice has to do with whether a sentence subject performs or receives the action stated in the verb. If the subject performs the action, as in

He **melted** the lead,

the sentence and the verb are in the **active voice**. If the subject receives the action, as in

The lead **was melted** (by him),

the sentence and the verb are in the **passive voice**. Almost all transitive verbs and many intransitive ones can be transformed from active to passive voice. Linking verbs and some intransitive verbs will not transform into the passive voice.

The transformation involves the following steps: (1) the addition to the verb of a form of *to be* as an auxiliary,[3] according to tense; (2) the change of the main verb form to the past participle, if necessary; (3) the shifting of the direct object or indirect object or, in some cases, the object of a preposition to the subject position; and (4) the shifting of the subject of the active-voice sentence to a *by* phrase (which is often suppressed). The object of the preposition *by* in the passive-voice sentence is then the doer of the action.

The passive transformation can be symbolized. The meanings of the symbols used in the next few pages (and which will also be used in Chapter 9) are as follows:

N *means* any noun or nominal
N^1, N^2, and N^3 *mean* nouns or nominals distinguished from one another by having different references as the superscripts indicate.
V-Tr *means* transitive verb
V-In *means* intransitive verb
Be *means* any form of *to be* as an auxiliary
Past Part *means* past participle
by *means* the preposition by
prep *means* any preposition
Have *means* any form of *to have* as an auxiliary
Poss Det *means* possessive determiner

Here are symbolizations of an active-voice sentence and a passive-voice transformation of it:

Active voice:
$N^1 + V\text{-}Tr + N^2$
Passive voice:
$N^2 + Be + Past\ Part + by + N^1$

The real sentences are such as these:

---

[3]The auxiliary *get* can sometimes substitute for *be* in a passive verb form. This is wholly a colloquial usage. Examples: *Sandy* **got shot** (by someone). *Louis* **gets punished** *often* (by his father).

The cat sees the bird.
The bird is seen by the cat.

All six regular tenses may be made passive and three different noun functions in active-voice sentences may become subjects in passive-voice sentences.

The Active-Voice Sentence with a Direct Object

When an active-voice sentence has a direct object as its only complement, the passive-voice transformation is as illustrated above. More examples, with the passive-voice verb in boldface:

Past tense:

The President gave a speech.
A speech **was given** by the President.

Future tense:

The captain will hunt polar bears.
Polar bears **will be hunted** by the captain.

Present perfect:

Someone has read this new book.
This new book **has been read** (by someone).

A modal tense:

Someone could have shot the intruder.
The intruder **could have been shot** (by someone).

In passive-voice sentences in everyday speaking and writing, the *by* phrase is often suppressed. Examples:

Much corn **is grown** in Iowa.
The victim **had been strangled**.
The building **was dedicated** to those killed in World War II.

In such sentences the writer suppresses the *by* phrase because he does not consider it important to mention the doer of the action.

The passive-voice verbs in such sentences as those above were transitive in their active-voice counterparts but have no direct objects in the passive-voice sentences. Yet they are still transitive verbs; the subject of the sentence is really also the verb's displaced direct object.

A few verbs that seem to be transitive with direct objects will not meaningfully transform into the passive voice. Examples:

That dress **suits** her temperament.

> That car **resembles** a Mercedes.
> This car **cost** a lot of money.
> I **have** one thousand books.
> This key **fits** that lock.

The passive transformation can be made (except perhaps with *cost*), but it is very awkward and almost meaningless. We do have the structure

> A good time **was had** by all,

but it is recognized as humorous and awkward. There are only a very few transitive verbs that will not transform into the passive voice.

The Active-Voice Sentence with a Direct and Indirect Object

When a transitive verb has both a direct and an indirect object, either object can become the subject of a passive-voice sentence and the other remains as the retained object. Examples:

> *Active voice*:
> Carnegie gave Dunfermline a public library.
> *Passive voice*:
> Dunfermline **was given** a public library (by Carnegie).
> *Passive voice*:
> A public library **was given** Dunfermline (by Carnegie).

> *Active voice*:
> Jerry tells me lies.
> *Passive voice*:
> Lies **are told** me by Jerry.
> *Passive voice*:
> I **am told** lies by Jerry.

The symbolic notations of these passive transformations are as follows:

> *Active voice:*
> $N^1 + V\text{-}Tr + N^2 + N^3$
> *Passive voice:*
> $N^3 + Be + Past\ Part + N^2 + by + N^1$
> *Passive voice:*
> $N^2 + Be + Past\ Part + N^3 + by + N^1$

The Active-Voice Sentence with a Direct Object and an Object Complement

This kind of sentence is as follows:

> The committee elected George chairman.

George is the direct object and *chairman* is the object complement and is the same as *George*. When such a sentence is transformed into the passive voice, only the direct object can become the subject:

George **was elected** chairman (by the committee).

Chairman is the **retained** object complement. The object complement cannot become the subject of a passive-voice sentence. For example,

*Chairman was elected George (by the committee)

is not grammatical.

The Intransitive Verb in the Active Voice

Some intransitive verbs, though they do not have direct objects to become subjects, can be transformed into the passive voice if they are followed by a preposition the object of which is really the object of the verb and the preposition together. Examples:

Intransitive verb:
Someone laughed at Milton.
Passive voice:
Milton **was laughed** at (by someone).

Intransitive verb:
Someone stared at Jane.
Passive voice:
Jane **was stared** at (by someone).

The symbolic notation of this transformation is as follows:

Active voice:
$N^1 + V\text{-}In + prep + N^2$
Passive voice:
$N^2 + Be + Past Part + prep + (by + N^1)$

In the first example sentence *Milton* is really the object of *laughed at* rather than of just *at*. When the N^2 of such an active-voice sentence is the object of the preposition only and not of the verb plus the preposition, the sentence will not transform into the passive voice. For example, such a sentence as

Mary walked at a fast pace

will not transform into the passive voice, for *pace* is not the object of *walked at*, but only of *at*.

Passive Voice in Nonfinite Verb Forms

Infinitive and past-participial verb forms may occur in the passive voice. Examples:

Being loved (by someone) is highly desirable.

The door not **having been closed** (by anyone), we were cold.
This is the topic **to be written on** (by the students).
I don't want that ball **to be thrown** (by anyone).

In the first sentence a past participle is in the passive voice; in the second, a past perfect participle; and in the last two, infinitive phrases. Note that a form of *to be* and a past participle must be used in any verb form in the passive voice.

The *Have* Transformation in the Passive Voice

Some active-voice sentences will not only transform into the regular passive voice but also into a sentence in a kind of half-active-half-passive voice with the verb *have* and, as a direct object of *have*, a non-finite predication in the passive voice. Example:

> *Active voice*:
>   Someone stole his wallet.
> *Passive voice*:
>   His wallet was stolen (by someone).
> *Active-passive voice with* have:
>   He had his wallet stolen (by someone).

This half-active-half-passive-voice transformation can occur (1) when the direct object in the active-voice sentence has a possessive pronoun or noun as a determiner; (2) when the direct object of the active-voice sentence is followed by a preposition the object of which is a personal pronoun or a proper noun; and (3) when the active-voice sentence has both a direct and indirect object.

Here is a second example of the first type:

> *Active voice*:
>   Someone damaged John's car.
> *Passive voice*:
>   John's car was damaged (by someone).
> *Active-passive voice with* have:
>   John had his car damaged (by someone).

Here are two examples of the second type:

> *Active voice*:
>   Someone spilled coffee on her.
> *Passive voice*:
>   Coffee was spilled on her (by someone).
> *Active-passive voice with* have:
>   She had coffee spilled on her (by someone).[4]

> *Active voice*:
> Someone threw rice at Susan.
> *Passive voice*:
> Rice was thrown at Susan (by someone).
> *Active-passive voice with* have:
> Susan had rice thrown at her (by someone).

And here are two examples of the third type:

> *Active voice*:
> Someone gave Steve a book.
> *Passive voice*:
> Steve was given a book (by someone).
> *Passive voice*:
> A book was given Steve (by someone).
> *Active-passive voice with* have:
> Steve had a book given him (by someone).

> *Active voice*:
> Someone bought her a ring.
> *Passive voice*:
> She was bought a ring (by someone).
> *Passive voice*:
> A ring was bought her (by someone).
> *Active-passive voice with* have:
> She had a ring bought her (by someone).

A sentence with an indirect object is the only kind that can have two regular passive transformations, as illustrated here. So, in effect, such a sentence can have three different passive transformations.

The analysis of the active-passive-voice sentence with *have* is that (in *Susan had rice thrown at her*, for example) *Susan* is the subject of the sentence and *rice thrown at her* is the direct object of *had*. In that phrasal direct object, *thrown* is a past participle with *rice* as its subject, and the whole phrase is in the passive voice (that is, *rice was thrown by someone*). Or for another example (with *she had a ring bought her*), *she* is the subject and *a ring bought her* is the direct object of *had*. In that phrasal direct object, *bought* is a past participle, *ring* is its subject, and *her* is its indirect object. The whole phrase is in the passive voice (that is, *a ring was bought for her by someone*).

---

[4] Sometimes the verb *get* can substitute for *have* in this construction, as in: *She **got** coffee spilled on her*.

The symbolic notations of the transformations when the direct object has a possessive determiner are as follows:

Active voice:
N¹ + V-Tr + Poss Det + N²
Passive voice:
Poss Det + N² + Be + Past Part + by + N¹
Active-passive voice with have:
N³ + Have + Poss Det + N² + Past Part + by + N¹

The **Poss Det** is a possessive determiner; the **N³** is that possessive determiner transformed into a personal pronoun or proper noun. Here is another example that you can apply these notations to:

Active voice:
Someone burned his cabin.
Passive voice:
His cabin was burned by someone.
Active-passive voice with have:
He had his cabin burned by someone.

As a prelude to work in Chapter 9, you might try to supply for yourself symbolic notations of the other two kinds of the *have* transformation. The active-passive-voice sentence with *have* is common in English.

EXERCISES

1. Identify the verb phrases in the following sentences and tell whether the verb headword (or head-phrase) is linking, intransitive, or transitive.

a. In the autumn some birds fly nonstop all the way from the arctic to summering grounds in South America.

b. Excluding the caribou, most members of the deer family do not make long migrations between hunting and breeding grounds.

c. The clerk had decided that he would not again take an insult from a customer and felt that he would be supported by his employer.

d. The Mottled Edsels could compose their own popular music, adapt classics to modern tastes, play six instruments each, and mainline horse with the best of them.

e. Professor Howard has been chosen leader of the Divertimento Club and will be traveling throughout the country seeking new members.

f . The Anthology of Pros were guilty of abetting the rioters who tried to block the Governor's cavalcade.

g. The Flat Tires remained the most popular rock group in the Rocky Mountain states.

h. At nine we returned to the demonstration grounds, where six guardsmen had been injured by flying rocks.

i. The local businessmen gave the President a reception that warmed the cockles of his heart.

j. There is no possible way in which we can erase the harm done by the militant minority on our campus.

2. See how many different combinations you can make with *could*, other auxiliaries, and either *lead*, *leading*, or *led* as the main verb form.

3. Conjugate the verb *to be* in the six regular simple and perfect tenses.

4. Comment on the tense possibilities in the verbs in the following sentences. What is the name of the tense of each verb?

a. I eat spinach ravenously.

b. I am leaving by stagecoach.

c. I am due in Calcutta next week.

d. I had almost been about to leave when she finally showed up.

e. Henry tells me you are as pretty as Susan.

5. List all the perfect and perfect progressive tenses of *to ride*.

6. Identify by name the tenses of the verbs in the following sentences. Consider both progressive and passive forms. If the actual time of occurrence in the verb does not agree with the tense name, comment on the discrepancy.

a. He has gone there frequently.

b. He had been there before.

c. What chapter will you have completed by midnight?

d. He thinks you are intelligent.

e. The car is being stolen.

f. The casino had been raided.

g. He was carrying too much insurance.

h. You will be receiving my letter soon.

i. The jerky has been eaten.

j. I am writing letters of application for a job as computer analyst.

7. Create a sentence that can use either the future perfect tense or the simple future tense with the same meaning.

8. Create a future progressive passive-voice form and a present perfect passive-voice form to show that they are not natural English forms.

9. Use both *could* and *should* in a form denoting present occurrence and one denoting future occurrence.

10. How many verb forms can you create with *be going to* in all its forms and the stem *cry*?

11. What is the tense in the italicized nonfinite verb forms in the following sentences? Take voice into consideration.

    a. *Drinking* coconut milk is a treat.
    b. Our car *having been stolen*, we had to walk.
    c. *To have heard* the cries of alarm must have been frightening.
    d. *Having read* the assignment, I went to bed.
    e. *To have been robbed* by a child was embarrassing.
    f. The sun *having set*, the mosquitos came out.
    g. *To be learning* Sanskrit is a joy.
    h. *To pray* is not *de rigueur* in some circles.
    i. *Having been told* a lie, I was unable to complete the survey.
    j. The house, *condemned* as a dwelling, stood vacant.

12. Identify the mood of the italicized verb form in each of the following sentences:

    a. I recommended that he *secure* his future with insurance.
    b. The turtle *had been left* to die.
    c. *Do* you *have* any incunabula?
    d. He *can play* offense or defense equally well.
    e. If he *were* coach, I *would resign* from the team.
    f. He *suggested* that I *be* the candidate.
    g. You *should stay* in college.
    h. Please do not *be* late.
    i. I wish I *was* a genius.
    j. Is it necessary that he *remain* in the infantry?

13. Demonstrate that *you* in the following sentence is not a subject:

    You be quiet.

14. Convert the following active-voice sentences to passive voice (two versions in sentence c).

    a. He sighted the eagle.
    b. Someone might have dialed the wrong number.
    c. Mother bought me a parrot.
    d. The club appointed Jack leader.
    e. Someone sat on this antique chair.

15. Following are two paragraphs chosen at random. Identify all the verbs in them and specify the tense, mood, and voice of each of them.

> Until the attitude of the northern ghetto dweller is understood, there is no hope for solving this nation's social problems. When the United States Supreme Court passed its famous ruling on school desegregation in 1954, all black folks took a psychological cop-out. We didn't really want to confront the white man, so we unconsciously said to ourselves, "I won't realize the benefits, but, thank God, life will be better for my children." We took the Supreme Court decision at face value and passed on the encouraging word to our kids. A teenager in 1954 is in his twenties now, like Stokely Carmichael and Rap Brown. He has lived for a decade and a half with his dream deferred and he can accept the vision of eventual betterment no longer. Today's black youth are demanding what their parents unwittingly taught them to expect. [Dick Gregory, *Write Me In!*]

> One motivational analyst who became curious to know why there had been such a great rise in impulse buying at supermarkets was James Vicary. He suspected that some special psychology must be going on inside the women as they shopped in supermarkets. His suspicion was that perhaps they underwent such an increase in tension when confronted with so many possibilities that they were forced into making quick purchases. He set out to find out if this was true. The best way to detect what was going on inside the shopper was a galvanometer or lie detector. That obviously was impractical. The next best thing was to use a hidden motion-picture camera and record the eye-blink rate of the women as they shopped. How fast a person blinks his eyes is a pretty good index of his state of inner tension. The average person, according to Mr. Vicary, normally blinks his eyes about thirty-two times a minute. If he is tense he blinks them more frequently, under extreme tension up to fifty or sixty times a minute. If he is notably relaxed on the other hand his eye-blink rate may drop to a subnormal twenty or less. [Vance Packard, *The Hidden Persuaders*]

16. Convert the following active-voice sentences into the regular passive voice and into the half-active-half-passive voice with *have*:

a. Someone shot buckshot at Jim.
b. Someone destroyed Bob's motorcycle.
c. Someone pitched hay on her.
d. Someone mussed Carol's hair.

e. Someone threw pennies at the comic.
f. Someone gave Bob a hard time.
g. Someone handed Jim a book.
h. Someone tossed a book at Jim.
i. Someone hit Jeannie's elbow.
j. Someone bought Sadie a box of candy.

8 COMPLEMENTS

This chapter is devoted to a study of the third component of a predication: **the complement of the verb.** Chapters 5, 6, 7, and 8, then, form a unit: an overview of predication and a study of the three parts of a predication—subjects, finite verbs, and complements.

Complementation: The Second Great Grammatical Function

In Chapter 5 we maintained that a hypothetical, beginning student of language would inductively discover that the first great grammatical function in English sentences is predication: the fitting of a subject to a predicate. If such an intelligent novice began with short sentences, as he undoubtedly would, he would then soon discover that the second half of a predication (the predicate) is sometimes composed of a verb only, but that more often the predicate will itself divide into two parts, the verb and a **complement**, or completer, of the verb. (Indeed, some verbs take two complements (some even three), as will be explained, but that would be a later discovery of our hypothetical language student.) After pondering this discovery, he would conclude that our second great grammatical function is **complementation**, the completion of a meaning initiated in the verb. He would see that such a predication would be incomplete without the complement—that the verb would be left hanging, so to speak. For example, he would see that if *the dress* were omitted from

> The seamstress scorched the dress

there would be incomplete predication.

We have already discussed complements in some detail, for our study of parts of speech and finite verbs required doing so. Now we will give an orderly presentation of all types of complements in English and will illustrate the different kinds of constructions that can function as complements.

Direct Objects

The complement with the highest frequency of occurrence in English is the **direct object**. It appears with a transitive verb and is the person or thing or even concept that receives the action of the verb. Here are simple sentences of this sort with the direct object in boldface:

> Mrs. Gundry // locked / the **door**.
> Kapp // throws / many **passes**.
> Grandfather // will carve / the **turkey**.

Double slashes (//) separate the subject from the predicate, and a single slash separates the verb from its complement.

In the above sentences simple direct objects are illustrated: nouns. An endocentric noun phrase may function as a full direct object with a simple object (the headword) within it. Examples:

> The preacher // discussed / **the undesirable effects of hidden sin on those who are afraid to confess publicly.**
> The orchestra // played / **a warmly received series of classical pieces which had only recently been discovered in Salzburg.**

In these sentences the simple direct objects are *effects* and *series*, but the whole endocentric structures are functioning as full direct objects, just as they could function as full subjects. Dependent clauses within an endocentric structure can have their own complements.

Pronouns and noun substitutes may function as direct objects. Examples:

> As the sinful congregation listened, the preacher // excoriated / **them**.
> You // have said / **enough**.

Them is a personal pronoun functioning as the direct object of *excoriated*, and the indefinite pronoun *enough* is functioning as a noun substitute as the direct object of *have said*.

Endocentric nominal phrases with pronouns or noun substitutes as headwords may also occur as full direct objects. Examples:

> The judge // eliminated / **those of the contestants who had not followed the rules set up by the Rules Committee.**
>
> The Dean // expelled / **many of the students who refused to vacate the Administration Building when the National Guardsmen moved in to restore order.**

In sentence one, *those*, a demonstrative pronoun, is the simple direct object and the whole boldface endocentric phrase is the full direct object of *eliminated*. In sentence two, *many*, an indefinite pronoun functioning as a noun substitute, is the simple direct object and the whole boldface endocentric phrase is the full direct object of *expelled*. Long endocentric phrases are rarely formed with a personal pronoun as the headword.

Various kinds of word groups can also function as direct objects. Here are examples of noun clauses so functioning:

> I // don't believe / **that you understand my purpose.**
> I // suggested / **that he not resort to violence.**
> I // know / **who will give the Ewing Lectures.**

It is easy for a beginner to confuse noun-clause direct objects with adjective clauses, since identical connectives can introduce both. The test to use is to see if either of the indefinite pronouns *something* or *someone* can be substituted for the clause. If so, the clause is a nominal and a direct object if it follows a verb. The test works in the above three sentences, as, for example, *I don't believe something*. But in

> I bought the hat **that suited me**

the clause is not a direct object, for *I bought the hat something* makes no sense. The clause is an adjectival modifying *hat*.

Infinitives and infinitive phrases can function as direct objects. Examples:

> No one // really likes / **to smoke.**
> John // wants / **to take nineteen units.**
> I // want / **you to drive this car.**
> This passage // will make / **your heart skip a beat.**

The direct object is defined as the person or thing that receives the action of the transitive verb. But though most word-group direct objects do not really receive any action—they just complete the meaning initiated in the transitive verb—they are nevertheless direct objects. In sentence three above, an infinitive phrase with a subject (*you*) is a direct object, and the same is true for sentence four except that the infinitive (*skip*) does not have the *to*. (The *to* is often omitted from an infinitive, but there are no rules applying to its elision.) Note that the nominals *something*, *this*, or *that* can replace the infinitive direct objects above, though only awkwardly in the last sentence.

Present participles and present-participial phrases can function as direct objects. Examples:

> I // like / **swimming**.
> This hunter // regretted / **having shot the doe**.
> He // found / **me eating watermelon**.

These participial direct objects can also be replaced with the nominal *something*. In the third sentence, the participial phrase has not only a direct object itself but also a subject (*me*). The entire phrase is a direct object, a rather common kind of construction.

A past participle with a subject can also function as a direct object. Examples:

> He // found / **the door lock broken**.
> He // had / **his car stolen**.

The entire boldface phrases are direct objects of *found* and *had*. *Door lock* is the subject of *broken*, and *car* is the subject of *stolen*. With the exception of *gone* and possibly one or two others, past participles in this kind of construction are all in the passive voice, as here: *the door lock was broken by someone*.

The direct object may appear in a different position in a sentence with reversed order, though usually only for emphasis in the second sentence of a pair. Examples:

> I tolerate unanimity. **Controversy** I love.
> He entertained the girls. The **boys** he ignored.

The order direct object-verb-subject almost never appears in English.

Some verbs are grammatically intransitive when logically they are transitive and would normally take a direct object. For example, the sentence

> John fought bravely

has no direct object and technically the verb *fought* is intransitive. But John must have fought something. The sentence may be analyzed as having an understood direct object, though such analysis is not mandatory. Note the difference between that sentence and

> He walked fast.

No understood object is possible here and the verb *walked* is logically as well as grammatically intransitive. Transitivity is mostly a grammatical, not a logical, function.

When an active-voice sentence with a direct object is transformed into the passive voice, the direct object often appears as the subject and the passive-voice verb may have no direct object so far as the grammar of the sentence goes. Example:

> *Active voice*:
> Several boys have broken this **window**.
> *Passive voice*:
> This **window** has been broken (by several boys).

Has been broken is still a transitive verb, and *window* may be called its displaced direct object, even though it is the grammatical subject of the passive-voice sentence. *Window* controls the verb; the doer of the action in the often suppressed *by* phrase no longer has an effect on the verb.

Indirect Objects

Some transitive verbs—especially *give*, *buy*, *tell*, *bring*, *do*, *pass*, *teach*, *play*, and *write*—can take an indirect as well as a direct object. The indirect object is of high frequency in English considering the limited number of verbs that can take it. It names the person or thing for whom or to whom an action is performed. It comes before the direct object.[1] Examples:

> Mother // gave / **John** / a raise in his allowance.
> Please buy / **me** / a record. (no subject)
> Terry // didn't bring / **Daddy** / his slippers.
> Professor Jones // taught / **Joan** / a lesson.

The slashes show how the predicate divides into three parts: verb, indirect object, and direct object.

The indirect object can always be transformed into a prepositional phrase with *to* or *for* which follows the direct object. Examples:

> Mother // gave / a raise in his allowance **to John**.
> Please buy / a record **for me**.
> Terry // didn't bring / Daddy's slippers **to him**.

The different grammatical analysis of these sentences—that the prepositional phrase modifies the verb rather than completes it—is technical only, not logical.

A number of verbs in English *can* take indirect objects but normally are used with prepositional phrases instead. For example, we would be

---

[1] In two active-voice constructions—*he wrote me* and *he told me*—an indirect object (*me*) can appear without a direct object being stated. Some direct object, such as *a letter* and *the rumor*, is understood.

more likely to say

> Conduct a quartet for me

rather than

> Conduct me a quartet.

The above examples illustrate simple indirect objects. In addition to these, endocentric noun phrases and occasionally noun clauses can function as indirect objects. Examples:

> The candidate // gave / **the young students who attended the meeting** / a lecture on temperance.
> Mr. Gay // bought / **all the boys in the band** / silver replicas of their instruments.
> Give / **whoever arrives first** / the door prize. (no subject)

In the first two sentences, *students* and *boys* are the simple indirect objects; the whole boldface phrases are full indirect objects. In sentence three, a noun clause is the indirect object, a rare usage in English. Rarely, a participial phrase can function as an indirect object. Example:

> The preacher // gave / **drinking whisky** / a bad time.

Apparently an infinitive cannot function as an indirect object.

Sometimes an indirect object can come first in reversed sentence order. Example:

> Professor Gordon gave Betty a C. **John**, he gave an A.

In the second sentence of this pair, *John*, the indirect object, is placed first for emphasis. *An A* is the direct object.

When an active-voice sentence with both an indirect and direct object is transformed into the passive voice, either the indirect or the direct object can become the subject. The other is left as the **retained object**. Example:

> *Active voice*:
> Calvin bought me a gift.
> *Passive voice*:
> I was bought a **gift** by Calvin.
> *Passive voice*:
> A gift was bought **me** by Calvin.

In the middle sentence, *gift* is the **retained direct object**. In the third sentence *me* is the **retained indirect object**.

Object Complements

A few transitive verbs—chiefly *elect*, *call*, *appoint*, *make*, *consider*, *think*, *choose*, *find*, *show*, and *select*—can take an object complement with the direct object. The object complement really completes the direct object rather than the verb. It cannot appear without a direct object, except when it is a retained object complement in a passive-voice sentence. There are **noun object complements** and **adjective object complements**. The object complement either renames the direct object in different terms (noun) or gives an adjectival description of the direct object (adjective).

Here are some typical noun object complements:

> The voters // elected / Walter Stern / **Senator.**
> Mary // called / Harriet / a **fool.**
> Tom // considered / Jim / a **malingerer.**

The object complement is what the direct object (usually a person) is elected, called, considered, or the like.

Endocentric noun phrases and even noun clauses can function as nominal object complements. Examples:

> The council // appointed / Lowell / **the grand dragon of the newly
>   formed Owls Club.**
> We // should elect / Paul / **whatever he wants to be.**

In the first sentence *dragon* is the simple and the entire boldface phrase the full object complement. The noun-clause object complement, as in the second sentence, is a rare usage.

Following are examples of adjective object complements:

> Muriel // made / me / **happy.**
> John // considers / Susan / **beautiful.**
> Frank // called / Professor Newly / **arrogant.**

The boldface adjectives complement the direct objects. They are what the direct objects are made, called, or considered. Note that the predication is incomplete without the object complement. Only a very few verbs can take an adjective object complement.

As you saw in the section on direct objects, a past participle with a subject can function as a direct object. This construction can be confused with a direct object followed by an adjective object complement. Compare these two sentences:

> We found Harry tied up.
> We found Harry tired.

They have a superficial similarity since seemingly a past participle follows *Harry* in each. But they are grammatically different. In the first, *Harry tied up* is the direct object of *found*. *Harry* is the subject of the past participle (of a verb-particle composite) *tied up*. In the second, *Harry* is the direct object of *found*, and *tired* is an adjective object complement. *Tired* is really an adjective since it will compare (*more tired*) and can be modified by *very*. Another way to tell the difference between the two constructions is to see that the past participle with a subject (the whole phrase functioning as a direct object) is a passive-voice construction which can be transformed into an active-voice construction. For example, in the first sentence the meaning is

Harry was tied up by someone,

which transforms into

Someone tied up Harry.

But the second sentence does not seem to mean

Harry was tired by someone

or

Someone tired Harry.

Hence the difference between the two constructions.
Here is another example:

Sue found Billy bedraggled.
I saw Jack murdered.

The meaning of the first sentence does not seem to be

Someone bedraggled Billy,

and thus *bedraggled* is an adjective object complement. But the meaning in the second sentence seems to be

Someone murdered Jack,

and thus *Jack murdered* in the original sentence is a past participle with a subject, the whole phrase being the direct object of *found*. Very few verbs can take this kind of direct object, and so there is not much chance of confusing the two constructions.

There are a few past participles, however, that do take subjects but that are not passive constructions. Examples are

We found **James gone**

and

> We found **Billy departed**.

The past participles here are not adjective object complements even though they are not in the passive voice. The whole phrases are direct objects. Note that *gone* and *departed* will not compare and cannot be modified by *very*.

Sometimes a sentence can be analyzed either way. Example:

> We found Jane excited.

Jane excited can be considered a passive construction; thus

> Jane was excited by someone.

But also *excited* can just be considered an adjective, since it will compare (*more excited*) and can be modified by *very*. So the sentence can be considered one with a direct object (*Jane*) and an adjective object complement (*excited*). Or it can be considered just as a sentence with a direct object (*Jane excited*).

Sometimes the infinitive *to be* occurs between a direct object and its object complement. Examples:

> I // consider / Susan / to be intelligent.
> We // found / John / to be a complainer.

Also *as* is sometimes used between a direct object and a noun object complement. Example:

> We // chose / George / as captain.

In these constructions, *to be* and *as* may be considered expletives. They can be omitted. Or with *to be* the grammatical analysis can be that an infinitive phrase is functioning as an object complement. When *as* is used with an object complement, reversed sentence order is possible. Example:

> As secretary, we selected Elena.

In this sentence *secretary* is an object complement in spite of its position.

A prepositional phrase can be an adjectival object complement. Examples:

> I // found / him / **in rare humor**.
> I // considered / him / **on the make**.

This construction occurs only when the prepositional phrase is an adjectival describing the direct object. For example, in

> I found him in the bar,

in the bar is an adverbial modifying *found* and is not completing the direct object *him*.

In some idiomatic constructions the object complement can come before the direct object. In such cases the direct object is always a noun clause or an infinitive phrase and an expletive *it* stands for the clause or phrase. Example with an infinitive phrase:

> I think it **necessary** to vote a straight party ticket.

This transforms into

> I // think / to vote a straight party ticket / **necessary,**

showing *necessary* to be an object complement. The infinitive phrase is the direct object of *think*. The sentence is equivalent to *I think something necessary*. Example with a noun clause:

> I thought it **odd** that Jane should snub me.

This transforms into

> I // thought / that Jane should snub me / **odd,**

showing that *odd* is an object complement. This idiom is not especially common in English. This kind of construction should not be confused with such sentences as

> It is true that John was drafted,

which transforms into

> That John was drafted is true,

showing that *true* is a predicate adjective, not an object complement.

When an active-voice sentence with an object complement is transformed into the passive voice, the direct object becomes the subject and the object complement is retained. Examples:

> *Active voice*:
> The club appointed me **treasurer.**
> *Passive voice*:
> I was appointed **treasurer** (by the club).

> *Active voice*:
> We considered him **irresponsible.**
> *Passive voice*:
> He was considered **irresponsible** (by us).

In the passive-voice sentences, *treasurer* and *irresponsible* are **retained object complements,** not a direct object or a predicate adjective. The object complement cannot be made into a subject. For example,

*Treasurer was appointed me (by the club)

is ungrammatical. This test shows that *treasurer* remains an object complement in the passive-voice sentence, for a direct object can almost always be made the subject of a passive-voice sentence.

Humorous ambiguity can arise when an indirect and direct object are taken as a direct object and object complement. An old joke illustrates this grammatical ambiguity:

Straight man:
"Call me a taxi."
Jokester:
"O.K. You're a taxi."

The grammatical explanation is that in the first sentence *me* can be an indirect and *taxi* a direct object, or *me* can be a direct object and *taxi* an object complement. Context always prevents such ambiguity from actually occurring.

Predicate Nouns

The linking verbs—chiefly *be*, *seem*, *remain*, *get*, *become*, *continue*, *feel*, *appear*, *taste*, *smell*, *stay*, and *look*—take **subjective complements**, which are either predicate nouns or predicate adjectives. Some linking verbs will take only predicate adjectives and some both predicate adjectives and predicate nouns. A predicate noun renames the subject; it completes the verb so that the subject is identified as whatever the speaker has in mind. Here are examples:

Joe Louis // was / the **champion**.
The jaguar // remained / a **killer**.
The river // became / a **torrent**.

Regardless of which linking verb is used, a form of *to be* can always be substituted for it with a retention of the basic meaning; for example, *the river* **was** *a torrent*. This test shows that the meaning of *to be* is contained in the linking verb. *To be* is by far the linking verb with the highest rate of occurrence.

Pronouns and noun substitutes can function as predicate nominals. Also endocentric noun phrases and noun clauses can function as predicate nouns or nominals. Examples:

Ernest Hemingway // was once / **the most popular author of stories celebrating the virtues of manly courage, virility, and stoic endurance in the face of adversity.**

As an old man Hans Reichenbach // remained / **what he had been in his youth**.

In the first sentence *author* is the simple predicate noun, but the entire boldface phrase is the full complement. In sentence two the predicate nominal is a noun clause, a rather common usage.

Very frequently with some of the linking verbs the infinitive *to be* is used with a predicate noun. Examples:

He // appeared / to be a clergyman.
She // continued / to be a flirt.
They // seemed / to be friends.

Undoubtedly *clergyman*, *flirt*, and *friends* are predicate nouns, for they rename the subjects. *To be* might be considered an expletive in these constructions, since it can be omitted and since it cannot be used with such linking verbs as *remain*, *become*, and *stay*. *To be* is also redundant since its meaning is contained in the linking verb. An alternate grammatical analysis is to call the whole infinitive phrase a predicate nominal. A more complicated structure of this sort is

He seemed to be considered a giant.

The whole infinitive phrase is a predicate nominal (telling what he seemed). The infinitive phrase itself is in the passive voice, and *giant* is actually a retained object complement, for the transformation is

Someone // considered / him / a giant,

in which *giant* is clearly the object complement.

Predicate Adjectives

The second kind of subjective complement taken by linking verbs is the predicate adjective, which appears in the predicate but modifies the subject. Here are some typical examples:

Jerome // was / **happy**.
I // feel / **bad**.
This ham // tastes / **smoky**.
The teacher // remained / **calm**.

Sentence two illustrates a point in usage. Most educated Americans now seem to *feel badly*; this construction, *badly* being an adverb, is a technical error in the meaning usually intended. But since custom determines usage, the erroneous construction must now be accepted.

A number of predicate adjectives, such as *necessary*, *true*, *easy*, and *hard*, may appear before the subject when the expletive *it* stands for the subject. Examples:

> It is **true** that the Chinese invented printing.
> It seemed **hard** for me to learn Sanskrit.

The transformations are

> That the Chinese invented printing // is / **true**

and

> For me to learn Sanskrit // seemed / **hard**,

showing that *true* and *hard* are predicate adjectives.

Prepositional phrases can function with some linking verbs as predicate adjectives or adjectivals. Examples:

> This suit // is / **of the finest material.**
> Jane // seemed / **in a happy mood.**
> Old Forester // remained / **of topmost quality.**

Only when such a prepositional phrase modifies the subject is it a predicate adjective. For example, in

> Dorman // is / in the bar

in the bar is an adverbial complement (see next section), for it does not modify *Dorman*.

When used with a form of *to be*, some *ed* words are verbs (past participles) and some are predicate adjectives (adjectives by form), and it is not always easy to tell which is which. If the *ed* word is a past participle, then the form of *to be* is an auxiliary. If the *ed* word is an adjective, then the form of *to be* is the main, linking verb. Examples:

> I am **tired.**
> She is **interested.**
> He was **confused.**
> He was **bullied.**
> The pie was **baked.**
> The suit was **cleaned.**

There are two tests which usually will distinguish the verb from the predicate adjective. First, if the *ed* word can be modified by *very* it is usually a predicate adjective; if not, it is usually a verb: *very tired* but not *very bullied*. Second, if the sentence can be transformed into the active voice, the *ed* form is a verb in a passive-voice sentence: *someone bullied him*. If the sentence cannot be so transformed, the *ed* form is usually a predicate adjective: *someone tired me* does not appear to be the meaning of the first sentence above. These tests are mostly reliable but in a few cases do not work. For example, in

> I am excited

excited would appear to be a predicate adjective since *very* can modify it. But also the sentence will transform into the active-voice form

> Someone excited me,

which might indicate that *excited* is a verb. The analysis would really depend on the meaning of *excited* (whether one became excited by himself or not). Also *engaged* in

> I am engaged

is certainly a predicate adjective, but it cannot be modified by *very* (because it is an absolute superlative which cannot be compared). But for the most part, verbs can be distinguished from predicate adjectives when they follow *to be*. Usually one can tell whether the *ed* form modifies the subject or not. Of the six examples in the group above, the first three have predicate adjectives and the last three past participles.

Some of the linking verbs may also function as intransitive verbs, and then they take adverbial modifiers instead of predicate adjectives. Examples:

> *Linking verb*:
> John looked curious.
> *Intransitive verb*:
> John looked curiously (at the exhibition).
>
> *Linking verb*:
> Susan appeared subdued.
> *Intransitive verb*:
> Susan appeared promptly.

Curious and *subdued* are predicate adjectives; *curiously* and *promptly* are adverbial modifiers. Usually when a verb will function as either linking or intransitive, different meanings are denoted. For example, in the *looked* sentences above the linking verb means "had the appearance of" and the intransitive verb means "glanced" or "used his eyes."

This dual function of some verbs in some cases makes for statements of identical meaning, whether a predicate adjective or adverbial modifier is used. In such cases the verbs have the same meaning whether they are used as linking or intransitive. Examples:

> He stood rigid.
> He stood rigidly.

> She acted strange.
> She acted strangely.
>
> They played fair.
> They played fairly.

Not many verbs will function in this dual capacity.

A few verbs that are normally intransitive can in special constructions be linking verbs and take predicate adjectives. Examples:

> The well ran **dry**.
> The dog went **mad**.
> John proved **reliable**.

The boldface words are predicate adjectives modifying the subjects; thus *dry well*, *mad dog*, *reliable John*. *Run*, *go*, and *prove* are rarely used as linking verbs but are in these constructions.

The infinitive *to be* frequently accompanies a predicate adjective. Examples:

> He seems to be intelligent.
> She appeared to be angry.
> I continued to be cooperative.

This construction seems to be the natural idiom in such sentences as these, but some linking verbs will not take *to be* at all. For example,

> *I remained to be cooperative

is not grammatical, whereas *I remained cooperative* is grammatical. When *to be* does appear in such constructions, it can be called an expletive (actually the linking verb contains its meaning so that *to be* is redundant) or it can be considered a part of the predicate-adjective structure.

Adverbial Complements

Very few grammarians have recognized the existence of adverbial complements. Traditionally, all adverbials have been considered modifiers. But that some adverbials complement rather than modify verbs cannot be questioned. As will be mentioned in Chapter 9, one of the common sentence patterns in English is

N + Be + Adv,

and in that pattern the **Adv** is undoubtedly a complement. Here are some examples:

The cat is **outside**.
The dance is **tonight**.
The book is **over there**.
The cook is **in the kitchen**.
He is **where he wants to be**.

All of these boldface constructions are adverbial complements, which may be single adverbials, prepositional phrases, or adverb clauses. These constructions are complements rather than modifiers because the predication is manifestly incomplete without them. *The cat is* is simply not a complete predication unless *is* means *exists*. When used with an adverbial complement, *to be* means something like "occur" or "be located," quite a different meaning from its use as a linking verb, in which use it is little more than an equals mark.

Whether other verbs can take adverbial complements is a moot question. For example, in

He goes **where his wife drives him**,

does the adverb clause modify or complement *goes*? *He goes* can be a complete predication, but it sounds incomplete, and perhaps the clause is a complement. Deciding which analysis is correct is complicated by the fact that a modifier, as well as a complement, can be mandatory. For example, in

They are lovers of art,

the prepositional phrase *of art* is a mandatory modifier (to preclude a completely different meaning). So probably the mandatory adverb clause in the *goes* sentence above is a modifier rather than a complement. The problem probably cannot be solved to every grammarian's satisfaction.

Our analysis will be that *to be* is the only verb that takes an adverbial complement. (*To be*, after all, is a very special case as a verb.) Adverbials with other verbs we will call modifiers. For example in

Johnny is **in the tree**,

we will call *in the tree* an adverbial complement. But in

Johnny played **in the tree**,

we will call *in the tree* an adverbial modifier of the verb *played*. This is a reasonable analysis, though not one that every grammarian will agree with.

Complements of the Adjective

Another kind of complement overlooked by most grammarians is the **complement of the adjective**. Usually it completes meaning initiated in a predicate adjective and thus helps form the third kind of sentence that has a double complement. It may, however, appear with adjectives in other positions, and occasionally it appears with an adjective object complement, making a sentence with three complements for one verb. Not many adjectives can take a complement. All such complements should be called nominals by function.

The complement of the adjective with the highest rate of occurrence is the noun clause. Examples:

> I // am / sure / **that you will succeed.**
> I // wasn't / aware / **that he had died.**
> They // are / undecided / **whether they will come.**
> Happy / **that John had proposed**, Miss Bildt began planning her trousseau.
> Jerry, aware / **that he had been rude,** formulated an apology.
> I // made / him / happy / **that he did not resign.**

Each of these noun clauses completes the meaning initiated in the adjectives *sure, aware*, and so on. Most grammarians have called such clauses adverbials on the grounds that they modify adjectives, but beyond doubt they are complements instead—they have no characteristics of adverbials. Note that the last sentence has a direct object (*him*), an adjective object complement (*happy*), and a complement of the adjective—three complements in a row. This sentence pattern is not common.

Infinitive phrases also frequently complement adjectives. Examples:

> Jack // appears / eager / **to see her.**
> He // was // content / **to be a plumber.**
> Glad / **to be useful**, Pam busied herself with household chores.
> I // made / Rollo / happy / **to leave early**.

These complements have no adverbial characteristics either. Usually when an infinitive functions as an adverbial, *in order* can be placed in front of it (for example, *waiting (in order) to see if she would speak* ...). Thus the above infinitives must be complements. They should not, however, be confused with the infinitive as a subject. For example, the sentence

> It is possible to go to Vancouver by water

has a predicate adjective (*possible*) and an infinitive phrase following it, but the transformation is

> To go to Vancouver by water is possible,

showing that the infinitive phrase is a subject, not a complement.

In one construction a noun or noun phrase can function as a complement of the adjective. Examples:

> This pamphlet // is / worth / a **dollar.**
> You // are not / worth / my **time.**
> Not worth / **all the effort we had put into the task**, our results were disappointing.

In the last example, the headword *effort* is the simple complement within the full complement. *Worth* seems to be the only adjective that will take a noun or noun phrase as a complement.

Prepositional phrases may be said to function as complements of the adjective. Examples:

> He // is / similar / **to his father.**
> I // am / sick / **of your vain bibble-babble.**
> He // remained / silly / **in the extreme.**

It is probably sounder analysis to call such phrases complements rather than modifiers, but not all grammarians would agree.

Not only complements but also adverbial modifiers can follow predicate adjectives. Examples:

> She was happy when he came.
> He became sick in the barroom.

The best test to differentiate complements from modifiers in such sentences is to see that the adverbials, but not the complements, can be shifted. Examples:

> When he came, she was happy.
> In the barroom he became sick.

But not

> *A dollar this pamphlet is worth

or

> *In the extreme he remained silly.

But this test leaves some apparent prepositional-phrase complements of the adjective in limbo, for

> Of your vain bibble-babble I am sick

is possible, though not convincing, word order. Prepositional-phrase complements of the adjective are likely to cause controversy for some time to come.

Internal Complements of the Verbal

As has already been demonstrated throughout this text, nonfinite verb forms—that is, various forms of present and past participles and infinitives—can function as subjects, complements, and modifiers, and also as the verbs of absolute phrases. In any of these functions the nonfinite verb may take a complement or complements. Often a verbal-phrase complement has within it a complement. Such a complement is known as the **internal complement of the verbal**, to differentiate it from the complement of a finite verb. But there is no difference in the complementation. It represents the same grammatical function whether it occurs with finite or nonfinite verbs. Following are examples. Direct objects:

> Planning a **party** is usually fun.
> I wanted to shoot a **bear**.

Retained direct object:

> John having been given a **car**, his brother Terry was jealous.

Indirect objects:

> She tried to give **him** a kiss.
> Buying **her** a mink coat didn't serve its purpose.

Retained indirect object:

> A car having been given **John**, his brother Terry was jealous.

Noun object complements:

> Having elected Harry **president**, the club adjourned.
> We promised to appoint Susan **treasurer**.

Retained noun object complement:

> Sally having been elected **secretary**, the older club members sighed with relief.

Adjective object complements:

> Making my wife **happy** is my aim.
> He didn't seem to consider her **beautiful**.

Retained adjective object complement:

His wife having been made **happy**, Andy went to the pub.

Predicate nouns:

Being a **coward**, Flourney ran home.
He wanted to remain **chairman**.

Predicate adjectives:

Staying **calm**, Joe controlled the mob.
He tried to appear **sober**.

Adverbial complements:

Being **outside**, Freddie didn't hear his mother.
Jess wants to be **in the band**.

Complements of the adjective:

Being happy **that he had studied**, Greg beamed at the professor.
He wanted to be sure **to pass the exam**.

Our second great grammatical function is almost as common with non-finite verb forms as it is with regular sentence verbs.

EXERCISES

1. In the following sentences, all complements are distinguished from other portions of the sentence by *italic* type and complements within complements by underlining in addition. The underlining isolates the latter from the word-group complements within which they occur. Your task is to identify by name all complements in these sentences. Some of them are retained objects.

    a. Abandoning *tradition* will cause *society to corrupt <u>itself</u>*.
    b. To elect a socialist *president* is the *aim* of the Whig Party.
    c. We are <u>*certain*</u> *that the polls will be 99 percent <u>accurate</u>*.
    d. The President gave one *reporter* an advance *copy* of his speech.
    e. The candidate receiving the largest *number* of votes will be declared the *winner* even if he doesn't receive a *majority*.
    f. Gold is *where you find <u>it</u>*.
    g. To rest *easy* is the *desire* of every crowned head.
    h. The chairman appointed *Fred* the *sergeant-at-arms*.
    i. We observed a *hippie* strewing *flowers* in the path of the magistrate.
    j. We were given a complimentary *pass* by the owner of the theater.

k. Glad of *his hard renown*, Aaron cast *slurs* on those who would pity *him*.
l. He wants *to be where he will be happy*.
m. To be chosen *queen* was her fondest *desire*.
n. Remaining *closeted* for an hour *with a producer* caused *her to lose her audience*.
o. He considered *her clever* enough *to win an Oscar*.
p. John Doe having been elected *vice-president*, the radical wing burned the *flag*.
q. A book was given *me* by my aunt.
r. I am *sure that she meant to be kind*.
s. I was given a *record* by my uncle.
t. I found *him glad to be of service*.
u. I made *him feel lucky to be alive*.
v. Making *John happy to stay overnight* made Shirley *happy*.
w. Remaining *steadfast in his purpose*, Corey recouped his *fortune*.
x. She is *where Saturn tends the years*.
y. Mary wanted *John to go home*.
z. We heard *the baby crying for its milk*.
aa. The baby was heard *crying for its milk*.
bb. The convict was seen *escaping*.
cc. The guard saw *the convict escaping*.
dd. Johnny was found *eating cheesecake*.

2. Here are two paragraphs chosen at random. Identify and name all complements in the paragraphs.

I was coming home from school, carrying my books by a strap, when I passed Gavin's poolroom and saw the big guys hanging around. They were standing in front near the windows, looking across the street. Gavin's has a kind of thick window curtain up to eye level, so all I saw was their heads. The guys were looking at Mrs. Oliver, who lately has started to get talked about. Standing in her window across the street, Mrs. Oliver was doing her nails. Her nice red hair was hanging loose down her back. She certainly is a nice-looking woman. She comes to my father's newspaper stand on the corner and buys five or six movie magazines a week, also the afternoon papers. Once she felt me under the chin, and laughed. My father laughed, too, stamping about in his old worn leather jacket to keep warm. My old man stamps a lot because he has leg pains and he's always complaining about a heavy cold in his head. [Albert Halper, *Prelude*]

No less revolutionary is the development of electronics, a field of research so new that the current meaning of the word has not yet reached the main body of all the standard dictionaries. New computers capable of combining thousands of separate items in a single formula, or solving mathematical equations that are beyond the control, or even the grasp, of the human mind, or directing the most complicated and delicate machines in the most complicated and delicate processes—these promise to extend the mental power of man as steam and electricity extended his physical power in the past. And already on the horizon—it is an alarming prospect—are computing machines that not only work on the material fed into them, but "think" for themselves, on subjects formulated for them. So far, happily, no machine has learned to think independently. [Henry Steele Commager, "A Quarter Century: Its Advances"]

BASIC SENTENCE PATTERNS

Variations on a Theme

We have been talking a great deal about sentences in the past eight chapters, and now it is time to give an orderly presentation of the basic sentence types in English. But before we present the concept of the limited number of basic sentence patterns, we should consider defining the term **sentence**. We have made no attempt so far to define the term, for anyone reading this book undoubtedly has "sentence sense" enough to recognize a sentence and does not need a definition. Yet common terms should be definable. Paradoxically, though, it seems that the more common the term, the harder it is to define. And *sentence* is certainly hard to define. One linguist claimed that he catalogued 123 different definitions of *sentence* and that none of them satisfied even a majority of linguists, much less all of them.

The common definition of the term given in school grammars is that "a sentence is a group of words expressing a complete thought." But this definition is not wholly satisfactory, for the word *complete* is not defined either in regard to grammar or to "thought." A school child who doesn't have sentence sense will not be helped by this definition. It would exclude, for example, the construction

He thought they could.

This construction would undoubtedly be accepted by those having sentence sense as a sentence, as an expression to begin with a capital

213

letter and to end with a period, but there is no complete thought to it. Neither *he* nor *they* nor *could* is meaningful without reference to preceding "thoughts." This same construction demonstrates the insufficiency of the definition that "a sentence is a group of words that contains a subject and predicate and that can stand alone." This definition is close to being satisfactory, but the "stand alone" excludes sentences that need reference to preceding sentences; and the stipulation of a subject excludes the imperative sentence, which has no subject.

Many linguists think that a proper definition of *sentence* should take in all meaningful human utterances regardless of whether they have subjects or predicates. From this approach the great Danish grammarian Otto Jespersen defined the term in this way: "A sentence is a (relatively) complete and independent human utterance—the completeness and independence being shown by its standing alone or its capability of standing alone, *i.e.*, of being uttered by itself."[1] But again, "complete" and "independent," not being clearly defined, leave unclear the matter of needed reference to past utterances. For example, can *I think so* be uttered completely by itself with meaning? Or why should *it could* be accepted as a sentence and *it being* not be accepted? Also "relatively" in this definition is not clear. But Jespersen's definition does allow such utterances as *good old Sam*, *just barely*, *nice day*, or *yes indeed* to be called sentences, as linguists prefer. But **meaningful utterances** might be a better term for these latter, saving *sentence* to refer to constructions that have subjects and predicates or that are request sentences.

For the study of grammar, then, and for teaching students, we need to talk about constructions that people with sentence sense recognize as sentences, and we need to talk about subjects, verbs, complements, and modifiers. We can get along without a definition, for most people perceive and agree on the grammatical completeness of the constructions we know as sentences. But a definition is a challenge. Here is a try at one: "A sentence is either (1) a group of words with a subject, which may or may not have pronominal or other reference to a previous utterance, and a predicate which (a) has either a finite verb form or a verbal auxiliary which carries full meaning through reference to a preceding utterance and (b) perhaps a complement, which may or may not have pronominal or other reference to a previous utterance; or (2) a verb-stem form, with or without complements, which issues a request. Any part of either of these two sentence types may have modifiers. A group of words with a subject and predicate is not a sentence if the verb form is nonfinite or if the construction is introduced

[1] *Philosophy of Grammar*, p. 307.

by a connective that subordinates it to another construction." To complete the definition, both finite and nonfinite verb forms and subordinating connectives would have to be defined and illustrated, as we have already done. True, this definition is somewhat unwieldy, but nothing less than this can define *sentence* as the term is used in grammar texts. Fortunately, however, most people early develop sentence sense so that the term *sentence* can be used meaningfully without definition.

Now back to our concern with basic sentence types. Though we have illustrated some of the various sentence types in English in discussing subjects, finite verbs, and complements, it will be rewarding to catalogue all the basic patterns here in order to reinforce what we have already learned and to provide an orderly scheme for reference. Also it will be valuable to give symbolic notations for sentence patterns.

The number of possible sentences in English is infinite. Always another modifier could be added to any sentence, no matter how long. But within this infinity only a dozen basic patterns reside. Thus every sentence, except a bare, kernel sentence, is a **variation on a theme**. The kernel sentence is the theme itself. We will present these themes here and give you practice in analyzing real sentences to see what the theme is. We will work with independent clauses (that is, with sentences) only, but every dependent clause also exhibits one of these themes. Fragmentary utterances, which linguists like to call sentences, are also based on these patterns if the understood part of the utterance is supplied. For example, the common utterance

> nice day

presupposes the construction

> It is a nice day,

which is a basic sentence pattern in English.

Pattern 1: N + V-In + (Adv)

> The girl // smiled (sweetly).
> The rich // (often) succeed (in their endeavors).
> Many // fail (miserably).
> Reading novels // satisfies.

The N of our notation stands for **nominal**, that is, for any noun or other form-class or structure-class word or word group functioning as a noun. The **V-In** stands for **intransitive verb** (no direct object), and the **Adv** stands for **adverbial**, with the parentheses indicating that it is optional in this pattern.

This kind of sentence breaks naturally into two parts: the subject with its modifiers (if any) and the verb with its modifiers (if any). No matter how extensive this sentence pattern becomes, it still divides into these two basic parts. Here is a normal sentence which follows this basic pattern:

> The ignorant **student** who said Pluto was a Greek philosopher //
> **talked** foolishly about the theory of forms.

The basic pattern is in boldface. The other constructions in the sentence are modifiers.

In the four example sentences at the beginning of this section, a noun (*girl*), an adjective (*rich*), a structure word or noun substitute (*many*), and a present-participial phrase (*reading novels*) are functioning as subjects. But only very rarely does a present participle or an infinitive serve as the subject in this sentence pattern. For the most part, only a noun or noun substitute does. But if a participial or infinitive phrase does serve as a subject (or complement) in *any* sentence pattern, the whole phrase, not a part of it, is the subject (or complement) and thus helps make a kernel or basic sentence. This fact will be illustrated in other patterns.

Some verbs are nearly always intransitive—*smile* and *talk*, for example—and they must function nearly always in this pattern (or a passive-voice variation thereof). Many other verbs, however, can readily function either transitively or intransitively, and the two patterns formed with them should not be confused. For example,

> He // banged (noisily)

and

> He // banged / the drum

are two different patterns, the second belonging to pattern 3 below. You can test for the difference. If you can substitute *him*, *her*, *it*, or *them* for the final word, you have a pattern 3 sentence. Otherwise you have pattern 1. The difference is between an adverbial modifier and a direct object.

As was explained in Chapter 8, it is an open question as to whether an adverbial following an intransitive verb can be a complement or whether it is always a modifier. For example, the adverbial in

> Someone // slept (in this bed)
> Someone // slept / in this bed

may be a modifier or an adverbial complement. If the latter analysis is correct, then we really should list a separate sentence pattern. But, as stated, we will take the traditional view that the adverbial (except after *to be*) is a modifier. This view seems reasonable and avoids a great deal of sticky grammatical analysis.

Many pattern 1 sentences with a prepositional phrase following the intransitive verb can be transformed into the passive voice. In this case the pattern transforms from

Active voice:
N¹ + V-In + (prep + N²),

which is a pattern 1 sentence, into

Passive voice:
N² + Be + V-In + prep + (by + N¹),

which is a variation of pattern 1. The superscripts on **N¹** and **N²** mean that the nominals have different referents. The sentences themselves are like these:

Active voice:
Someone slept in this bed.
Passive voice:
This bed has been slept in (by someone).

Active voice:
Mischa laughed at me.
Passive voice:
I was laughed at (by Mischa).

The passive-voice sentences represent a variation on the pattern 1 theme. The auxiliary **has** in the first passive sentence is a part of **V-In** even though it comes before **Be.**[2]

The *by* phrase is often suppressed in a passive-voice sentence. This option is indicated by the parentheses in the pattern notation and in the examples.

Pattern 2: N + Be + Adv

Mother // is / inside.
The bear // was / in the tree.
He // was / where the police put him.

---

[2]The half-active-half-passive-voice transformation with *have* has been discussed fully on pages 184–186. It will not be repeated in this chapter on basic sentence patterns. To refresh your memory, however, here is one repetition of that pattern: *Active voice: Someone threw a kiss at Susan. Passive voice: A kiss was thrown at Susan (by someone). Half-active-half-passive-voice with* have: *Susan had a kiss thrown at her (by someone).* For other examples and symbolic notations of this kind of passive-voice sentence, refer to the pages mentioned above.

This sentence pattern is of course similar to pattern 1, except that in pattern 2 the **Adv** is demanded; but *to be* is a special case as a verb in this pattern and unquestionably takes an adverbial complement, as was explained in Chapter 8. In this pattern *to be* means "occur" or "be located" or some such meaning. *Mother is* is simply not a complete predication with this meaning of *to be*; the adverbial is needed to complement *is*, not to modify it. Only adverbials of time and place, prepositional phrases, and adverb clauses can function as adverbial complements in this pattern. An *ly* adverb by itself cannot complement **Be** in this pattern. For example, **he was courageously* and **it is indefinitely* are not grammatical. True, such a sentence as

> It is completely

might be uttered, but the *completely* would be referring to—actually modifying—a word from the previous utterance. The verb *to be* can be modified, even with an *ly* adverb, when the form of *to be* has a complement. Examples:

> Debbie **certainly** is a character.
> That man is **probably** in trouble.

In this modification the *ly* adverb can precede or follow a form of *to be*. But in the kernel sentences at the head of this section, *to be* is being complemented by adverbials, not being modified.

This sentence pattern breaks naturally into two parts: subject and predicate. And the predicate breaks into two parts: verb and complement. The slashes show these divisions. Even when a prepositional phrase or adverb clause is used as the complement in this pattern, the result is still a kernel or basic sentence, since nothing can be left out of it. The sentence with the adverb clause is complex, but it is still a basic sentence. Here is a normal sentence using this pattern:

> The old farmer's unused 1920 **Model T Ford** // **is** / **in his hayloft**
> above the remains of three others that he wore out.

The boldface constructions show the kernel sentence within the long sentence.

Pattern 3: N¹ + V-Tr + N²

> The student // read / his lesson.
> Making good grades // requires / studying hard.
> To finish the race // demands / stamina.
> He // tramples / whoever opposes him.

He // wants / me to drive.
He // found / me studying Latin.

The N^1 and N^2 are nominals of different referents. **V-Tr** stands for **transitive verb**, one that has a direct object; N^2 is the direct object. This pattern breaks naturally into two parts: subject and predicate. And the predicate breaks naturally into two parts: the verb and its complement. Even those sentences with word-group subjects and objects are basic or kernel sentences, since nothing can be left out of them. In the last two examples, an infinitive and a present participle with a subject are functioning as N^2, the direct object—what he wants and what he found. Here is a normal sentence with this basic pattern of subject-verb-direct object:

The enraged **postman** who had been bitten severely by the dog //
threw / a **rock** at it as it disappeared around the house.

The boldface words form the basic pattern, and the remaining constituents are modifiers.

This pattern 3 sentence transforms into the passive voice with this pattern:

$N^2 + Be + V\text{-}Tr + (by + N^1)$
The lesson // was read by the student.

The passive sentence of this type breaks naturally into two parts, since the *by* phrase is a modifier, not a complement. Even when the *by* phrase is lacking (*The lesson was read.*), the passive verb is still transitive, and the subject may be said to be its displaced object.

Sometimes it appears that a *from* or *in* phrase rather than a *by* phrase can be used in a passive-voice sentence. Examples:

Active voice:
The shape of the head // can foretell / events.
Passive voice:
Events // can be foretold **from** the shape of the head.

Active voice:
This course // requires / a term paper.
Passive voice:
A term paper // is required **in** this course.

Actually, however, these passive-voice sentences are not faithful transformations of those in the active voice. The doers of the action in the active-voice sentences are *the shape of the head* and *this course*; the doers of the action in the passive-voice sentences are others not specified—they might be supplied:

> Events can be foretold from the shape of the head (by a phrenologist).
> A term paper is required in this course (by the professor).

But the true and faithful transformations are:

> Events // can be foretold **by** the shape of the head.
> A term paper // is required **by** this course.

And these sentences must have the **by** phrase.

When a pattern 3 sentence has an infinitive or participial phrase as its subject, it will not transform into the passive voice with a normal *by* phrase taking the subject of the active-voice sentence as its object. For example:

> *Active voice:*
> Getting a divorce // requires / a lawyer.
> *Passive voice:*
> *A lawyer // is required by getting a divorce.

> *Active voice:*
> To earn a Ph.D. degree // demands / stamina.
> *Passive voice:*
> *Stamina // is demanded by to earn a Ph.D. degree.

Other transformations are required to make grammatical passive-voice sentences in such cases. Examples:

> *Passive voice:*
> A lawyer is required (by someone) for getting a divorce.
> *Passive voice:*
> Stamina is demanded (for anyone) for earning a Ph.D. degree.

These passive-voice transformations are grammatically quite complex.

If the subject of a pattern 3 sentence is a noun and the direct object is an infinitive or participial phrase without a subject, then the sentence will transform into the passive voice. Example:

> *Active voice:*
> This course // requires / studying two hours a day.
> *Passive voice:*
> Studying two hours a day // is required by this course.

The passive sentence is awkward but nevertheless grammatical.

If the infinitive- or participial-phrase direct object in a pattern 3 sentence has a subject of its own, the normal passive transformation is impossible. Example:

> *Active voice:*
> He // found / me studying Latin.
> *Passive voice:*
> *Me studying Latin // was found by him.

To be grammatical, the passive transformation must be

> I was found studying Latin (by him).

The grammar of this passive-voice transformation is also quite complex.

When the subject or direct object of a pattern 3 sentence is a noun clause that denotes a person, the passive transformation is possible. Example:

> *Active voice:*
> He // tramples / whoever opposes him.
> *Passive voice:*
> Whoever opposes him // is trampled (by him).

The passive sentence is fully grammatical.

Naturally when an original sentence is the passive-voice variation of a pattern 3 sentence, it will transform into the active voice as the normal pattern 3 sentence. For example, the passive-voice sentence

> The succulent peaches on our backyard trees // were eaten by several
> dozen blackbirds

might appear in anybody's friendly letter. It will transform into

> Several dozen **blackbirds** // **ate** / the succulent **peaches** on our
> backyard trees,

which is a normal active-voice pattern 3 sentence.

Pattern 4: $N^1 + V\text{-}Tr + N^2 + N^3$

> My mother // bought / me / a car.
> Playing football // gave / me / what I desired.
> Our minister // gave / drinking liquor / a hard time.
> Sherry // gave / whoever came to the meeting / a booklet.

This is the subject-verb-indirect object-direct object pattern. The verb is transitive, and all three nominals have different referents. The sentence as a whole breaks into its two parts and the predicate in turn breaks into three parts, since the verb has two complements. In this pattern the nominals are almost always nouns or pronouns, though word groups can function as subjects and indirect objects, and noun clauses can function as direct objects, as the last three examples illustrate. Apparently, infinitive and participial phrases almost never function as direct objects in pattern 4 sentences. Here is a normal sentence with this basic pattern:

> The old **gentleman** on crutches // gratefully **gave** / the first redcap **porter** on the scene / a **tip** that made his day.

The boldface words illustrate pattern 4. The verbs that will function in this pattern are few in number, the chief ones being listed on page 195. This pattern, however, is of high frequency in our language.

This pattern 4 sentence will usually transform into a pattern 3 sentence with the indirect object becoming the object of the preposition *to* or *for*. Examples:

> My mother // bought / a car for me.
> Sherry // gave / a booklet to whoever came to the meeting.

Now the basic structure is subject-verb-direct object (pattern 3), and the prepositional phrases are modifying the verbs. When the indirect or direct object of this pattern is a word group, the transformation with a *to* or *for* phrase may be quite awkward, as it would be in sentences two and three at the head of this section. However, word groups are not often used in pattern 4 sentences.

The construction

> Tom // wanted / me to date Jane

should not be confused with the pattern 4 sentence, for the whole infinitive phrase *me to date Jane* (which has both a subject and a direct object) is the direct object of *wanted*, making a pattern 3 sentence. *Me* is not an indirect object here, for an indirect object is always the person or thing to or for whom something is done (except for the very rare cases in which a participial phrase functions as an indirect object). Note that the normal pattern 4 transformation

> *Tom // wanted / to date Jane for me

is ungrammatical, or at least different in meaning. And if *for me* is placed in front of the infinitive, the *for* is an expletive. The original sentence is definitely pattern 3, not pattern 4.

Pattern 4 sentences will transform into two kinds of passive-voice sentences, with either the indirect or direct object becoming the subject of the passive sentence. Examples:

    $N^2 + Be + V\text{-}Tr + N^3 + (by + N^1)$
    I // was bought / a car (by my mother).

    $N^3 + Be + V\text{-}Tr + N^2 + (by + N^1)$
    A car // was bought / me (by my mother).

In these passive-voice transformations of pattern 4, either the direct or indirect object becomes the **retained object** while the other is the subject. The *by* phrase (often suppressed) modifies the verb. Though grammatical, these passive-voice variations on a theme might not be stylistically desirable.

Pattern 5: $N^1 + V\text{-}Tr + N^2 + N^2$

    We // elected / Harry / president.
    The police // considered / Morretti / to be a thief.
    They // chose / helping the poor / as their project.
    She // made / her husband / what she wanted him to be.

This is the subject-verb-direct object-(noun)-object complement pattern, the two nominal complements having the same referent. The expletives *as* and *to be* can precede the object complement, as in sentences two and three. Usually the three nominals in this pattern are nouns, but they can be word groups, as in sentences three (participial phrase) and four (noun clause). The verbs that can function in this pattern are few in number, the chief ones being listed on page 197. However, this sentence pattern is of rather high frequency in English. Here is a normal sentence based on this pattern:

    The badly shaken and disappointed **Dean** // quickly **appointed** /
        Professor Roberts / the **chairman** of the new Basic Studies
        program.

The predicate of this pattern falls into three parts because of the two complements.

Since it has a direct object, a pattern 5 sentence will transform into the passive voice. The symbolic notation is this:

    $N^2 + Be + V\text{-}Tr + N^2 + (by + N^1)$
    Harry // was elected / president (by us).

In this transformation only the direct object (even if it is a participial phrase), not the object complement, may become the subject of the passive-voice sentence. For example, the construction

    *President was elected Harry by us

is ungrammatical. In the grammatical passive sentence the object complement is retained; it does not become a direct object or a predicate noun. The verb, however, is still transitive, with its displaced direct object as its subject.

Pattern 6: N¹ + V-Tr + N² + Adj

> The beauty shop // made / Susan / beautiful.
> We // consider / helping the poor / praiseworthy.
> They // proved / what he did / culpable.

This pattern is the same as pattern 5 except that the object complement is an adjective instead of a noun. The adjective object complement describes N^2, the direct object. Strictly speaking, however, the adjective does not modify that nominal, but complements it. The nominals in this pattern are usually nouns, though the direct object can be a word group, as sentences two (participial phrase) and three (noun clause) illustrate. Because of the nature of the few verbs which can function in this pattern (see page 197), the sentence subject is usually a noun or pronoun, though such a word group as *playing football* can serve as the subject of the verbs *make* and *prove* when they have a direct object and an adjective object complement. For example,

> Playing football // made / Harry / strong

is a common type of sentence, a pattern 6. Here is a normal sentence of pattern 6:

> The new **testimony** turned up by the defense counsel // **proved** / the **defendant** / **innocent** of all the charges made against him by the district attorney.

As with pattern 5, the predicate of this pattern breaks into three parts. Pattern 6 will also transform into the passive voice:

> **N² + Be + V-Tr + Adj + (by + N¹)**
> Susan // was made / beautiful (by the beauty shop).

Beautiful is the retained object complement, not a predicate adjective. This is the only passive transformation possible with this pattern.

Pattern 7: N¹ + V-Tr + N² + Adj + N³

> John // made / Susan / happy / that she married him.
> Mary // considered / Bill / lucky / to be a teacher's son.
> The will // made / Ted / worth / a million dollars.

This sentence pattern is something of a curiosity, being the only sentence pattern in English with three complements for one verb: a direct object, an adjective object complement, and a complement of the adjective, in that sequence. It is not a commonly used pattern but is perfectly natural and occurs more frequently than one might think. In this pattern, N^3 must be a noun clause or infinitive phrase unless the adjective object complement is *worth*. A single noun will function in this position only with *worth*. The structure of the sentence is such that it seldom occurs in expanded form. It is a theme with few variations.

The pattern will transform into a passive-voice sentence:

N^2 + Be + V-Tr + Adj + N^3 + (by + N^1)
Susan // was made / happy / that she married John (by him).

Though grammatical, this passive transformation seldom occurs.

Pattern 8: N^1 + V-L + N^1

My sister // remained / an old maid.
The poor // may be / the chosen.
To be rich // is / to be envied.
Playing in the band // became / my passion.
He // appeared / (to be) what everyone had thought.

This pattern, one of the commonest in English, is made with a **linking verb**, one of a small group of verbs (see page 201) that contain the meaning of *to be* plus other denotations. *To be* is by far the most commonly used of all linking verbs. The superscripts on the nominals show that they have the same referent.

The second nominal is called a **predicate noun**, or **predicate nominal** if it is a word group. The generic term for it is **subjective complement**, which includes the predicate adjective of pattern 9. The linking verb joins the two nominals to show that they are the same. Word groups can function in either of the nominal positions, as the last three sentences illustrate. Also adjectives by form can function in both nominal positions, as sentence two illustrates. If an adjective in the second nominal position is accompanied by a determiner, it may be considered a predicate nominal. For example, in

Billy // was / the most courageous,

the most courageous is thought of as a nominal rather than an adjectival.

Sometimes *to be* may be used as an expletive with the second nominal, as in sentence five above; at times it seems to be required, as perhaps it is in sentence five. Here is a normal sentence based on pattern 8:

> The **student** who seemed to show the least promise // actually **became** / the **valedictorian** of his high-school graduating class.

No passive-voice transformation is possible with this pattern, since the linking verb does not express an action or have a direct object.

Sometimes a pattern 8 sentence has in the predicate-noun position an infinitive phrase which really does not rename the subject, as a predicate noun usually does. Here are some examples:

> Billy // seemed / **to show the most promise.**
> John // continued / **to have the greatest resistance.**
> Roy // appeared / **to look guilty.**

These infinitive phrases are nominals in the subjective-complement position and are therefore to be considered predicate nominals. Since the passive transformation is impossible with such sentences, they cannot be considered pattern 3 sentences with direct objects. For example,

> *To show the most promise was seemed by Billy

is ungrammatical. Hence the original sentence must be pattern 8. Such infinitive predicate nominals do not occur with the linking verb *to be*. In such a sentence as

> Henry is to show his prize calf,

the *is to* is an auxiliary and *show* is the main verb (see page 101).

Pattern 9: N + V-L + Adj

> Those flowers // look / fresh.
> Going in debt // is / possible.
> What he did // appeared / insane.
> Sarah // was / in the pink.
> George // seemed / like a good fellow.

This very common pattern, like pattern 8, uses a linking verb, and its subjective complement is a **predicate adjective** or **predicate adjectival**. Word groups, as in sentences two and three, can be used in the subject position, but the predicate adjectival is most often an adjective by form. A prepositional phrase may function as the predicate adjectival, as in sentences four and five. In those sentences *in the pink* modifies *Sarah* and *like a good fellow* modifies *George*. The predicate adjective or adjectival may be said to modify the subject, even though they are called complements.

Adjectives in the comparative degree may function in this pattern. Examples:

> This cloth // is / coarser (than yours).
> Henry // appears / (to be) better.

An adjective in the superlative degree in this position would take a determiner and would be a nominal, thus forming a pattern 8 sentence.

Sometimes the infinitive *to be* may accompany the predicate adjective, as in

> The policeman // seemed / to be calm.

In such a construction the *to be* can be considered an expletive, since it redundantly repeats meaning contained in the linking verb. Or the whole infinitive phrase can be called a predicate adjective. Here is a normal sentence based on pattern 9:

> The **crew** of the ship which had been at sea for six months //
> **became** / **sick** because of spoiled food.

Pattern 9 will not transform into the passive voice.

Pattern 10: N¹ + V-L + Adj + N²

> I // am / sure / that you will understand.
> Henry // seemed / happy / to be of service.
> Being cooperative // appeared / certain / to pay dividends.
> This material // feels / worth / a fortune.

This pattern is like pattern 9 except that its predicate adjective has itself a **complement of the adjective**. That complement is always a nominal; hence the N^2 of the symbolic notation. The N^2 is usually a noun clause or infinitive phrase, as in sentences one, two, and three, but it can be a noun when the predicate adjective is *worth*, as in sentence four. A word group can be the subject in this pattern, as sentence three illustrates. Only a limited number of adjectives can function in this pattern, chiefly *sure, certain, happy, worth, confident, sad, overwhelmed, surprised, overjoyed, upset,* and *concerned.* These will all follow such a linking verb as *seem* and will take complements of the adjective. Sentences of this pattern are not usually elaborated beyond the noun clauses and infinitive phrases that end them. (Pattern 10 should not be confused with pattern 12, which seems to have a similar structure but does not.)

Pattern 11: There + V-L + N-endo

There / is // no way to solve this problem.
There / were // several cases of fraud.
There / seem to be // several avenues of approach.

There are several **There** patterns but we will consider them all under pattern 11 since they all start with *there*, though all but this first one are really transformations of other basic patterns. In the above symbolic notation **There** is an expletive and **N-endo** stands for endocentric noun phrase, since a single noun seldom occurs in this pattern. One notable exception is

There is one God.

Other sentences of this sort do occur occasionally, but not often enough to change our **N-endo** symbol. The **N-endo** is the subject of the **There** sentence.

This pattern is not a transformation of any of the basic patterns discussed heretofore in this chapter, for an elimination of the expletive *there* does not produce normal English sentences. Transformation produces these sentences:

No way to solve this problem // is.
Several cases of fraud // were.
Several avenues of approach // seem to be.

Such sentences are not normal in English, and thus the above **There** pattern is a separate one by itself. *To be* is by far the linking verb most used in this **There** pattern, but other linking verbs, as *seem* in the third example, can occur in it. In the third sentence the *to be* is an expletive, for it redundantly repeats meaning already contained in *seem*. *Seem to be* is functioning as a unit. This is just an English idiom. All the other **There** patterns discussed below are transformations of basic sentence patterns illustrated earlier in this chapter.

Some authorities on usage have maintained that **There** sentences should be avoided, but the transformations in the preceding paragraph show that they can't be, for those transformations sound strange. **There** sentences of all sorts represent fully acceptable usage and need not be avoided.

Another **There** pattern is a transformation of pattern 1, which, you will remember, is **N + V-In + (Adv)**. The **There** pattern is

There + Be + N + V-In + Adv
There / were // two big dogs // lying / in the back of the room.
There / was // a policeman // staying / with the injured man.

A grammatical curiosity here is that a noun (which is the subject of the sentence) comes between the main verb and its auxiliary (*be*). This position occurs only in a **There** pattern. This **There** pattern is a transformation of pattern 1, except that the **Adv** is more or less demanded rather than optional. Reversion to pattern 1 brings

> Two big dogs // were lying in the back of the room.
> A policeman // was staying with the injured man.

As these reversions to pattern 1 show, this **There** pattern lends some credence to the grammatical analysis that says an intransitive verb can take either an adverbial modifier or an adverbial complement, but we will continue with the analysis explained on pages 205ff, since the adverbial prepositional phrases seem to modify rather than complement the intransitive verbs. The alternate analysis brings almost unsolvable grammatical problems.

Still another **There** pattern is a transformation of pattern 1. The difference is that it uses an intransitive verb without *be* as an auxiliary. Its pattern is

> **There + V-In + N + (Adv)**
> There / occurred // a strange event last night.
> There / came // a time for meditation.

N is of course the subject of the sentence. The **Adv** after **N**—such as *last night* in the first of the two sentences—is common, but sometimes the N itself is modified by an adjectival—such as *for meditation* in sentence two. Reversion to pattern 1 brings

> A strange event // occurred last night
> A time for meditation // came.

Though not common, such **There** sentences as these do occur, and they are not only grammatical but respectable.

Another **There** pattern is a transformation of pattern 2, which, you will remember, has **Be** as the main verb with an adverbial complement. The pattern is

> **There + Be + N + Adv**
> There / are // two students // on the Dean's List.
> There / was // a patrol car // at the top of the hill.

The N is the subject of the **There** sentence. The reversion to pattern 2 is as follows:

> Two students // are / on the Dean's List.
> A patrol car // was / at the top of the hill.

The prepositional phrases are adverbial complements of **Be**, since *to be* definitely takes a complement in this position (see page 205).

Another **There** pattern is a transformation of the passive-voice transformation of pattern 3. Pattern 3 is $N^1 + V\text{-}Tr + N^2$ and its passive-voice version is $N^2 + Be + V\text{-}Tr + (by + N^1)$. Only the passive-voice, not the active-voice, pattern 3 will transform into a **There** pattern. The pattern is

> **There + Be + N^2 + V-Tr + (by + N^1)**
> There / were // several spectators // hurt in the crash (by the cars).
> There / are // two term papers // required (by this course).

Here also a noun (the subject) comes between the main verb and its auxiliary (*be*). This noun must be N^2, since in the active-voice version of the sentence it is the direct object of the transitive verb. The *by* phrase with N^1 is usually suppressed in such **There** sentences. The **V-Tr** may have an adverbial modifier, such as *in the crash* in the first sentence. Reversion to pattern 3 can be stated in either the active or passive voice:

> *Active voice:*
> In the crash the cars // hurt / several spectators.
> *Passive voice:*
> Several spectators // were hurt in the crash (by the cars).

> *Active voice:*
> This course // requires / two term papers.
> *Passive voice:*
> Two term papers // are required (by this course).

In spite of the fact that these regular pattern 3 sentences are for the most part natural, the **There** transformation is common. Presumably it is common because speakers sometimes like to delay the emphatic parts of their utterances. These three different patterns with identical meanings illustrate the flexibility of English grammar.

Note that an attempt to transform an active-voice pattern 3 sentence into a **There** pattern, such as

> *There hurt several spectators in the crash the cars,

is wholly ungrammatical.

The passive-voice version of pattern 4 can also transform into a **There** pattern, but it very seldom does. The pattern is

> **There + Be + N^3 + N^2 + (by + N^1)**
> There / was // a car // bought / me (by my mother).

Though such a sentence is grammatical, it is not very useful to native speakers, who would instead use an active- or passive-voice version of pattern 4.

The passive-voice version of pattern 5 can also transform into a **There** pattern. The active-voice version of pattern 5 is N^1 + **V-Tr** + N^2 + N^2, and the passive-voice version is N^2 + **Be** + **V-Tr** + N^2 + (**by** + N^1). The **There** pattern is

> **There + Be + N^2 + V-Tr + N^2 + (by + N^1)**
> There / were // two players // designated / captains (by the team).
> There / was // a Black // chosen / as Homecoming Queen (by the students).

The first N^2 is the subject of the sentence and the second N^2 is the object complement. In the second sentence, *as* is an expletive. This pattern is rare in our usage, but still more common than the awkward **There** pattern in the preceding paragraph. The pattern can revert to pattern 5 in both the active and the passive voice:

> *Active voice:*
> The team // designated / two players / (as) captains.
> *Passive voice:*
> Two players // were designated / captains (by the team).

The active-voice version cannot transform into a **There** pattern.

Pattern 9, which is **N** + **V-L** + **Adj**, can transform into a **There** pattern, with or without a modifier of the **Adj**. The pattern is

> **There + V-L + N + Adj**
> There / was // a passenger // sick in the aisle.
> There / remained // one soldier // unaccounted for.
> There / happened to be // a fight // going on.

Both *unaccounted for* and *going on* are adjectivals coined from the verb-particle composites *to account for* and *to go on* (see Chapter 3). In the third sentence, *happened* is being used as a linking verb (a rare usage) and *to be* is just an expletive, redundantly repeating meaning already included in *happened*. Reversion to pattern 9 brings

> A passenger // was / sick in the aisle.
> One soldier // remained / unaccounted for.
> A fight // happened to be / going on.

Sick, *unaccounted for*, and *going on* are predicate adjectivals modifying the subjects. An alternate analysis is to consider *to be going on* an infinitive phrase functioning as a predicate adjectival. *To be* is by far the linking verb most used in this **There** pattern, as in the first sentence (*was*). This **There** pattern is not uncommon at all, for it is as natural as the pattern 9 sentence.

The similar pattern 10, which is $N^1 + V\text{-}L + Adj + N^2$, also transforms into a **There** pattern, which is

There + Be + N^1 + Adj + N^2
There / were // two students // happy / to come early.
There / was // one policeman // glad / that he was armed.

N^1 is the subject of the sentence and N^2 is the complement of the adjective, which is usually a noun clause or infinitive phrase. In this pattern *to be* is the only linking verb normally used. Reversion to pattern 10 brings

Two students // were / happy / to come early.
One policeman // was / glad / that he was armed.

This **There** pattern is rather common in our usage, considering the few adjectives that can function in the predicate-adjective position and also take a complement of the adjective.

It is not possible to transform patterns 6, 7, and 8 into **There** patterns. Nevertheless, the number of **There** patterns available in English is rather astonishing.

Pattern 12: It + V-L + Adj + N

It / is / lucky // that you arrived early.
It / seems / sad // that he was divorced.
It / is / unclear // whether he was guilty.
It / is / hard // to fly a jet.
It / seems / easy // to marry rich.
It / is / easy // for you to say no.
It / appears / hard // for her to please her date.

In this very common pattern the **It** is an expletive, the **N** is the subject of the verb, and the **Adj** is a predicate adjective. The **N** is always either a noun clause (sentences one, two, and three), a simple infinitive phrase (sentences four and five), or an infinitive phrase with a subject and introduced by the expletive *for* (the last two sentences). The whole *for* phrase in these last two examples can alternatively be considered a prepositional phrase functioning as a nominal. The linking verb *to be* is by far the most common one used in this pattern. Only a limited number of adjectives will function in the **Adj** position, some of them being *lucky, true, untrue, correct, easy, hard, sad, tough, certain, apparent, obvious, clear, unclear, distressing, incomprehensible, believable,* and *unbelievable.* Some of the adjectives will function only with noun clauses, not with *for* phrases. The adjective *unclear* seems to be the only one that will function with a noun clause introduced by *whether*.

Pattern 12 is a transformation of pattern 9, which is $N + V\text{-}L + Adj$. Reversion to pattern 9 brings

> That you arrived early // is / lucky.
> For you to say no // is / easy.
> That he was divorced // seems / sad.

We are so used to the **It** pattern that it often sounds more natural than some of the original pattern 9 sentences.

This **It** pattern should not be confused with pattern 10—$N^1 + V\text{-}L + Adj + N^2$—in which the N^2 is a complement of the adjective. The N of pattern 12 seems to be in the same position, but it is the subject of the verb rather than the complement of the adjective. Pattern 10 has a real subject, not an expletive, in the subject position.

A very similar pattern, which we will consider only as a variation of pattern 12, is

> **It + V-L + N^1 + N^1**
> It / is / a fact // that helium is inert.
> It / seems to be / a certainty // that Japan is no longer warlike.

Fact, *certainty*, and *truth* seem to be the only nouns normally used in this pattern; they really function just as the predicate adjective *true* does, showing that this kind of construction is for all practical purposes a pattern 12 sentence. Only a noun clause will fill the second N^1 position. Technically, this pattern is a transformation of pattern 8, which is $N^1 + V\text{-}L + N^1$. Reversion to pattern 8 brings

> That helium is inert // is / a fact,

showing that in the original the second N^1 is the subject and the first N^1 (*fact*) a predicate noun. In sentence two above, *to be* is just an expletive accompanying *seems*, which already contains the meaning of *to be*.

Another **It** pattern which we will consider only as a variant of pattern 12 is a transformation of pattern 3, which is $N^1 + V\text{-}T + N^2$. The N^1 (subject) in this **It** pattern may be a noun clause, an infinitive phrase, or an infinitive phrase with a subject introduced by *for*. Examples:

> **It + V-T + N^2 + N^1**
> It / pleases / Susan // that Jack is her steady.
> It / annoys / Bill // to always be the scapegoat.
> It / grieves / me // for you to insult me that way.

The **It** is an expletive, the N^1 is the subject of the transitive verb, and the N^2 is the direct object. Reversion to pattern 3 brings

N¹ + V-T + N²
That Jack is her steady // pleases / Susan.
To always be the scapegoat // annoys / Bill.
For you to insult me that way // grieves / me.

This **It** pattern is not as common as the first one listed under pattern 12 (page 232).

Another **It** pattern, a transformation of pattern 1, occurs with only a very few intransitive verbs. Examples:

It + V-In + N
It / doesn't matter // whether you come.
It / doesn't matter // how you earn the money.
It / matters // that you are my friend.
It / helps // that you understand.
It / hurts // that you should dislike me.

Several other connectives—such as *why*, *what*, and *when*—can introduce the noun clauses that serve as subjects in this pattern. Reversion to pattern 1 brings

N + V-In
Whether you come // doesn't matter.
That you understand // helps.
That you should dislike me // hurts.

This **It** pattern, especially in the negative with the verb *to matter*, is very common in our speech.

Miscellaneous Patterns with *It*

The general-purpose word *it* also appears in a number of sentences with such meanings as "the weather," "the general situation we are in." "the decision," and so on. Here are common examples:

It's raining.
It's a nice day.
It's all right
It doesn't matter.
It's up to you.

In these examples *it* is a nominal, not an expletive. Such sentences therefore conform to patterns already discussed. To demonstrate:

Pattern 1:
N + V-In
It // is snowing.
It // doesn't matter.

To snow and *to matter* are intransitive verbs.

Pattern 2:
N + Be + Adv
It // is / up to you.

Pattern 8:
N¹ + V-L + N¹
It // is / foul weather.

Pattern 9:
N + V-L + Adj
It // looks / foggy.
It // is / all right.

All such sentences can just be called miscellaneous *It* patterns.

The Comparative-Comparative Pattern

The harder he works, the richer he gets.
The more I study, the less I know.
The bigger they are, the harder they fall.

This two-part sentence pattern is a double transformation of patterns 1, 3, or 8. Examples:

Pattern 1:
N + V-In + Adv
He // works / harder.

Pattern 8:
N + V-L + Adj
He // gets / richer.

Harder is modifying *works*, and *richer*, a predicate adjective, is modifying *he*.

Pattern 1:
N + V-In + Adv
I // study / more.

Pattern 3:
N¹ + V-Tr + N²
I // know / less.

More is modifying *study*, and *less* is the direct object of *know*.

Pattern 8:
N + V-L + Adj
They // are / bigger.

Pattern 1:
N + V-In + Adv
They // fall / harder.

Bigger is a predicate adjective modifying *they*, and *harder* is modifying *fall*. Through transformation of these basic patterns we get the comparative-comparative pattern.

In these sentences, *the* is not a determiner but a qualifier. It is an adverbial, historically an entirely different word, used with comparative forms of adverbs and adjectives in the sense of *so much, by so much, that much, thus much.* Hence

Thus much harder he works, thus much richer he gets.
He works thus much harder, he gets thus much richer.

The sentence-pattern analyses are not affected by this qualifier. It remains current in use without being fully understood. Complete dictionaries define it and give its etymology and examples of its use.

Questions

All of the basic sentence patterns 1 through 12 can be transformed into questions, which retain the underlying basic patterns. There are two kinds of questions: *yes-no questions* and *QW questions*.

Yes-No Questions

One kind of question is asked with the expectation of an answer *yes* or *no*. These questions begin with a form of *to be* as the main verb or with a form of *to be, to have, to do,* or any of the modals as an auxiliary. There are few departures from these modes for introducing a yes-no question, although variations are possible. For example, one can ask

Have you a match?

in which *have* is a main verb and not an auxiliary. But almost everyone says instead

Do you have a match?

which makes use of the auxiliary *do*.

Here are the various **transformed** sentence patterns which produce yes-no questions. Compare them with the sentence patterns already discussed to see that they really are transformations of those patterns, not new patterns.

Pattern 1:
Be + N + V-In + (Adv)
Was he lying to you?

Do + N + V-In + (Adv)
Did she arrive early?

Have + N + V-In + (Adv)
Has he come to town?

Modal + N + V-In + (Adv)
Will he arrive soon?

These are all transformations of

N + V-In + (Adv)
He // lied (to you).
She // arrived (early).
He // came (to town).
He // arrives (soon).

The passive transformation of pattern 1 may also be transformed into a question:

Be + N² + V-In + prep + (by + N¹)
Was she laughed at (by anyone)?

This is a transformation of the passive form of pattern 1:

N² + Be + V-In + prep + (by + N¹)
She // was laughed at (by someone).

Pattern 2:
Be + N + Adv
Was he there?

Modal + N + Be + Adv
Should she be at home?

These are transformations of

N + Be + Adv
He // was / there.
She // is / at home.

Pattern 3:
Do + N¹ + V-Tr + N²
Did he hurt his hand?

Have + N^1 + V-Tr + N^2
Has she bought a car?

Modal + N^1 + V-Tr + N^2
Can they pick beans?

These are transformations of

N^1 + V-Tr + N^2
He // hurt / his hand.
She // bought / a car.
They //pick / beans.

The passive transformation of pattern 3 also can be transformed into a question:

Be + N^2 + V-Tr + (by + N^1)
Was his hand hurt (by himself)?

This is a transformation of

N^2 + Be + V-Tr + (by + N^1)
His hand // was hurt (by himself).

It should be clear now that all yes-no questions are transformations of basic sentence patterns. Here are questions based on all the other patterns. Supply the symbolic notations for yourself.

Pattern 4, active voice:
Did she give him a kiss?
Pattern 4, passive voice:
Was he given a kiss (by her)?
Pattern 4, passive voice:
Was a kiss given him (by her)?
Pattern 5, active voice:
Did they choose Harry captain?
Pattern 5, passive voice:
Was Harry chosen captain (by them)?
Pattern 6, active voice:
Did John make Susan happy?
Pattern 6, passive voice:
Was Susan made happy (by John)?
Pattern 7, active voice:
Did the professor make John happy to be in the course?
Pattern 7, passive voice:
Was John made happy to be in the course (by the professor)?
Pattern 8:
Did Frank become a doctor?

Pattern 9:
   Has Betty remained sick?
Pattern 10:
   Was Mary happy that she was invited?
Pattern 11:
   Is there no way to solve this problem?
Pattern 12:
   Was it hard for Nancy to say no?

The variations of patterns 11 and 12 and the miscellaneous *It* patterns may similarly be transformed into yes-no questions. It will be instructive for you to analyze each of these questions to see that it is formed from a basic pattern.

QW Questions

   The QW questions, which ask for information other than a *yes* or *no* answer, are introduced by *who, whom, which, what, where, when, why,* and *how* and also use as auxiliaries forms of *to be, to have, to do,* or the modals. They are transformations of basic sentence patterns.

Pattern 1:
QW + Do + N + V-In + (Adv)
How did Joan smile?

QW + modal + N + V-In
When will Evan arrive?

These are transformations of

N + V-In + (Adv)
Joan // smiled (how).
Evan // will arrive (when).

   With eight different QW words and many auxiliaries, including the modals, the variety of possible QW questions is enormous. Here is a sample transformed from each of the other basic patterns. You can provide symbolic notations for yourself.

Pattern 2:
   Where will he be?
Pattern 3:
   When did she buy a car?
Pattern 4:
   What will she buy him?
Pattern 5:
   Why did they elect Harry captain?

Pattern 6:
How did he make Susan happy?
Pattern 7:
How did she make Dave happy that he came?
Pattern 8:
Why is he the chief?
Pattern 9:
Why is he sick?
Pattern 10:
Why is he happy to be here?
Pattern 11:
Why is there no way to solve this problem?
Pattern 12:
Why is it easy for you to say no?

The passive-voice transformations of patterns 1, 3, 4, 5, 6, and 7, the variations of patterns 11 and 12, and the miscellaneous *It* patterns can all be transformed into QW questions. It will be instructive for you to apply the basic patterns to each of the above questions.

Exclamatory Sentences

Exclamatory sentences are such utterances as

How you rant!
What a gem you are!
How pretty Jane is!

Normally only the exclamatory words *how* and *what* are used in such sentences. These, too, are transformations of basic patterns. Examples:

Pattern 1:
How + N + V-In + (Adv)
How you rant (on and on)!

This is a transformation of

N + V-In + (Adv)
You // rant (on and on).

Pattern 8:
What + N^1 + N^1 + V-L
What a gem you are!

This is a transformation of

N^1 + V-L + N^1
You // are / a gem.

Pattern 9:
How + Adj + N + V-L
How pretty Jane is!

This is a transformation of

N + V-L + Adj
Jane // is / pretty.

Other basic patterns can be transformed into exclamatory sentences, though the above three patterns are most frequently used. Examples:

Pattern 2:
How he was at home!
Pattern 3:
What a car he bought!
Pattern 4:
What a start you gave me!
Pattern 5:
(Almost never used)
Pattern 6:
How happy he made Susan!
Pattern 7:
How he made George glad that he came!
Pattern 10:
How lucky he was to escape!
Pattern 11:
How there was a complete debacle!
Pattern 12:
How fortunate it was that you applied for the job!

It will be instructive for you to apply the symbolic notations to see that these are transformations of the basic patterns.

Imperative Sentences

Imperative, or request, sentences are also forms of the basic patterns, through the subject part (N^1) of each sentence is missing (see page 177). Only the verb stem (first form in the verb paradigm, or the infinitive without the *to*) can function in these sentences. The passive transformation is impossible. Examples:

Pattern 1:
V-In + (Adv)
Come to my house.

Pattern 2:
Be + Adv
Be outside the gate.

Pattern 3:
V-Tr + N²
Buy that car.

Pattern 4:
V-Tr + N² + N³
Buy me a drink.

Pattern 5:
V-Tr + N² + N²
Appoint Harry captain.

Pattern 6:
V-Tr + N² + Adj
Make Susan happy.

Pattern 7:
V-Tr + N² + Adj + N³
Make Susan happy that she came.

Pattern 8:
V-L + N¹
Be a good sport.

Pattern 9:
V-L + Adj
Remain faithful.

Pattern 10:
V-L + Adj + N²
Be happy that you weren't injured.

Pattern 11:
(not possible)

Pattern 12:
(not possible)

The transformation that produces these sentences drops the first **N¹** and changes the verb form to the verb stem.

Basic Patterns in Dependent Clauses

Dependent clauses (to be discussed in Chapter 11) occur with the same basic patterns that independent clauses have. Here are examples. Reviewing them will help reinforce the basic patterns in your mind. The basic pattern in the dependent clause is in boldface and slashes indicate the structure.

Pattern 1:
  N + V-In + (Adv)
  We don't know **who** // **came** (**early**).

Pattern 2:
  N + Be + Adv
  Call **whoever** // **is** / **outside**.

Pattern 3:
  N¹ + V-Tr + N²
  The policeman saw **who** // **threw** / the **bomb**.

Pattern 4:
  N¹ + V-Tr + N² + N³
  Henry, **who** // **bought** / **me** / a **drink**, was himself stoned.

Pattern 5:
  N¹ + V-Tr + N² + N²
  I resigned because **they** // **elected** / **Harry** / **president**.

Pattern 6:
  N¹ + V-Tr + N² + Adj
  Since **John** // **makes** / **Susan** / **happy**, I tolerate him.

Pattern 7:
  N¹ + V-Tr + N² + Adj + N³
  We invited Mim, **who** // **makes** / **Bob** / **happy** / **to be a part of the crowd**.

Pattern 8:
  N¹ + V-L + N¹
  Since **Crandel** // **became** / a **cop**, there is no living with him.

Pattern 9:
  N + V-L + Adj
  We visited Rosalind, **who** // **was** / **sick**.

Pattern 10:
  N¹ + V-L + Adj + N²
  Since **we** // **were** / **lucky** / **to be invited**, we behaved ourselves.

Pattern 11:
  There + Be + N-endo
  Since **there** / **was** / **no way out**, we surrendered.

Pattern 12:
  It + Be + Adj + N
  When **it** / **is** / **lucky** / **for you to gamble**, gamble big.

EXERCISES

1. Distinguish between pattern 1 and pattern 3 sentences in the following group. Indicate the symbolic notations.

    a. He talked intelligently.
    b. She urged us on.
    c. She spoke her part.
    d. She spoke musically.
    e. He succeeded in his youth.
    f. He succeeded his father.
    g. He walked home.
    h. She walked the dog.
    i. He phoned the caretaker.
    j. He phoned yesterday.

2. Distinguish between pattern 2 and pattern 9 sentences in the following group. Indicate the symbolic notations.

    a. He is well.
    b. He is up.
    c. She has been home.
    d. She has been miserable.
    e. They were effective.
    f. They were where the taxi left them.
    g. He was foolish.
    h. He was upstairs.
    i. She was at sea.
    j. He was silent.

3. Distinguish between pattern 4 and pattern 5 sentences in the following group. Indicate the symbolic notations.

    a. He gave her a hard time.
    b. They designated her representative to the parent organization.
    c. The chairman appointed John comptroller.
    d. They selected Bill as sergeant-at-arms.
    e. They bought Bill a gift.
    f. They secured John a sinecure.
    g. He hired his wife a maid.
    h. We considered Joy a fool.
    i. We obtained Harry a term-paper subject.
    j. They thought me a bore.

4. Distinguish between patterns 6, 7, and 10 sentences in the following group. Indicate the symbolic notations.

   a. She made him content.
   b. He was lucky that she loved him.
   c. He made her happy to be alive.
   d. She found him glad that he had invited her.
   e. She found him secluded.
   f. He remained sad that he had failed.
   g. He was delighted to buy the stamps.
   h. He considered her dizzy-headed.
   i. He found her overwhelmed to be the star pupil.
   j. The jury found him guilty.

5. Distinguish between pattern 8 and pattern 9 sentences in the following group. Indicate the symbolic notations.

   a. He remained an idiot.
   b. He grew idiotic.
   c. The spring ran dry.
   d. He grew a beard.
   e. He became a dentist.
   f. He became sulky.
   g. He appeared to be jealous.
   h. He appeared to be a lunatic.
   i. He was master of the events.
   j. He was mad at the events.

6. Distinguish between pattern 3 and pattern 8 sentences in the following group. Indicate the symbolic notations.

   a. The suit became him.
   b. The suit became a wreck.
   c. He bought a card.
   d. He remained a card.
   e. He became a sight for sore eyes.
   f. He lost a sight of money.
   g. He appeared a good risk.
   h. He envied his mother.
   i. He became a minister.
   j. He offered himself.

7. Distinguish between pattern 2 and pattern 9 sentences in the following group. You must decide whether the prepositional phrase is an adverbial (usually denoting time, place, or manner) complementing *be* or an adjectival modifying the subject and thus a predicate adjectival. It is sometimes hard to make this distinction, so don't feel frustrated if you feel unsure.

a. He is of topmost character.
b. He is in the way.
c. He is in the house.
d. She is at the dentist's.
e. They are of unusually high effectiveness.
f. He is in a league by himself.
g. She is on my mind.
h. She is in a bad way.
i. He is in a happy mood.
j. He is at the top of his class.

8. Transform each of these active-voice sentences into the passive voice. Give the symbolic notation for both the active- and passive-voice versions, and indicate the pattern number.

a. She gave me a thrill.
b. They elected June Bear chief.
c. The professor made the class sad.
d. The governor vetoed the bill.
e. He made her glad that he had called.
f. His mother gave him a spanking.
g. The salesman sold the soldier a jeep.
h. He considered her foolish.
i. He considered her a fool.
j. He found Nan glad to participate.

9. Transform each of these passive-voice sentences into the active voice. Give the symbolic notation for both the passive- and active-voice versions, and indicate the pattern number. You may have to supply your own *by* phrase.

a. The car was sold to John.
b. A bottle of perfume was given Susan by her boyfriend.
c. Susan was made happy.
d. Bill was made glad that he studied.
e. The spectators were trampled.
f. She was made happy to be a part of the play.
g. He was found contented.
h. He was thought to be a Serbian.
i. She was found an apartment.
j. The soldier was shot.

10. List all the linking verbs you can think of that are not mentioned in the text (page 201).

11. List all the verbs you can think of (not mentioned on page 197) that will function in patterns 5, 6, and 7.

12. List from the *Oxford English Dictionary* or *Webster's Third New International Dictionary* all the meanings of the verb *to be*.

13. Give the pattern number and symbolic notation for each of the following sentences.

    a. He considered her beautiful.
    b. The dog is upstairs.
    c. Father gave me a dollar.
    d. This cat died early.
    e. Children play in the sand.
    f. It is clear that she loves me.
    g. Harry kissed my girl.
    h. They chose me captain.
    i. There is a rat in the kitchen.
    j. John became a pest.
    k. Bill milked the cows.
    l. Penner owned a duck.
    m. The policeman seemed a good fellow.
    n. The berries tasted sweet.
    o. The doctor is out.
    p. It is hard to be a good Christian.
    q. We were happy to leave.
    r. We were happy.
    s. We were happiness itself.
    t. He found her a pig.
    u. We made Cowan glad that he had resigned.
    v. We made John the scapegoat.
    w. We made John sulky.
    x. We brought him a tire.
    y. We called him a liar.

14. Determine the basic sentence pattern that each of these questions is a transformation of and give the symbolic notation.

    a. Why did you give him a carrot?
    b. Why did you call him a carrot-top?
    c. Did you make Bill happy?
    d. Did you make Bill a voting member?
    e. Did you make Bill a tree house?
    f. How did you make Earl glad to be a member of your group?
    g. Why did you find her a pig?
    h. Were you afraid?
    i. Were you a dunderhead?
    j. Why were you afraid to leave?
    k. Why is it difficult to please Professor Hooker?

    l. Why is mother away?

    m. When did the performance seem best?

    n. Who seemed to be the best actor?

    o. How did you become a Phi Beta Kappa?

    p. Why does that dress become Susan?

    q. Why is there always a catch in your proposals?

    r. Who did they appoint Dean?

    s. Why is it not clear that Della loves you?

    t. Why did your dog die young?

    u. Why do children like to play in the sand?

    v. How did Jerry manage to rob a bank?

    w. What did you do to Terry?

    x. When will the concert be over?

    y. What does it matter whether you pass the course?

15. Write five **There** sentences that you think are different from each other and then try to pair them off with the symbolic notations under pattern 11.

16. Write four different kinds of **It** sentences and give their pattern number and symbolic notations.

17. Here are two paragraphs chosen at random. Copy down each independent and dependent clause in each (leaving off superfluous modifiers) and give the pattern number and symbolic notation of each.

> Automobiles, like women, can be fun, but they are expensive. Since I sold the family hag to the knacker, I have not only enjoyed the bachelor's irresponsible freedom but have also become the richer by more than $1000 a year. Moreover, instead of one car, I now have a dozen. On hot summer days, I use the convertible to drive to the shore. When taking guests to the theater, I tell the chauffeur when the limousine will be required. For camping trips, the station wagon is most useful. For parties in suburbia, one of the new compacts usually meets the need; but if my wife and I take another couple with us, we use one of the larger sedans. Meanwhile, I change no tires, put on no chains. Someone does this for me, free of charge. Frozen gas lines, insurance premiums, license tags, state inspections, antifreeze, grease jobs, oil, gasoline, car washings, garage bills, battery checks, and front-end adjustments are but dimly remembered nightmares of the past. I now enjoy happy motoring, and not the least of my driving pleasure is the thought that money is piling up in the bank. In brief, I rent. [John Keats, "Ask the Man Who Doesn't Own One," *The Atlantic Monthly*, December 1962]

> Most of our knowledge, acquired from parents, friends, schools, newspapers, books, conversation, speeches, and television, is received

verbally. All our knowledge of history, for example, comes to us only in words. The only proof we have that the Battle of Waterloo ever took place is that we have had reports to that effect. These reports are not given us by people who saw it happen, but are based on other reports: reports of reports of reports, which go back ultimately to the firsthand reports given by people who did see it happening. It is through reports, then, and through reports of reports, that we receive most knowledge: about government, about what is happening in Korea, about what picture is showing at the downtown theater—in fact, about anything that we do not know through direct experience. [S. I. Hayakawa, *Language in Action*]

10 MODIFIERS AND APPOSITIVES

Modification: The Third Great Grammatical Function

As we explained in earlier chapters, an intelligent beginning student of the structure of English would undoubtedly discover inductively that our first two great grammatical functions are predication—the fitting of a subject to a predicate—and complementation—the completing of a meaning initiated in a verb. His next inductive discovery would be that the third great grammatical function is **modification**. He would also quickly conclude that modification is the most complex of all grammatical functions, and he would probably spend months, or even years, trying to work out its details. Actually, such a hypothetical student of language working inductively is not as unlikely as might be thought. In about 350 B.C. an Indian named Pānini did exactly that kind of study of Sanskrit and inductively analyzed its primary grammatical functions. His is the oldest known existing grammar and it is still thought to be a very accurate one.

We have throughout this book already used the term *modification* frequently, for anyone studying this book has at least an elementary understanding of modifiers. Now we need to present an orderly, thorough analysis of the function of modification and its manifold variations. But first it is time to give a usable definition. A **modifier** is a word or word group that describes, limits, intensifies, restricts, changes, adds to, or subtracts from the meaning of another word or word group.

Modifiers are structures that flesh out the basic sentence patterns we saw in Chapter 9. These basic patterns—sometimes called **kernel sen-**

250

tences—consist of simple subjects, verbs, and complements. Though they sound perfectly natural and are fully grammatical, they really don't appear especially often in either our speech or writing. Instead, we use **expanded sentences**, and the expansion is mostly due to modification. The modifiers are **subordinate structures**, which means that they are "arranged under" the words they modify. The reason why many sentences are long even though the basic patterns are mostly short is that modifiers modify modifiers modifying modifiers, to paraphrase Gertrude Stein. For example, consider this apparently simple construction:

> The girl swimming in the pool owned by Mr. Sullivan, who loves girls in bikinis, . . .

Swimming modifies *girl*; *in the pool* modifies *swimming*; *owned* modifies *pool*; *by Mr. Sullivan* modifies *owned*; and *who loves girls in bikinis* modifies *Mr. Sullivan*. Such structures can be extended almost indefinitely. This simple illustration shows why sentences become long and also why our hypothetical language student would consider modification the most complex of the grammatical functions he would discover.

Modification is normally thought of as occurring within a sentence only. But a distinction can be made between logical dependence and grammatical dependence. For example, such a construction as

> when we finish

is obviously to be grammatically dependent in any sentence it appears in. The subordinating conjunction *when* prevents the clause from functioning with grammatical independence. But there can be grammatical independence combined with logical dependence. For example, the sentence

> He told me I should try then

is grammatically independent. Anyone with sentence sense would call it a sentence. But it has logical dependence on a preceding sentence or sentences. *He*, *should try*, and *then* depend on the preceding sentence or sentences for clear meaning. Is, therefore, modification involved from sentence to sentence? In a sense it is, in a reverse way. The first sentence modifies the logically dependent words in the second sentence to give them meaning. But this kind of modification comes under the heading of **reference** and is usually treated only in discussion of usage.

Also an entire sentence can modify a preceding sentence. Example:

> The study of grammar at the college level is becoming increasingly

prevalent. Such study not only provides students with insight into
one of the most interesting areas of humane knowledge but also
increases their ability to function in an increasingly verbal world.

The first sentence is a generality which is modified by less broad gen-
eralities in the second sentence. Then a third sentence would be a
further modification of these sentences. In effect, in any extended discourse sentences modify preceding sentences. This kind of modification, however, is not grammatical but logical and semantic.

We will be concerned only with grammatical modification within a
sentence. Thus this chapter will analyze **adjectivals**, **adverbials**, and
sentence modifiers, which are the three broad kinds of modifiers that
occur within sentences, and it will also include a section on **appositives**,
which, though not modifiers strictly speaking, are very like modifiers
and not extensive enough to merit a chapter of their own. However,
this chapter will not deal with dependent clauses, for their functions as
modifiers and nominals are complex enough to warrant a separate
chapter for them.

Predication can be confused with modification and hence before we
begin our analysis of modification we should review this potential
trouble spot. The predication in a simple declarative sentence or
dependent clause cannot be confused with modification. But three of
the nonfinite predicative structures we saw in Chapter 5 can be mistaken for modifying structures. Here is a review of them. The first is
the infinitive with a subject. Examples:

Sue wanted me to kiss her.
I asked Jack to leave.

Until one becomes somewhat skilled in grammatical analysis, he might
think that *to kiss her* modifies *me* and that *to leave* modifies *Jack*. But
such is not the case. *Me* and *Jack* are subjects of the infinitives, the
whole infinitive phrases being the direct objects of *wanted* and *asked*.
Also in

Don left her waiting,

waiting is not modifying *her*, but *her* is the subject of the present participle *waiting*. The whole phrase *her waiting* is the direct object of *left*.
And in

We found Jim shot,

shot does not modify *Jim*, but instead *Jim* is the subject of the past
participle *shot*, the whole phrase *Jim shot* being the direct object of
found.

In Chapter 4 we studied structure words, many of which function as modifiers. Structure words as modifiers can be called adjectivals, adverbials, and sentence modifiers. For example, in *this book*, *this* can be called an adjectival since it modifies a noun, but usually it is just called a demonstrative pronoun or determiner. In *very sleepy*, *very* can be called an adverbial since it modifies an adjective, but it is usually just referred to as a qualifier. In *however, we kept silent*, *however* can be called a sentence modifier, but it is most commonly referred to as a conjunctive adverb. But these and some other structure words are certainly modifiers. For example, consider these two sentences:

Henry **could** be a great pianist if he practiced.
John **may** be at home now.

Could as a modal auxiliary is modifying *be* with the meaning of possibility in the future. *May* is modifying *be* with the meaning of possibility now. But the meanings of the modals as verb modifiers are so various that the modals in these two sentences could actually be exchanged without a change in meaning if the verb *practiced* were changed to *practices*. There is, then, a great range of modification in structure words. But we will not here repeat material from Chapter 4, since reference to that chapter will give sufficient information about structure words as modifiers.

A useful way to think of modification is to see **what goes with what**. Usually **meaning** shows us word relationships so that we know what modifies what, but also **position** and **formal clues** can be used to tell what a modifier goes with. First consider meaning:

John was just sitting there, **disconsolate**.

It is only by meaning that we know *disconsolate* modifies *John*; neither position nor formal clues give us any insight into this modification. In this sentence, *disconsolate* cannot be a predicate adjective, for this *sitting* is not a linking verb, and also there is juncture before *disconsolate*. The meaning of the sentence could be expressed in

Disconsolate, John was just sitting there

or

John, disconsolate, was just sitting there,

but these constructions do not sound entirely natural to our ears.

Especially with adverbials is meaning necessary to show what goes with what. Example:

Jerry jumped into the pool **with great delight**.

Though *with great delight* is placed next to *pool*, meaning, not position or formal clues, shows that it modifies *jumped*. That is, *jumped with great delight* makes sense, but *pool with great delight* doesn't make sense.

Position can, however, establish word relationship in modification. Example:

> Job, **burdened with sorrow**, replied to Elihu.

Elihu could of course be burdened with sorrow, but the position of the phrase in the sentence shows us that it modifies *Job*. Similarly, formal clues can establish the pattern of modification. Example:

> The first six chapters of A Review of Nuclear Physics, **which were recommended reading**, are written in layman's language.

The clause *which were recommended reading* is shown by the formal clue *were* to modify *chapters* and not the book title. If the clause modified the book title, the verb would be *was*. Here is another example of formal clues establishing the pattern of modification:

> Professor Tucker **courageously** and **patiently** faced the complaining students.

The inflectional suffix *ly* is a formal clue showing that these two modifiers go with the verb *faced*, not with the nominal *Professor Tucker*. The word relationship is *faced courageously and patiently*. But the sentence can be changed to

> Professor Tucker, **courageous** and **patient**, faced the complaining students.

Now that the *ly* is missing, the modifiers are seen to go with *Professor Tucker*. The adjective-forming derivational suffix *ous* acts as a formal clue to show this, though *patient* does not have such a clue.

Often two or even all three of the indicators establish word relationship in modification. Example:

> John's aunt, **who is his favorite relative**, bought him a car.

The boldface clause is shown by meaning, by position, and by two formal clues (*is* and *his*) to modify *aunt*. But normally it is meaning that establishes word relationships, especially with adverbials. The only formal clues that establish the pattern of modification are verbs and pronouns in adjective clauses (to be discussed in Chapter 11), the *ly* on adverbs, and adjective-forming derivational suffixes.

Sometimes neither meaning nor position nor formal clues establish the pattern of modification and then ambiguity results. Example:

> He mentioned meeting me **also** in San Francisco.

Does *also* modify *me*, so that he met me and others? Or does *also* modify *in San Francisco*, so that he met me there as well as somewhere else? None of the three indicators will solve the problem. Another example:

> John **only** donated $500.

Does *only* modify *John*, so that John alone donated $500? Or does it modify *$500*, so that John donated that small an amount? Of course in speech, intonation would give us the meaning; but in writing, the sentence is ambiguous. Another example:

> John had the nerve to talk about food **in the kitchen**.

Is *in the kitchen* an adjectival modifying *food* or an adverbial modifying *talk*? Context only would tell. In the sentence by itself neither of the three indicators will establish the word relationship. Still another example (from a television ad):

> Don't wait until you're itching **to get at it**.

Does *to get at it* modify the verb *wait* or the verb *itching*? Even intonation will not clear up this ambiguity; only reference to a preceding sentence will. In the ad *it* referred to dandruff, and the phrase was intended to modify *wait*. Still, those listeners especially adept at language study were quite aware of the ambiguity.

Another kind of ambiguity sometimes results when an adjective precedes a noun which modifies a noun. Example:

> a **coarse** nylon carpet

Does *coarse* modify *nylon* or *carpet*? Only context would tell and even context might not tell. Also a possessive noun as a determiner can be involved in such ambiguity. Example:

> **colorful** girls' blouses

Are the girls or the blouses colorful? Some authorities have advanced rules to cover such possibly ambiguous constructions. For example, one authority maintained that the ad language

> **imperfect** boys' orlon sweaters

is ungrammatical and should have been

> boys' **imperfect** orlon sweaters

But in fact confusing ambiguity seldom arises from such constructions. *Boys' orlon sweaters* is a noun unit that can be modified, and certainly the original ad is grammatical, though people interested in language might have fun with it.

Adjectivals

An adjectival is a word or word group that modifies a noun or pronoun—usually a noun, for nouns are modified much more often than are pronouns. Structure words (see above and Chapter 4), form-class words, and various kinds of word groups can function as adjectivals. All of these kinds of adjectivals (except structure words) will be discussed below. The predicate adjective, however, will not be discussed again in this chapter, since it has been fully treated as a complement in Chapter 8. Also, adjective clauses will be discussed in Chapter 11.

Position of Adjectivals

There are three positions for adjectivals: **prenominal**, **postnominal**, and **shifted**. Almost all prenominal adjectivals are single words or word compounds, unless the adjectival is a phrase set off from the noun by punctuation or voice pause, both of which represent terminal juncture. Examples of prenominal adjectivals:

> **Black** cats cause **bad** luck.
> **Printed** books make good **debating** texts.
> **College** texts are profitable for **book** publishers.
> **Ten-year-old** girls like **rich-food** lunches.

In the last sentence the hyphenated constructions are functioning as single adjectivals (see Compound Adjectivals, pages 274–276). More than one adjectival can occur in front of a noun. Examples:

> a **pretty college** coed
> **tasty, refreshing, nourishing** sandwiches

All these boldface words are separate adjectivals, not word groups modifying nouns. Theoretically, there is no limit to the number of single adjectivals that can precede one noun, though there is a grammatical restriction on word order. As has been mentioned, a word group almost never precedes the noun it modifies unless there is terminal juncture between it and the noun. For example, such constructions as

> *The swimming in the river girl is Joan

and

> *The on the street man always has an opinion

are not grammatical. Conceivably, these word-group adjectivals could be hyphenated and then precede the nouns, but they would still sound very strange.

Often a word-group adjectival occurs in the prenominal position when it is separated from its noun by juncture. Examples:

> **Happy to be of service,** Carol busied herself with housework.
> **Not seeing the patrol car,** Ann kept speeding.
> **Elevated to a full professorship,** Dr. Clark began more research.

The boldface adjectival phrases are modifying *Carol*, *Ann*, and *Dr. Clark*. The commas indicate terminal juncture. This is a common adjectival position. And occasionally a single adjectival can function in this prenominal position. Examples:

> **Satisfied,** Bert left the complaint department.
> **Angry,** George stomped out of the room.

Such single adjectivals in the prenominal position with juncture are almost nonexistent in ordinary conversation and rare in writing.

In the postnominal position both single-word and word-group adjectivals can occur. Single-word postnominal adjectivals are rather rare, the most common ones being present or past participles by form. Examples:

> The girl **swimming** is . . .
> The students **talking** are . . .
> The evidence **gathered** proved . . .
> The events **recalled** were . . .

Not all present and past participles can function in this postnominal position. For example, we can say

> The girl **listening** is . . .

but not

> *The girl **hearing** is . . .

We can say

> The meal **served** was . . .

but not

> *The meal **finished** was . . .

There are no apparent rules governing which verbs can function as postnominal adjectivals. Note, however, that a participial phrase might function as a postnominal adjectival when a participle by itself cannot. For example, we can say

> The girl **hearing us** is . . .

The addition of the direct object *us* for *hearing* changes its capacity to be a postnominal adjectival.

Only rarely does a single-word adjective by form serve as a postnominal adjectival. Usually such modification occurs only after an indefinite pronoun. Examples:

> Something **valuable** was stolen from my office.
> Someone **intelligent** is needed for this job.

But such a construction as

> *A watch **valuable** was ...

almost never occurs. There are, however, a few fixed phrases with single-word adjectives by form as postnominal adjectivals. Examples:

> the heir **apparent**
> accounts **receivable**
> the body **politic**
> God **Almighty**
> the devil **incarnate**
> the first person **singular**
> deuces **wild**

Phrases based on these patterns can be invented. Examples:

> Miracles **unbelievable** were ...
> Love **uncontrollable** is ...

But such constructions do not often occur.

Nouns in a postnominal adjectival position are rare also. The chief possibilities are

> operation **breadbasket** (and other nouns)
> the party **outdoors**
> the affair **indoors**
> a trip **overseas**
> the room **upstairs**
> the man **downstairs**

Though the last five modifiers may be considered nouns, they also have adverbial characteristics. In these constructions they are adjectivals.

Adjectives in pairs are frequently used in the postnominal position. Examples:

> The night nurse, **pale** and **weary**, was ....
> The winner, **confident** and **jubilant**, prepared to ....
> Alfred, **tired** but **happy**, was ....

For some unknown reason we accept such postnominal adjectivals in pairs but not singly. For example,

> The winner, **confident**, prepared to . . . .

would sound somewhat unnatural to our ears.

Usually word-group adjectivals occupy the postnominal position, though as seen above they can also occur in the prenominal position with juncture. Here are examples:

> The man **in the street** is often happy.
> The boy **throwing rocks** is a delinquent.
> Jerry, **talking through his nose**, regaled his friends.
> The man **executed yesterday** was innocent.
> Paul, **executed by firing squad**, was brave to the end.

Note that the adjectivals in sentences three and five could be shifted to the prenominal position, since they would be set off by juncture. More discussion of all these adjectival constructions will be given below. Here we are just illustrating positions.

The shifted position for adjectivals is a place not either directly before or directly after the noun modified. It is a rather rare position. Here are examples of single-word adjectivals in the shifted position:

> The teacher just sat there, **angry**.
> Christine bowed her head, **subdued**.

Angry and *subdued*, modifying *teacher* and *Christine*, are shifted from the more usual adjectival positions. Note that they are set off by juncture. Word groups, including endocentric adjective phrases (see page 260), may also occupy a shifted position. Examples:

> We were all hurrying along, **happy to be on our way**.
> There John stood, **singing for all he was worth**.

The boldface phrases modify *we* and *John* and thus are adjectivals in the shifted position. An adjectival phrase can also come in a shifted position at the beginning of a sentence. Example:

> **Being of a capricious nature**, sometimes and without warning Jane
> would defy her parents.

The boldface adjectival is shifted away from *Jane*, the noun it modifies.

Now with the three adjectival positions in mind, we will study the form-class words and word groups that function as adjectivals.

Adjectives as Adjectivals

Statistically, the adjectival of greatest frequency is the adjective by form, as one might expect. Perhaps we should review adjectives by form here, for review in grammar, as in mathematics, is of great importance in reinforcing concepts in students' minds. Here is the adjective paradigm:

STEM	ER/MORE	EST/MOST	LY	NESS
sad	sadder	saddest	sadly	sadness
able	abler	ablest	ably	—
morbid	more morbid	most morbid	morbidly	morbidness
early	earlier	earliest	—	earliness

If a stem fits into the slots of columns two and three and *either* four *or* five, it is an adjective by form.

Also derivational suffixes mark adjectives. To refresh your memory here are a few of the most common ones:

> courage + ous = courageous
> comfort + able = comfortable
> pity + ful = pitiful
> emotion + al = emotional
> fortune + ate = fortunate
> guilt + less = guiltless
> combat + ive = combative
> athlete + ic = athletic
> boy + ish = boyish
> shine + y = shiny
> love + ly = lovely
> devote + ed = devoted
> interest + ing = interesting

For a fuller list and suffixes with bound roots, see pages 24–25. These examples are just for refreshing your memory.

Giving examples of single adjectives modifying nouns is needless here because such illustration would be too elementary. But adjectives can function in **endocentric adjective phrases**, the whole phrase, regardless of its own internal structures of modification or complementation, modifying a noun. The simple adjective is the headword of the endocentric structure. The headword will often not function grammatically as the whole phrase does, since there are restrictions on the placement of single adjectives and since the whole phrase, unless it is a complement, is usually nonrestrictive, whereas single adjectives are not usually nonrestrictive. But we will still call the phrase endocentric since it has a headword. The occurrence of a headword is really the determining characteristic of an endocentric phrase. Here are some examples of endocentric adjective phrases with the headword *happy*:

seemingly very	happy	in his ignorance of the facts in the case
inordinately	happy	that his invention was accepted for production
not especially	happy	with his wife

happy   in the knowledge that his loan had saved
           his friend

The second example has a complement of the adjective as a part of its structure. The other three examples have adverb and qualifier modifiers and apparently prepositional-phrase modifiers.[1] Such endocentric adjective phrases may modify nouns in any of the three adjectival positions.

Here are endocentric adjective phrases functioning in sentences:

> **At the most barely tolerant of his son's erratic behavior,** Mr. Bryant was reluctant to advance him more cash.
> John, **almost bereft of dignity,** bowed his head in shame.
> Winton resigned his chairmanship, **quite secure in his belief that he had given the club his best effort.**

These three boldface adjective phrases are, respectively, in the prenominal, postnominal, and shifted positions. The adjective headwords are *tolerant*, *bereft*, and *secure*, and they modify, in order, *Mr. Bryant*, *John*, and *Winton*. All three of the phrases are nonrestrictive, as such endocentric adjective phrases usually are.

Nouns as Adjectivals

A noun modifying a noun occupies almost exclusively the prenominal position. Here are constructions of this sort taken from a brief segment of a contemporary article:

> **Negro** spiritual
> **newspaper** headlines
> **television** commentator
> **record** numbers
> **armchair** anthropologist
> **future** plans
> **disaster** clause
> **suicide** rate

Such adjectival modification by nouns is so common in our language that only a few lines contributed these examples. Many languages do not have the linguistic phenomenon of a noun modifying a noun; instead they use connectives between two nouns or convert the modifier into a non-noun form. For example, in Spanish a noun never modifies another noun. In that language such a phrase as

---

[1] We say apparently because some grammarians maintain that prepositional phrases in this position are also complements of the adjective and thus nominals (see page 208). Either analysis is acceptable, for grammarians are likely never to agree.

future disaster

must be

desastre del futuro,

the *del* being a connective between the two nouns. Basque illustrates another mode of connecting nouns so that one noun does not modify another. In that language

a stone house

must be

eche arrizko,

the *ko* on the second word being a connective meaning *of*. Literally, the Basque phrase is

house stone-of

No one knows for sure, but probably only a small percentage of the world's 3000 to 5000 languages permit the modification of a noun by a noun. English has evolved, however, so that the phenomenon is probably as common as it is in any other language. Early traditional grammar confused grammatical analysis by calling such nouns adjectives in their modification, confusing such structures as *future plans* and *satisfactory plans*. Identifying parts of speech by form and by function, however, clears up the confusion caused by early English grammarians.

Anytime a noun modifies a noun in English, a grammatical transformation into another structure is possible, usually, though not always, involving a prepositional phrase. Transformations of the above structures are these:

spiritual of Negroes
headlines in a newspaper
commentator on television
numbers constituting a record
anthropologist in an armchair
plans for the future
clause providing for disaster
rate of suicides

When an adjective by form modifies a noun, only one transformation is possible: an adjective clause. For example, *a pretty girl* transforms into *a girl who is pretty* and *a dirty house* transforms into *a house which is dirty*. A noun modifying a noun will not undergo this transformation. For example, *suicide rate* will not transform into *a rate which is suicide*. This difference in transformations shows that there is a considerable grammatical difference between a noun modifying a noun and an adjective modifying a noun.

A noun may modify a noun when other adjectivals also modify the noun, but in such cases the noun modifier is always the last adjectival before the noun headword. Examples:

>an old **iron** fence
>an expensive new **stone** house

Such constructions as *an iron old fence* and *an expensive stone new house* are ungrammatical. When a verb by form functioning as an adjectival accompanies a noun modifying a noun, it too must come before the noun modifier. For example, *an old rusting iron fence* is grammatical, but *an old iron rusting fence* is ungrammatical (unless *rusting fence* were considered a compound noun). *Rusting* is a present participle, not an adjective.

Adverbs as Adjectivals

The "pure" *ly* adverb can modify a noun in the prenominal position only when the modified noun is an appositive. Examples:

>Mr. Bodford, **officially** Grand Dragon of the Mystic Knights of the Sea, detests ritual.
>Sarah Cleeford, **nominally** a Christian, likes to attend Buddhist ceremonies.

Technically, the adverbs *officially* and *nominally* modify the nouns *Grand Dragon* and *a Christian* and thus are adjectivals. This construction, however, comes from the fact that the appositive is a transformed sentence: for example, *Sarah Cleeford is nominally a Christian*. And in the sentence the adverb modifies the verb *is*, for it can be placed before *is*. But in the appositive, the adverb functions as an adjectival.

Ly adverbs can also modify a few nouns in the postnominal position. Examples:

>The difference **graphemically** was that an x was used instead of a ks.
>The edge **financially** was held by Jay Gould.

These boldface adverbs are modifying the nouns *difference* and *edge*, not the verb *was*. This is demonstrated by the facts that the adverbs cannot be placed after *was* and that there is terminal juncture (though no comma) after the adverbs. Note that if the adverbs are placed in the prenominal position they convert to adjectives. Very few nouns can be modified in this way by the *ly* adverbs. These modifying adverbs are adjectivals by function.

Some of the miscellaneous adverbs of time and place may modify

nouns, sometimes in the prenominal position, sometimes in the postnominal, and sometimes in either. The shifted position is not possible
with these adjectivals. Here are examples of some of the adverbs that
can function as adjectivals:

> the **above** question
> the question **above**
> the **back** row
> the night **before**
> the apartment **below**
> a **clockwise** movement
> a **forward** movement
> the **in** group
> the **now** generation
> the day **thereafter**

Other adverbs that can function similarly as adjectivals are *behind*,
inside, *outside*, *out*, *upward*, *backward*, *headlong*, *overhead*, and *ahead*.
None of these adverbs has any characteristics of the adjective by form.
They must be considered adverbs functioning as adjectivals. The clue
to understanding this function is to see that all these adverbs are words
of place and time. Only when a noun can have the attribute of place
or time can it be modified by one of these adverbs

Prepositional Phrases as Adjectivals

A prepositional phrase can modify any noun in a sentence except a
noun that is modifying another noun. For example, in *future plans* and
meat sandwich neither *future* nor *meat* can be modified by a prepositional phrase. A noun in any other sentence position, however, may be
modified by a prepositional phrase, which is thereby an adjectival.
Such phrases are almost always in the postnominal position.

Here are noun subjects modified by prepositional phrases:

> The man **in the grey flannel suit** is a panhandler.
> The cost **of this car** is prohibitive.

Here are noun direct objects modified by prepositional phrases:

> He found a car **of 1905 vintage**.
> She bought a Bible **with a concordance**.

Here are noun indirect objects modified by prepositional phrases:

> She gave the man **in the sportscoat** a poppy for his lapel.
> I told the student **with the lisp** that he should seek therapy.

Here are noun object complements modified by prepositional phrases:

> We elected Henry president **of the club**.
> The president appointed Dr. Howard dean **of students**.

Here is a complement of the adjective modified by a prepositional phrase:

> Your book is not worth a dollar **of my money**.

Worth is the only predicate adjective that takes a noun complement of the adjective. Here are noun objects of prepositions modified by prepositional phrases:

> I went to the chief **of the bureau**.
> I bet on the team **with the best chance** of winning.

Here are predicate nouns modified by prepositional phrases:

> He is a man **of means**.
> She remained an old maid **with crotchety manners**.

Here is a retained direct object modified by a prepositional phrase:

> I was given a testimonial **of regard** by my colleagues.

Here is a retained indirect object modified by a prepositional phrase:

> A coat-of-arms was awarded Mr. Hunter **of Bear Creek Flats** by the Lions Club.

Here is a retained noun object complement modified by a prepositional phrase:

> Paul was chosen manager **of the Cubs**.

And here are noun appositives modified by prepositional phrases:

> Connie Sultan, the girl **of the month**, won a scholarship.
> Jeanie, Homecoming Queen **for the football game**, is also an A student.

In all these examples the prepositional phrase comes directly after the noun it modifies.

Adjectival prepositional phrases can pile up in sequence, with one modifying the object of a preceding prepositional phrase and in turn having its object modified. Examples:

> the man with a look of confidence in himself
> the author of a series of stories about banditry in Corsica

In the first example, *with a look* modifies *man*, *of confidence* modifies *look*, and *in himself* modifies *confidence*. In the second example, *of a series* modifies *author*, *of stories* modifies *series*, *about banditry* modifies *stories*, and *in Corsica* modifies *banditry*. Such piling up of adjectival prepositional phrases is very common.

A word of warning, however. A prepositional phrase coming directly after a noun does not necessarily modify that noun. Examples:

> John abused Joan **in a particularly severe way**.
> We took our boxer **to a kennel**.

In a particularly severe way is modifying the verb *abused*, not the noun *Joan*, and is therefore an adverbial. Similarly, *to a kennel* modifies the verb *took*, not the noun *boxer*. This is a very common pattern of modification. In analyzing modification, always ask "What does the modifier go with?" As you can see, *took to the kennel* makes sense, but *boxer to the kennel* doesn't. Ambiguity can occur in this kind of structure. For example, in

> John talked to the man in the car,

was John in the car talking, or was he just leaning against the car and talking to the man inside? In other words, is the word relationship *talked in the car* or *man in the car*? Actually, such ambiguity seldom arises.

Prepositional phrases often modify indefinite and interrogative pronouns, and when they do they are adjectivals. Examples:

> Only somebody **out of his mind** would challenge Freddie.
> Something **of note** happened last night.
> Much **of the beer** was green.
> Who **in the freshman class** can debate well?
> What **in the world** are you doing?
> Which **of these two** do you want?

These boldface phrases modify the indefinite and interrogative pronouns that they follow directly.

Prepositional phrases seldom modify personal and relative pronouns. For example, in

> He **in his turn** ordered cognac

and

> Joan, who **in her haste** burned the steaks, was abashed,

in his turn modifies the verb *ordered* and *in her haste* modifies *burned*. Such is almost always the case in constructions of this sort. But prepositional phrases in the shifted position sometimes modify personal pronouns, as will be shown in the next paragraph.

Prepositional adjectival phrases occasionally occupy the prenominal and shifted positions. Examples of phrases in the prenominal position:

In the best of health, John passed his physical easily.
With a heart of gold, Rose made the soldiers feel at home.

The boldface phrases are modifying *John* and *Rose*. Always in the prenominal position a prepositional phrase is followed by terminal juncture. Examples of phrases in the shifted position:

There she sat, **in a gay mood.**
He continued reading, **at peace with the world.**

The boldface phrases modify *she* and *he*. Prepositional phrases do not often function in this shifted position, and when they do they are accompanied by juncture. It is in the prenominal and shifted positions that prepositional phrases are most likely to modify personal pronouns.

Nonfinite Verb Forms as Adjectivals

On page 18 are listed twelve different nonfinite verb forms. All twelve fall into the three classifications of infinitives, present participles, and past participles, and we will just use those three terms, for the technical names of the different types are not important. All three of these nonfinite verb forms (and phrases made with them) can function as adjectivals.

1. *Infinitives and infinitive phrases as adjectivals.* Infinitives as adjectivals always take the postnominal position. For example, in

To get your good will, John praised you to others,

the boldface infinitive phrase modifies *praised*, not *John*, and is therefore an adverbial. Note that *in order* could precede the phrase, a sure sign that it is an adverbial. The shifted position for an infinitive as an adjectival is also impossible. Usually the noun an infinitive modifies is a subject or direct object.

Here are examples of simple infinitives as adjectivals:

The steak **to buy** is porterhouse.
The best book **to read** is the Bible.

The boldface infinitives are modifying *steak* and *book*. Infinitive phrases with complements and/or modifiers can also function as adjectivals. Example of an adjectival infinitive with a modifier:

Crowly is the man **to see about political appointments.**

The infinitive *to see* is modified by an adverbial prepositional phrase. The whole boldface infinitive phrase is an adjectival modifying *man*. Example of an adjectival infinitive with a direct object:

The first **to break Campbell's record** was Lookman.

The boldface infinitive phrase is an adjectival modifying the noun substitute *first*. *Record* is the direct object of *to break*. Example of an adjectival infinitive with direct and indirect objects:

> The last teacher **to give me a C** was Miss Humphrey.

Me is the indirect and *C* the direct object of *to give*. The whole boldface phrase is an adjectival modifying *teacher*. Example of an adjectival infinitive with a direct object and object complement:

> Bishop was the one **to appoint Joe captain**.

The boldface infinitive phrase is modifying the noun substitute *one*. Example of an adjectival infinitive with a predicate noun:

> The only woman **to remain chairman** was Professor Overly.

Chairman is a predicate noun following the linking verb *to remain*, the whole infinitive phrase modifying woman. Example of an adjectival infinitive with a predicate adjective:

> The athlete **to remain calmest** was Broxnik.

Example of an adjectival infinitive with both a complement and modifiers:

> The woman **first to bake a cake with buckwheat flour** was a Mrs. Rogers.

The infinitive *to bake* is modified by *first* and has the direct object *cake*, which in turn is modified by a prepositional phrase. The whole boldface phrase is an adjectival modifying *woman*. And here are examples of passive, perfect, and progressive infinitives functioning as adjectivals:

> The case **to be solved first** was the Jackson murder case.
> The only suspect **to have been seen at Murdo's** was Smith.
> The show **to be watching** is "Sesame Street."

Such complex infinitives are used much less frequently than simple ones.

Here is a kind of adjectival infinitive that might cause puzzlement in analysis:

> The man **to talk to** is Mr. Finlinson.
> The opportunity **to leap at** is the chance to go to Harvard.

The preposition after the infinitive is the puzzle. The whole boldface phrases are transformations of *to whom to talk* and *at which to leap*. Each of these is a prepositional phrase in which the object is an infinitive (*to talk*, *to leap*) with a subject (*whom*, *which*). The whole prepositional phrases, if used, would be adjectivals modifying *man* and *oppor-*

tunity. In the example sentences we just say that an infinitive phrase with a preposition is modifying a noun.

2. *Present participles and participial phrases as adjectivals.* Present participles and present-participial phrases can as adjectivals occupy the prenominal, postnominal, and shifted positions. Example of a simple present participle in a prenominal position:

> The **running** boy tripped on a wire.

Though a verb, *running* is modifying *boy* and is therefore an adjectival. But a word of caution is needed here, for there is a possibility of mistaking a present participle for a prenominal adjectival when it is really a part of a participial phrase functioning as a nominal. For example, in

> Running steers is likely to reduce their weight,

running is not a prenominal adjectival, but the whole phrase *running steers* is a subject and therefore a nominal. *Steers* is the direct object of *running.* Note that the verb (*is*) is singular even though *steers* is plural. This formal cue means that the whole participial phrase is the subject, not just *steers.* Example of a simple present participle in the postnominal position:

> The girl **swimming** is a paralytic.

Swimming is modifying *girl* and is therefore an adjectival. Example of a simple present participle in the shifted position:

> Jim just walked away, **grinning**.

Grinning is modifying *Jim.* A present participle in the shifted position is almost always accompanied by juncture.

A distinction needs to be made between simple present participles of the sort just illustrated and *ing* words that are adjectives by form, not verbs. For example, in

> An **interesting** book is worth more than money

and

> A **confusing** situation arose,

interesting and *confusing* are adjectives by form, not verbs. The difference is that an adjective ending in *ing* can be compared (*more, most*) and can be modified by *very*, whereas an *ing* verb cannot. For example, in

> A **talking** dog doesn't exist,

talking cannot be compared nor modified by *very* and is therefore a present participle, not an adjective, functioning as an adjectival.

Present-participial phrases can also function as adjectivals in all three positions. When the phrase is in the prenominal position it is always accompanied by juncture. Examples:

> **Arguing heatedly,** Jack gave evidence for his case.
> **Taking a five-minute break,** the patrol relaxed uneasily.
> **Having been seeing Joan nightly,** Jerry thought it time to propose.

These boldface present-participial phrases are in their entirety adjectivals. Within the phrases are modifiers and complements. For example, in sentence one, *heatedly* is an adverbial modifying the verb *arguing*, and in sentence two, *break* is the direct object of the verb *taking*. Participial phrases always have their own internal structure.

In the postnominal position the adjectival participial phrase may or may not be accompanied by juncture. Those without juncture are called **restrictive** and those with juncture are called **nonrestrictive**. Commas or other punctuation mark this juncture. Examples:

> The dog **biting the postman** is rabid.
> The boy **jogging around the golf course** is a star athlete.
> Janie, **feeling that she had been insulted,** left in a huff.
> Mr. Smith, **gleefully watching his team score another touchdown,** reached for another beer.

In the first two sentences the boldface present-participial phrases are restrictive (needed to identify the nouns they modify) and in the last two they are nonrestrictive (not needed to identify the nouns they modify). The whole phrases are adjectivals, but they have complicated internal structures of their own. For example, in the last sentence, *gleefully* is an adverbial modifying the verb *watching*; *his team score another touchdown* is an infinitive phrase functioning as the direct object of *watching*; *team* is the subject of the infinitive *score* (which omits the *to*); and *touchdown* is the direct object of *score*.

A present-participial-phrase adjectival in the shifted position is always accompanied by juncture and almost always comes at the end of a sentence. Examples:

> Jerry studied the question, **wondering whether he could fake an answer.**
> Mr. Jones refused his partner another loan, **being sure that he would not even repay the first one.**

The boldface participial phrases modify *Jerry* and *Mr. Jones* and thus are in the shifted adjectival position. These participial phrases have their own internal structure. For example, in the last sentence, *sure* is the predicate-adjective complement of the linking verb *being* and *that he would not even repay the first one* is a noun-clause complement of the adjective.

A present-participial-phrase adjectival, particularly in the prenominal position, is sometimes introduced by a logical connective.   Here are examples:

> After **studying until three o'clock,** Harlen slept through his exam.
> By **following the doctor's orders to the letter,** Mary was well within a week.
> Through **investing wisely,** Mr. Aranian made a fortune.
> The coach had an all-winning season, thereby **endearing himself to the alumni.**

Phrases like those in the first three sentences have been called prepositional, on the grounds that *after*, *by*, and *through* are prepositions. But *thereby* has never been called a preposition, and it certainly introduces its phrase in the same way that *after*, *by*, and *through* do. Clearly, these words are logical connectives expressing the relationship of cause-and-result (and also time in the case of *after*).   They are subordinating conjunctions, just like those that introduce adverb clauses (see page 90).   The participial phrases in the four sentences above are still adjectivals, modifying the nouns *Harlen, Mary, Mr. Aranian,* and *coach.*   These participial phrases are not objects of prepositions, though such a phrase can be.   For example, in

> He was finished with **playing golf,**

the participial phrase *playing golf* is the object of the preposition *with*, which does not express the relationship of cause-and-result as *after*, *by*, *through*, and *thereby* do in the sentences above.   Such logical connectives can also introduce past-participial phrases, which are discussed in the next section.

A grammatical peculiarity that sometimes accompanies a present-participial phrase (and also occasionally past-participial and other kinds of adjectival and adverbial phrases) is known as the **dangling modifier.**   As you noticed above, a participial phrase in the prenominal position modifies the noun subject of the sentence that follows.   When a prenominal phrase does not modify that noun subject, it dangles.   Here are three examples:

> **While investigating the burglary,** another house was robbed.
> **Being unused to such attention,** the hotel service was wonderful.
> **Having numerous dangerous curves,** Jane drove carefully over the mountain road.

The boldface phrases seem to modify *house, hotel,* and *Jane,* whereas they should modify words that are not in the sentences, perhaps *police, I,* and *road.*   Or the sentences could be recast completely to remedy the dangling.   The syntax in such faulty sentences certainly tells something about the mental processes of those who write them.

3. *Past participles and participial phrases as adjectivals.* The simple past participle may function as an adjectival in the prenominal, post-nominal, and shifted positions. Examples of simple past participles in the prenominal position:

> The **printed** book is one of man's great inventions.
> My **repaired** car was delivered to my door.

Both *printed* and *repaired* are verbs modifying *book* and *car* and are thus adjectivals. Examples of simple past participles in the postnominal position:

> The man **executed** was denied a reprieve.
> A girl **rejected** is a dangerous foe.

This is a rare pattern of modification in English; usually adjectival past participles take the prenominal position unless they form phrases. Simple past participles in the postnominal position are always passive, for the implied constructions are *the man was executed* (*by someone*) and *the girl was rejected* (*by someone*). Examples of simple past participles in the shifted position:

> There she sat at the church, **jilted**.
> She was all alone at home, **deserted**.

This is a rare pattern of modification too, but when a simple past participle is in the shifted position, it is always accompanied by juncture and is always passive.

Sometimes an *ed* word is an adjective by form rather than a verb. Examples:

> a **devoted** mother
> an **interested** customer
> an **excited** dog

Usually such *ed* adjectives will compare (*more*, *most*) and can be modified by *very*, whereas a past participle will not compare nor take *very*. For example, you can't say **a more printed book* or **a very printed book*. But this method of distinguishing between adjectives and past participles is not foolproof. For example, *excited* can be thought of as a past participle: *Someone excited the dog.* Still, it will compare and can be modified by *very*.

Various kinds of past-participial phrases will function as adjectivals in all three positions. Examples of such phrases in the prenominal position:

> **Educated at Harvard**, John was able to pick his job.
> **Having been cheated before**, Perry was on his guard.

> **Having seen too many good soldiers die uselessly,** Paul became a
> pacifist.

Such prenominal past-participial phrases are always accompanied by
juncture and always modify the noun subject that they immediately
precede. The third example shows how complex the internal structure
of such a phrase can be. The perfect past participle *having seen* has
as its direct object the entire infinitive phrase *too many good soldiers
die uselessly*; the infinitive *die* (without the *to*) has *soldiers* (which is
modified) as its subject and is also modified by the adverb *uselessly*.
The whole past-participial phrase, however, is an adjectival.

In the postnominal position a past-participial phrase may or may not
be accompanied by juncture. Examples:

> The suspect **jailed by the deputies** refused to talk.
> The player **thrown out of the game** was fined $50.
> Joan, **having been received graciously**, felt quite at home.
> Mr. Gordon, **having seen the students cheating**, refused to accept
> their tests.

When a postnominal past-participial phrase is restrictive, as in the first
two sentences, it is in the passive voice. For example, the two transformations to the active voice are

> The deputies jailed the suspect

and

> The umpire threw the player out of the game.

The reason for this kind of phrase being passive is that it modifies a
noun that received the action expressed in the phrase. If such a postnominal phrase is nonrestrictive, as in the last two sentences, it may or
may not be in the passive voice (in sentence three it is passive, but
in sentence four it is active). The boldface adjectival phrase in sentence
four illustrates the internal complexity that such phrases can have. The
perfect past participle *having seen* has *the students cheating* as its direct
object, and in that direct object the present participle *cheating* has
students as its subject. The whole past-participial phrase is an adjectival.

In the shifted position past-participial phrases are always accompanied by juncture. Examples:

> John just stood there, **awed by the size of the General Sherman
> tree.**
> Mr. Pananides withdrew from the committee, **having already given
> more of his time than he could spare.**

The boldface phrases, adjectivals in their entirety, modify *John* and *Mr. Pananides*. In this position the phrase may be passive, as in the first sentence, or active, as in the second.

A few past participles of verb-particle composites can also function as adjectivals. Examples:

> The **turned-off** neon signs looked eerie in the moonlight.
> The **stirred-up** wasps were stinging everything in sight.
> The **worn-out** coat sold for fifty cents.
> The actor stood in the wings, **made up** to look like Mark Twain.

These boldface past-participial adjectivals are derived from the composites *to turn off*, *to stir up*, *to wear out*, and *to make up* and all are in the passive voice; for example, *the signs were turned off by someone*. Not many past participles derived from composites will function as adjectivals. For example, **the run-across old friend* is not grammatical even though *to run across* is a verb-particle composite.

Compound Adjectivals

When two or more words of any form or structure classes function in the prenominal position as a single adjectival, they should be hyphenated to show that they are functioning as a unit. Many peculiar, and sometimes puzzling, structures occur because writers often do not follow this rule. For example, an ad in *Harper's* once mentioned a stereo with

> two-35 watt amplifiers.

This expression is gibberish. The ad should have specified

> two 35-watt amplifiers,

which has a cardinal number and a noun compounded to make an adjectival. Another ad once mentioned

> the new embedded in plastic printed wiring circuit

This is confusing on first reading. Of course it should have been

> the new embedded-in-plastic, printed-wiring circuit,

which has the two necessary compound adjectivals. Also a publication called *School Days* spoke of

> word analysis-skills.

Of course it should have been

> word-analysis skills.

Various combinations of form- and structure-class words can pro-

duce compound adjectivals. Here are a few of the many possibilities.
Noun plus noun:

> the law-school faculty
> a steel-mill strike

Noun plus structure word plus noun:

> cradle-to-grave needs
> martini-and-steak lunches

Adjective plus noun:

> civil-rights battle
> high-pressure steam

Adjective plus past participle:

> a soft-spoken type
> quick-dried tobacco

Verb stem plus past participle:

> freeze-dried coffee

Verb stem plus verb stem:

> look-say method

Adjective plus present participle:

> a bitter-tasting cola

Cardinal number plus pseudo past participle:

> a two-fisted gesture

Indefinite pronoun plus qualifier plus adjective:

> all-too-human attributes

Noun plus past participle:

> state-supported schools

Noun plus present participle:

> a catharsis-giving experience

Present participle plus noun:

> a biting-dog court case

Past participle plus noun:

> frozen-custard dessert

Cardinal number plus noun:

> a three-year course

Cardinal number plus noun plus adjective:

> an eight-year-old girl

Compound noun:

> shade-tree culture

The variations of form- and structure-class words in compound adjectivals are almost endless. The hyphens contribute to clarity in their use.

Modification of Compound Nouns

On pages 9–10 it was demonstrated that many compound nouns in English are spelled as two words. Such compound nouns can take adjectival modifiers just as ordinary nouns do. Not one part of the compound but the entire compound is modified. Examples of adjectives modifying compound nouns:

> the **leafy** shade tree
> an **ancient** spinning wheel
> a **formal** dining room

Not *shade* nor *tree* but the whole compound *shade tree* is being modified by *leafy*, and the same analysis applies to the other two examples. Examples of present participles modifying compound nouns:

> a **burning** high school
> a **leaking** radiator hose

Examples of past participles modifying compound nouns:

> a **broken** funny bone
> a **repaired** hot rod

Examples of compound adjectivals modifying compound nouns:

> an **all-meat** hot dog
> a **walnut-wood** rocking chair

In all of these examples the last two words are compound nouns and the boldface adjectivals are modifying the whole compounds. Of course when a compound noun is spelled as one word—as are *handyman* and *blackbird*—no misunderstanding of modification would occur.

Adverbials

An adverbial is a word or word group that modifies a verb, an adjective, an adverb, or an adjectival or adverbial word group—usually a verb, for verbs are much more often modified than adjectives, adverbs, or word groups. Verbs excepted, a modified single word must be an adjective or adverb by form, not an adjectival or adverbial, for the modifier to be an adverbial. For example, in

a **coarse** cotton shirt

the modifier *coarse* is not an adverbial even though it is modifying the adjectival *cotton*; the modifier is required to be an adjectival because *cotton* is a noun by form. *Cotton's* being an adjectival by function does not require or permit its modifier to be an adverbial; the phrase **a coarsely cotton shirt* is ungrammatical. And in

Early yesterday he arrived

the modifier *early* is not an adverbial even though it is modifying the adverbial *yesterday*; it is an adjectival because *yesterday* is a noun by form. Though *yesterday* is an adverbial it does not admit of an adverbial modifier. Thus a word that modifies a single-word adjectival or adverbial (*cotton* or *yesterday*) is not necessarily itself an adverbial. To be an adverbial, a word must modify an adjective or adverb by form rather than a single-word adjectival or adverbial; or it may modify a verb (*He arrived early.*), for any word or word group modifying a finite or nonfinite verb is an adverbial.

But when an adjectival or adverbial word group is modified, the modifier is an adverbial. For example, in

He arrived **early** in the day,

early is an adverbial because it is modifying the adverbial prepositional phrase *in the day*. And in

He arrived **long** after we had left,

long is an adverbial because it is modifying the adverbial clause *after we had left*. This difference between modifiers of single-word adjectivals and adverbials which are nouns by form and word-group adjectivals and adverbials is demonstrated by the use of form-class adjectives and adverbs. For example, in

a **coarse** cotton shirt

we use a form-class adjective, not the adverb *coarsely*, to modify the adjectival *cotton*. And in

> He came **immediately** after we left,

we use the form-class adverb, not the adjective *immediate*, to modify the word-group adverbial *after we left*. This series of examples shows the difference between the modification of a single-word adjectival or adverbial and the modification a word-group adjectival or adverbial.

Position of Adverbials

The possible positions of adverbials in sentences are so numerous that no simple, comprehensible list of them can be given, as the list can be given for adjectivals. Here are some of the main adverbial positions. Before a verb:

> He **carefully** considered his options.

Within a verb form with auxiliaries:

> He could **scarcely** see the road.

After a verb:

> He walked **cautiously** along the path.

After a direct object:

> He threw the ball **carelessly**.

After two complements:

> They chose Louis captain **without thinking**.

After an adverbial prepositional phrase:

> He walked into the room **casually**.

All of these positions of adverbials modifying verbs can also occur with nonfinite verbs. Examples:

> **Carefully** inspecting the gun, James found a flaw.
> Edging **carefully** along the path, Bill avoided the booby trap.
> Having **hungrily** eaten the pie, George asked for more.
> Throwing the ball **carelessly**, Billy hit Susan.
> Electing Clive president **quickly**, the club adjourned.
> Walking out of the house **disgustedly**, Jean started for school.

And when the modification is not of a verb there are still other positions. Before a prepositional phrase:

> He hit the nail **right** on the head.

Before an adverb clause:

> He arrived **barely** before we did.

There is also another position when the adverbial modifies a verb. This is the position before a sentence:

> **Cautiously,** Fern edged into the alley.

The adverbial in this presentence position should not be confused with a sentence modifier. In the above sentence *cautiously* modifies *edged*. But in

> **Luckily,** I found my wallet,

luckily modifies the whole sentence, not *found* (see the section on sentence modifiers later in this chapter). There are other miscellaneous adverbial positions, but it is not necessary to get any of the positions in mind in order to identify adverbials. The only test that need be used is to see what the modifier goes with. Also keep in mind that we are discussing a function class, not a form class.

The difficulty of identifying adverbials by position, and the uselessness of trying to memorize positions, is illustrated by the mobility of the adverbial. Example:

> **Cautiously,** Fern edged into the alley.
> Fern **cautiously** edged into the alley.
> Fern edged **cautiously** into the alley.
> Fern edged into the alley **cautiously**.

All of these positions sound completely natural. Prepositional-phrase adverbials, however, do not have as much mobility. For example,

> **Into the alley** Fern edged cautiously

does not sound natural to our ears. And

> Fern **into the alley** edged cautiously

would strike many as ungrammatical. Mobility within the sentence is, however, one of the chief characteristics of single-word adverbials.

Adverbials can pile up just as adjectivals can. Example:

> He walked **carelessly into the jungle without giving danger a thought**.

There are three adverbials piled up here:

> walked **carelessly**
> walked **into the jungle**
> walked **without giving danger a thought**

Remember, the way to test for modification is to see *what goes with what*. Clearly, the *ly* adverb and the two prepositional phrases above go with the verb *walked* and are thus adverbials. The last of the prepositional phrases is illustrative of how complex a prepositional phrase can be. *Giving danger a thought* is a present-participial phrase serving as the object of *without*. In that participial phrase *danger* is the indirect object of *giving* and *thought* is its direct object.

When three or more modifiers pile up after a verb, as in the example sentence in the last paragraph, not all need be adverbials. For example, in

> He walked carelessly into the jungle of the Amazon,

the word relationships are

> walked **carelessly,**
> walked **into the jungle,**

and

> jungle **of the Amazon.**

So *of the Amazon* is an adjectival modifying the noun *jungle*. Note that *walked of the Amazon* makes no sense. In over 99 percent of the cases the simple test to see what goes with what will identify adjectivals and adverbials.

However, ambiguity can occur between adjectivals and adverbials and even between adverbials and adverbials. Consider this sentence from a newspaper article:

> The United States has not always been able to present clear evidence of their alleged illegal activities **in Swiss courts.**

Is the word relationship

> present in Swiss courts

or

> activities in Swiss courts?

If the first, the prepositional phrase is an adverbial, and if the second, an adjectival. The context of the article tells, but the sentence by itself might be considered ambiguous. Or consider this sentence, also from a news item:

> Maheu has been told his services are no longer required **by the Hughes Tool Company.**

Is the word relationship

> told by the Hughes Tool Company

or

> required by the Hughes Tool Company?

In both cases the prepositional phrase is an adverbial, but the ambiguity remains. Actually, anyone reading the sentence would assume that the modification is *required by the Hughes Tool Company*, which is not what the writer intended. When such ambiguity can be cleared up by shifting a modifier, the original sentence has the syntactic flaw known as the **misplaced modifier**.

Adverbs as Adverbials

Most adverbs by form modify verbs, though occasionally they modify adjectives, adverbs, and word groups. The "pure" *ly* adverb presents little difficulty in identification. True, as was illustrated above, it may occupy many positions when it modifies a verb, but the pattern of word relationship is almost always clear, even when the adverb is far removed from the verb it modifies. Examples:

> The little boy climbed up the rugged, prickly branches of the old
> pine tree **cautiously**.
> Read the directions to the test on modification **carefully**.

Though most writers and speakers would probably place these adverbs closer to the verbs, *cautiously* and *carefully* quite clearly modify *climbed* and *read*. And so it goes with *ly* adverbs, unless one is placed ambiguously. For example, in

> The little boy ran toward the vase placed out of his reach **quickly**,

quickly might modify *ran* or it might modify *placed*. But such instances of ambiguity are not especially common and can be cleared up by repositioning the adverb.

Though adverbs modify verbs much more frequently than they do adjectives and adverbs, they can modify adjectives and adverbs. Here are examples of adverbs modifying adjectives:

> He was **cautiously** prudent.
> She is **completely** unprejudiced.

Here *cautiously* and *completely* are modifying the adjectives *prudent* and *unprejudiced*. But an adverb coming directly before an adjective does not necessarily modify that adjective. For example, in

> He was **soon** dissatisfied,

soon modifies *was*, not *dissatisfied*. The fact that *soon* can be placed before *was* shows its pattern of modification. But an *ly* adverb before an adjective almost always modifies the adjective. Adverbs are even less frequently modified by adverbs than adjectives are. Examples:

> He peered around the corner **extremely** cautiously.
> **Probably** soon it will rain.

Usually, however, adjectives and adverbs are modified by qualifiers rather than by adverbs. Only when a modifier of an adjective or adverb is an *ly* word should it be called an adverb. Most other words modifying adjectives and adverbs are qualifiers (see Chapter 4).

Adverbs can also modify prepositional phrases and adverb clauses, and then they are adverbials. Examples:

> He arrived **soon** after dinner.
> He was **completely** in the right.
> **Soon** after we left, John arrived.
> **Barely** before we arrived, the rainstorm struck.

These boldface adverbs are modifying the word groups that they directly precede. Note that repositioning the adverbs produces awkward or ungrammatical sentences. For example, *he arrived after dinner soon* and *he completely was in the right* do not sound grammatical. This test shows that the adverbs are modifying *after dinner* and *in the right*.

Adverbs do not participate in endocentric phrases to the extent that the other three form-class words do. Often a short endocentric adverb phrase occurs when an adverb is modified by a qualifier or another adverb. Examples:

> very selfishly
> quite contentedly
> extremely carefully

The adverbs *selfishly*, *contentedly*, and *carefully* are headwords in these short endocentric structures and will function grammatically as the whole structures do. For example, *he acted very selfishly* and *he acted selfishly* are equally grammatical. Prepositional phrases so rarely modify adverbs that they can be dismissed as participating in endocentric adverb phrases. Don't be led astray in analysis by thinking that such a phrase as

> quite indignantly at the professor

is an endocentric adverb phrase, for in a sentence such as

> He stared quite indignantly at the professor

the word relationships are *stared quite indignantly* and *stared at the professor*, the adverb and the phrase equally modifying *stared*, not forming a unit of their own.

The *ly* adverb, then, presents few problems in identification, but for the record here are some examples of miscellaneous adverbs modifying verbs:

> Charlie runs **fast**.
> His car runs **well**.

Bill is here **now**.
They will arrive **there soon**.
Sue went **ahead**.
She came **back**.
It **seldom** rains **here**.
He will go **anywhere**.
Call me up **sometime**.
Still he didn't come.
He fell **headlong**.
I've **already** eaten.
He is **indeed** sarcastic.
I spoke **offhand**.

There are only three or four dozen adverbs of this sort altogether. Generally it is easy to perceive their modification of verbs. When they modify nouns, as in *a headlong plunge*, the adjectival modification is clear. Remember, always ask what goes with what.

Nouns as Adverbials

One noun of place and several nouns of time may function as adverbials by modifying verbs. Examples:

He took her **home**.
She arrived **yesterday**.
The ship sails **Tuesday morning**.

The boldface nouns by form are functioning as adverbials since they modify the verbs *took*, *arrived*, and *sails*. Such nouns of time as the months of the year, the days of the week, *today*, *tomorrow*, and so on frequently function as adverbials. In the third example above, *Tuesday morning* is a noun of time modifying a noun of time, the whole functioning as an adverbial. But noun phrases seldom function as adverbials. *Home* seems to be the only noun of place that functions as an adverbial. In such a sentence as *the children played house*, *house* is really a direct object, just as *a game* would be. With nouns of place other than *home*, a prepositional phrase functions as an adverbial. For example, **I took her town* is ungrammatical; only *I took her to town* is grammatical. *To town* is an adverbial, just as is *home* in the first example sentence above. Nouns, then, are severely limited in their capacity to function as adverbials.

Adjectives as Adverbials

Adjectives are not extensively used as adverbials, for the good reason that most adjectives can be made into adverbs by the addition of *ly*.

But we do have some adjectives that can modify verbs and thus be adverbials. The most common instances of adjectives functioning as adverbials are these:

> Drive **slow**.
> Talk **louder**.
> Run to the store **quick**.
> My car runs **good**.

These are colloquial usages. Most professional writers would use *slowly*, *more loudly*, *quickly*, and *well*. Historically, it is accurate to call *slow* an adverb as well as an adjective, for both *slowe* and *slowlich* existed side by side as adverbs in the Old English period (about 800 A.D.). The other colloquial usages developed later.

We also frequently use adjectives to modify the verb *think*. Examples:

> Think **young**.
> Think **big**.
> Think **hard**.

Note that if you change *young* to *in a young manner*, its adverbial nature is clear. It might be thought that we use these adjectives as adverbials because our language lacks the corresponding *ly* adverbs, but that explanation will not suffice. Though *hardly* and the obsolete *bigly* do not correspond to *hard* and *big*, there is the rare word *youngly*. And most of us would accept

> Think **beautiful**

as a similar construction, though *beautifully* is available. Thus these adjectives must be accepted as natural adverbials.

Another peculiar idiom using adjectives as adverbials is our traditional admonition

> If you study **long**, you study **wrong**.

Both *long* and *wrong* are adjectives functioning as adverbials, since they modify the verb *study*. Despite dictionaries we rarely use the adverb *longly*, and to achieve the obvious rime the natural form *wrongly* was not used in the above saying.

Sometimes *ed* adjectives modify verbs and thus function as adverbials. Examples:

> They romped **naked**. (= thus)
> He drove **plastered**. (= thus)

These *ed* words are not past participles, for no verb now exists for them. The fact that *thus* can be substituted for them shows that they are adverbials of manner.

The words *early* and *late* pose something of a problem in analysis. Both are words of time and thus might be considered adverbs by form. But they both freely modify both nouns and verbs, and they also fit into the adjective paradigm. So it is probable that they are adjectives that can function as adverbials. We do not have the form **earlily*, but *earliness* is a good word and thus, since *early* also compares, it fits into the adjective paradigm. Also note that adverbs do not normally take the derivational suffix *ness* to make nouns. It may be that the possible adverb **earlily* did not develop because it is so awkward to pronounce. The comparable *friendlily* is listed in the dictionary as an adverb, but very few use it because of its awkward pronunciation. Probably the accurate analysis, then, is that in such sentences as

> They arrived **early**

and

> Spring came **early** this year,

early is an adjective functioning as an adverbial. A possible alternate analysis is to accept *early* as both an adjective and an adverb by form.

Late also fits into the adjective paradigm, for it compares and also makes the forms *lately* and *lateness*. However, *lately* has a specialized meaning so that *he arrived lately* and *he arrived late* have different meanings. Probably, however, in such a sentence as

> We reached our destination **late** in the afternoon,

late is an adjective functioning as an adverbial, since it modifies the adverbial prepositional phrase *in the afternoon*. As with *early*, a possible alternate analysis is to consider *late* both an adjective and an adverb by form.

In general it can be said that not many adjectives by form function as adverbials in our language.

Nonfinite Verb Forms as Adverbials

All three of the nonfinite verb forms in the verb paradigm—infinitives, present participles, and past participles (and phrases made with them)—can function as adverbials.

1. *Infinitives as adverbials.* Actually, most of the time when an infinitive functions as an adverbial by modifying a verb it is a deletion transformation of a prepositional phrase beginning with *in order*. Example:

> I went to the registrar **to inquire about my transcript**.

The boldface infinitive phrase modifies the verb *went* and thus is an adverbial, but note that *in order* could precede it. Thus the understood adverbial is a prepositional phrase, the preposition being this suppressed *in order* and the infinitive phrase being its object. But our syntax has omitted the *in order* for so long that it is accurate just to call the infinitive an adverbial. Using *in order*, however, is a simple test to see if an infinitive is functioning as an adverbial (though some infinitive adverbials will not take *in order*). Here are some additional examples:

> I studied hard **to see whether I could improve my grade**.
> I donated generously **to give the poor a better Christmas**.
> I sipped the water **to test its purity personally**.

The boldface infinitive phrases are adverbials since *in order* could be used with them and since they are modifying the verbs. The phrases have their own internal structure. In sentence one, a noun clause is the direct object of *to see*. In sentence two, *poor* is an indirect and *Christmas* a direct object of *to give*. And in sentence three, *purity* is a direct object and *personally* an adverbial modifier of *to test*.

Such infinitive phrases can also take a presentence position. Examples:

> **To get a good view**, climb the stairway.
> **To avoid credit difficulties**, pay your bills on time.
> **To insure his admission to college**, Brian applied to six universities.

Note that *in order* could precede each of these phrases and that each modifies the sentence verb. For example, the word relationships are *climb in order to get a good view* and the like.

With some passive-voice verbs, infinitives function as adverbials without being able to take *in order*. Examples:

> I was heard **to utter an imprecation**.
> I was made **to believe his lie**.

These infinitive phrases are not direct objects, for a passive-voice sentence can have a retained direct object only when the active-voice sentence has also an indirect object. In the active-voice sentence

> Someone heard **me utter an imprecation**,

the whole boldface phrase is a direct object. Thus in the passive-voice sentences the boldface infinitive phrases are adverbials modifying the verbs *was heard* and *was made*. However, in such active-voice sentences as

> He found me to be a liar

and

> He thought me to be a genius,

liar and *genius* are noun object complements with *to be* an expletive (note that it can be left out). Therefore in the passive-voice sentence

> I was found to be a liar,

liar is a retained object complement and *to be* is an expletive.

Infinitives functioning as complements should not be confused with infinitive adverbials. Examples of infinitives as direct objects:

> She wanted **to go to the prom.**
> I decided **to buy a Mercedes.**
> He hoped **to make an A average.**

Note that these boldface phrases are not modifying the verbs and that *in order* cannot precede them. *Something* can be substituted for them, showing that they are nominals. Also infinitives can function as complements of the adjective. Examples:

> That latch is hard **to reach.**
> She was happy **to be of service.**
> This problem is impossible **to understand.**

These boldface infinitives are not modifying the adjectives but are complementing them. Note that *in order* cannot precede them.

2. *Present participles as adverbials.* Present participles and present-participial phrases occasionally function as adverbials. Examples:

> I like to eat **standing.** (= thus)
> He stood **ogling the girls.**
> He came in **limping.**
> He died **laughing.**

Though these present participles denote actions performed by the subjects of the sentences, they are, nevertheless, grammatically modifying the verbs (an infinitive in the first sentence). Note that the possibility of substituting *thus* for the present participles shows their adverbial nature. In the third sentence *came in* is a verb with a modifying adverb, not a verb-particle composite.

Present participles following a few passive-voice verbs also function as adverbials. Examples:

> I was caught **drinking whisky.** (= thus)
> I was heard **telling lies.**
> I was found **checking out books.**

The fact that *thus* can be substituted for these present-participial phrases shows their adverbial nature. In the active-voice version, such as

> Someone caught **me drinking whisky,**

the whole participial phrase (with a subject and a direct object) is the direct object of *caught*.

Present participles as direct objects should not be confused with those functioning as adverbials. Examples:

> He likes **ogling the girls**.
> He disliked **limping**.

Note that since not *thus* but *something* can be substituted for these present participles, they are nominals (direct objects).

3. *Past participles as adverbials*. Past participles and past-participial phrases also occasionally function as adverbials. Here are examples:

> He finished the fight **battered to a pulp**. (= thus)
> The senatorial candidate ran **scared**.
> He began his tenure **condemned to misery**.
> They sat **frozen by the north wind**.

It might be thought that these past participles are really adjectives, but they are past participles in the passive voice: *he was battered (by someone)*, *he was scared (by his opposition)*, *he was condemned to misery (by his public office)*, and *they were frozen by the north wind*. The fact that *thus* could be substituted for the boldface past-participial phrases shows that they are adverbials and are modifying the verbs *finished*, *ran*, *began*, and *sat*.

Prepositional Phrases as Adverbials

Probably the majority of written sentences in English have at least one prepositional phrase modifying a finite or nonfinite verb form. Such phrases are adverbials. Here are examples of prepositional phrases modifying verbs:

> He came walking **into the saloon by himself**.

The word relationships are *came into the saloon* and *came by himself*. Also note that *walking* is an adverbial.

> The dog tore the pants of the mailman **in three places**.

The word relationship is *tore in three places*. Note that the wide separation of the phrase from the verb does not prevent it from modifying the verb.

> The little boy bit **into the middle** of the cake **with all his force**.

The word relationships are *bit into the middle* and *bit with all his force*. *Of the cake* modifies *middle* and is therefore an adjectival.

> Hitting the first pitch of the inning **with all his force**, Greenberg showed that he still thought his team could win.

The word relationship is *hitting with all his force*. Remember that in analyzing modification patterns you should always ask *what goes with what*.

As was mentioned in the section on endocentric adjective phrases on page 260, prepositional phrases may be said to modify adjectives, though some grammarians maintain that in such constructions the phrases are complements of the adjective. When (and if) a prepositional phrase modifies an adjective, it is an adverbial by function. But aside from the possibility of such phrases being complements rather than modifiers, care must be taken in identifying prepositional phrases that modify adjectives. For example, in

> He was contented **in a half-hearted way**

the boldface phrase does not modify the adjective *contented* even though it comes next to it. Shifting the phrase to

> In a half-hearted way, he was contented

shows that it really modifies *was*. Also in

> He arrived early **in the afternoon**

the boldface prepositional phrase does not modify the adjective *early*, but vice versa, making *early* an adverbial. The word relationship is *arrived in the afternoon*, showing that the phrase modifies the verb.

But at other times prepositional phrases do seem to modify adjectives (if the phrases are not complements). Examples:

> I am contented **with my salary**.
> We were sad **in the extreme**.
> She was bitter **about being jilted**.
> Courageous **in his principles**, Bill stood his ground.
> Angry **at the world**, I could only sulk.

These prepositional phrases may plausibly be said to modify the adjectives preceding them (they certainly do not modify the verbs) and thus may be called adverbials. But if someone insists on calling them complements of the adjective, just agree with him, for the sake of peace in the grammatical family.

Prepositional phrases do not modify *ly* adverbs. For example, in such sentences as

> Morally **in the right**, Burns felt secure

and

> Barely **in his right senses**, Odgen had difficulty giving orders,

morally and *barely* are modifying the prepositional phrases, not vice versa. And in such a sentence as

> He acted normally **in his accustomed role,**

the word relationships are *acted normally* and *acted in his accustomed role*, showing that the phrase does not modify *normally* but that the adverb and the phrase modify the verb equally.

The same analysis applies to most prepositional phrases that might appear to modify non-*ly* adverbs. For example, in such a sentence as

> He is still **in trouble,**

still is modifying the prepositional phrase, not vice versa. And in such a sentence as

> They found him somewhere **in the building,**

the word relationships are *found somewhere* and *found in the building*, showing that both the adverb and the phrase are modifying the verb equally. Two possibilities of prepositional phrases modifying adverbs are

> He ran ahead **of the crowd**

and

> He is behind **in his work.**

The boldface prepositional phrase *of the crowd* is modifying the adverb *ahead*, for *ran of the crowd* is not the word relationship. Also the phrase *in his work* is modifying the adverb *behind*, for *is in his work* is not the word relationship. But it can be said that prepositional phrases rarely modify adverbs.

Sentence Modifiers

In the past sections of this chapter we have seen that within a sentence single words and all verb forms, prepositional phrases, and dependent clauses can be grammatically modified. Also within a sentence the sentence itself can be modified. We will consider dependent-clause sentence modifiers in the next chapter; here we will discuss single-word and phrase modifiers of sentences.

In general, analysis of sentence modification is a sticky matter. Grammarians disagree about which structures are sentence modifiers and which are not, just as they disagree as to whether prepositional phrases modify or complement adjectives. Probably there are constructions which can with equal validity be called either sentence modifiers or adjectivals or adverbials. But there are many unquestionable instances of sentence modification, and we will concentrate on those.

One clue to the sentence modifier is its dissociation from the sentence by terminal juncture. This juncture must always be present whether the modifier takes a presentence, postsentence, or interior position and whether or not the modifier is set off by a comma or commas (a few sentence modifiers, such as *of course*, are so commonly used and have their juncture so minimized that many writers no longer separate them with commas). But the chief clue to the sentence modifier is *its application to the whole idea of the sentence instead of to a single word or word group within the sentence.*

Single-Word Sentence Modifiers

Single-word sentence modifiers are usually adverbs by form and thus have adverbial characteristics, but their meaning applies to the sentence as a whole, not just to its verb. The same adverb form that functions as a sentence modifier, however, can instead modify the sentence verb and thus be an adverbial rather than a sentence modifier. In some such cases the sentence modifier and the adverbial have different meanings and sometimes they have similar meanings. First, consider these two sentences:

> I love you **truly**.
> **Truly**, I love you.

In the first sentence *truly* is an adverbial (without juncture) modifying the verb *love* with the meaning "in a true manner." In the second sentence *truly* is a sentence modifier (with juncture) with the meaning "of a certainty" or "in accordance with fact" or, simply, "I mean it." In this meaning *truly* modifies the entire statement, not just the verb. Note that the sentence modifier could take the postsentence position with juncture:

> I love you, **truly**.

Not all modifiers accompanied by juncture are sentence modifiers, but here the juncture marks the sentence modifier and indicates its difference in meaning from the adverbial.

Now consider these two sentences:

> He is **apparently** sane.
> He is sane, **apparently**.

In the first sentence *apparently* is an adverbial modifying the adjective *sane* with the meaning "according to appearances." In the second sentence *apparently* is a sentence modifier, set off by juncture so that it cannot be modifying *sane* alone, but also with the meaning "according to appearances." The major difference between the two sentences is grammatical structure, not meaning. Thus sometimes sentence modi-

fiers and adverbials identical in form have different meanings and
sometimes the same meaning.

Here are a number of other examples to help you develop a feel for
identifying single-word sentence modifiers:

> *Adverbial:*
>> He acted **naturally** at the party. (= in a natural manner)
>
> *Sentence modifier:*
>> **Naturally**, he acted at the party. (= of course)

> *Adverbial:*
>> He is **undeniably** competent.
>
> *Sentence modifier:*
>> **Undeniably**, he is competent.

> *Adverbial:*
>> Arnold left **happily**. (= He was glad to leave.)
>
> *Sentence modifier:*
>> **Happily**, Arnold left. (= We were glad he left.)

More single-word sentence modifiers:

> **Luckily**, Bill could swim.
> **Truthfully**, I can't remember the night.
> The merger was for the best, **institutionally**.
> **Concurrently**, we ran a warehouse sale.
> Jerry didn't graduate from college, **unfortunately**.
> **Remarkably**, the accident caused no injuries.
> **Anyway**, you had the last word.

Each of these sentence modifiers applies its meaning to the sentence as
a whole, not just to the sentence verb.

Adverbs in the presentence position with juncture may be adverbials
rather than sentence modifiers. Examples:

> **Cautiously**, Mac peered around the corner.
> **Greedily**, Gertrude grabbed the last piece of chicken.
> **Patiently**, Marie repeated her explanation.

The boldface adverbs are modifying the verbs *peered*, *grabbed*, and *repeated* and thus are adverbials. Note that if the adverbs were shifted to
the preverb, postverb, or postsentence position they would not be accompanied by juncture. In none of those positions would they modify
the whole sentence. The determining characteristic of the sentence
modifier is that its meaning applies to the whole statement, not just to a
word or word group within the statement.

Phrasal Sentence Modifiers

As with a single-word sentence modifier, a phrase is a sentence modifier when its meaning applies to the whole statement, not to an individual word or word group in the statement. Phrasal sentence modifiers are accompanied by juncture and may variously occupy pre-sentence, postsentence, and interior positions. The kind of phrase most commonly used as a sentence modifier is prepositional. Examples:

> **In fact,** Rory was not even at the party.
> The salesman's spiel was, **of course,** inaccurate.
> **Under the circumstances,** we should conserve our principal.
> **In theory,** the maximum speed possible for matter is the speed of light.
> The play did very well, **considering the circumstances.**
> **Barring a depression,** our product should sell well.

In the last two sentences, *considering* and *barring* are now regarded by most grammarians as prepositions (see page 79), but a possible alternate analysis is to call the phrases present-participial phrases functioning as sentence modifiers. Note that there is no actor named in the sentences to do the considering and barring, so that the phrases are sentence modifiers.

Examples of infinitive phrases as sentence modifiers:

> **To be sure,** I understood the message.
> I didn't want her, **to tell the truth.**

Note that in both sentences *in order to* is not the meaning. Instead, set expressions are being used as sentence modifiers. Also note the great difference between the last sentence and

> I didn't want her to tell the truth.

Juncture makes the difference. Example of a present-participial phrase as a sentence modifier:

> **Strictly speaking,** the appositive is a noun repeater, not a modifier.

Note that there is no one in the sentence to do the speaking, so that the phrase is obviously a sentence modifier. Example of a past-participial phrase as a sentence modifier:

> **Everything considered,** the party was a success.

The boldface phrase is really a nonfinite predication, for *everything* is the subject of the passive past participle *considered*. The implied construction is *everything was considered by us.* The whole phrase functions as a sentence modifier.

Here are additional examples of various sorts of phrases functioning as sentence modifiers. Some of them could be shifted to other sentence positions.

Regardless of what you say, I'll marry her.
Profit aside, we enjoyed the work.
Needless to say, the judge was impartial.
Contrary to our assumption, the sermon was not well received.
Yes, indeed, we are open for business.
Just perhaps, Mona may be coming.
Aside from that one danger, it looks like clear sailing.
For example, we give a three-year warranty.
More than likely, the ABCA will absorb the CPYU.
Over and above our salaries, the project made money.

The adverbial nature of sentence modifiers often makes the dividing line between adverbials and sentence modifiers not very clear. For example, in the last two sentences above the boldface phrases might be analyzed as modifying *absorb* and *made*, in which case they would be adverbials. When there is genuine doubt in your mind as to whether a construction is a sentence modifier or an adverbial, either analysis is probably accurate.

The absolute phrase is a sentence modifier. Examples:

The polls having closed, we went home to hear the returns.
The riots not having diminished, more troops were called in.

Since such absolute phrases have their own subjects and nonfinite verbs, they must be sentence modifiers. The entire independent clause is the result of the action in the absolute phrase, showing the sentence modification.

Some grammatical debate has occurred as to whether or not pre-sentence infinitive and present-participial phrases are sentence modifiers. Examples:

To get the best job, register with an employment agency.
After going over the accounts, we found one sizable error.

On page 286 we maintained that the introductory infinitive phrase (which could have *in order* placed in front of it) is an adverbial modifying the sentence verb. That is, *register in order to get the best job* is the word relationship. And on page 270 we maintained that an introductory present-participial phrase, with or without a connective, is an adjectival modifying the immediately following sentence subject, since it is that subject which performs the action in the participial phrase. That is, the implied word relationship is *we, going over the accounts,....* We will stick to these analyses, recognizing that not all grammarians will agree. In the next chapter we will also see that it is often difficult to determine whether a dependent clause is a sentence modifier or an adverbial. Unfortunately, grammar is so complex that complete analysis with 100-percent certainty is not possible.

Appositives

Though there are many complexities in the whole matter of appositives, essentially an appositive is a **noun repeater** and is a nominal. It represents one of the eight primary functions of the noun. Since nouns may modify nouns, it might seem reasonable to call the appositive an adjectival—a modifier of a noun—but the grammatical transformation of an appositive shows that it is a nominal. When a noun modifies a noun, as in

> freedom fighters,

the transformation usually is a prepositional phrase or, less often, a verbal phrase, such as

> fighters for freedom

or

> fighters making a fight for freedom.

This kind of transformation shows that a noun is modifying a noun, not that it is repeating a noun. But the only transformation possible with an appositive is a pattern 8 sentence: *Subject-be-predicate noun.* For example, here is a sentence with a typical appositive:

> Neutron stars, **heavenly bodies with a diameter of only a few miles**, were discovered in the 1970's.

The boldface construction is an endocentric noun phrase in apposition to *neutron stars.* With the addition of a form of *be* the two constituents will make a pattern 8 sentence:

> Neutron stars are heavenly bodies with a diameter of only a few miles.

This is the transformation that most appositives[2] will undergo: the appositive, the noun or noun substitute it is in apposition to, and a form of *to be* will normally make a pattern 8 sentence. This test shows that as a noun repeater the appositive is a nominal, not a modifier. But we are including this section on appositives in the chapter on

---

[2]In the case of pronouns—especially indefinite pronouns—as appositives, the transformation is very awkward. Also when the appositive is in apposition to the noun substitute *that* or *this*, the transformation requires a little tinkering. See below.

modifiers because appositives are very like modifiers and are not extensive enough to warrant a chapter of their own.

Most appositives are endocentric noun phrases, most are non-restrictive, and most occupy the postnominal position. Examples of typical appositives:

> Ecology, **the study of the mutual relationship between organisms and their environment**, now attracts widespread interest.
> Walt Kelly, **the creator of the comic strip "Pogo,"** is an acute political satirist.

The headwords of the boldface endocentric appositive phrases are *study* and *creator*; the phrases directly follow the nouns they are in apposition to—*ecology* and *Walt Kelly*; and the commas denote that the phrases are nonrestrictive, that is, that they are not necessary to identify the nouns they are in apposition to. Note that with the use of a form of *be* the appositives and the nouns they are in apposition to will form pattern 8 sentences. These are typical appositives, but many variations from this pattern occur.

Single nouns—especially proper names—sometimes function as appositives. Examples:

> The instigator of the court action against Professor Twerly—**Dean Hoag**—was himself fired.
> The world's most important animal—**the earthworm!**—is responsible for continued soil fertility.

Personal pronouns, usually in conjunction with a proper name, sometimes function as appositives. Examples:

> The two of us—**Bob and I**—constructed the float by ourselves.
> We should get married, **you and I.**

Bob and I is in apposition to *us*, and *you and I* is in apposition to *we*. In the last sentence the appositive is in a shifted position. Some indefinite pronouns also may function as appositives. Examples:

> We **all** phoned Harriet.
> They are **both** astronauts.
> Father gave us **each** a cat.
> Our cats, **most of them**, have their front claws removed.

The boldface appositives are in apposition to *we*, *they*, *us*, and *cats*. The pattern 8 sentence transformation is awkward with such appositives as these. In the first three examples the appositives are not really restrictive even though they are not set off by commas. Since they are not needed to identify the noun substitutes they are in apposition to, they are nonrestrictive appositives. But they are not accompanied by juncture and thus do not need separation by commas or dashes. These are highly idiomatic appositives.

Present participles and participial phrases and infinitives and infinitive phrases may function as appositives. Examples of present participles as appositives:

> Her first love—**eating wild mushrooms**—was her last act.
> His hobby—**racing cars at the Salt Flats**—is expensive.
> That was the cause of our terror—**the tent flapping in the rain.**

In the last example the boldface appositive is in apposition to *that* and is in a shifted position. In the first and second examples the present participles have direct objects (*mushrooms* and *cars*) and in the third example a subject (*tent*). Examples of infinitives as appositives:

> His one desire—**to act**—went unfulfilled.
> That's his constant goal—**to score the highest on every test.**
> Were those his only thanks—**to say he didn't care?**
> **To be great in his own field**—that is all a man can ask.

In the second example the boldface appositive is in apposition to *that* and is in a shifted position. In the fourth sentence the infinitive appositive is in apposition to *that* (the grammatical subject) and is in a pre-sentence position. In sentences two and three the appositive infinitives have direct objects. In sentence four *great* is a predicate adjective following the linking verb *to be*. Both the participial and infinitive appositives in this paragraph are nominals by function. Note that they will make pattern 8 sentences: for example, *her first love was eating wild mushrooms*. When *that* (or *this*) is the noun substitute that an appositive is in apposition to, the pattern 8 sentence is formed with the appositive and the predicate noun accompanying *that*: for example, *the cause of our terror was the tent flapping in the rain*.

An appositive can be in apposition to a nominal implied by a verb phrase. Examples:

> He conceded the election, **a gesture that not many of his backers approved of.**
> He was known to have supported the subversive Committee for Democratic Principles, **a fact that hurt his political career.**

In sentence one the boldface appositive is in apposition to the implied nominal *his concession of the election* and in sentence two to the implied nominal *his support of the subversive Committee for Democratic Principles*. Note that with these implied nominals pattern 8 sentences can be formed; for example, *his concession of the election was a gesture not many of his backers approved of.*

Appositives are sometimes accompanied by appositive conjunctions (see page 89). Examples:

> We brought the necessities—that is, **beer and cheese**.
> The follicle widens into a bulb—or **hair root**—at its deep end.
> You should engage in many activities, such as **singing, bowling, skiing, and debating**.

That is, *or*, and *such as* are appositive conjunctions introducing the boldface appositives.

Sometimes appositives—generally titles or proper names—are restrictive and thus not set off by commas or dashes. Examples:

> The movie **The Great Train Robbery** started the tradition of the western.
> Sinclair Lewis's novel **Arrowsmith** won him a Pulitzer Prize, which he refused.
> Britain's jabbery novelist **Eric Stotts** is due to visit America.
> Highes's general flunky **Ed Cordon** was fired unceremoniously.

The boldface appositives are needed to identify the nouns they are in apposition to: *movie*, *novel*, *novelist*, and *flunky*. Thus they are restrictive and not set off by commas or dashes. Note that these appositives will make pattern 8 sentences: for example, *the novel* (under discussion) *is* Arrowsmith.

EXERCISES

1. In the following sentences identify the italicized constructions as nonfinite predications, or complements that are not nonfinite predications, or modifiers.

> a. The lawyer wanted *her to tell the truth*.
> b. I went over the mountain *to see what I could see*.
> c. I wanted *to see what I could see*.
> d. We found *her eating*.
> e. I urged John to try *skiing*.
> f. John was there *grinning from ear to ear*.
> g. We found *Jim jailed*.
> h. Jim was just sitting there, *jailed*.
> i. Having wanted *to go too*, Perry was disappointed.
> j. I resigned *to take a higher-paying position*.
> k. The wolf is *at the door*.
> l. His mother made him *stingy*.

    m. He is alive *to tell the tale.*
    n. I'm sorry *that you are sick.*
    o. He went to court *to tell the truth.*

2. In the following sentences establish whether meaning or position or formal clues or a combination of these tells what the italicized modifiers modify.

    a. I went into the classroom *with trepidation.*
    b. Boris just sat there, *meditating.*
    c. In the first three houses of the tract, *which was financed by FHA loans,* extra appliances were included.
    d. Petrov, *unable to control his temper,* lashed out at Manski.
    e. The first three books of the set, *which were badly worn,* were offered free.
    f. Professor Morris examined the test papers *carefully* and *patiently.*
    g. Professor Morris, *careful* and *patient,* examined the test papers.
    h. John read Bill's account of tracking cheetahs *in Uganda.*
    i. Bill's Siamese, *which is his favorite cat,* bore four half-breeds.
    j. Jerry and Gail, *who is his fiancee,* decided to stay in separate hotels for the vacation.

3. Compose six sentences illustrating adjectivals in the prenominal, postnominal, and shifted positions.

4. Compose a sentence with a present-participial adjectival that cannot occupy the postnominal position singly but that can occupy it when the present participle takes an object. Do the same for a past participle.

5. Compose three sentences with restrictive present-participial-phrase adjectivals in the postnominal position and three with such adjectivals that are nonrestrictive.

6. Compose three sentences with restrictive past-participial-phrase adjectivals in the postnominal position and three with such adjectivals that are nonrestrictive.

7. Compose five sentences with adjectivals in the shifted position.

8. Compose three sentences with endocentric adjective phrases.

9. Give a transformation for each of the following constructions in which a noun modifies a noun.

a record album	a steel trap
a tenement flat	a linen dress
frog legs	Hollywood sins
a feather duster	freeway traffic
an adult conversation	a neutron star

10. In the following sentences identify the form class of each italicized adjectival.

a. The *crying* boy had a *broken* toy.
b. The *unnerving* incident was caused by a *wildcat* strike.
c. The *mystic* night calls for an *upward* look.
d. The *overhead* projector showed *cryptic* graphs.
e. The *rubber* tire blew out on the *concrete* pavement.
f. A *prejudiced* minister is not a *Godly* man.
g. The man *outside* is an *encyclopedia* salesman.
h. The *shifted* position is one for *descriptive* adjectivals.
i. An *annoying* dog should be a *banned* pest.
j. *Barking* dogs are *increasing* nuisances.

11. In the following sentences identify adjectival and adverbial prepositional phrases.

    a. The mouth of the creek in Coosa County remained in the hands of its original owners.
    b. By diving into the pool at its deep end one can glide submerged for thirty feet.
    c. The president of the student body was elected by a narrow margin of three votes out of fifteen hundred cast.
    d. Jim began by tracing on a map the probable escape route of the robbers.
    e. Joan bought a coat of mink with a savings bond given to her by her uncle.
    f. An adverb modified by a prepositional phrase is a rarity in English and may be rare in other languages.
    g. The man to see about a job is the personnel officer of the biggest company in town.
    h. Printed in lavender, the book became a great favorite with the hippies of North Beach.
    i. Happy about his new job, Ronald planned to save for the future by depositing ten dollars in the bank on every Friday.
    j. Depressed by the failure of his plans, Evan resolved to engage in a new series of activities in hopes of re-establishing an image of success.

12. In the following sentences differentiate between present participles as adjectivals and present participles which are part of a nominal construction. Don't confuse a present participle with an adjective by form.

    a. Beating children is a crying shame.
    b. Smiling foxes are often after laying hens.
    c. Interesting the students is a challenge for all striving teachers.
    d. Interesting students are appreciated by demanding teachers.
    e. Grinding jobs sometimes call for grinding stones.

13. Which of the following italicized adjectivals or adverbials can be shifted to another position in its sentence? Explain why each can or cannot be shifted. Tell which is an adjectival and which an adverbial.

    a. I went straight to the professor *to be sure that I understood why I failed.*

    b. *Angrily replying*, Joe proved that he had a short temper.

    c. The boy *angrily replying* is the brother of the beleaguered quarterback.

    d. *To get my money's worth*, I shop at Sage.

    e. I decided not to go swimming, *not wanting to catch cold.*

    f. I was discovered *eating the Christmas cake.*

    g. Clyde, *to insure his safe retirement*, took out an annuity.

    h. Mr. Smith, *wondering if his job were secure*, decided to talk to the company president.

    i. Peter, *elected by the narrowest of margins*, decided to allow a recount.

    j. The officer *elected by the narrowest margin* decided to resign his post.

14. Rewrite the following sentences to eliminate dangling modifiers.

    a. By doing right all the time, your conscience will feel at ease.

    b. Coming at an inconvenient time, I rather resented my parents-in-law's visit.

    c. Besides offering a great deal of entertainment, people can sometimes improve their educational status by watching television.

    d. By teaching the dangers of communism, our citizens can learn to protect our freedoms better.

    e. The game between the Rams and the Forty-niners was quite exciting, not having seen a professional football game before.

    f. Not having been refilled after the last draining, we just sunbathed around the pool's edge.

    g. The rescue team could hardly be seen, having been nearly blinded by the flash of the explosion.

    h. Intently searching his underside for parasites, the zoo attendant showed us a rare South American species of monkey.

    i. Being exaggerated, anybody can see through most advertisements.

    j. While making a sandwich, the doorbell rang.

15. Make up five compound adjectivals which have combinations of form- and structure-class words not given in the text (pages 274–276).

16. Write four versions each of two sentences with an adverb in a different position in each of the sentences in each group.

17. Show how repositioning modifiers in the following sentences can eliminate ambiguity.

a. I had to go to work when my father died because my mother needed money.
b. We found a picture of her swimming with him after he died.
c. He showed us how to bartend clearly.
d. All modifiers ending in *ly* are not adverbs.
e. The coach even agreed that the team had shown poor sportsmanship.
f. The prisoner resisted the efforts of his inquisitor to break him down steadfastly.
g. Half of the naturalized citizens cannot understand the Constitution in this country.
h. We must confess our wrongdoings to the priest.
i. You can easily prepare to be a diesel engineer for GM in a technical school.
j. I was not able to understand just what he intended to do clearly.

18. In the following sentences distinguish between sentence modifiers and adverbials. The word or phrase in question is italicized.

a. *Indubitably*, we will have a recession if the whigs take office.
b. *For peace of mind*, go to church regularly.
c. *Excluding Handel*, most eighteenth-century composers were poor.
d. *Inevitably*, we failed to reach the theater in time.
e. We were *unavoidably* detained.
f. *Fortunately*, the steel chain held.
g. He was, *fortunately*, near his home at the time of the accident.
h. *To conserve cash for emergencies*, use your credit cards on trips.
i. He was, *in effect*, a charlatan.
j. *Moodily*, Austin skulked through the alleys.
k. *Amusingly*, we went to the wrong address.
l. Jeanie is *amusingly* different.
m. Clara did not sing *happily*.
n. *Happily*, Clara did not sing.
o. *Regarding the accident*, Otho said he would share the blame.

19. Combine each of the following pairs or triplets of sentences into one sentence with an appositive.

a. Las Vegas has a sometimes oddsmaker. He is Bela Torino. He was indicted for skimming.
b. William Faulkner is considered by many to be America's greatest author. He is a writer of prose fiction.
c. W. Somerset Maugham wrote a novel. It is *Of Human Bondage*. It is considered one of the finest naturalistic novels of its age.
d. Man is in many ways built like his furry relatives. They are the gorilla, the orangutan, and the chimpanzee.

e. Programed learning is the newest educational technique. It seems most successful when adapted to machine teaching.

f. William Burroughs is one of the "black" humorists. He writes always as though he is in a total rage at the universe.

g. Mrs. X is in jail on a morals charge. She is the mother of three teen-agers.

h. Morphemes are composed of one or more phonemes. Morphemes are the smallest meaningful units in language.

i. The pupils gave very creditable performances in the play. The pupils were mostly fifth-graders.

j. The eccrine glands secrete water. The eccrine glands are the source of most of man's sweat.

20. Following are two paragraphs chosen at random. Identify all the adjectivals, adverbials, and sentence modifiers in them except for dependent clauses and structure words.

An understanding of this basic, universal language is of key importance when it comes to milking, for neither bells, bruises, nor moral suasion will induce a cow to let down her milk. She will part with just as much, or as little, as she pleases. I have a simple program for keeping milk production at phenomenal levels. The program begins the moment I decide a heifer calf is worth raising. Aside from her social aspirations a cow is a rational being. Unloved and unlovely, she is too cynical to hope for happiness, but she does like to be comfortable. An empty stomach and an overstrained udder make her physically uncomfortable, so I explain to my cows that a full milk pail earns a full feed bucket. Cows are particular to the point of being absolutely meticulous about anything which affects them; they know to within an ounce when their feed ration is slighted. For the benefit of Behaviorists, however, I will explain that in hand-raising my heifer calves, I am careful to show them that gaining my approval earns soft words and extra grain, but that misbehavior evokes, "Ouch, dammit!" and a whack. By the time a calf is a month old, it understands the words "good" and "bad" and what they portend. By milking age, my cow has the hearing vocabulary of a three-year-old child, but I can snatch away the feed bucket if it does not obey. [J. O. Harvey, "All Cows Are Mean"]

But never before in history have absurd notions regarding nutrition enjoyed such widespread popularity as in our present modern 20th century. Based on misstatements of the facts on nutritional disease, food faddism has emerged as a whopping multimillion dollar business, observes Dr. Kenneth L. Milstead, of the Food and Drug Administration (FDA), adding that "it has become the most widespread kind of quackery in the United States." An estimated 10 million duped Americans—more than one out of every 17 persons—contribute handsomely to the perpetuity and prosperity of swindlers and crackpots, estimates Philip L. White, Sc.D., director of the Department of Foods and Nutrition, American Medical Association. The faddists have mounted an immense effort to undermine public confidence in the nutritional value of the food supply of the best-fed and best-nourished nation on earth. [Ralph Lee Smith, "The Bunk About Health Foods"]

11 DEPENDENT CLAUSES AS NOMINALS AND MODIFIERS

The Concepts of Subordination and Dependence

An **independent clause** is in effect a sentence and has grammatical independence even though for specific meaning it may need to refer to a previous sentence or sentences. It has a subject, which may be any of a variety of words or word groups functioning as a nominal, and a predicate, which must contain either a finite verb form or a verb auxiliary with reference and which may or may not contain one or more complements. It may be introduced by a coordinating connective (such as *but* or *therefore*) but cannot be introduced by a subordinating connective (such as *when* or *since*). This definition of an independent clause is in effect a repetition of our definition of *sentence* given on page 214.

A **dependent clause** has the same kind of structure as an independent clause so far as the subject and predicate are concerned but differs from the independent clause in that it is introduced by a subordinating connective, either expressed or understood, which prevents the clause from standing by itself as a grammatically independent sentence. For example, the construction

But he could

must be considered an independent clause and thus a sentence even though the subject and the modal auxiliary must get their meaning from a previous utterance. The coordinating connective *but* does not affect the grammatical independence of the clause. People with sen-

305

tence sense will recognize this three-word construction as a sentence even though it can have no specific meaning by itself. But the construction

When he could

does not have the same grammatical independence. The subordinating connective *when* makes the construction grammatically *dependent*, for even with reference to a preceding utterance it still must participate as a nominal or modifier in a grammatically independent sentence if it is to carry specific meaning. All people with sentence sense will recognize that the construction cannot be called a sentence. As school grammars have said for centuries, it cannot "stand alone" and hence is dependent. It is a dependent *clause* because it has a subject-predicate combination —that is, because it exhibits the grammatical function of predication.

Such constructions as the last illustrated have frequently been called *subordinate clauses* on the grounds that they must be "arranged under" another constituent in a sentence. But such clauses are not always subordinate and should have only the generic term **dependent clause** applied to them as a group. Such a clause is subordinate only when it functions as a modifier, for being subordinate means functioning as a modifier. For example, in

the **angry** man

angry, an adjective and adjectival, is subordinate to the noun it modifies. Similarly, in

the man **who was angry,**

who was angry, an adjective clause and an adjectival, is also subordinate to the noun it modifies. But consider this sentence:

The **man** was unknown.

Is *man* subordinate to any other constituent in the sentence? By no means. It is instead a part of the basic sentence pattern (the subject) and not subordinate in any way. Thus in

Who was angry is unknown,

who was angry is by no means subordinate. It is the sentence subject, a part of the basic sentence pattern. It is not a modifier and therefore is not subordinate. But it is a *dependent* clause, for, since it is introduced by a subordinating connective, it cannot stand by itself with grammatical independence (unless it were a question). Thus the terms *subordinate clause* and *dependent clause* are not always interchangeable. All subordinate clauses are dependent but not all dependent clauses are subordinate. When a dependent clause functions as a subject, as a complement, or as an object of a preposition, it is not subordinate. When it functions as a modifier (adjectival, adverbial, or sentence modifier) or as an appositive, it is subordinate grammatically.

By form there are three kinds of dependent clauses: **noun**, **adjective**, and **adverb**. They are given these names because of the usual functions they have, just as the form-class words derive their names from their usual functions in sentences. But like the form-class words, the dependent clauses can cross over into each other's territory. Thus the dependent clauses, like the form-class words, should be classified by both **form** and **function**. Noun clauses can have not only the usual nominal functions of being subjects, complements, objects of prepositions, and appositives but also may occasionally function as sentence modifiers and in one case as an adjectival. Adjective clauses can function as adjectivals and as sentence modifiers. And adverb clauses can function as adverbials, adverbial complements, adjectivals, sentence modifiers, and nominals. However, not all dependent clauses in any one classification can have all the functions mentioned. For example, a noun clause introduced by *who* cannot function as a sentence modifier, but one introduced by *whether* can. Or an adverb clause introduced by *because* cannot function as an adjectival but one introduced by *when* can. On page 72 and pages 89–94 we listed the subordinating connectives (structure words) that can introduce each of the three kinds of dependent clauses. These connectives will be reviewed in the following pages.

Noun Clauses

Review of the Subordinating Conjunctions that Introduce Noun Clauses

For easy reference here again is a list of the connectives that introduce noun clauses. They are usually called subordinating conjunctions even though the clause one of them introduces may not be subordinate in its sentence.

who	whatever	whensoever
whom	whatsoever	which
whoever	where	whichever
whosoever	wherever	why
whomever	wheresoever	how
whomsoever	when	whether
whose	whenever	that
what		

As was demonstrated in Chapter 4, many of these connectives also fit into other classifications. *Who*, *whom*, *whose*, and *which* also fit into the classification of relative pronouns that introduce adjective clauses. But here they belong in a separate classification, for in adjective clauses the relative pronouns have reference within their own sentences, whereas in noun clauses these connectives have reference only outside their own sentences. *That* as a connective introducing a noun clause is an entirely different word from *that* as a relative pronoun, for when it introduces a noun clause it has no reference at all. *When*(*ever*) and *where*(*ever*) fit into this group as well as into the group of subordinating conjunctions that introduce adverb clauses. *Who*, *whom*, *whose*, *what*, *where*, *when*, *which*, *why*, and *how* also fit into the QW (question-forming) structure class. When these words form questions they do not introduce dependent clauses. Thus we have words that individually appear to be identical but that fit into separate classifications. This point was emphasized in Chapter 4.

The Functions of the Connectives in Their Own Clauses

Most of the connectives that introduce noun clauses function grammatically in their own noun clauses, but two function as connectives only. Here are connectives functioning as the subjects of their clauses:

> **Who** will come is not yet known.
> **Whatever** happens is sure to be a surprise.

Who is the subject of *will come*, with the whole being a noun clause functioning as the subject of *is*. *Whatever* is the subject of *happens*, and that two-word noun clause also functions as the subject of *is*. Only the *who*, *what*, and *which* connectives can function as subjects in their own clauses.

Here are connectives functioning as direct objects in their own clauses:

> I don't know **what** you mean.
> **Whomever** you call will probably say he's busy.

What is the direct object of *mean*, for the transformation is *you mean what*. The whole noun clause is the direct object of *know*. *Whomever* is the direct object of *call*, for the transformation is *you call whomever*. The whole noun clause is the subject of *will say*. Only the *who*(*m*), *what*, and *which* connectives can function as direct objects in their own noun clauses.

Here are connectives functioning as determiners in their own clauses:

> **Whose** woods these are, I think I know.
> Do this by **whatever** means are necessary.

Whose is a possessive determiner for *woods* but still serves as the connective to introduce the noun clause, which as a whole is the direct object of *know*. *Whatever* is functioning as a determiner modifying *means*; it also is the connective introducing the noun clause, which as a whole is the object of the preposition *by*. Only *whose* and the *what* and *which* connectives can function as determiners in their own noun clauses.

Here are connectives functioning as adverbial modifiers and as an adverbial complement in their noun clauses:

> I don't know **when** he will come.
> I don't see **how** you can do it.
> He is **wherever** he should be.

In its own clause (the equivalent of *he will come then*), *when* functions not only as a connective but also as an adverbial modifier of *come*. In sentence two, *how* is also functioning as an adverbial modifier of *can do* (the equivalent of *thus* in *you can do it thus*). In sentence three *wherever* functions as an adverbial complement in its own clause (the equivalent of *there* in *he should be there*). Only when the verb of a noun clause is a form of *to be* can the connective serve as an adverbial complement, according to our system of analysis. The *when* and *where* connectives and *how* and *why* can serve as adverbial modifiers in their own clauses and the *where* connectives can serve as adverbial complements.

Here are connectives functioning as object complements:

> I am **what** my Alma Mater made me.
> You will be **whatever** God selects you to be.

The transformations of the clauses are *my Alma Mater made me what* and *God selects you to be whatever*. *What* and *whatever* are object complements of *me* and *you*. In the second sentence, *to be* is an expletive. *What* and *whatever* are the only connectives normally used in this function.

The connectives *that* and *whether* play no grammatical role within their own noun clauses but serve as connectives only.

Noun Clauses as Subjects

A common function of the noun clause is to serve as a subject, and then it is necessarily a nominal by function. As a review of Chapter 9, here are examples of noun clauses as subjects of some of the basic sentence patterns:

Pattern 1:
N + V-In + (Adv)
Whoever sees that show // laughs hysterically.

Pattern 2:
N + Be + Adv
What you want // is / outside.

Pattern 3:
N¹ + V-Tr + N²
Whether I cut class // affects / my professor's morale.

Pattern 4:
N¹ + V-Tr + N² + N³
What he said // gave / me / a shock.

Pattern 5:
N¹ + V-Tr + N² + N²
Whatever you do // will make / me / a nervous wreck.

Pattern 6:
N¹ + V-Tr + N² + Adj
What you did // made / Nancy / sad.

Pattern 8:
N¹ + V-L + N¹
How you became the top student // remains / a puzzle.

Pattern 9:
N + V-L + Adj
That you were to blame // finally became / clear.

Pattern 12:
It + Be + Adj + N
It / was / true // **that Willie had absconded.**

These are very common usages in our language, and most of the connectives will function in noun clauses in this position.

Noun clauses can also function as the subjects of dependent clauses. Examples:

Since **whoever is guilty** did not confess, we will have an investigation.
The stamps which **whoever is guilty** stole were not really valuable.
We are sure that **whoever planted the bomb** strengthened the hand of the police.

In sentence one the adverb clause *since whoever is guilty did not confess* is functioning as a sentence modifier, and the noun clause *whoever is guilty* is the subject of *did confess* in that adverb clause. In sentence two the adjective clause *which whoever is guilty stole* is modifying *stamps*, and the noun clause *whoever is guilty* is the subject of *stole* in that adjective clause. In sentence three the noun clause *that whoever planted the bomb strengthened the hand of the police* is the complement of the predicate adjective *sure*, and the noun clause *whoever planted the bomb* is the subject of *strengthened* in that noun clause. In effect, in the last sentence we have a noun clause serving as the subject of a noun clause. Such usages as those illustrated in these example sentences are not uncommon in our language.

Noun clauses can also function as subjects of nonfinite verb forms. Examples:

> **What we needed** having been gathered, we prepared to set out.
> I am willing for **whoever is available** to drive the car.
> We caught **who(m) you mentioned** stealing the petty cash.

In sentence one, *what we needed* is the subject of the past perfect participle, passive voice, *having been gathered*. In sentence two, *whoever is available* is the subject of the infinitive phrase *to drive the car*. And in sentence three, *who(m) you mentioned* is the subject of the present-participial phrase *stealing the petty cash*. Such usages are not particularly common, but they are entirely grammatical.

Noun Clauses as Complements

Noun clauses can function as five different kinds of nominal complements, just as other nominals can.

1. *Noun clauses as direct objects.*

> We bought only **what we needed.**
> I didn't know (**that**) **you had arrived.**
> We wondered **why you brought Cathy.**

The boldface noun clauses are the direct objects of the transitive verbs *bought*, *know*, and *wondered*. These are very common usages, and most of the connectives will function in noun clauses in this position. In this function and some others, the connective *that* can be omitted, as the parentheses indicate.

2. *Noun clauses as indirect objects.*

> Give **whoever comes first** the best seat.
> Buy **whomever you like best** the most expensive gift.

These usages are uncommon but nevertheless fully grammatical. Normally, only the *who(m)* connectives will function in noun clauses in this position.

3. *Noun clauses as object complements.*

> The Military Academy made Louis **what he wanted to be.**
> We'll elect Charles **whatever officer he desires to be.**
> You'll find Julia **what every man desires.**

These usages are uncommon also. Normally only the *what* connectives will function in noun clauses in this position, though the *who(m)* connectives can be awkwardly forced to.

4. *Noun clauses as predicate nominals.*

> Perry remained **what he had been in his youth.**
> Joe appeared to be **whatever his colleagues thought he was.**
> Betty is **who(m) you saw.**

What, whatever, and *who(m)* are the only connectives that will function in this uncommon usage. In sentence two, *to be* is an expletive.

5. *Noun clauses as complements of the adjective.*

> I am happy **(that) you agree with me.**
> John was glad **(that) Bill could come.**
> I was not sure **where you would be.**

This is a common usage, but *that* and *where* (rarely) are the only connectives that will function in noun clauses in this position. In this construction the connective *that* can be omitted, as the parentheses indicate.

Noun Clauses as Objects of Prepositions

Like a simple noun, a noun clause can function as the object of a preposition. Examples:

> Give this package to **whoever calls first.**
> Travel by **whatever modes of transportation are available.**
> Go with **whomever you want to.**

The boldface noun clauses are the objects of *to, by,* and *with* and thus are nominals. Note that in sentence one the subjective form *whoever* is used because not the connective by itself but the whole noun clause is the object of *to*. *Whoever* is the subject of *calls* within the noun clause itself. In sentence three *whomever* is technically correct because it is not functioning as a subject (but *whoever* would sound more natural). Actually, not only the whole noun clause in that sentence but also the connective *whomever* is the object of *with*, for the transformation of the clause is *you want to go with whomever*. The *who(m), what,* and *which* connectives are the only ones normally used in noun clauses that function as objects of prepositions.

Noun Clauses as Appositives

Noun clauses, usually introduced by *that,* can function as appositives. There is a danger, however, of confusing this construction with an adjective clause introduced by the relative pronoun *that*. Consider these two sentences:

> The belief **that like produces like** is a superstition.
> The belief **that John holds** is a superstition.

The boldface noun clause in sentence one is an appositive; the boldface adjective clause in sentence two is an adjectival. The two *that*s are entirely different words. The difference is that in sentence one the clause tells what the belief is, but in sentence two the clause gives only side information about the belief. Two tests can be used to demonstrate the difference. First, with the appositive a sentence can be made by using a form to *to be* with the appositive and the noun it is in apposition to—here, *the belief is that like produces like.* Such a construction cannot be created with the adjective clause; **the belief is that John holds* is ungrammatical. The second test is to see that in the adjective clause *which* can be substituted for *that* but that in the noun clause it cannot be substituted for *that.*

Noun-clause appositives introduced by *that* can accompany only such nouns as *belief, suggestion, claim, concept, idea, assumption,* or their likes. The appositive tells what the belief, suggestion, and so on is. Such appositives may be either restrictive or nonrestrictive. Examples:

> The suggestion **that we adjourn** was met with cheers.
> My first suggestion—**that we invest in real estate**—was rejected.
> The assumption **that men have more endurance than women** is false.
> John's assumption—**that Mr. Winer would be elected**—proved wrong.

The noun-clause appositives set off by dashes are nonrestrictive because *my first* and *John's* identify the nouns *suggestion* and *assumption* The clauses without the dashes are restrictive because they are needed to identify the nouns *suggestion* and *assumption.* The connective *that* is not normally omitted in appositives. Such noun-clause appositives are rather common in our written language.

Who(so)ever, whichever, and *what(so)ever* can introduce noun-clause appositives when the appositives are in apposition to pronouns and are in a shifted position. Examples:

> **Whosoever follows my creed,** give him a gold star.
> **Whichever is the correct answer,** mark it in red.
> **Whatever it was,** it gave me a start.

The boldface noun clauses are in apposition to *him, it,* and *it.* Note that the noun clause can replace the pronoun it is in apposition to: *give whoever follows my creed a gold star.* Such noun-clause appositives are rarely used.

Noun Clauses as Sentence Modifiers

The connectives *whether* (commonly) and *whatever* (rarely) can introduce noun clauses which function as sentence modifiers. Examples:

Whether you propose or not, I am going to marry you.
Whether it rains or not, we will play the game.
Whatever you do, don't miss taking a course from Professor Longueil.

These boldface noun clauses modify the whole ideas of the independent clauses and are thus sentence modifiers. Note that the *or not* is demanded with the *whether* clause functioning as a sentence modifier. The noun clause as a sentence modifier can come at the end of its sentence with or without juncture. For example, in

I'm going to the game **whether you like it or not,**

the boldface noun clause is a sentence modifier, since it applies to the entire independent clause.

The Noun Clause as Adjectival

One connective—*why*—can introduce a noun clause which functions as an adjectival. Example:

The reason **why I failed** is that I did not study.

Why I failed is modifying the noun *reason* and is therefore an adjectival. Note that the noun clause is not an appositive, for *the reason is why I failed* does not make sense. *Reason* is the only noun such a noun clause will modify. This construction is a commonly used but nevertheless a singular idiom in English.

Adjective Clauses

Review of the Relative Pronouns

The subordinating connectives that introduce adjective clauses are the relative pronouns: *who, whom, whose, which, that,* and (rarely) *who(m)ever* and *whichever.* These words also fall into other classifications, as was discussed on pages 76 and 93. When they function as relative pronouns, they refer to specific nouns (often to a whole idea in the case of *which*) within their own sentences. In other uses for other classifications these words do not have such reference. Thus it is clear that as relative pronouns they belong to a separate classification. The noun which the relative pronoun refers to is its **antecedent**. Examples:

The **student who** is guilty should confess.
My **car, which** is registered as a horseless carriage, is valued at $5000.

Student is the antecedent of *who* and *car* is the antecedent of *which*, and the whole adjective clauses modify those nouns. If the antecedents are substituted for the relative pronouns, the adjective clauses become independent clauses: *the student is guilty* and *my car is registered as a horseless carriage.* These connectives are called *relative* pronouns because they refer (relate) to specific antecedents.

A relative pronoun, in addition to functioning as a subordinating connective, always has a grammatical function within its own adjective clause. Examples of relative pronouns as subjects:

> Are you the waitress **who** serves this table?
> That's the dog **that** bit me.
> That's the house **which** has been sold.

In sentence one, *who* is the subject of *serves* and the whole adjective clause modifies *waitress*. Note that *who* in this sentence is not a QW word, for it is the independent clause, not the *who*, which asks a question. In sentence two, *that* is the subject of *bit* and the whole adjective clause modifies *dog*. In sentence three, *which* is the subject of the passive-voice verb *has been sold*. When relative pronouns are subjects, they cannot be omitted from their clauses.

Examples of relative pronouns as direct objects:

> He's the professor [**who(m)**] I interviewed.
> The Bible is the book (**that**) I read most often.
> Brown betty is the dessert (**which**) we recommend.

Who(m), *that*, and *which* are respectively the direct objects of *interviewed*, *read*, and *recommend*. The transformations are *I interviewed whom, I read that, we recommend which*. If in this transformation the antecedent is substituted for the relative pronoun, a simple independent clause results, as *I interviewed the professor*. The relative pronouns as direct objects function also as subordinating connectives. The parentheses indicate possible omissions; very frequently when the relative pronoun is a direct object it is omitted, even in professional writing (but only when its clause is restrictive; see page 318 below). *Who* is quite commonly used for *whom* in the speech even of educated people, though professional writers still distinguish between *who* and *whom*.

Examples of relative pronouns as objects of prepositions:

> She is the secretary to **whom** I gave the letter.
> Football is the sport (**that**) I am most interested in.
> This is a car (**which**) you should not tinker with.

In the first sentence, *whom* is the object of the preposition *to* and *to whom I gave the letter* is an adjective clause modifying *secretary*. Arbiters of usage used to insist that for correct grammar the preposition must precede the relative pronoun, but, as is illustrated in sentences two and three, almost everyone nowadays puts the preposition at the end of the clause, especially in conversation. In sentences two and three, *that* and *which* are the objects of the prepositions *in* and *with*. Either the objects or the prepositions may be regarded as displaced; in any event, the objects cannot come at the ends of the sentences:

> *Football is the sport I am most interested in that.
> *This is a car you should not tinker with which.

When the preposition comes at the end of the clause, the relative pronoun is often omitted, as the parentheses indicate. In sentences two and three, *sport* and *car* are the nouns which the relative pronouns refer to, and of course the relative pronouns in all three sentences are connectives introducing dependent clauses.

The relative pronoun *whose* functions as a determiner in its own adjective clause. Examples:

> Professor Dick is the one **whose** classes always fill up first.
> I have yet to find a book **whose** index is really usable.

In these sentences *whose* is a possessive determiner as are *his* and *its* in *his classes* and *its index*. But *whose* is still a connective introducing an adjective clause. It can never be omitted. It can refer to inanimate objects, as it does in sentence two.

Adjective Clauses as Adjectivals

The large majority of adjective clauses function as adjectivals by modifying a specific noun or noun substitute. The noun or noun substitute which is modified need not be in an independent clause. Examples:

> I am looking for a partner, one **who can furnish capital.**
> Bill Turner, who turned in the same term paper **that I did**, escaped undetected.

In sentence one the boldface adjective clause modifies *one*, which is in apposition to *partner*. Thus the clause is part of an appositive phrase. In sentence two the boldface adjective clause (which has a verb substitute as its predicator) modifies *paper*, a constituent within a longer adjective clause. Similarly, adjective clauses can function in noun and adverb clauses, in verbal phrases, and in miscellaneous sentence modifiers by modifying nouns within those constructions.

Adjective clauses always take the postnominal position, though they can be separated by phrases from the nouns they modify. Examples:

> The Playmate of the Month pictured in the July issue of *Playboy*, **who had waited two years for the honor,** directly became engaged.

> The manager of the West Division of the Bank of the Palouse, **who started out as a messenger**, is expected to be appointed president.

Technically the boldface adjective clauses modify *Playmate* and *manager* and thus are in separated positions; but since the phrases modifying *Playmate* and *manager* are parts of endocentric noun phrases, the adjective clauses are really in the postnominal position, as they always are. Note that in both sentences the relative pronoun *who* serves as a formal clue to show that the clauses modify *Playmate* and *manager*, and not *Playboy* or *Bank*.

Adjective clauses are either **restrictive** or **nonrestrictive**. When they are restrictive they are needed in their sentences to identify the nouns they modify and they are not set off by commas. All of the five main relative pronouns may introduce restrictive clauses. Examples:

> Teachers **who play favorites** are despised by perceptive pupils.
> The preacher **whom you mentioned** is planning to resign.
> The girl **whose date you insulted** was very embarrassed.
> The test question **which gave me the most trouble** was the one about pulsars.
> Industries **that pollute the environment** are now subject to closure.

The boldface adjective clauses are needed to specify which teachers, preacher, girl, question, and industries are being discussed and thus are restrictive. For example, without the clause the first sentence would say *teachers are despised by perceptive pupils*, which is of course not what any speaker or writer would mean. The clauses are part of endocentric noun phrases and can be omitted grammatically, but they cannot be omitted logically. The relative pronoun *that* can be used only in restrictive clauses.

When adjective clauses are nonrestrictive they give only side information about nouns or noun substitutes which are already fully identified, and they are separated by commas. All of the relative pronouns except *that*, including *who(m)ever* and *whichever*, may introduce nonrestrictive clauses. Examples:

> Phi Beta Kappas, **who must earn nearly an A average in college**, claim they have nothing in common but brains.
> Professor Claude Jones, **whom the students loved**, was refused promotion.
> My first sweetheart, **whose parents guarded her severely**, finally eloped with a carnival man.
> The east wind, **which blows all summer in our part of the country**, often brings in rain.

Take either Joan or Julia, **who(m)ever you like best**.
This car is guaranteed for thirty days or 300 miles, **whichever comes first**.

The nouns which these boldface nonrestrictive clauses modify are fully identified without the clauses; the clauses can be omitted and fully meaningful sentences will remain. In sentence three the determiners *my first* identify *sweetheart* and in all the other sentences the nouns modified are specific names or time or measure designations. (A specific name does not have to be a proper noun; *the east wind* is a specific name even though *wind* is a common noun.) When an adjective clause is nonrestrictive, its relative pronoun cannot be omitted regardless of its grammatical function in its own clause.

Since the relative pronoun *that* can introduce only a restrictive clause, if it can be substituted for *who, whom,* or *which* in an adjective clause, then the clause must be restrictive. For example, in

The girl **whom** I love best is Sadie,

that can be substituted for *whom*, which is complete proof that the adjective clause is restrictive. But in

Sadie, **whom** I love best, plans to be an actress,

that cannot be substituted for *whom*, showing that the adjective clause is nonrestrictive. *Who(m)ever* and *whichever* as relative pronouns may introduce only nonrestrictive clauses. If a clause introduced by one of these words is not set off by a comma, as in

Take **whomever you like best**,

the connective is a subordinating conjunction introducing a noun clause, not a relative pronoun introducing an adjective clause, since there is no antecedent in the sentence.

Adjective Clauses as Sentence Modifiers

The relative pronoun *which* may introduce an adjective clause which does not modify a single noun in its sentence but modifies the whole idea of an independent clause, a dependent clause, an absolute phrase, or a verbal phrase. In such a case the *which* refers to an implied nominal and thus its clause is clearly an adjective rather than a noun or adverb clause, but that adjective clause functions as a sentence modifier rather than as an adjectival. Here is a typical example:

John made several mistakes on his math exam, **which was to be expected**.

Three points are to be noted here. First, such an adjective clause is always nonrestrictive, which means that it will be set off by a comma or commas. Second, the clause often (though not always) comes next to a noun and might, at first glance, be thought to modify that noun (*exam* in the above sentence). But the content of the clause quickly shows that it does not modify that noun. When the content of the clause does not immediately show that the clause does not modify the noun in question, ambiguity results. Example:

> **John was thrown by a horse, which hurt him.**

If the boldface clause modifies the noun *horse* as an adjectival, the meaning seems to be that the horse itself hurt John, presumably after he was thrown. But if the clause is a sentence modifier, it was the being thrown that hurt John, not the action of the horse after he was thrown. Actually, such ambiguities do not often arise. The third point to be noted about the first example sentence is that the antecedent of *which* is the implied nominal *John's making several mistakes*, for that is what was to be expected. If that implied nominal is substituted for *which*, the result is the independent clause *John's making several mistakes was to be expected*. The fact that the *which* clause modifies a whole idea instead of a single noun makes the clause a sentence modifier rather than an adjectival.

Here is another example of an adjective clause modifying an independent clause:

> **An Oscar Meyer once memorized the entire New York City telephone directory, which must be a record for useless memorization.**

The boldface clause modifies the implied nominal *the memorization of the entire New York City telephone directory* (*by an Oscar Meyer*) and thus is a sentence modifier. Note that if the implied nominal is substituted for *which* in the adjective clause a simple independent clause will be formed.

Sometimes more complexity than this is involved with an adjective clause functioning as a sentence modifier. Example:

> **Whoever scores in the 90th percentile on SCAT, which I did, is put in an honors program.**

The relative pronoun *which* has as its antecedent the implied nominal *scoring in the 90th percentile on SCAT*, but this implied nominal cannot be grammatically substituted for *which*, since the predicator of the adjective clause is a verb substitute which also refers to the verb *scores*. The transformation of the adjective clause is *I scored in the 90th percentile on SCAT*. So the transformation of the whole sentence is

> **Whoever scores in the 90th percentile on SCAT—I scored in the 90th percentile on SCAT—is put in an honors program.**

In the original sentence, however, the adjective clause is a sentence modifier, since it modifies a whole idea rather than a single noun.

Here is an adjective clause modifying the whole idea of another adjective clause:

> Anyone who makes an A in Organic Chemistry, **which is hard to do**, is eligible for a scholarship.

The boldface adjective clause modifies the nominal *the making of an A in Organic Chemistry*, which is implied in the adjective clause introduced by *who*. Since it modifies an entire idea rather than a single noun, the *which* clause is a sentence modifier. Here is an adjective clause modifying the whole idea of an adverb clause:

> When you come to Texas, **which will probably be years from now**, drop in to see us.

The implied nominal which the boldface clause modifies is *your coming to Texas*, and thus the clause is a sentence modifier.

Here is an adjective clause modifying an absolute phrase:

> The plant having shut down, **which we all expected**, we had to go on welfare.

The absolute phrase itself is a kind of nominal for the *which* clause to modify. The clause should still be called a sentence modifier, for it modifies a whole idea rather than a single noun.

Here is a *which* clause modifying a nonfinite predication with a past participle:

> Joan had coffee spilled on her, **which disgusted her**.

The *which* clause modifies the implied nominal *coffee's being spilled on her*, which could substitute for *which* to make an independent clause. The *which* clause is a sentence modifier. And here is a *which* clause modifying an infinitive phrase.

> Sally asked me to return her letters, **which I did**.

To return her letters is a part of the nonfinite predication *me to return her letters*. It implies the nominal *the returning of her letters*, and the *which* clause is a sentence modifier since it modifies a whole idea.

Note that the *which* adjective clause as a sentence modifier is not like a noun clause as a sentence modifier. In such a sentence as

> **Whether you like it or not**, I'm leaving,

the boldface noun clause is a sentence modifier of the whole independent clause, but it has no reference in that clause. The adjective clause as a sentence modifier has implied reference in the clause or phrase that it modifies, as has been demonstrated above.

The *which* clause as a sentence modifier is sometimes called a **loose adjective clause**. It has been condemned as bad usage by some self-styled arbiters of correctness, but it has appeared in the writings of the best authors for hundreds of years. Its **broad reference** is entirely grammatical.

Adverb Clauses

Review of the Connectives that Introduce Adverb Clauses

The syntactic functions of adverb clauses are more complex than those of noun and adjective clauses, as is witnessed in the greater number and variety of subordinating connectives that introduce them. The chief difference between this group of subordinating conjunctions and the connectives that introduce noun and adjective clauses is that the latter (with a few exceptions for noun clauses) do not express logical relationship but instead have reference, whereas the former express logical relationships. Adverb clauses are more truly "complicating" clauses than are noun and adjective clauses. The subordinating conjunctions that introduce adverb clauses can be grouped according to the relationships they express, and as a review we will so list them here. There are eight such divisions.

Cause-and-Result

because	since
inasmuch as	so . . . that
in that	in case
now that	

Time (with Cause-and-Result often included)

after	once
as	until
as soon as	when
before	whenever
since	while

Contrast

although	while
though	however (much)
whereas	no matter how

Condition or Concession

if	provided (that)
unless	since (*concession only in this use*)

Manner
> as   as though
> as if   like

Purpose
> so that   in order that
> so

Place
> where   wherever

Comparison
> as . . . as   *comparative adjective or adverb +*
> more . . . than   than (*such as* earlier than)
> less . . . than

Most of these subordinating conjunctions serve as logical connectives only, without playing a grammatical role in their own clauses. The *place* and *time* connectives can be said to function grammatically in their adverb clauses. Examples:

> Your briefcase is **where** you put it.
> I'll come **when** I can.

The transformations of these adverb clauses are *you put it where* (*there*) and *I can come when* (*then*), making the connectives adverbial modifiers of the verbs *put* and *can come*. But in general the subordinating conjunctions that introduce adverb clauses are just connectives and need not be thought of as playing a grammatical role in their own clauses.

Adverb Clauses as Adverbials

Noun clauses most frequently function as nominals and adjective clauses most frequently as adjectivals, though on occasion both function as sentence modifiers. The contrary is the case with adverb clauses: They infrequently function as adverbials and most frequently as sentence modifiers. (Also, as will be seen, adverb clauses can function as nominals, adjectivals, and adverbial complements.) An adverb clause functions as an adverbial only when it modifies a nonfinite verb form; when the adverb clause modifies the whole idea of another clause, as it usually does, it functions as a sentence modifier.

As an adverbial, an adverb clause always modifies a nonfinite verb form, and the whole phrase formed with the nonfinite verb and the adverb clause functions as a nominal, adjectival, or adverbial. Here is an example to illustrate this rather complex syntactical function:

> Smiling **when you are angry** takes guile.

When you are angry is an adverb clause modifying the present participle *smiling*, and it is therefore functioning as an adverbial just as any other modifier in that position would. For example, in

> Smiling **sweetly** is a social grace,

sweetly is an adverbial modifying the present participle *smiling*; the same analysis must apply to the adverb clause *when you are angry* in the sentence above. Note that the clause is modifying a single verb form by itself, not a whole clause. It is only in this kind of function that an adverb clause is an adverbial. In the above sentence the whole present-participial phrase *smiling when you are angry* is the subject of *takes* and therefore a nominal.

Here are other examples of adverb clauses functioning as adverbials within verb phrases that function as nominals:

> Staying **until he has worn out his welcome** is a habit of John's.
> Jerry tried escaping **while the guard was away**.
> Mary's worst habit—lingering **after the other guests have left**— is hard to tolerate.

In sentence one the present-participial phrase *staying until he has worn out his welcome* is the subject of *is* and therefore a nominal, and in that phrase the boldface adverb clause is an adverbial modifying the present participle *staying*. In sentence two the whole present-participial phrase beginning with *escaping* is the direct object of *tried* and therefore a nominal. Within that nominal the boldface adverb clause is an adverbial modifying *escaping*. In sentence three the present-participial phrase is an appositive in apposition to *habit*, and the boldface adverb clause is an adverbial modifying *lingering*.

Here are examples of adverb clauses functioning as adverbials in verb phrases that function as adjectivals:

> Crowing **as the sun rose,** the rooster looked for his hens.
> Having passed out **when carbon monoxide entered his car,** Harry was in extreme danger.

In sentence one the present-participial phrase *crowing as the sun rose* is an adjectival modifying *rooster*, and the boldface adverb clause is an adverbial modifying *crowing*. In sentence two, *having passed out* is a perfect past participle of a verb-particle composite and is thus a single verb form. The boldface adverb clause modifying it functions as an adverbial. The whole verb phrase is an adjectival modifying *Harry*.

And here are examples of adverb clauses functioning as adverbials within verb phrases that function as adverbials:

> Billy stood gaping **while the ship sank.**
> Rose was found hiding **after the party was over.**

Both the present-participial phrases *gaping while the ship sank* and *hiding after the party was over* are adverbials modifying the verbs *stood* and *was found* (= thus), and within those adverbials the boldface adverb clauses are also adverbials, since they modify the present participles *gaping* and *hiding*. Thus adverb clauses function as adverbials only when they modify nonfinite verb forms. When they modify whole predications, either finite or nonfinite, they are sentence modifiers.

Adverb Clauses as Sentence Modifiers

Though adverb clauses function in a variety of ways, they most frequently serve as sentence modifiers. The reason is that the subordinating conjunctions which introduce adverb clauses usually express a logical relationship between two whole clauses so that the dependent adverb clause modifies the other clause in its entirety. This relationship to the other clause makes the adverb clause a sentence modifier, for, as you will remember from earlier discussion, when a modifier applies to the whole idea of a clause or of a nonfinite predication rather than to a single word, it is a sentence modifier.

Perhaps this concept can be made clearer with further illustration. Consider this sentence:

The car **which I bought** was a lemon.

The boldface adjective clause has a relationship only to *car*, that word being the antecedent of *which*. So the adjective clause is not a sentence modifier but an adjectival modifying a single noun. Now consider this sentence:

I went hungry **so that I could buy another record**.

The connective *so that* does not relate its clause (*I could buy another record*) to any single word such as *went* or *hungry*. Instead, it expresses the relationship of cause-and-result between two whole ideas. *I went hungry* is the cause and *I could buy another record* is the result. So the entire boldface adverb clause in the example sentence is a sentence modifier modifying the whole independent clause. This is the most common function of the adverb clause: to serve as a sentence modifier with the subordinating conjunction expressing a relationship between two whole clauses. We will further illustrate adverb clauses functioning as sentence modifiers by giving examples of the various kinds of relationship expressed by the subordinating conjunctions. Remember, it is the fact that these conjunctions link whole clauses that makes adverb clauses so frequently function as sentence modifiers.

Here are adverb clauses with connectives that express the relationship of cause-and-result:

Inasmuch as you have already called a taxi, I won't take you to the airport.

The cause is *you have already called a taxi*; the result is *I won't take you to the airport. Inasmuch as* expresses this relationship and clearly the adverb clause is a sentence modifier.

In case you want to read it, I will leave this book with you.

The cause is *you (may) want to read (this book)*; the result is *I will leave this book with you.* Again, the subordinating conjunction shows a relationship between two whole ideas and thus introduces a sentence modifier. In these examples the cause is expressed in the dependent clause and the result in the independent clause. With the connective *so . . . that* the cause is expressed in the independent clause and the result in the adverb clause. Example:

The election is **so** far in the past now **that we can forget our differences.**

The cause is *the election is far in the past now* (independent clause) and the result is *we can forget our differences* (dependent clause). *So* is not a qualifier in this sentence but a part of the subordinating conjunction. Note that the *so* could be placed next to the *that*, but the result would not sound natural to us. If you test, you will find that all the connectives of cause-and-result can function in any of these three example sentences, though some adjustments in syntax might be necessary.

Here are adverb clauses with connectives that express the relationship of contrast, which includes such concepts as opposition, contradiction, and paradox:

Though there is a world of evidence for the theory of evolution, many people still oppose it.
The bids ended at $50, **whereas I thought they would begin at $100.**
However much you study, you can still make no more than a B in Professor Kendall's classes.

There is a contrast or opposition between the two whole ideas in such sentences as these, and the subordinating conjunctions express that contrast. Clearly the adverb clauses are modifying the whole independent clauses and are thus sentence modifiers.

Here are adverb clauses that express the relationship of condition or concession:

If the storm abates, we can set out again.
We can't set out again **unless the storm abates.**
I will buy your car **provided you have it tuned up.**

Again, the subordinating conjunctions express a logical relationship between whole clauses, and thus the adverb clauses are sentence modifiers. The first two sentences express condition and the third both condition and concession. *If* also can imply concession as well as condition. Example:

If you will have your car tuned up, I will buy it.

A condition is stated, but the speaker is also making a concession. Also *since* can imply concession as well as cause-and-result. Example:

I will buy your car, **since you had it tuned up.**

Both cause-and-result and concession are expressed here. Condition and concession go so closely together that they can hardly be separated; hence we included both in one category in our lists above of subordinating conjunctions. There are many subtleties in the kinds of relationships expressed by the subordinating conjunctions that introduce adverb clauses, just as there are subtleties in the modal auxiliaries.

Here are adverb clauses with connectives that express the relationship of manner or method:

He curses **as if he were a demon.**
She drives **as I would like to.**
She drives **like I would wish to.**

These connectives express the relationship of *how*, but the connective *how* cannot function in their place: **I want to drive how you do* is ungrammatical. As a connective, *how* can introduce only noun clauses and infinitives. In the third sentence *like* as a conjunction is completely grammatical, though there seems to be a folk superstition that it is ungrammatical. The sentence modification in these examples is clearly apparent. For example, in the first sentence *as if* expresses the relationship between the whole clauses *he curses* and *he* (*may be*) *a demon.*

Here are adverb clauses with connectives that express the relationship of purpose:

I want to go to Fordham University **so that I will be close to the New York theaters.**
In order that I may have a secure old age, I have taken out an annuity.

The boldface adverb clauses express the purpose of the action in the independent clauses, and the adverb clauses are sentence modifiers. *So* without *that* is a connective colloquially used to express purpose, as it could in the first sentence.

Here are adverb clauses with connectives that express a comparison between two ideas:

> Shirley is **as** pretty **as she is intelligent.**
> Bimbo bought **more** books **than I did.**
> I always get up earlier **than my wife does.**

In the first sentence there are two ideas: *Shirley is pretty* and *Shirley is intelligent*. The connective *as . . . as* equates them, showing that the adverb clause is a sentence modifier. In the third sentence, *earlier* is not only a part of the independent clause (*I always get up early*) but also its comparative suffix (*er*) is a part of the connective, as *more* is in the second sentence. Often in the comparative structure a part of the dependent clause is omitted and just understood. Examples:

> George studies hard**er than I.**
> Father buys Stevie **more than me.**

In the first sentence, *study* is understood so that *than I study* is the understood dependent clause. In the second sentence the understood dependent clause is *than he buys me*. These understood adverb clauses are sentence modifiers.

Here are adverb clauses with connectives that express time or time plus cause-and-result:

> **Before you register**, talk to Professor Swedenberg.
> **Once Philbert has completed payments on his car**, he promptly buys a new one.
> **When the petition failed**, several students left school.

In sentence one, *before* expresses only a simple time relationship, but in sentences two and three, *once* and *when* express not only time but also cause-and-result: the students left school not only *when* but also *because* the petition failed. When the restrictor *only* precedes an adverb clause introduced by *when*, *if*, *unless* and a few others, the subject and verb auxiliary of the independent clause are reversed in sequence and there is no terminal juncture. Example:

> Only when men perform their hereditary duties **does society** function properly as an element of the universe.

If the *only* were dropped, the subject and verb in the independent clause would resume their normal order. Note that cause-and-result as well as time is expressed by *when* in this sentence.

Finally, here are adverb clauses with connectives that express the relationship of place:

> I stood **where I could see the parade best.**
> **Wherever you are**, I will find you.

In the first sentence the connective *where* expresses the relationship between *I stood* and *I could see the parade best*, and thus the adverb clause is a sentence modifier. And in the second sentence, *wherever you are* is clearly modifying the independent clause.

Adverb clauses can also modify nonfinite predications, and in that function they are best called sentence modifiers. Examples:

> John having dropped his tools **when the whistle sounded**, the fore-man docked him an hour's pay.
> I want you to play golf every day **after you get well**.

In sentence one the boldface adverb clause is modifying the absolute phrase *John having dropped his tools*, which is a nonfinite predication. In sentence two *you to play golf every day* is also a nonfinite predica-tion (an infinitive with a subject and complement) and is modified by the boldface adverb clause. Since these adverb clauses are modifying whole ideas (even though they are not stated finitely), they are sentence modifiers, just as are the *which* clauses are on pages 318–320.

Adverb Clauses as Adverbial Complements

Our pattern 2 sentence—N + Be + Adv—is the only one that defi-nitely contains an adverbial complement (it's an open question as to whether other intransitive verbs can take adverbial complements). A typical pattern 2 sentence is

> Timmy is outside,

in which *outside* is an adverbial complement. Similarly in

> Timmy is **where you left him**

the boldface adverb clause is an adverbial complement, the clause filling the **Adv** slot in a pattern 2 sentence. An adverb clause introduced by *wherever* can function in a similar manner. Example:

> Bea will be **wherever you direct her to be**.

Will be is complemented by the adverb clause.

Adverb Clauses as Adjectivals

Adverb clauses introduced by *when*, *where*, *before*, and *after* fre-quently modify nouns of time and place, and when they do they func-tion as adjectivals. On pages 263–264 we showed that adverbs can modify nouns, as in

> an **outside** movie
> the **now** generation

and

> the example **above**.

In such uses the adverbs are functioning as adjectivals. Thus adverb clauses that modify nouns are also adjectivals. Examples:

> The day **when you pick up a check** is the day I'll celebrate.
> The road **where the accident occurred** is not on the map.
> A month **after I graduated** a depression set in.
> The week **before she got married** she acquired a new stepfather.

These boldface adverb clauses are obviously very different in function from those that function as sentence modifiers, for in these sentences they modify the nouns *day*, *road*, *month*, and *week*, not whole independent clauses. However, they are not adjective clauses, as they have been called, for, like some of the form-class adverbs, these adverb clauses are crossing over into the territory of the adjectival. Classification by form and function is the clue to understanding the adjectival nature of these adverb clauses.

The dependent clauses in the previous examples were all restrictive, for they were needed to identify the nouns they modified. Adverb clauses can also function as nonrestrictive adjectivals. Examples:

> Last Sunday, **when three football games were scheduled**, my TV set broke down.
> Appleton Boulevard, **where I was stopped for speeding**, is certainly suitable for high-speed traffic.

The time and place nouns modified by these boldface adverb clauses are fully identified by the determiner *last* and by name, and thus the adverb clauses are nonrestrictive adjectivals.

Adverb Clauses as Nominals

Adverb clauses of time can function as the objects of the prepositions *until* and *since*, and in that function they are nominals. Examples:

> I wasn't sure what I would do until **after you called**.
> I haven't bought a new car since **before disk brakes became standard**.

In these sentences, *until* and *since* are prepositions and the boldface adverb clauses are their objects. Thus the adverb clauses are functioning as nominals.

Also adverb clauses introduced by *if*, *because*, and *when* can function colloquially as nominals. Examples with *if*:

> I don't know **if I can pass this course**.
> I wonder **if you will help me**.

The two boldface adverb clauses are functioning as the direct objects of the verbs *know* and *wonder* and thus are nominals. Though very common, such usage is colloquial; professional writers would use *whether* instead of *if*, thereby using noun clauses as nominals.

Examples with *because*:

> Just **because you're so intelligent** is no reason for you to be conceited.
>
> The reason I left was **because Jenny came.**

In sentence one the adverb clause introduced by *because* is the subject of *is* and in sentence two it is a predicate nominal equal to *reason*, as in a pattern 8 sentence: $N^1 + V\text{-}L + N^1$. For a long time prescriptive grammarians railed against these usages, on the grounds that an adverb clause cannot function as a noun. But these usages, though perhaps colloquial, are very common, and certainly in them adverb clauses are functioning as nominals.

The notorious *is when* sentence also must be analyzed as containing an adverb clause functioning as a nominal. These sentences are universally condemned by all stylists and authorities on usage, but they are commonly used by the less literate. Since they are natural grammatical structures for some native speakers, they should be analyzable. They in fact form pattern 8 sentences. Examples:

> Courage is **when you are scared but don't admit it.**
>
> Bossism is **when politicians give all their allegiance to one man.**

The *when* adverb clauses are predicate nominals equal to *courage* and *bossism*. Our analysis of these sentences should not be taken as our approval of them.

EXERCISES

1. In the following sentences, identify the connective that introduces each of the italicized noun clauses and tell what its grammatical function is in its own clause. The natural *who* form may be used instead of the technically correct *whom* form.

> a. *Whoever you select* will no doubt be acceptable.
> b. I didn't know *that you were a Mason.*
> c. Return the money to *whoever lost it.*
> d. Did you find out *whose book this is?*
> e. I wonder *when it will rain again.*
> f. I want to be *where the angels are.*
> g. You can be *whatever your friends consider you to be.*

    h. I think I know *which teams will win.*

    i. I know *who you have a crush on.*

    j. *Who you sit by* makes a difference.

2. In the following sentences tell the grammatical function within the whole sentence of each of the italicized noun clauses. If a clause is a complement, tell what kind.

    a. It's clear *that you don't understand.*

    b. I found *what I was looking for.*

    c. He is *what his wife made him.*

    d. *When you leave* is of no concern to me.

    e. Earn your money by *whatever means you can.*

    f. *Whether you know it or not,* you are Professor Burk's favorite.

    g. The conclusion *that might makes right* is un-Christian.

    h. You made me *what I am today.*

    i. Give *whoever asks first* the complimentary pass.

    j. We are sure *that you will qualify.*

3. Create five sentences with noun clauses functioning as each of the five different kinds of nominal complements.

4. Create five sentences with noun clauses as objects of prepositions.

5. Create five sentences with noun clauses as restrictive appositives.

6. Create five sentences with noun clauses as nonrestrictive appositives.

7. Distinguish between noun and adjective clauses in the following sentences.

    a. The opinion *that Shakespeare was the world's greatest dramatist* is almost universal.

    b. The opinion *that Matt expressed* seemed absurd.

    c. We know *that your opinion is false.*

    d. That's the teacher *to whom I complained.*

    e. Give the money to *whoever is neediest.*

    f. Give the money to those *who ask for it.*

    g. I don't wonder *that you were upset.*

    h. It's understandable *that you were upset.*

    i. A belief *that hurts others* is despicable.

    j. The belief *that Christ originated the golden rule* is false.

8. Tell the grammatical function in its own clause of the relative pronoun that introduces the italicized adjective clause in the following sentences. The natural *who* form may be used instead of the technically correct *whom* form. The connective may be omitted; if so, supply it.

    a. Is she the girl *you are interested in*?
    b. "Busby" is the show *which got the highest rating*.
    c. That's the dog *I shot at*.
    d. That's the dog *I kicked*.
    e. That's the policeman *whose beat is on skid row*.
    f. The Bible is a book *that I read often*.
    g. Are you the one *who took my book*?
    h. Poe could swim twenty miles without stopping, *which is hard to do*.
    i. She's a girl *everyone wants to go out with*.
    j. Continuous creation is the theory *that Hoyle favors*.

9. In the following sentences distinguish between restrictive and non-restrictive adjective clauses. *No punctuation is supplied.* Relative pronouns may be omitted. The clauses are not italicized. There may be ambiguities; if you find one, explain it.

    a. The course I wanted to follow was also favored by the president.
    b. Jake's opinion which we all agreed with originated with his father.
    c. The first cheerleader who was reluctant to serve was voted homecoming queen.
    d. The first cheerleader that I saw was Cheri Slikker.
    e. The novel of Faulkner's that I like best is *The Hamlet*.
    f. Faulkner's first novel which was written in New Orleans is entitled *Soldier's Pay*.
    g. My brother who is an airline pilot learned to fly in the Air Force.
    h. Quitting smoking which is hard to do is being attempted by many thousands.
    i. The best movie that I recall seeing was "Genevieve."
    j. My first course in calculus which almost caused me to drop out of college was taught by Professor Nielsen.

10. Create five sentences with adjective clauses or noun clauses functioning as sentence modifiers.

11. Create five sentences with adverb clauses functioning as sentence modifiers.

12. Create five sentences with adverb or noun clauses functioning as adjectivals.

13. Create five sentences with adverb clauses functioning as adverbial complements or nominals.

14. Following are three paragraphs chosen at random. Identify all dependent clauses in them by both form and function. Tell the grammatical role, if any, that each subordinating connective plays in its own clause. If a connective is omitted, tell what it would be if supplied.

    Similarly, it is the writers of fashion copy who see through the shadows and mists of native puritanism and recognize that the shoe, which traditionally has played no recognized part in American love-making, has recently acquired an aura of erotic value such as it has not had since Solomon, or whoever wrote the *Song of Solomon*, sang the finest bit of advertising copy yet: "How beautiful are thy feet with shoes, O prince's daughter!" In a comparably rapturous vein, the Wohl Shoe Company of St. Louis offered young women, via the February 15, 1959, issue of *Vogue*, a pump described as a "dream of a shoe," and spelled out the dream visually: a lovely young miss leaned upon the manly chest of a masked *caballero*. No prosaic considerations of arch support or hygienic insole for her; the shoe is no longer a piece of utilitarian clothing, but a *laissez-passer* to the wondrous fantasy world of romance. Underwear, too, according to the testimony of the Madison Avenue confraternity, has an equally transporting effect. A case in point is a message some of them produced for Seamprufe, Inc. in a recent issue of *Seventeen*. In this instance, the journey took place in time as well as in space: the ad showed a medieval knight in chain mail, mounted upon a white charger, in the act of sweeping up with one arm a damsel improbably clad only in a lace-trimmed slip of nylon tricot. If, indeed, lingerie produces such reveries in American women, one can only be struck with admiration at the strength of character they show in getting past the state of deshabille and actually arriving at their jobs or starting their housework. [Morton M. Hunt, "Love According to Madison Avenue"]

A number of studies have shown that while people may protest about some social change, when the change actually takes place most will fall silently and willingly into line. It's the rare examples of change being resisted with violence that unfortunately receive most publicity. A psychologist interested in this phenomenon once made an amusing study of the differences between what people say they'll do and what they really do in a particular situation that evokes prejudice. Traveling across the country with a Chinese couple, he found that the three of them were received in 250 hotels and restaurants with great hospitality—and only once were refused service. When the trip was over, he wrote to each of the hotels and restaurants and asked if they would serve Chinese people. Ninety-two percent of those who had actually served them said they would not do so! [Ian Stevenson, "People Aren't Born Prejudiced"]

The present situation is utterly unfair to the individual physician who believes that the relief of suffering is one of his principal duties. Many medical practitioners undoubtedly resort to euthanasia, but since they do so secretly it is impossible to say how many. They feel compelled to commit a technical "murder" even though they must bear the whole responsibility. That is the unfair part. Situations like the recent one in New Hampshire must arise frequently, and why in that case the doctor reported his act is difficult to understand. (Why, too, did he inject air instead of merely giving an overdose of morphine?) Bigots and sticklers for legal technicalities will always try to prevent or punish humanitarian action by an individual physician. Since the decision rests with him alone, the doctor will rarely ask for the consent of either the patient or the relatives. The mercy killing is therefore done furtively, when it should be done candidly, serenely, and lawfully. [Harry Benjamin, "Euthanasia—A Human Necessity"]

12   COORDINATION

The Fourth Great Grammatical Function

Predication, complementation, and modification are truly the great grammatical functions in English. They are the functions that weld a wide variety of structures into sentences. Our fourth great grammatical function—**coordination**—is of a different order from those three and not so "great" as they. It simply involves the compounding[1] of a sentence constituent which is already involved in predication, complementation, or modification. But, though not of the same order or magnitude as the other three, coordination provides the fourth grammatical function needed to round out a scheme for the analysis of the surface structure of English sentences.

To coordinate means "to arrange together," and in coordination two or more sentence constituents that are alike in structure or function are placed in equal arrangement with each other, usually, though not always, joined by a coordinating connective. All sentence constituents except a few structure words can be coordinated. Predications, sub-

---

[1]A word of caution about our use of the word *compounding*. Coordination does result in compounding, for two or more structures are joined to make a unit, at least in a sense. But we also use the word *compounding* to indicate that a unit has been formed even though coordination has not taken place. For example, *high school* is a compound noun, but the two words are not coordinated. Also, *but nevertheless* is a compound coordinating connective, but has no coordination itself. But this double use of the word *compound* causes no ambiguity, for we are all used to both meanings of the word in many fields.

335

jects, complete predicates, finite verbs, auxiliaries, complements, and most modifiers can be coordinated into double or multiple structures. In our illustrations to follow, we will use only two constituents in each coordinated structure, but of course three, four, or even more constituents can be coordinated. In fact, theoretically there is no limit to the number of, say, adjectivals that can be coordinated in one structure.

A few structure words cannot be coordinated. For example, the determiner *the* in

> **the** pretty girl

cannot be coordinated into any such structure as

> *the and this pretty girl.[2]

Or, for another example, the coordinating conjunction *and* in such a construction as

> **the coach** *and* **all the players**

cannot undergo coordination. It can, however, be compounded without coordination, as in

> **the coach** *and also* **all the players**.

Some structure words, however, can be coordinated. For example,

> **any** *and* **all** alligators

and

> those **in** *and* **out of** office

illustrate determiners and prepositions being coordinated. In general, then, all nonstructure words and word groups and many structure words can be coordinated.

The chief reason for the existence of coordination in language is to permit the speaker or writer to circumvent tedious repetition. For example, one could say

> The car skidded. The car crashed.

But even a three-year-old would have command enough of coordination to know that

> The car **skidded** *and* **crashed**

is more economical and pleasing phrasing than the tedious repetition

---

[2]In all of our illustrations of coordination that follow, the two structures that are coordinated will be in boldface type and the connectives used to coordinate the structures will be italicized. Any other part of a sentence will be in ordinary type.

of the subject *car*. He would not know that he had deleted a repetitious subject and coordinated two verbs, but he would have utilized a grammatical function that, though apparently simple, takes a place of importance with the other three major grammatical functions.

Not all coordinated structures involve **deletion**. For example, when two simple predications, such as

The whip cracked *and* **the lion jumped,**

are coordinated, no deletion has occurred—only the compounding of two statements. But in most other cases of coordination deletion occurs. For example, the underlying (or deep) structure of such a simple sentence as

I want **to eat** *and* **drink**

is

I want to eat. I want to drink,

or perhaps even simpler structures leading to those. Deletion of a subject, a finite verb, and the *to* of an infinitive and coordination of two infinitives result in the surface sentence. But we will not be concerned with the deletion transformation. That function is the province only of advanced linguistic study, whereas we are concerned only with grammatical analysis which provides a basis for the discussion among students and laymen of our surface language as it actually appears in our speech and writing.

In Chapter 4 we gave an accounting of the coordinating connectives and the logical relationships they express and also examples of their use. That section was a part of our classification of structure words. Now we will repeat and expand that material in order to give a thorough analysis of the grammatical function of coordination, and *in doing so we will take the opportunity to review many of the concepts presented in previous chapters.* Since almost all structures in English can be coordinated, it will be convenient briefly to run through those structures again as we present the relatively simple function of coordination. Such review is very helpful in the learning process.

First, we will list again, grouped according to the logical relationships they express, the coordinating connectives, which usually are categorized as coordinating conjunctions, correlatives, and conjunctive adverbs.[3]

---

[3]Transitional phrases such as *for example, in addition, in effect,* and *in the same way* in a sense participate in coordination when they come between two sentences or two independent clauses. But we consider them sentence modifiers rather than coordinating connectives and so will exclude them in the illustrations in this chapter.

Addition *or* **Accumulation** (*with* **Cause-and-Result** *sometimes included*)

and	furthermore
not only . . . but also	besides
both . . . and	also
moreover	

Contrast

but (not)	nevertheless
yet (not)	still
not . . . but	otherwise
however	

Condition

or	otherwise
or else	

Addition *and* **Contrast** *combined*

but also	and yet

Cause-and-Result

for	hence
accordingly	so
consequently	thus
therefore	

Alternatives

or	whether . . . or
either . . . or	

Time

afterward(s)	later
earlier	then

Exclusion

nor	not . . . nor
neither . . . nor	never . . . nor

Occasionally a few of these connectives are themselves compounded (but not coordinated). For example, we often hear such combinations as *but nevertheless*, *and yet*, *not . . . but still not*, *and accordingly*, and *so therefore*. Such compounding is usually for the purpose of intensifying the expression of relationship. For example, *so therefore* emphasizes the relationship of cause-and-result that is to be expressed. The subtleties of connectives rival those of the modal auxiliaries, and we will not attempt a categorization of all possibilities.

The conjunctive adverbs and the connective *for* in these lists can coordinate only independent clauses. The coordinating conjunctions and correlatives can coordinate various kinds of structures and will necessarily be the connectives we use most in our illustrations.

In addition to these verbal connectives, terminal juncture must also be considered a coordinating device. For example, such a construction as

> They were not Americans, they were French

contains the comma splice given so much notoriety in handbooks. But in constructions of this sort the comma splice is entirely acceptable, for the comma represents the terminal juncture which coordinates the two short, closely related statements. Such juncture can also be denoted by a semicolon (which would be the choice of many writers) with the same effect of coordination. The coordination of most of the so-called coordinate adjectives is also denoted by juncture rather than by a connective. Example:

> a morose, miserly hermit

The juncture, denoted by the comma, substitutes for the connective *and*, and therefore it is surely a coordinating device. For a number of years *Time* magazine promoted the use of juncture to denote coordination in such constructions as these:

> The sprinter increased his speed, gained ground on his rival.
> The infantryman whirled suddenly, gave a burst from his M-16.

This kind of substitution of juncture for a connective was not well received by the reading public (much as reformed spelling was rejected by the readers of the *Chicago Tribune*) and *Time* gave up promoting its stylistic innovation. The device is rarely seen in any professional writing nowadays. But juncture is frequently used in conjunction with *not* to denote coordination. Examples:

> He is a **Serb**, *not a* **Croat**.
> We were really **sad**, *not* **happy**.

The nouns *Serb* and *Croat* and the adjectives *sad* and *happy* are coordinated with the relationship of contrast. This junctural device is so common that some grammarians consider *not* itself a coordinating connective, but juncture is surely a part of the coordinative structure here. Yet *not* must be given its due as an instrument in coordination, as it is in our listings above of the coordinating connectives.

The examples in the following sections (which, as has been stated, are given here as much to provide review as to illustrate coordination) will draw at random from the various coordinating connectives. No attempt will be made to illustrate all of them in any one section. The connectives most frequently used in our natural language will be the ones most frequently used in our illustrations to follow.

Coordination of Independent Clauses

Independent clauses are often coordinated when there is a close relationship between them. Actually, of course, there is a close relationship between any two consecutive sentences in good writing, and often a sentence will begin with a connective that relates it to and coordinates it with the previous sentence. Example:

> The promotional literature announced that the festival would be attended by at least ten nationally famous groups. *But* I decided not to go anyway.

The *but* expresses the logical relationship between the two sentences and in effect coordinates them. Actually, a comma rather than a period could separate the two independent clauses. So coordination of independent clauses is subject to individual styles in the use of punctuation and connectives. But in this section and throughout this chapter we will be concerned only with coordination within one sentence, that is, within a structure that begins with a capital letter and ends with a period. We will not consider coordination from sentence to sentence.

Independent clauses are most frequently coordinated with the connectives *and* and *but*. Examples:

> **Mother screamed** *and* **I came running.**
> **The siren sounded** *but* **Mosely refused to slow down.**

Note that in the first example the connective *and* denotes not only addition but also cause-and-result. *But*, as in the second sentence, is the connective most commonly used to denote a contrast between independent clauses.

The correlative *not only ... but also* is used in various ways to coordinate independent clauses. Examples:

> *Not only* **did I pass** *but also* **I gained grade points.**
> **John** *not only* **ignored the warning** *but* **he** *also* **increased his speed.**
> **The social worker** *not only* **delivered the welfare check; he** *also* **gave the family extra money of his own.**

In the first sentence the subject and auxiliary of the first clause are reversed because *not only* comes first; when the *not only* comes after the subject, as in sentence two, the subject and verb are not reversed. Sentence one shows *but also* coming together, but sentence two shows the two words separated. In sentence three the *but* part of the correlative is omitted, the juncture denoted by the semicolon taking its place. Also other variations in the use of this correlative are possible.

The conjunctive adverbs are thought by some stylists to be rather heavy words for use in coordinating independent clauses, but they are nevertheless much used. Examples:

> **The depositors demanded the withdrawal of their savings;** *therefore* **the bank could only close its doors.**
> **Interest rates dropped; the stock market,** *however,* **did not make a gain.**
> **I want you to leave now,** *and furthermore* **I don't want you to come again.**

When used singly, the conjunctive adverbs (except *so*) require a semicolon rather than a comma between the independent clauses. Sentence two shows how the connective can sometimes be shifted to the interior of the second clause. Sentence three illustrates the compounding of coordinating connectives for emphasis.

Juncture, denoted by either a comma (when the clauses are very short) or by a semicolon, can also coordinate independent clauses. Examples:

> **The rain came in sheets, the lightning flashed, the thunderbolts rolled.**
> **We withdrew our support from the Blackwood faction; it seemed the best way to regain unity.**

More and more professional writers are using "comma splice" sentences, as illustrated in the first example, but they use them with care. No professional writer, for example, would use a comma splice like this:

> He refused to talk reason, that is why I left in a huff.

Only a semicolon is acceptable if the two clauses in a sentence of this sort are to be in one sentence. In the second sentence above, the semicolon not only coordinates the two clauses but also implies the relationship of cause-and-result.

Questions and imperative sentences also can be coordinated. Examples:

> **Are you going to the convention** *and* **will you give a paper?**
> **Come early** *but* **don't bring a gift.**

Questions are coordinated almost exclusively with the connective *and* and imperative sentences with *and* or *but*.

Coordination of Basic Sentence Constituents

The basic sentence types in English (except the imperative sentence) first break naturally into subjects and predicates, and then a predicate may break naturally into a finite verb and one or more complements.

All of these constituents—subjects, predicates, finite verbs, and complements—can be coordinated.

Coordination of Subjects

Form-class words, some structure-class words, endocentric noun phrases, and various kinds of word groups may function as subjects and may be coordinated. Some examples:

> **His daughter** *but not* **his son** agreed to his new rules.
> **Swimming** *and* **hiking** are our favorite sports.
> *Neither* **the rich** *nor* **the poor** will like this bill.
> *Either* **outside** *or* **inside** is good enough for me.
> *Both* **more** *and* **less** is now demanded of students.

In order in these five sentences we have (1) nouns, (2) present participles, (3) adjectives, (4) adverbs, and (5) noun substitutes coordinated as subjects. Note that in the last sentence the singular verb *is* sounds natural even though the two parts of the subject are compounded. In sentence four the two subjects are really not compounded, for the *either . . . or* correlative signifies exclusion of one or the other.

Endocentric noun phrases may similarly be coordinated. Examples:

> **The mystery surrounding the disappearance of the twins** *and* **the strange antics of the private investigator brought in to solve the mystery** gave the newspapers ample copy of sensational journalism.
> *Neither* **the student whose house was raided on the basis of an anonymous tip** *nor* **the street person who provided the drugs and brought in strangers** was found guilty.

In the first sentence *mystery* and *antics* are the headwords in the co-ordinated noun-phrase subjects. In the second sentence *student* and *street person* are the headwords of the two phrases. The verb (*was found*) must be singular because the correlative expresses exclusion.

Prepositional phrases are probably the word-group subjects least likely to appear in a coordinated structure, but the phenomenon is grammatically possible. Example:

> *Either* **in the sun** *or* **in the shade** is fine with me.

The prepositional phrases as subjects are nominals by function. Noun clauses are more often compounded in the subject position. Examples:

> **What you do** *and* **where you go** are of no concern to me.
> **Whether he is solvent** *or* **whether he is in debt** remains unknown.

In the first example the verb *is* would be colloquially acceptable even though the connective *and* technically makes a plural subject. The singular verb is mandatory in the second sentence because of the connective *or*.

Infinitive and present-participial phrases can also be coordinated in the subject position. In such functions the phrases are nominals. Examples:

> **To have an IQ of 140** *and yet not* **to be able to learn calculus** hurts a student's ego.
>
> **Accepting welfare funds** *but* **refusing to work** seems to be a way of life with some people.

Both the infinitives and the present participles in these sentences have direct objects, thus forming phrases. Note that singular verbs (*hurts* and *seems*) are proper for these coordinated subjects, though coordinated verbal phrases often take a plural verb. For example, in

> **To dream of perfect love** *and* **to seek perfect solitude** are two of life's contradictory pleasures,

the coordinated verbal subjects require the plural verb *are*. In coordination of infinitives, the *to* for the second one is often omitted. Example:

> **To eat onions** *but not* **use a mouthwash** is perilous for playboys.

When a verb stem, such as *use* in this sentence, is not functioning as a finite verb, it is always an infinitive even though the *to* is omitted.

Coordination of Whole Predicates

The second half of a sentence often contains both a finite verb and one or more complements, which together make the predicate of the sentence (of course a finite verb by itself can be a predicate). These whole predicates can be coordinated. Examples:

> The detective **examined the disarrayed apartment** *and* **took fingerprints from several objects.**
>
> The club members **elected Harry secretary for social affairs** *but* **directed him not to plan an evening of entertainment for several months.**

In the first sentence, coordination of the two predicates (each with a finite verb and direct object) allows one subject to serve both. In the second sentence the first predicate has a direct object (*Harry*) and an object complement (*secretary*) for its finite verb (*elected*), and the second predicate has a nonfinite predication (*him not to plan an evening . . .*) as the direct object of its finite verb (*directed*). Such coordination of whole predicates is very common.

Coordination of Finite Verbs

Finite verbs of sentences may be coordinated when other parts of the predicate are not. Examples:

> The renegade grizzly bear **sniffed** *and* then **ate** the poisoned bait.
> The sixth-grade pupils **couldn't understand** *but* **would memorize** many of the poems in the text.

In sentence one the finite verbs *sniffed* and *ate* share the direct object *bait* so that only the verbs are coordinated. In the second sentence, finite verb forms containing auxiliaries (*couldn't understand* and *would memorize*) share the direct object *many* .... Also in both sentences the finite verbs share the same subject.

A finite verb with an auxiliary and one without an auxiliary can also be coordinated. Example:

> George **could have been** *and* maybe **was** the culprit.

In such coordination the two finite verb forms must come from the same verb stem, as *could have been* and *was* in this sentence both come from *to be. Maybe* is an adverbial, not an auxiliary. Both finite verbs share the same subject and predicate noun.

Sometimes only the main verb forms of sentence verbs are coordinated, with one auxiliary applying to both of the main verbs. Examples:

> The boxer wouldn't **swing at** *or* even **approach** his opponent.
> Dogberry has been **working** *and* **saving** all his life.

In sentence one, *or* coordinates *swing at* and *approach*, the auxiliary *wouldn't* serving both verbs. *Opponent* serves as the object of the preposition *at* that goes with *swing* and also as the direct object of *approach*. Such structures are entirely grammatical. In sentence two, only the main verb forms *working* and *saving* are coordinated, the auxiliary *has been* serving both to make two finite verb forms. Repetition of the auxiliary would be tedious indeed.

Auxiliaries alone may also be coordinated, with a single main verb form for both auxiliaries. Examples:

> Freddie **could have** *and* perhaps **ought to have** sent the letter of complaint.
> George **has been** *and* maybe still **is** going regularly to cell meetings.

In the first sentence *could have* and *ought to have* are coordinated auxiliaries for the past participle *sent*, and in sentence two *has been* and *is* are coordinated auxiliaries for the present participle *going*. Thus there are two finite verbs in each sentence, though only one main verb form in each.

Coordination of Complements

All eight kinds of complements can be coordinated.

1. *Coordination of direct objects.*   Many different kinds of structures can serve as direct objects and all can be coordinated.   Examples of coordinated nouns as direct objects:

> The handyman repaired the **faucet** *but not* the electric **switch.**

Faucet and *switch* are coordinated direct objects of *repaired.*   Example of coordinated endocentric noun phrases as direct objects:

> The Chairman of the Board greeted *both* **the shareholder who had objected to his plan to merge with two other companies** *and* **the entrepreneur who was secretly buying large blocks of shares in an attempt to control the company.**

Shareholder and *entrepreneur* are the headwords of these coordinated noun-phrase direct objects of *greeted.*   Example of coordinated noun substitutes as direct objects:

> You have said *not only* **plenty** *but too* **much.**

Plenty and *much* (with a qualifier) are noun-substitute direct objects of *said.*   Example of coordinated noun clauses as direct objects:

> In ambiguous terms she told him **where she had been** *and* **what she had done.**

The *where* and *what* noun clauses are coordinated direct objects of *told* (which has *him* as a single indirect object).

In all the above examples both the forms and the functions of the coordinated constituents have been the same.   But the forms can vary if the functions are the same.   Example:

> She told him the **title** of the book *and* **where he could find it.**

Here a noun (*title*) and a noun clause (*where he could find it*) can be coordinated since they have the same function (direct objects of *told*).

Example of coordinated present-participial phrases as direct objects:

> She likes **dining in expensive restaurants** *but not* **making the evening pleasant afterwards.**

The first present participle (*dining*) has only a prepositional-phrase modifier, but the second (*making*) has a direct object (*evening*), an adjective object complement (*pleasant*), and a modifier (*afterwards*). The internal construction of all kinds of participial and infinitive phrases and nonfinite predications has no bearing on their capability of being coordinated. Example of coordinated infinitive phrases as direct objects:

The angry professor planned **to give a surprise exam** *and* **count it as one-fourth of the course grade**.

The coordinated infinitive phrases *to give* . . . and (*to*) *count* . . . are direct objects of *planned*, and also *to give* and *count* themselves have direct objects (*exam* and *it*).

Three different kinds of nonfinite predications can function as direct objects. Example of coordinated infinitive phrases with subjects functioning as direct objects:

George wanted **me to issue the invitations** *and* **Bill to buy the party supplies**.

Each of the coordinated infinitives (*to issue* and *to buy*) has a subject (*me* and *Bill*) and a direct object (*invitation* and *supplies*). Both the whole nonfinite predications are direct objects of *wanted*. Example of coordinated present-participial phrases with subjects functioning as direct objects:

When I approached the apartment, I was sure I would find **Pete playing jazz** *or* **Susie playing up to Pete**.

The present participle *playing* has a subject (*Pete*) and a direct object (*jazz*) and the present participle of the verb-particle composite *to play up to* has a subject (*Susie*) and a direct object (*Pete*). Both nonfinite predications are coordinated direct objects of *would find*. Example of coordinated past participles with subjects functioning as direct objects:

I saw **Richard kissed** *and* **Norman slapped** by Carol.

Richard is the subject of the past participle *kissed* and *Norman* of *slapped*. Both nonfinite predications, the direct objects of *saw*, are served by the prepositional phrase *by Carol*. Both of these nonfinite predications are in the passive voice, for the implied structure is *Richard was kissed by Carol* and *Norman was slapped by Carol*.

2. *Coordination of indirect objects.*

Clara gave **me** *and* **Chester** a date for the same evening.

Though *gave* has a single direct object (*date*), it has coordinated indirect objects (*me* and *Chester*). Indirect objects are almost always personal pronouns or proper nouns, and hence no further illustration of this kind of coordination is necessary.

3. *Coordination of noun object complements.*

The President appointed Dean Clark **Chairman** of the Curriculum Committee *and* **Representative** to the CCJCA.

Chairman and *Representative* are the compounded object complements of the direct object *Dean Clark*. Since only a limited number of nouns normally function as object complements, no further illustration of this kind of coordination is necessary.

4. *Coordination of adjective object complements.*

> Marian made Clint *both* **happy** *and* **sad** at the same time.

The sentence has only one direct object (*Clint*) but compounded adjective object complements (*happy* and *sad*) for that direct object. In a sentence of this type both the direct object and the object complement can be compounded. Example:

> Mother found **Damon furious** *and* **Carl contented**.

Damon is one direct object with *furious* as its adjective object complement, and *Carl* is a second direct object with *contented* as its adjective object complement, both constructions being served by one subject and one verb.

5. *Coordination of predicate nouns.*

> Lee Jacoby remained a **Vice-President** *but not* **a Board Member** of the firm.
> Don Moody appeared to be a **con man** *but also* **what the club needed**.

Usually predicate nouns are nouns by form, but the second sentence shows a noun (*con man*) and a noun clause (*what the club needed*) coordinated as predicate nominals. Structures that function alike but are different in form can often be coordinated. In the second sentence, *to be* is an expletive. In the first sentence *of the firm* modifies each of the predicate nouns.

6. *Coordination of predicate adjectives.*

> Debbie seemed **agitated** *and yet* **happy**.
> The old man was **bright-eyed** *and* **in good humor**.

In the first sentence *and yet* expresses addition, for Debbie was both agitated and happy, but it also denotes contrast, for it is not expected that one would be both agitated and happy. It takes a compound coordinating connective to express both kinds of relationship at the same time. In the second sentence a compound adjectival (composed of an adjective plus a pseudo past participle) is coordinated with a prepositional phrase, showing again that the form of coordinated constituents need not be identical.

7. *Coordination of adverbial complements.*

> Billy was **outside** *and* **inside** all day long.

> The deer was **out of range** *but* **in sight.**
> The pliers were not **in their usual place** *but* **where you had absent-mindedly left them.**

To be is the only verb, in our analysis, that takes an adverbial complement. Usually such complements are words, phrases, or clauses of place. The third example above shows a prepositional phrase and an adverb clause coordinated.

8. *Coordination of complements of the adjective.*

> We were sure **that you had heard the rumor** *but* **that you hadn't squelched it.**
> I'll be happy **to meet you at the airport** *and* **drive you to your hotel.**

Noun clauses in sentence one and infinitive phrases in sentence two are coordinated complements of the predicate adjectives *sure* and *happy*. Note that in such a sentence as

> I was sure that you **had received my message** *and* **would come**

complements of the adjective have not been coordinated but only the predicates of the noun clause introduced by *that*, which as a whole serves as one complement of the adjective *sure*.

Coordination of Internal Complements of the Verbal

You will remember that nonfinite verb forms—infinitives, present participles, and past participles—can function as nominals, adjectivals, and adverbials, and that in doing so they can take all of the complements that finite verbs can take. These internal complements of the verbal can be coordinated just as complements of finite verbs can. We will not run through all of the possibilities again but will give only a few examples:

> Knowing **Latin** *and* **Greek** is a great help in studying any area of the humanities.
> I wanted to elect **Harriet secretary** *but not* **Cuthbert treasurer.**
> Being *both* **naive** *and* **soft-hearted**, Professor Wooster accepted my excuse.

In sentence one *Latin* and *Greek* are coordinated direct objects of the verbal *knowing*, and the whole present-participial phrase functions as the subject of *is* and therefore is a nominal. In sentence two the infinitive phrase beginning with *to elect* is the direct object of *wanted* (and therefore a nominal), and it itself has coordinated direct objects and noun object complements. In sentence three the present-participial phrase beginning with *being* is an adjectival modifying *Professor Wooster*, and *being* as a verbal is taking coordinated predicate adjectives. *Soft-hearted* is a compound adjectival composed of an adjective and a pseudo past participle. This is just a small sample of the possibilities of coordinated internal complements of the verbal.

Coordination of Adjectivals

All kinds of adjectivals except for a few structure words can be coordinated

Coordination of Single-Word and Prepositional-Phrase Adjectivals

In coordination, adjectivals can be either added together or contrasted, as can other structures. They can also be coordinated in any of the three adjectival positions: prenominal, postnominal, and shifted. Examples:

> *Both* **angry** *and* **bewildered**, Daniel could only fume.
> Anybody **single** *and* **rich** is welcome to join our club.
> Morris sat in his car, **grinning** *but not* really **pleased**.

In sentence one, two adjectives in the prenominal position with juncture are coordinated by the correlative *both . . . and*, which shows addition. In sentence two, adjectives in the postnominal position are also added together. In sentence three, the two contrasted adjectivals are in the shifted position, one (*grinning*) being a present participle and the other an adjective.

In the prenominal position without juncture, adjectivals are usually coordinated with only juncture between them. Example:

> The **exuberant, beaming** cheerleader decided to twirl three batons.

Note that there is no juncture separating the two adjectivals from the noun headword *cheerleader*, but that the adjective *exuberant* and the present participle *beaming* are separated by juncture, which denotes their coordination. Such structures are known as **coordinate adjectives** or **adjectivals**. The connective *and* could replace the junctural comma, but the construction would then not sound wholly natural. But prenominal adjectivals can be naturally coordinated with *and*. Example:

> The **stately** *and* **well-cared-for** mansion is a delight to visitors.

Here the *and* sounds as natural as juncture would. *Well-cared-for* is a compound adjectival formed from a verb-particle composite.

Sometimes two or more adjectivals in the prenominal position are not coordinated and do not have connectives or juncture between them. Examples:

the red steel horseshoes
the stoop-shouldered old woman

Note that the connective *and* would sound strange between the two adjectivals in each of these phrases, showing that they are not really coordinated. The adjectivals *steel* (a noun) and *old* (an adjective) in some indefinable way modify the noun headwords so that *steel* and *old* are not coordinate with *red* and *stoop-shouldered*. It might be maintained that *steel horseshoes* and *old woman* are constructions that lie somewhere between an adjectival modifying a noun and a compound noun. *Stoop-shouldered* is a compound adjectival composed of a verb stem and a pseudo past participle.

Sometimes coordination of adjectivals can occur with the noun headword coming after the first adjectival and followed by the connective. Examples:

He is a **brilliant** student *but not* **hard-working**.
Georgia is a **beautiful** girl *and* **rich** too.

Brilliant and *hard-working* are coordinated to modify *student* and *beautiful* and *rich* to modify *girl*, but for rhetorical effect the second adjectival is delayed. *Hard-working* is a compound adjectival composed of an adjective and a present participle.

Single-word adjectivals can be coordinated with prepositional phrases in most positions. Examples:

Bitter *and* **in a nasty mood**, Joe insulted everyone.
Carol stalked toward her car, **resentful** and **out of humor**.
Anybody **rich** *but not* **in good health** is really to be pitied.

This kind of coordination does not occur in the prenominal position without juncture. For example, **the rich and in good health man ...* is ungrammatical.

Adjectival prepositional phrases themselves can be coordinated. Examples:

In debt *and* **without a friend**, Joey pondered his fate.
A man **of wealth** *but* **without friends** may still be happy.

Note, however, that in such a sentence as

A man with **credit cards** *but* **no cash** may have to go hungry

prepositional phrases are not coordinated but instead two objects (*cards* and *cash*) of the preposition *with* are coordinated. This is a common type of coordination but so simple that we need not illustrate it further.

Coordination of Verbal-Phrase Adjectivals

Infinitive, present-participial, and past-participial phrases may function as adjectivals and may be coordinated. Examples of coordinated infinitive adjectival phrases:

> The best argument **to advance against anti-intellectuals** *and* **to use to substantiate the need for early scientific training in school** is the evidence that a civilization declines when its learning declines.
>
> Alger was the only man **to take on the Jack Acid Society** *and* **defeat it in the courts.**

In sentence one the infinitive phrases *to advance* ... and *to use* ... are coordinated adjectivals modifying *argument*. In the second of these two infinitive phrases, the included infinitive phrase beginning with *to substantiate* is the direct object of *to use*, and *need* is the direct object of *to substantiate*. This internal complexity of a verbal phrase of course has no effect on its capability of being coordinated. In sentence two the infinitive phrases *to take on* ... and (*to*) *defeat* ... are coordinated adjectivals modifying *man*. *To take on* is a transitive verb-particle composite with *the Jack Acid Society* as its direct object.

Here are examples of coordinated present-participial phrases functioning as adjectivals:

> The student **sitting in the front row** *and* **asking the ponderous questions** is just trying to impress the professor.
>
> **Appointing Jose acting president** *and* **adjourning the meeting immediately thereafter,** Faculty Advisor Tucker caused some resentment.

In sentence one the present-participial phrases *sitting* ... and *asking* ... are modifying *student* in the commonly used postnominal position. The phrases are restrictive. In sentence two the two present-participial phrases modifying the sentence subject *Faculty Advisor Tucker* are in the prenominal position with juncture and are thus nonrestrictive. *Appointing* has both a direct object (*Jose*) and an object complement (*acting president*).

Also present-participial phrases can be coordinated with adjectivals of other forms. Examples:

> The book **with a torn binding** *and* **containing early woodcuts** will be auctioned off.
>
> Very **pretty** *but not* **smelling exactly of roses,** Joy did not appeal to the boys.

In sentence one a prepositional phrase and a present-participial phrase and in sentence two an adjective (with a qualifier) and a present-participial phrase are coordinated adjectivals, modifying *book* and *Joy*.

Here are examples of coordinated past-participial phrases functioning as adjectivals:

> The student **arrested by three plainclothesmen** *and* **charged with dope pushing** was actually an undercover agent himself.
> The last book, **printed in Latin** *and* **bound in leather**, sold for $1000.

In sentence one, *arrested* and *charged* and in sentence two *printed* and *bound* are headwords of past-participial phrases functioning as adjectivals modifying *student* and *book*. The first coordinated pair is restrictive and the second nonrestrictive. These headwords are past participles and not adjectives, for they cannot be compared or be modified by *very*.

A past-participial phrase can also be coordinated with other structural forms. Example:

> The large picture, **cracked in three places** *and* **dripping paint**, was the obvious object of vandalism.

A past-participial phrase (*cracked in three places*) and a present-participial phrase (*dripping paint*) are coordinated as adjectivals modifying *picture*. Many different combinations of forms can be coordinated provided their function is the same.

Coordination of Dependent-Clause Adjectivals

As we saw in Chapter 11, adjective, adverb, and noun clauses can function as adjectivals, and in such functions they can be coordinated. Examples of coordinated adjective clauses as adjectivals:

> Janice Vanata, **who earned the highest GPA** *but* **whose modesty prevented her from applying for a scholarship**, did not enter graduate school.
> Any student **who earns a GPA of 3.00** *and* **who is in financial need** will receive a scholarship.

In the first sentence the two adjective clauses coordinated by *but* are nonrestrictive and also illustrate the fact that the coordinated clauses need not have the same structure; note in that sentence that the relative pronoun *who* of the first clause functions as a subject but that the relative pronoun *whose* in the second functions as a determiner. Note that if, in the second sentence, the *who* of the second adjective clause were omitted the coordination then would be of two whole predicates (*earns a GPA of 3.00* and *is in financial need*) in one adjective clause.

Example of coordinated adverb clauses functioning as adjectivals:

> The day **when the earth melts** *and* **when the jaws of hell open**
> will come sooner than most expect.

The *when* clauses are adverb by form but function here as adjectivals modifying the noun *day*. The second *when* could be understood, but the sentence would still have two coordinated adjectivals. Also an adverb and an adjective clause can be coordinated as adjectivals. Example:

> The building **where the unexploded bomb was found** *but* **which**
> **has no connection with war or other government activity** is
> to have its security guard doubled.

The *where* clause is adverb by form and the *which* clause adjective by form, but both are coordinated as adjectivals modifying the noun *building*. But dependent clauses are very seldom coordinated with structures of other forms.

Noun clauses introduced by the connective *why* can function as adjectivals and can be coordinated. Example:

> The reason **why the moon shot was aborted** *and* **(why) the tele-**
> **scope on the craft was parachuted back to earth** was that the
> malfunction-detection system predicted that an oxygen tank would
> explode.

Since they modify the noun *reason*, the coordinated *why* clauses are functioning as adjectivals. In such a construction the second *why* would usually just be understood, as the parentheses indicate.

Coordination of Adverbials

Coordination of Single-Word and Prepositional-Phrase Adverbials

Adverbials are not as often coordinated as nominals, finite verbs, and adjectivals, but there are many grammatical possibilities. Here are some examples of coordinated single-word adverbials:

> John wrote **hastily** *and* **sloppily**.
> Perry ran *neither* **behind** *nor* **ahead**.
> Speak **loud** *and* **clear**.
> We will arrive **tomorrow** *or* **Wednesday**.
> **To grow** *and* **(to) prosper**, a firm should diversify.
> Johnny stood **fidgeting** *and* **squirming**.
> The deer was found **shot** *but* *not* **cut up**.

In these seven sentences the adverbials coordinated are, in order, (1) *ly* adverbs, (2) adverbs of place, (3) adjectives (colloquially used), (4) nouns of time, (5) infinitives (*in order* will go with them), (6) present participles (= thus), and (7) past participles (= thus). The seventh sentence is in the passive voice, its active-voice form being

> Someone found the deer shot but not cut up,

in which the phrase *the deer shot but not cut up* is a nonfinite predication functioning as the direct object of *found*. In the passive-voice sentence (the last example) the past participles function as the adverbial substitute *thus* and hence are to be analyzed as adverbials. *Cut up* is a verb-particle composite.

Single-word and prepositional-phrase adverbials can be coordinated. Examples:

> Fred walked **rapidly** *but* **with a limp.**
> Your package will arrive **soon** *and* **in good condition.**

Since *rapidly* is functioning the same as *with a limp* and *soon* the same as *in good condition*, the pairs can be coordinated. They modify the verbs *walked* and *will arrive*.

Adverbial prepositional phrases can also be coordinated. Examples:

> Come *either* **in the Mercedes** *or* **in the Rolls Royce.**
> Jack ate **with good manners** *but* **without gusto.**

The coordinated prepositional phrases are modifying *come* and *ate*. But in such a sentence as

> He spoke with **deliberation** *but not* **clarity,**

just the objects (*deliberation* and *clarity*) of one preposition (*with*) are coordinated, not two prepositional phrases. In the first example sentence in this paragraph, the second *in* could be omitted, changing the coordination but not the meaning.

Coordination of Adverb Clauses as Adverbials

As we saw in Chapter 11, adverb clauses do not often function as adverbials, being mostly used as sentence modifiers. But adverb clauses as adverbials can be coordinated. Examples:

> Talking **while you are chewing** *and* **when you have an unwilling audience** is rude.
> We advise investing **when the market is rising** *but not* **when it is mixed.**

In sentence one the *while* and *when* adverb clauses are modifying the present participle *talking* and are thus coordinated adverbials. The whole present-participial phrase beginning with *talking* is the subject of the verb *is*. In sentence two the *when* and *when* adverb clauses are modifying the present participle *investing* and are thus coordinated adverbials. The whole participial phrase *investing when . . .* is the direct object of *advise*.

Coordination of Verbal Phrases as Adverbials

In the above section we saw single infinitives, present participles, and past participles as coordinated adverbials. Phrases formed with these nonfinite verb forms can also function as adverbials and be coordinated. Example of coordinated adverbial infinitive phrases:

> Elmer Gantry would do anything **to advance up the hierarchy of clerical positions** *and* **to seduce the wives of his fellow ministers.**

The infinitive phrases *to advance . . .* and *to seduce . . .* are coordinated adverbials modifying the verb *would do*. The first of these phrases has prepositional-phrase modifiers and the second a direct object and a modifier. Note that *in order* could precede these infinitive phrases.

Example of coordinated adverbial present-participial phrases:

> The star walked out **swinging her hips** *and* **crying crocodile tears**.

The two present-participial phrases, each with a direct object, modify the verb-plus-modifying-adverb *walked out*. They are equal to the adverbial substitute *thus*.

Example of coordinated adverbial past-participial phrases:

> The victim was seen **pinned down by part of the cargo** *and also* **punctured in the chest by a steel bar.**

The past participles *pinned down* and *punctured* are headwords of phrases modifying the verb *was seen*. The phrases are equivalent to the adverbial substitute *thus*. *Pinned down* is a verb-particle composite.

Coordination of Sentence Modifiers

Coordination of Single-Word and Phrasal Sentence Modifiers

Sentence modifiers in general are not often coordinated, but here are some possibilities:

> **Conclusively** *and* **undeniably,** the sharp break in the stock market had driven out most small investors.
>
> **Unluckily** *but* **as expected,** the roll of the dice turned against Van Osdel.
>
> **Regardless of your opinion** *and* **of a certainty,** I will endorse Throckmorton for Vice President.

The coordinated words and phrases relate only to the whole idea of the following independent clauses, not to single words in those clauses, and are thus sentence modifiers. In sentence two a single word (adverb by form) and a past participle with a connective word are coordinated. In sentence three an adjective phrase and a prepositional phrase are coordinated. The forms are different but the functions are the same.

Coordination of Absolute Phrases and Dependent Clauses as Sentence Modifiers

The absolute phrase, which grammatically is a sentence modifier, can be coordinated with either the logic of addition or contrast. Examples:

> **It being near tavern closing time** *and* **my money having vanished**, I decided to call it a day.

> **The trial being over** *but* **the verdict not having been reached**, all the attorneys took a break.

Such compounding of absolute phrases is rare, though perfectly grammatical.

Here are coordinated noun clauses functioning as sentence modifiers:

> **Whether or not it snows** *and* **whatever the temperature is,** I intend to go to Yosemite National Park next week.

The *whether* and *whatever* clauses modify the whole independent clause. Here are coordinated adjective clauses functioning as sentence modifiers:

> Pinelli came racing in first, **which won him the top prize money for that race** *but* **which did not complete the points he needed to qualify for the Winton Stakes.**

The two *which* adjective clauses modify the whole idea of the independent clause and are thus sentence modifiers. And here are coordinated adverb clauses functioning as sentence modifiers:

> **After the processional begins** *but* **before the first graduates enter the auditorium,** we plan to block the entrance.

Here, too, the *after* and *before* adverb clauses are modifying the whole independent clause. But in general sentence modifiers are not frequently compounded.

Coordination of Appositives

Appositives, which are noun or nominal repeaters, can be coordinated. Examples:

The two greatest predators of the Kalahari Desert, **the lion** *and* **the cheetah**, are dwindling in numbers.

Shovlov, **holder of the record for deep-sea diving** *and* **runner-up in long-distance swimming**, refuses to go sightseeing in foreign countries.

My two greatest desires—**to climb Anapurna** *and* **to spend a week in a sea lab**—seem contradictory.

Joseph's two most strenuous activities—**sparring with Ahmed Abou** *and* **jogging twice around the golf course each day**—keep him in top shape.

Two beliefs of the Australian Aborigines—**that ritual dances bring rain** *and* **that fire is sacred**—are shared by some other tribes.

Faulkner's novels **The Hamlet, The Town,** and **The Mansion** form a trilogy.

The coordinated appositives in these six sentences are, in order, (1) two single nouns, (2) two endocentric noun phrases with headwords *holder* and *runner-up*, (3) two infinitive phrases, (4) two present-participial phrases, (5) two noun clauses, and (6) three titles. In the sixth sentence the titles are restrictive appositives. Appositives are more often coordinated than are sentence modifiers.

— — — — — — — — — —

This concludes our chapter on the fourth of the great grammatical functions in English—**coordination**. The chapter not only illustrates the range of coordination but also gives a review in capsule form of many of the various kinds of structures that make up English sentences. The exercise to follow will be specifically on coordination but it will also serve as a review of the other three major grammatical functions in English.

EXERCISE

Following are five paragraphs chosen at random. First identify each coordinating connective in each of the paragraphs, but do not consider connectives that join two separate sentences (each with a capital letter and period). Then identify the function of the two or more constituents coordinated by the connective: whole predications, subjects, whole predicates, finite verbs or auxiliaries, complements (there are eight kinds), adjectivals, adverbials, sentence modifiers, and appositives. And finally, identify the form of each of these constituents.

To answer such questions we must consider mankind's hereditary endowment as a whole and the distribution of this endowment among individuals. Let us assume, as we may for the purpose of this discussion, that the human germ cell has exactly 20,000 genes. That means that every one of the more than two billion people on earth today has acquired a set of 20,000 genes from the father and a similar set from the mother. These are shuffled like two decks of cards to produce new sets of 20,000 genes in the individual's own germ cells. Everyone has the same 20,000 kinds of genes but some genes appear in more than one form. Many probably occur in only one variety and are the same for everyone; others may show two, three, four, and up to 100 varieties. In any case, the total pool of genes in the earth's population at present is some 80 trillion (two billion people times 20,000 pairs of genes each). This is the storehouse from which the genetic future of man will be furnished. [Curt Stern, "Man's Genetic Future"]

The primary focus of the teen culture, however, is the teen-age hero who, like heroes of all cultures, represents the final expression of those values by which it lives. The seven aforementioned heroes are the Apollos and Zeuses of Teen-Land. A few years ago, the movies supplied most of the heroes for adolescent Americans. Marlon Brando and James Dean were two, but the former's receding hairline and the latter's death disconnected them from the young. Chances are they would have faded anyway, because rock-and-roll was bigger than both of them. Now, except for Dick Clark, every first-class teen-age hero is a recording star. No athlete, politician, businessman, or intellectual is accorded comparable esteem, nor could he be, given the teen-agers' demand for safety. The ideal athlete is admired for courage, the politician for principles, the businessman for enterprise, and the intellectual for devotion to hard truths—all represent values that tend to separate the individual from the crowd, that expose him, and that lead him into an uncertain and dangerous future. Teenagers make virtues of conformity, mediocrity, and sincerity. It is a simple matter of survival; there's safety in the crowd. They can express themsélves through their safe-sex heroes, each one of whom represents his own brand of sex—rebellious sex, sincere sex, clean sex, low-down sex, motherly sex, cool sex—at no risk. It's perfect: It's sex, but it's safe. Without leaving the warmth and security of the crowd, you can say what you want to say to the world. [Thomas B. Morgan, "Teen-Age Heroes"]

We had a good week at the camp. The bass were biting well and the sun shone endlessly, day after day. We would be tired at night and lie down in the accumulated heat of the little bedrooms after the long hot day and the breeze would stir almost imperceptibly outside and the smell of the swamp drift in through the rusty screens. Sleep would come easily and in the morning the red squirrel would be on the roof, tapping out his gay routine. I kept remembering everything, lying in bed in the mornings—the small steamboat that had a long rounded stern like the lip of a Ubangi, and how quietly she ran on the moonlight sails, when the older boys played their mandolins and the girls sang and we ate doughnuts dipped in sugar, and how sweet the music was on the water in the shining night, and what it had felt like to think about girls then. After breakfast we would go up to the store and the things were in the same place—the minnows in a bottle, the plugs and spinners disarranged and pawed over by the youngsters from the boys' camp, the fig newtons and the Beeman's gum. Outside, the road was tarred and cars stood in front of the store. Inside, all was just as it had always been, except there was more Coca-Cola and not so much Moxie and root beer and birch beer and sarsaparilla. We would walk out with a bottle of pop apiece and sometimes the pop would backfire up our noses and hurt. We explored the streams, quietly, where the turtles slid off the sunny logs and dug their way into the soft bottom; and we lay on the town wharf and fed worms to the tame bass. Everywhere we went I had trouble making out which was I, the one walking at my side, the one walking in my pants. [E. B. White, "Once More to the Lake"]

Basic research on the nature of space and its gravitational and magnetic fields, as well as on the fundamental nature of matter and its distribution in space, is being advanced very greatly by use of special instrumentation carried aboard spacecraft. Earth-based astronomy, for instance, is seriously hampered by the atmosphere. The earthbound astronomer is like a man standing at the bottom of a pool of murky water, trying to observe what goes on above the surface. While the seventy-five-mile-thick envelope of air and dust surrounding the earth effectively protects living organisms from lethal radiation coming from the sun and other sources in space, this same layer severely limits our ability to observe much of outer space by optical or radio telescopes. What light does get through the atmosphere is often so seriously distorted that the image of a distant star appears as though it were observed through the turbulent air rising above a hot pavement on a sunny day. Space astronomy, by freeing scientific observation from the earth's atmosphere, will increase manyfold the knowledge that can be gained from the solar system and intergalactic space. In ways that are yet unknown, this new knowledge will surely be of great benefit to mankind. For it is significant that the basic laws of Newtonian mechanics, without which the machine age could never have occurred, were evolved from astronomical observations; and the basic concepts of the atomic age were developed by Einstein and others from observations of stars and planets. [Franklin A. Lindsay, "The Costs and the Choices"]

The arguments in favor of medicare are simple and overwhelming. Good medical care is, and is bound to be, expensive. In the years ahead, as the science of medicine expands, it will become more expensive. It follows that most people will be unable to pay the full cost in cash at the time they receive treatment. Common sense tells us to spread the cost of our episodes of illness over our entire earning life. This means we must insure. But for most of us the heaviest costs are inevitably in infancy and old age, outside our normal working and earning span. This means family and whole-life insurance. During a period of, say, forty working years, we have to pay for risks spread over seventy or more years. But there is another difficulty. Because of their heredity or upbringing or work some people are better risks than others. Through no fault of their own, the bad risks simply cannot carry their own burden. Nor indeed is it possible to isolate the bad risks in advance. The only fair thing to do is to pool all our risks. But even if we do this, a flat per capita payment will be unfair. A uniform flat payment will have little effect on the $40,000 a year man, but will seriously reduce the standard of living of the man earning one-tenth of this amount, and this in turn may reduce his family's level of health. It follows that, if we want everyone to have the best possible medical care at his time of need, everyone must pay according to his capacity throughout his entire earning life. In a modern society this presents no inherent technical difficulty. It simply means that the cost of medicare is added to the income tax or other graduated taxes. That is what we have done in Britain. Of our weekly per capita contributions of about $2 for national insurance, a small part only goes toward the cost of the health service. Something like seven-eighths of the cost of the service comes out of general taxation— mainly income tax, purchase (or sales) tax and excise tax. [Lord Taylor, "America's Medical Future: A Briton's View"]

INDEX

continued

continued

continued

continued

continued

continued